10-10-00

To my Son, Russ
on this fourth

Love,
Dad & Russ

Christ
Triumphant

To order additional copies of *Christ Triumphant,* or other books by Ellen G. White, call 1-800-765-6955.

Visit us at *www.rhpa.org* for more information on Review and Herald products.

Christ Triumphant

Devotional Meditations on the
GREAT CONTROVERSY STORY

By
Ellen G. White

"The fallen world is the battlefield for the greatest conflict the heavenly universe and earthly powers have ever witnessed. It was appointed as the theater on which would be fought out the grand struggle between good and evil, between heaven and hell. Every human being acts a part in this conflict. No one can stand on neutral ground."

—*Manuscript 56, 1899* (Lift Him Up, *p.253*).

INCLUSIVE LANGUAGE EDITION
(See Foreword)

REVIEW AND HERALD® PUBLISHING ASSOCIATION
HAGERSTOWN, MD 21740

Bible texts credited to NRSV are from the New Revised Standard Version of the
Bible, copyright © 1989 by the Division of Christian Education of the National Council
of the Churches of Christ in the U.S.A. Used by permission.

This book was
Copyedited by James Cavil
Designed by Bill Kirstein
Electronic make-up by Shirley M. Bolivar
Typeset: Minion 11/13

PRINTED IN U.S.A.

03 02 01 00 99   5 4 3 2 1

R&H Cataloging Service
White, Ellen Gould Harmon, 1827-1915.
    Christ triumphant.

    I. Devotional calendars—Seventh-day Adventists.
                            242.2

ISBN 0-8280-1351-9

FOREWORD

*T*HE general theme of this book is the great controversy between Christ and Satan. Every person is involved in it. Ellen White was personally reminded of this when she suffered a stroke of paralysis at the age of 30 as she was about to write out her first account of the vision she had been given at Lovett's Grove, Ohio, in March 1858. The Lord told her that the paralysis was an attempt by Satan to kill her so she could not write what she had seen. The little book of 219 pages that she produced that year, based on this vision, is *Spiritual Gifts*, volume 1, which today can be found as a part of *Early Writings*. This marked the beginning of a lifetime of writing on the controversy theme that was to continue to the last year of her life as she completed *Prophets and Kings*.

The great controversy theme is well covered in the five books of the Conflict of the Ages series. This devotional book complements these major works. It begins where the great controversy began—with Lucifer in heaven. It traces that controversy through to the end. The entry for January 1 comes from the first page of *Patriarchs and Prophets,* and the last entry, for December 31, is found in the last pages of *The Great Controversy.* It is interesting to note that the first and last phrases are identical: "God is love."

Nearly 90 percent of this book has been drawn from Ellen White's letters, sermons, and manuscripts. Portions of these materials will be familiar to frequent readers of her books, as some extracts have been used in the many compilations prepared since her death. These compilations include devotional books that have been published during the past 50 years. Other materials can be found in *Manuscript Releases*, volumes 1 to 21, and in *Sermons and Talks*, volumes 1 and 2.

In general, the text for each day's devotional study has been taken from the King James Version of the Bible. This was the version most used by Ellen White, though occasionally she used others.

The prophets whom God inspired to write the books of the Bible used the languages of their day—Hebrew, Aramaic, and Greek. But these languages were not understood by all, hence translations were needed. To make the Old Testament available to people unacquainted with Hebrew and Aramaic, Jewish scholars several centuries before the time of Christ produced a Greek version known as the Septuagint. From this beginning the Scriptures have been translated into more than a thousand languages. And beyond that, numerous versions have been produced in a single language. Among the English language versions the New Revised Standard Version (NRSV) uses gender-inclusive language without in any way changing the meaning of the text. A few of the Scripture texts for the daily devotionals in this book have been selected from this version.

Like the Bible writers, Ellen White used the language of her day. However, writing styles change, as do meanings of words. Thus, when the *Comprehensive Index to the Writings of Ellen G. White* was published in 1963, a "Glossary of Obsolete and Little Used Words and Terms With Altered Meanings" was included at the end of volume 3. The purpose was to help readers understand better what Mrs. White was saying. In her time, words such as "he," "man," "men," and "mankind" were accepted as generic terms that included both men and women. Today this is not so common. Thus, without making any change in Mrs. White's thought, this devotional book uses gender-inclusive language.

As an example, note the February 12 reading: "The difference between a good person and a wicked person is not always caused by natural goodness of disposition." The original reads: "The difference between a good man and a wicked man is not always caused by natural goodness of disposition." In the February 3 reading, note the line that begins: "As the years of human beings have decreased, and their physical strength has diminished, so their mental capacities have lessened." The original reads: "As the years of man have decreased, and his physical strength has diminished, so his mental capacities have lessened."

It is our prayer that this devotional book will help every reader be better prepared for the second coming of Christ and be among those who in eternity will enjoy the fruits of Christ's victory in the great controversy.

THE TRUSTEES OF THE ELLEN G. WHITE ESTATE

January 1
"GOD IS LOVE"

♦ *God is love; and he that dwelleth in love dwelleth in God, and God in him.* 1 John 4:16.

*G*OD is love." His nature, His law, is love. It ever has been; it ever will be. "The high and lofty One that inhabiteth eternity," whose "ways are everlasting," changeth not. With Him "is no variableness, neither shadow of turning." Isaiah 57:15; Habakkuk 3:6; James 1:17.

Every manifestation of creative power is an expression of infinite love. The sovereignty of God involves fullness of blessing to all created beings. . . . The history of the great conflict between good and evil, from the time it first began in heaven to the final overthrow of rebellion and the total eradication of sin, is also a demonstration of God's unchanging love.

The Sovereign of the universe was not alone in His work of beneficence. He had an associate—a coworker who could appreciate His purposes, and could share His joy in giving happiness to created beings. "In the beginning was the Word, and the Word was with God, and the Word was God." . . . Christ, the Word, the only begotten of God, was one with the eternal Father—one in nature, in character, in purpose—the only being that could enter into all the counsels and purposes of God. . . .

The Father wrought by His Son in the creation of all heavenly beings. "By him were all things created . . . whether they be thrones, or dominions, or principalities, or powers: all things were created by him, and for him." . . . The Son, the anointed of God, the "express image of his person," "the brightness of his glory," "upholding all things by the word of his power," holds supremacy over them all. . . .

The law of love being the foundation of the government of God, the happiness of all intelligent beings depends upon their perfect accord with its great principles of righteousness. God desires from all His creatures the service of love—service that springs from an appreciation of His character. He takes no pleasure in a forced obedience, and to all He grants freedom of will, that they may render Him voluntary service.—*Patriarchs and Prophets*, pp. 33, 34.

January 2
**THE NEW
CREATION**

◆ *And God saw every thing that he had
made, and, behold, it was very good. And the
evening and the morning were the sixth day.
Genesis 1:31.*

*H*OW beautiful the earth was when it came from the
Creator's hand! God presented before the universe a world in which even
His all-seeing eye could find no spot or stain, no defect or crookedness.
Each part of His creation occupied the place assigned it and answered the
purpose for which it was created. Like the parts of some great machine,
part fitted to part, and all was in perfect harmony. . . . There was no disease . . . and the vegetable kingdom was without taint of corruption. God
looked upon the work of His hands wrought out by Christ and pronounced it "very good." He looked upon a perfect world, in which there
was no trace of sin, no imperfection.

But a change came. Satan tempted Adam, and he fell. He who in
heaven had become disloyal and had been cast out made lying reports of
God to the beings He had created, and they listened to his reports and believed his lie. And sin entered the world, and death by sin.—Letter 23,
1903 (see also *Review and Herald,* July 21, 1904).

When Christ saw that there was no human being able to be humanity's intercessor, He Himself entered the fierce conflict and battled with
Satan. The First Begotten of God was the only one who could liberate
those who by Adam's sin had been brought in subjection to Satan.

The Son of God gave Satan every opportunity to try all his arts upon
Him. The enemy had tempted the angels in heaven, and afterward the first
Adam. Adam fell, and Satan supposed he could succeed in ensnaring
Christ after He assumed humanity. All the fallen host looked upon this engagement as an opportunity to gain the supremacy over Christ. They had
longed for a chance to show their enmity against God. When the lips of
Christ were sealed in death, Satan and his angels imagined that they had
obtained the victory. . . .

In the death struggle the Son of God could rely only upon His heavenly Father. All was by faith. He Himself was a ransom, a gift, given for the
freeing of the captives. By His own arm He has brought salvation to humanity; but at what a cost to Himself!—Manuscript 125, 1901 (*The
Upward Look,* p. 357).

January 3
**"PERFECT IN
THY WAYS"**

◆ *Thou wast perfect in thy ways from the
day that thou wast created, till iniquity was
found in thee. Ezekiel 28:15.*

So long as all created beings acknowledged the allegiance of love, there was perfect harmony throughout the universe of God. It was the joy of the heavenly host to fulfill the purpose of their Creator. They delighted in reflecting His glory and showing forth His praise. And while love to God was supreme, love for one another was confiding and unselfish. There was no note of discord to mar the celestial harmonies. But a change came over this happy state. There was one who perverted the freedom that God had granted to His creatures. Sin originated with him who, next to Christ, had been most honored of God and was highest in power and glory among the inhabitants of heaven. Lucifer, "son of the morning," was first of the covering cherubs, holy and undefiled. He stood in the presence of the great Creator, and the ceaseless beams of glory enshrouding the eternal God rested upon him. . . .

Little by little Lucifer came to indulge the desire for self-exaltation. . . . Though all his glory was from God, this mighty angel came to regard it as pertaining to himself. Not content with his position, though honored above the heavenly host, he ventured to covet homage due alone to the Creator. Instead of seeking to make God supreme in the affections and allegiance of all created beings, it was his endeavor to secure their service and loyalty to himself. And coveting the glory with which the infinite Father had invested His Son, this prince of angels aspired to power that was the prerogative of Christ alone. . . .

To dispute the supremacy of the Son of God, thus impeaching the wisdom and love of the Creator, had become the purpose of this prince of angels. To this object he was about to bend the energies of that master mind, which, next to Christ's, was first among the hosts of God. But He who would have the will of all His creatures free left none unguarded to the bewildering sophistry by which rebellion would seek to justify itself. Before the great contest should open, all were to have a clear presentation of His will, whose wisdom and goodness were the spring of all their joy.—*Patriarchs and Prophets*, pp. 35-37.

January 4
**A TRAGIC
CHANGE**

◆ *He was a murderer from the beginning,
and abode not in the truth, because there is
no truth in him. John 8:44.*

ONCE Satan was in copartnership with God, Jesus Christ, and the holy angels. He was highly exalted in heaven and was radiant in light and glory that came to him from the Father and the Son, but he became disloyal and lost his high and holy position as covering cherub. He became the antagonist of God, an apostate, and was excluded from heaven. . . . He invited all the powers of evil to rally about his standard, in order to form a desperate companionship of evil to league against the God of heaven. He worked perseveringly and determinedly to perpetuate his rebellion, and to cause members of the human family to turn from Bible truth, and to stand under his banner.

As soon as the Lord through Jesus Christ created our world and placed Adam and Eve in the Garden of Eden, Satan announced his purpose to conform to his own nature the father and mother of all humanity, and to unite them with his own ranks of rebellion. He was determined to efface the image of God from the human posterity, and to trace his own image upon the soul in the place of the divine image. He adopted methods of deception by which to accomplish his purpose. He is called the father of lies, an accuser of God and of those who maintain their allegiance to God, a murderer from the beginning. He put forth every power at his command to win Adam and Eve to cooperate with him in apostasy, and succeeded in bringing rebellion into our world. . . .

Through generation after generation, from age to age, Satan has gathered human agencies through whom to work out his diabolical purposes, and to bring about the enforcement of his plans and devices in the earth. The great putrid fountain of evil has been continually flowing through human society. Though unable to expel God from His throne, Satan has charged God with satanic attributes and has claimed the attributes of God as his own. . . . Through his serpentine sharpness, through his crooked practices, he has drawn to himself the homage that human beings should have given to God, and has planted his satanic throne between the human worshiper and the divine Father.—Manuscript 39, 1894 (*Review and Herald,* Apr. 14, 1896).

January 5
**NO EXCUSE
FOR SIN**

◆ *Thine heart was lifted up because of thy beauty, thou hast corrupted thy wisdom by reason of thy brightness. Ezekiel 28:17.*

HE sin of Lucifer is unexplainable. He was disloyal to God. His mourning and complaining aroused sympathy among the angelic hosts, and many took the same position as did Satan [Lucifer]. How did the Lord break the force of these accusations?

Because of Satan's accusing power, it was not the plan of God to deal with him as he deserved. The tempter would throw all the blame of his course upon others who were below him. He would make it appear that if he could have moved according to his own judgment all this demonstration of rebellion would have been avoided.

The condemning power of Satan would lead him to institute a theory of justice inconsistent with mercy. He claims to be officiating as the voice and power of God, claims that his decisions are justice, are pure and without fault. Thus he takes his position on the judgment seat and declares that his counsels are infallible. Here his merciless justice comes in, a counterfeit of justice, abhorrent to God.

But how shall the universe know that Lucifer is not a safe and just leader? To their eyes he appears right. They cannot see, as God sees, beneath the outward covering. They cannot know as God knows. To work to unmask him and make plain to the angelic host that his judgment is not God's judgment, that he has made a standard of his own and exposed himself to the righteous indignation of God, would create a state of things that must be avoided.

It was on account of Satan's deceiving power that many angels became disloyal to God. God was true and right. Satan was wrong and he was convinced that he was wrong. He must now choose, either by submission to place himself on the Lord's side, or by lying to sustain himself. By sophistry and fraud he appeared to gain an advantage, but it was only for a short time. God cannot lie; He moves in a direct line. Lucifer could speak the truth when it served his purpose best, but he could move in a crooked course to avoid humiliation and defeat. . . .

Satan could not be presented to the universe at once in his real character. His crooked course must be allowed to continue until he should reveal himself as an accuser, a deceiver, a liar, and a murderer. In the latter act, Satan uprooted himself from the affection of the loyal universe. In the death of the Son of God the deceiver was unmasked.—Letter 16a, 1892.

January 6
SATAN'S
TACTICS EXPOSED

◆ *How art thou fallen from heaven, O Lucifer, son of the morning! how art thou cut down to the ground, which didst weaken the nations! Isaiah 14:12.*

EJECTING with disdain the arguments and entreaties of the loyal angels, he [Satan] denounced them as deluded slaves. . . . He would never again acknowledge the supremacy of Christ. He had determined to claim the honor that should have been given him, and take command of all who would become his followers; and he promised those who would enter his ranks a new and better government, under which all would enjoy freedom. Great numbers of the angels signified their purpose to accept him as their leader. . . .

Still the loyal angels urged him and his sympathizers to submit to God, and they set before them the inevitable result should they refuse: He who had created them could overthrow their power and signally punish their rebellious daring. . . .

Many were disposed to heed this counsel, to repent of their disaffection, and seek to be again received into favor with the Father and His Son. But Lucifer had another deception ready. The mighty revolter now declared that the angels who had united with him had gone too far to return; that he was acquainted with the divine law, and knew that God would not forgive. . . . The only course remaining for him and his followers, he said, was to assert their liberty, and gain by force the rights that had not been willingly accorded them.

So far as Satan himself was concerned, it was true that he had now gone too far to return. But not so with those who had been blinded by his deceptions. . . . But pride, love for their leader, and the desire for unrestricted freedom were permitted to bear sway, and the pleadings of divine love and mercy were finally rejected. . . .

God could employ only such means as were consistent with truth and righteousness. Satan could use what God could not—flattery and deceit. . . . God permitted him to demonstrate the nature of his claims, to show the working out of his proposed changes in the divine law. His own work must condemn him. Satan had claimed from the first that he was not in rebellion. The whole universe must see the deceiver unmasked.

Even when he was cast out of heaven, Infinite Wisdom did not destroy Satan. Since only the service of love can be acceptable to God, the allegiance of His creatures must rest upon a conviction of His justice and benevolence.—*Patriarchs and Prophets*, pp. 40-42.

January 7
OUR CHOICES DETERMINE OUR DESTINY

◆ *Sometimes there is a way that seems to be right, but in the end it is the way to death. Proverbs 16:25, NRSV.*

HE principles of the character of God were the foundation of the education constantly kept before the heavenly angels. These principles were goodness, mercy, and love. Self-evidencing light was to be recognized and freely accepted by all who occupied a position of trust and power. They must accept God's principles and convince all who were in the service of God, through the presentation of truth and justice and goodness, [that] this was the only power to be used. Force must never come in. . . .

These principles are to be the great foundation of education in every administration on the earth. The rules given by God are to be observed and respected in every church. God has enjoined this. His government is to be moral. Nothing is to be done by compulsion. Truth is to be the prevailing power. All service is to be done willingly and for love of the service of God. All who are honored with positions of influence are to represent God, for when officiating they act in the place of God. . . .

Satan's representations against the government of God, and his defense of those who sided with him, were a constant accusation against God. These murmurings and complaints were groundless. Yet God allowed Satan to work out his theories. He could have handled Satan and all his sympathizers as easily as one can pick up a pebble and cast it to the earth. But by this He would have given a precedent for the violence of human beings that is so abundantly shown in our world in the compelling principles.

The Lord's principles are not of this order. All the compelling power is to be found under Satan's government. God would not work in this line. He would not give the slightest encouragement for any human being to set himself up as God over another human being, and cause him mental or physical suffering. This principle is wholly of Satan's creation. . . .

In the councils of heaven it was decided that principles must be acted upon that would not at once destroy Satan's power, for it was His [God's] purpose to place things upon an eternal basis of security. . . . God's order must be contrasted with the new order after Satan's devising. The corrupting principles of Satan's rule must be revealed. The principles of righteousness expressed in God's law must be demonstrated as unchangeable, eternal, perfect.—Manuscript 57, 1896 (*Manuscript Releases,* vol. 18, pp. 360, 361).

January 8
BY THEIR FRUITS

◆ *Wherefore by their fruits ye shall know them. Matthew 7:20.*

WHEN those who are in God's service resort to accusation, they are adopting Satan's principles to cast out Satan. It never will work. Satan will work. He is working upon human minds by his crooked principles. These will be adopted and acted upon by those who claim to be loyal and true to God's government. How shall we know that they are untrue, disloyal? "By their fruits ye shall know them."

The Lord saw the use that Satan was making of his power, and He set before him truth in contrast with falsehood. Time and again during the controversy Satan was ready to be convinced, ready to admit that he was wrong. But those he had deceived were ready to accuse him of leaving them. What could he do—submit to God, or continue in a course of deception? He chose to deny truth, to take refuge in misstatements and fraud. The Lord allowed Satan to go on and demonstrate his principles.

God did establish Himself, and He carried the worlds unfallen and the heavenly universe with Him, but at a terrible cost. His only begotten Son was given up as Satan's victim. The Lord Jesus Christ revealed a character entirely opposite to that of Satan. As the high priest laid off his gorgeous, pontifical robes, and officiated in the white linen dress of a common priest, so Christ emptied Himself and took the form of a servant and offered sacrifice, Himself the priest, Himself the victim.

By causing the death of the Sovereign of heaven, Satan defeated his own purposes. The death of the Son of God made the death of Satan unavoidable. Satan was allowed to go on until his administration was laid open before the worlds unfallen and before the heavenly universe. By shedding the blood of the Son of God, he uprooted himself [from sympathy], and was seen by all to be a liar, a thief, and a murderer.

God sees that the same course of action is being pursued the world over. Men and women come to the place where the road diverges: it is either right or wrong. Thousands upon thousands clothe themselves in what they suppose to be an impenetrable disguise, and choose the wrong. . . . God does not force anyone. He leaves all free to choose. But He says, "By their fruits ye shall know them." The Lord will not write as wise those who cannot distinguish between a tree that bears thorn berries and a tree that bears olives.—Manuscript 57, 1896 (*Manuscript Releases,* vol. 18, pp. 361-363).

January 9
WORSHIP THE CREATOR AND REDEEMER

◆ *Thou shalt worship the Lord thy God, and him only shalt thou serve. Matthew 4:10.*

*I*T is those who obey that will be blessed of God. He says that He will bless your children and your lands and all that you lay your hand unto. Do you think that Satan is going to allow this without making a struggle for the mastery?

The enemy is working just as sharply and decidedly now as he worked upon the minds of Adam and Eve in Eden. The people are gathering under his banner, and he is encircling them with his power. But everyone who sees that the law of God is changeless in its character will decide on the side of Christ. If God could have changed one precept of His law to meet the fallen human race, then Jesus Christ need never have come to our earth to die.

Did Christ die to let loose the whole of humanity to worship idols instead of God, when the commandment said, "Thou shalt worship the Lord thy God, and him only shalt thou serve"? And "the Lord made heaven and earth," and what then? "And rested the seventh day" and "sanctified it," and gave it to you to observe as God's memorial—a memorial that He is the living God who created the heavens overhead and the earth upon which we stand. He made the lofty trees and put the covering upon every flower. He gave to each one its tints, and the Lord of heaven made human beings and gave them the Sabbath. What for? For all the posterity of Adam; it was a gift to all his posterity. If they had always obeyed the fourth commandment there never would have been an infidel in the world, because it testified that "the Lord made heaven and earth, the sea, and all that in them is.". . .

His hands are over His created works. Can you wonder that the devil wants to make void the law of God, the standard of His character? It will be the standard in the judgment when the books shall be opened and every person judged according to the deeds that are done. And the names are written—what does He say?—engraven "upon the palms of my hands." The marks of the crucifixion have engraven them. Humans are His property, and they are God's by creation and by redemption. . . .

What do we give to Satan when we concede the point that the law of God needs to be taken away? We give the whole creative universe a defective God, a God that made a law and it was so defective that He had to take it away. That is all Satan wants. Can we afford to be working on any side but that of God?—Manuscript 10, 1894 (*Sermons and Talks,* vol. 1, pp. 232-235).

January 10
SETTING ASIDE DIVINE AUTHORITY

◆ *Thou hast defiled thy sanctuaries by the multitude of thine iniquities. Ezekiel 28:18.*

HE high honors conferred upon Lucifer were not appreciated as the gift of God and called forth no gratitude to the Creator. He gloried in his brightness and exaltation, and aspired to be equal with God. He was beloved and reverenced by the heavenly host. Angels delighted to execute his commands, and he was clothed with wisdom and glory above them all. Yet the Son of God was the acknowledged Sovereign of heaven, one in power and authority with the Father. In all the councils of God, Christ was a participant, while Lucifer was not permitted thus to enter into the divine purposes. "Why," questioned this mighty angel, "should Christ have the supremacy? Why is He thus honored above Lucifer?"—*The Great Controversy,* p. 495.

To the very close of the controversy in heaven, the great usurper continued to justify himself. When it was announced that with all his sympathizers he must be expelled from the abode of bliss, then the rebel leader boldly avowed his contempt for the Creator's law. He denounced the divine statutes as a restriction of their liberty, and declared that it was his purpose to secure the abolition of law. With one accord, Satan and his host threw the blame of their rebellion wholly upon Christ, declaring that if they had not been reproved, they would never have rebelled.

Satan's rebellion was to be a lesson to the universe through all coming ages, a perpetual testimony to the nature and terrible results of sin. The working out of Satan's rule, its effects upon both humans and angels, would show what must be the fruit of setting aside the divine authority. It would testify that with the existence of God's government and His law is bound up the well-being of all the creatures He has made. Thus the history of this terrible experiment of rebellion was to be a perpetual safeguard to all holy intelligences, to prevent them from being deceived as to the nature of transgression, to save them from committing sin and suffering its punishment.

At any moment God can withdraw from the impenitent the tokens of His wonderful mercy and love. Oh, that human agencies might consider what will be the sure result of their ingratitude to Him and of their disregard of the infinite Gift of Christ to our world! If they continue to love transgression more than obedience, the present blessings and the great mercy of God that they now enjoy, but do not appreciate, will finally become the occasion of their eternal ruin.—Manuscript 125, 1907 (*Sermons and Talks,* vol. 1, pp. 388, 389).

January 11
THE CONTROVERSY RECALLED

◆ *Thou hast sinned: therefore I will cast thee as profane out of the mountain of God: and I will destroy thee, O covering cherub, from the midst of the stones of fire. Ezekiel 28:16.*

I am writing out more fully the volume of *Great Controversy,* containing the history of the fall of Satan and the introduction of sin into our world, and I can have a more vivid sense of this great controversy between Christ, the Prince of light, and Satan, the prince of darkness, than I have ever had before. As I see the various devices of Satan to compass the ruin of erring people and make them like himself, a transgressor of God's holy law, I would that angels of God could come to earth and present this matter in its great importance.

Then I feel so intensely for souls who are willfully departing from light and knowledge and obedience to God's holy law. As Adam and Eve believed the lie of Satan, "Ye shall be as gods," so these souls hope through disobedience to rise to greater heights, to gain some flattering position. I am so anxious that, while others are sleeping, I spend hours in prayer that God will work in mighty power to break the fatal deception upon human minds and lead them in simplicity to the cross of Calvary. Then I quiet myself with the thought that all these souls are purchased by the blood of the Lord Jesus. We may have love for these souls, but Calvary testifies how God loves them. This work is not ours, but the Lord's.

We are only the instruments in His hands to do His will, not our own. We look at those who are doing despite to the Spirit of grace, and tremble for them. We feel sorry, and are disappointed, that they prove untrue to God and the truth; but we feel a deeper sorrow as we think of Jesus, who has purchased them with His own blood. We would give all our possessions to save one, but we find we cannot do this. We would give life itself to save one soul unto life eternal, but even this sacrifice would not do the work.

The one great sacrifice has been made in the life, the mission, and the death of Jesus Christ. Oh, that minds would contemplate the greatness of that sacrifice! Then might they be better able to comprehend the greatness of salvation.—*Testimonies for the Church,* vol. 5, pp. 625, 626.

January 12
SIGNIFICANCE OF THE SABBATH

◆ *Thus the heavens and the earth were finished, and all the host of them. And on the seventh day God ended his work which he had made; and he rested on the seventh day from all his work which he had made. Genesis 2:1, 2.*

HUMAN philosophy declares that an indefinite period of time was taken in the creation of the world. Does God state the matter thus? No; He says, "It is a sign between me and the children of Israel for ever; for in six days [not six indefinite periods of time, for then there would be no possible way for us to observe the day specified in the fourth commandment] the Lord made heaven and earth, and on the seventh day he rested, and was refreshed." Please read carefully the fifth chapter of Deuteronomy. God says again, "Remember [do not forget] the sabbath day, to keep it holy. . . . For in six days the Lord made heaven and earth, the sea, and all that in them is, and rested the seventh day: wherefore the Lord blessed the sabbath day, and hallowed it."

Yet with the living oracles before them, those who claim to preach the Word present the suppositions of human minds, the maxims and commandments of humans. They make void the law of God by their traditions. The sophistry in regard to the world's being created in an indefinite period of time is one of Satan's falsehoods. God speaks to the human family in language they can comprehend. He does not leave the matter so indefinite that human beings can handle it according to their theories. When the Lord declares that He made the world in six days and rested on the seventh day, He means the day of twenty-four hours, which He has marked off by the rising and setting of the sun.

God would not pronounce the death sentence for a disregard of the Sabbath unless He had presented before His people a clear understanding of the Sabbath. . . . When the foundation of the earth was laid, the foundation of the Sabbath was laid also. When the morning stars sang together and all the sons of God shouted for joy, God saw that a Sabbath was essential for Adam and Eve, even in Paradise. In giving them the Sabbath, God considered their spiritual and physical health.

God made the world in six literal days, and on the seventh literal day He rested from all His work which He had done, and was refreshed. So He has given human beings six days in which to labor. . . . By thus setting apart the Sabbath, God gave the world a memorial. He did not set apart one day and any day in seven, but one particular day, the seventh day. And by observing the Sabbath, we show that we recognize God as the living God, the Creator of heaven and earth.—Letter 31, 1898.

January 13
FIRST TRANSGRESSION INEXCUSABLE

◆ *I made the earth, and created humankind upon it; it was my hands that stretched out the heavens, and I commanded all their host. Isaiah 45:12, NRSV.*

ADAM and Eve received knowledge through direct communion with God, and they learned of Him through His works. All created things, in their original perfection, were an expression of the thought of God. To Adam and Eve nature was teeming with divine wisdom. But by transgression the human family was cut off from learning of God through direct communion and, to a great degree, through His works. . . . Upon every page of the great volume of His created works may still be traced His handwriting. Nature still speaks of her Creator. Yet these revelations are partial and imperfect. And in our fallen state, with weakened powers and restricted vision, we are incapable of interpreting aright. We need the fuller revelation of Himself that God has given in His written word.—*Education*, pp. 16, 17.

All heaven took a deep and joyful interest in the creation of the world and of Adam and Eve. Human beings were a distinct order. They were made "in the image of God," and it was the Creator's design that they should populate the earth. They were to live in close communion with heaven, receiving and assimilating power from the great Source of power. Upheld by God, they were to live sinless lives.

Satan determined to defeat God's plan. We need not try to understand the motives that prompted the being next to Christ in the heavenly courts to bring envy and jealousy into the ranks of the angels. To many he communicated his disaffection, and there was war in heaven, which ended in the expulsion of Satan and his sympathizers. We need not puzzle our minds for a reason that Satan acted as he did. Could a reason be found, there would be excuse for sin. But there is no excuse. There is no reason human beings should travel over the same ground that Satan traveled. . . .

After Satan was thrust from heaven, he determined to set up his kingdom on this earth. Through him sin entered the world, and death by sin. By listening to his misrepresentation of God, Adam fell from his high estate, and the floodgates of woe were opened upon our world.

There is no excuse for Adam's transgression. All his wants were generously supplied. He had need of nothing more. Only one prohibition was laid upon him. . . . This prohibition Satan used as a means of insinuating suggestions of evil.—*Manuscript 97, 1901.*

January 14
LABOR NECESSARY EVEN IN EDEN

◆ *But of the tree of the knowledge of good and evil, thou shalt not eat of it. Genesis 2:17.*

*I*N creating Adam and Eve, God designed that they should be active and useful. The holy pair was placed in Paradise and surrounded with everything that was pleasant to the eye or good for food. A beautiful garden was planted for them in Eden. In it were stately trees of every description, all that could serve for use or ornament. Flowers of rare loveliness, and of every tint and hue, perfumed the air. Merry songsters of varied plumage caroled joyous songs of praise of the Creator.

Paradise delighted the senses of the holy pair, but this was not enough; they must have something to call into play the wonderful human organism. He who formed them knew what would be for their good; and had happiness consisted in doing nothing, they, in their state of holy innocence, would have been left unemployed. But no sooner were our first parents created than God appointed them their work. They were to find employment and happiness in tending the things which God had created, and their wants were to be abundantly supplied from the fruits of the garden.

Work of brain and muscle is beneficial. Each faculty of the mind and each muscle of the body has its distinctive office, and all require exercise to develop them and give them healthful vigor. Each wheel in the living mechanism must be brought into use. The whole organism needs to be constantly exercised in order to be efficient and meet the object of its creation.—Manuscript 58, 1890.

Christ is called the second Adam. In purity and holiness, connected with God and beloved by God, He began where the first Adam began. But the first Adam was in every way more favorably situated than was Christ. The wonderful provision made in Eden for the holy pair was made by a God who loved them. Everything in nature was pure and undefiled. Fruits, flowers, and beautiful, lofty trees flourished in the Garden of Eden. With everything that Adam and Eve required, they were abundantly supplied.

But Satan came and insinuated doubts of God's wisdom. . . . Eve fell under the temptation, and Adam accepted the forbidden fruit from his wife's hand. He fell under the smallest test that the Lord could devise to prove his obedience, and the floodgates of woe were opened upon our world. . . . By one man's disobedience many were made sinners.— Manuscript 20, 1898 (*Manuscript Releases,* vol. 8, pp. 39, 40).

January 15
TEMPTATION SOMETIMES DISGUISED AS PLEASURE

◆ *Yea, hath God said, Ye shall not eat of every tree of the garden? Genesis 3:1.*

*I*N order to accomplish his work unperceived, Satan chose to employ as his medium the serpent—a disguise well adapted for his purpose of deception. The serpent was then one of the wisest and most beautiful creatures on the earth. It had wings, and while flying through the air presented an appearance of dazzling brightness, having the color and brilliancy of burnished gold. Resting in the rich-laden branches of the forbidden tree and regaling itself with the delicious fruit, it was an object to arrest the attention and delight the eye of the beholder. Thus in the garden of peace lurked the destroyer, watching for his prey.

The angels had cautioned Eve to beware of separating herself from her husband while occupied in their daily labor in the garden; with him she would be in less danger from temptation than if she were alone. But absorbed in her pleasing task, she unconsciously wandered from his side. On perceiving that she was alone, she felt an apprehension of danger, but dismissed her fears, deciding that she had sufficient wisdom and strength to discern evil and to withstand it. Unmindful of the angels' caution, she soon found herself gazing with mingled curiosity and admiration upon the forbidden tree. The fruit was very beautiful, and she questioned with herself why God had withheld it from them.

Now was the tempter's opportunity. As if he were able to discern the workings of her mind, he addressed her: "Yea, hath God said, Ye shall not eat of every tree of the garden?" Eve was surprised and startled as she thus seemed to hear the echo of her thoughts. . . . To the tempter's ensnaring question she replied: "We may eat of the fruit of the trees of the garden: but of the fruit of the tree which is in the midst of the garden, God hath said, Ye shall not eat of it, neither shall ye touch it, lest ye die. And the serpent said unto the woman, Ye shall not surely die: For God doth know that in the day ye eat thereof, then your eyes shall be opened, and ye shall be as gods, knowing good and evil.". . .

Such has been Satan's work from the days of Adam to the present, and he has pursued it with great success. He tempts people to distrust God's love and to doubt His wisdom. He is constantly seeking to excite a spirit of irreverent curiosity, a restless, inquisitive desire to penetrate the secrets of divine wisdom and power. In their efforts to search out what God has been pleased to withhold, multitudes overlook the truths that He has revealed, and that are essential to salvation.—*Patriarchs and Prophets*, pp. 53-55.

January 16
**SATAN URGES
DEPENDENCE
ON SELF**

◆ *God doth know that in the day ye eat thereof, then your eyes shall be opened, and ye shall be as gods, knowing good and evil. Genesis 3:5.*

*B*Y listening to the tempter, our first parents lost their beautiful Eden home. Satan found Eve willing to listen to his temptations, and [he] read a disposition to distrust the word of God. . . .

Satan desired to make transgression appear a real blessing to them, and that in prohibiting them from taking of the fruit of the tree God was withholding from them great good. If you eat, your eyes shall be opened, he said, and you shall be as gods. You will be like God Himself in knowledge and in power. . . .

But what an opening it was! "Ye shall be as gods knowing good and evil." That knowledge was obtained, but what a knowledge it was! The curse of sin was the knowledge they gained. Eve coveted the thing God had forbidden. She revealed a distrust of God and His goodness, and a desire to be independent and do as she thought best. Eve offered the fruit to Adam and became his tempter. She would be a god. She would be a law unto herself. She would acknowledge no restraint. But that apparently smallest of sins constituted her a transgressor of the law of God. . . .

The Lord Jesus came into our world and was tempted by the same enemy. He passed over the ground where Adam fell, but He was steadfast. He resisted the devil, and in behalf of the human race was Conqueror. The universe of heaven triumphed. Satan came to Christ with his specious temptations to induce Him to question the plans and law of God, and to make Him occupy an independent position; but the tempter was foiled. Christ would enter into no controversy with Satan. He met the enemy of God with the Word of God—"It is written."

"Know ye not that . . . ye are not your own? For ye are bought with a price." And what a price it was—the sacrifice of Christ to save a perishing world. . . . All who are united with Christ will come out of the world and be separate. They will not enter into the world from any choice of their own. They will not by their associations place themselves in the way of temptation. They will not be educated in worldly lines. They will choose to come into the school of Christ and learn of the great Teacher. He invites every soul, "Come unto me, all ye that labour and are heavy laden, and I will give you rest."—Manuscript 21, 1898.

January 17
WARNING AGAINST COUNTERFEIT KNOWLEDGE

◆ *And when the woman saw that the tree was . . . pleasant to the eyes, and a tree to be desired to make one wise, she took of the fruit thereof, and did eat, and gave also unto her husband with her; and he did eat. Genesis 3:6.*

THERE is a spurious knowledge, the knowledge of evil and sin, which has been brought into the world by the cunning of Satan. The pursuit of this knowledge is prompted by unsanctified desires, unholy aims. Its lessons are dearly bought, but many will not be convinced that they are better left unlearned. . . .

In educational pursuits as in all others, selfish, earthly aims are dangerous to the soul. In educational lines many ideas are advanced which proceed not from the High and Holy One who inhabiteth eternity, but from those who make scholastic studies an idol and worship a science that divorces God from the education. Yet because these errors are clothed in an attractive garb, they are widely received. . . .

It is well to gain a knowledge of the sciences. But the acquirement of this knowledge is the ambition of a large class who are unconsecrated, and who have no thought as to the use they will make of their attainments. The world is full of men and women who manifest no sense of obligation to God for their entrusted gifts. . . . They are eager for distinction. It is the object of their lives to obtain the highest place. . . .

There are people whom God has qualified with more than ordinary ability. They are deep thinkers, energetic and thorough. But many of them are bent upon the attainment of their own selfish ends, without regard to the honor and glory of God. Some of these have seen the light of truth, but because they honored themselves, and did not make God first and last and best in everything, they have wandered away from Bible truth into skepticism and infidelity.

When these are arrested by the chastisements of God, and through affliction are led to inquire for the old paths, the mist of skepticism is swept from their minds. Some of them repent, return to the old love, and set their feet in the way cast up for the ransomed of the Lord to walk in. . . . When this amazing change is wrought, the thoughts are directed by the Spirit of God into new channels, the character is transformed, and the aspirations of the soul reach out toward heavenly things. . . . The grace which Christ imparts . . . will lead them to the cross of Jesus as active, devoted, loyal workers for the advancement of the truth of heaven.—Manuscript 51, 1900 (*Manuscript Releases*, vol. 20, pp. 40, 41).

January 18
VALUE IN COMPARING EDEN AND GETHSEMANE

◆ *As by one man's disobedience many were made sinners, so by the obedience of one shall many be made righteous. Romans 5:19.*

HE life of Christ is to be carefully meditated upon, and to be constantly studied with a desire to understand the reason He had to come at all. We can form our conclusions only by searching the Scriptures as Christ has enjoined upon us to do, for He says, "They . . . testify of me." We may find by searching the Word the virtues of obedience in contrast with the sinfulness of disobedience. "As by one man's disobedience many were made sinners, so by the obedience of one shall many be made righteous."

The Garden of Eden, with its foul blot of disobedience, is to be carefully studied and compared with the Garden of Gethsemane, where the world's Redeemer suffered superhuman agony when the sins of the whole world were rolled upon Him. Listen to the prayer of the only begotten Son of God, "O my Father, if it be possible, let this cup pass from me: nevertheless not as I will, but as thou wilt." And the second time He prayed saying, "O my Father, if this cup may not pass away from me, except I drink it, thy will be done."

And the third time He prayed saying the same words. It was here the mysterious cup trembled in the hands of the Son of God. Shall He wipe the bloody sweat from His agonized countenance and let the human race go? The wail, wretchedness, and ruin of a lost world rolls up its horrible picture before Him.

"And being in an agony he prayed more earnestly: and his sweat was as it were great drops of blood falling down to the ground." "And there appeared an angel unto him from heaven, strengthening him." The conflict is ended; Jesus consents to honor His Father by doing His will and bearing His curse, the consequence of humanity's transgression. He was obedient unto death, even the death of the cross. Here was what was involved in Adam's disobedience and what the obedience of the Son of God means to us. . . .

The happiness of human beings is in their obedience to the laws of God. In their obedience to God's law they are surrounded as with a hedge and kept from the evil. No one can be happy and depart from God's specified requirements, and set up a standard of their own, which they decide they can safely follow.—Manuscript 1, 1892 (*Manuscript Releases,* vol. 6, pp. 336-338).

January 19
THE CONSEQUENCES OF SIN

◆ *And Adam and his wife hid themselves from the presence of the Lord God amongst the trees of the garden. Genesis 3:8.*

DAM did not consider all the consequences resulting from his disobedience. He did not set his mind in defiance against God, nor did he in any way speak against God; he simply went directly contrary to His express command. And how many today are doing the very same thing, and their guilt is of much greater magnitude because they have the example of Adam's experience in disobedience, and its terrible results, to warn them of the consequences of transgressing the law of God. So they have clear light upon this subject, and no excuse for their guilt in denying and disobeying God's authority. . . .

Adam yielded to temptation, and as we have the matter of sin and its consequences laid so distinctly before us, we can read from cause to effect and see the greatness of the act is not that which constitutes sin; but the disobedience of God's expressed will, which is a virtual denial of God, refusing the laws of His government. . . .

The law of self is erected, human will is made supreme, and when the high and holy will of God is presented to be obeyed, respected, and honored, the human will wants its own way, to do its own promptings, and there is a controversy between the human agent and the Divine.

The fall of our first parents broke the golden chain of implicit obedience of the human will to the Divine. Obedience has no longer been deemed an absolute necessity. The human agents follow their own imaginations, which the Lord said of the inhabitants of the old world were evil and that continually. The Lord Jesus declares, "I have kept my Father's commandments." How? As a man. "Lo, I come to do thy will, O God." To the accusations of the Jews He stood forth in His pure, virtuous, holy character and challenged them, "Which of you convinceth me of sin?". . .

We are not to serve God as if we were not human, but we are to serve Him in the nature we have, that has been redeemed by the Son of God; through the righteousness of Christ we shall stand pardoned before God, and as though we had never sinned. We will never gain strength in considering what we might do if we were angels. We are to turn in faith to Jesus Christ, and show our love to God through obedience to His commands.—Manuscript 1, 1892 (*Manuscript Releases,* vol. 6, pp. 337-342).

January 20
RESULTS OF OPPOSING GOD'S PLANS

◆ *And the Lord God said unto the woman, What is this that thou hast done? And the woman said, The serpent beguiled me, and I did eat. Genesis 3:13.*

*I*T was God's purpose to repopulate heaven with the human family if they would show themselves obedient to His every word. Adam was to be tested, to see whether he would be obedient, as the loyal angels, or disobedient. If he stood the test, his instruction to his children would have been only of loyalty. His mind and thoughts would have been as the mind and thoughts of God. . . .

Satan, the fallen prince, was jealous of God. He determined through subtlety, cunning, and deceit to defeat God's purpose. He approached Eve, not in the form of an angel, but as a serpent, subtle, cunning, and deceitful. With a voice that appeared to proceed from the serpent, he spoke to her. . . . As Eve listened, the warnings God had given faded from her mind. She yielded to the temptation, and as she tempted Adam, he also forgot God's warnings. He believed the words of the enemy of God. . . .

The lie that Satan told Eve, "Ye shall not surely die," has been sounding through the centuries from generation to generation. Thus Satan tempted our first parents, and thus he tempts us today. . . .

Adam and Eve were driven out of Eden, and an angel with a flaming sword guarded the way to the tree of life, that the disloyal, disobedient pair might not gain access to it and thus immortalize transgression. Mark this point. The Lord did not place in Adam fallen and disobedient the confidence He placed in Adam loyal and true, living by every word that proceedeth out of the mouth of God. . . .

The eyes of Adam and Eve were indeed opened, but to what? To see their own shame and ruin, to realize that the garments of heavenly light that had been their protection were no longer around them as their safeguard. Their eyes were opened to see that nakedness was the fruit of transgression. . . .

All who today allow themselves to be used as Satan's instruments to lead others to disregard the commandments of God are under the curse of God. Our safety lies in a wholehearted belief in a "Thus saith the Lord." This is the declaration of truth. Those who are led away from the truth from any motive, however great may have been their supposed wisdom and exaltation, and venture in a path of their own choosing, are following a false leader and will be led by him into false paths.—Letter 91, 1900.

January 21
**SIN FORCED
CHANGE IN
GOD'S PLANS**

◆ *Thy desire shall be to thy husband, and he shall rule over thee. And unto Adam he said . . . Cursed is the ground for thy sake; in sorrow shalt thou eat of it all the days of thy life. Genesis 3:16, 17.*

EVE was told of the sorrow and pain that must henceforth be her portion. And the Lord said, "Thy desire shall be to thy husband, and he shall rule over thee." In the creation God had made her the equal of Adam. Had they remained obedient to God—in harmony with His great law of love—they would ever have been in harmony with each other; but sin had brought discord, and now their union could be maintained and harmony preserved only by submission on the part of the one or the other.

Eve had been the first in transgression; she had fallen into temptation by separating from her companion, contrary to the divine direction. It was by her solicitation that Adam sinned, and she was now placed in subjection to her husband. Had the principles enjoined in the law of God been cherished by the fallen race, this sentence, though growing out of the results of sin, would have proved a blessing to them. But man's abuse of the supremacy thus given him has too often rendered the lot of woman very bitter and made her life a burden.

Eve had been perfectly happy by her husband's side in her Eden home. But, like restless modern Eves, she was flattered with the hope of entering a higher sphere than that which God had assigned her. In attempting to rise above her original position, she fell far below it. . . .

To Adam the Lord declared: "Because thou hast hearkened unto the voice of thy wife, and hast eaten of the tree, of which I commanded thee, saying, Thou shalt not eat of it: . . . in the sweat of thy face shalt thou eat bread, till thou return unto the ground; for out of it wast thou taken: for dust thou art, and unto dust shalt thou return."

It was not the will of God that the sinless pair should know aught of evil. He had freely given them the good, and had withheld the evil. But, contrary to His command, they had eaten of the forbidden tree, and now they would continue to eat of it—they would have the knowledge of evil— all the days of their life. From that time the race would be afflicted by Satan's temptations. Instead of the happy labor heretofore appointed them, anxiety and toil were to be their lot. They would be subject to disappointment, grief, and pain, and finally to death.—*Patriarchs and Prophets*, pp. 58, 59.

January 22
GOD PUT SATAN ON NOTICE

♦ *And I will put enmity between thee and the woman. Genesis 3:15.*

*T*HERE is a strife between the forces of good and evil, between the loyal and the disloyal angels. Christ and Satan are not at an agreement, and they never will be. In every age the true church of God has engaged in decided warfare against satanic agencies. Until the controversy is ended, the struggle will go on between wicked angels and wicked people on the one side, and holy angels and true believers on the other.

The battle that is raging will grow more fierce as the end approaches. Those who are in unity with satanic agencies are designated by the Lord as the children of darkness. There is not, and cannot be, a natural enmity between fallen angels and fallen humans. Both are evil. Through apostasy both cherish evil sentiments. Wicked angels and wicked people are leagued in a desperate confederacy against the good. Satan knew that if he could induce the human race, as he had induced angels, to unite with him in his rebellion, he would have a strong force with which to carry on his rebellion.

In the hosts of evil there is jarring and discord, but they are all firm allies in fighting against heaven. Their one aim is to disparage God, and their great numbers lead them to entertain the hope that they will be able to dethrone Omnipotence.

When Adam and Eve were placed in the Garden of Eden, they were innocent and sinless, in perfect harmony with God. Enmity had no natural existence in their hearts. But when they transgressed, their nature was no longer sinless. They became evil, for they had placed themselves on the side of the fallen foe, doing the very things that God specified they should not do. Had there been no interference on the part of God, fallen humans would have formed a firm alliance with Satan against heaven. But when the words were spoken, "I will put enmity between thee and the woman, and between thy seed and her seed; it shall bruise thy head, and thou shalt bruise his heel," Satan knew that although he had succeeded in making human beings sin, although he had led them to believe his lie and to question God, although he had succeeded in depraving human nature, some arrangement had been made whereby the beings who had fallen would be placed on vantage ground, their nature renewed in godliness. He saw that his actions in tempting them would react upon himself, and that he would be placed where he could not become conqueror. . . .

God pledged Himself to introduce into the hearts of human beings a new principle—a hatred of sin, of deception, of pretense, of everything that bears the marks of Satan's guile.—Manuscript 72, 1904.

January 23
**ENMITY
BETWEEN CHRIST
AND SATAN**

♦ *And I will put enmity between . . . thy
seed and her seed; it shall bruise thy head,
and thou shalt bruise his heel. Genesis 3:15.*

HE Lord said concerning Satan, that old serpent, that he should bruise the heel of Christ, but Christ would bruise his head. Thank God, he cannot touch the head. "With the mind I myself serve the law of God," said the apostle. The mind and heart are enlisted in the service of Christ, while Satan has enlisted humans and fallen angels to join in his company to league against good. They can bruise only the heel, while in the very act, when Satan seems to have triumphed in putting them to torture and death, the faithful who stand in defense of the law of Jehovah are wounding the head of the great rebel.

This prophecy of enmity between Satan and Christ is far-reaching. It is a delineation of an unwearied conflict between Christ and His followers, Satan and his angels, and fallen humans united in a desperate companionship to reproach, bruise, wound, and exterminate the followers of Christ to the close of time. This controversy between Satan and Christ was carried on here in this world. Satan was constantly afflicting the Son of God and creating prejudice in the minds of people. Not only were Christ's doctrines and teachings perverted, misinterpreted, and wrested from their true meaning, but falsehoods followed Him everywhere. The misrepresentations that the chief priests, Pharisees, and Sadducees poured into the ears of the people appealed to the worst passions of adulterers, fornicators, and the dishonest, exciting a burning prejudice that made it almost impossible for Him to live upon the earth for even three and a half years after His public ministry began.

Why, then, Christ has said, should those who bear the truth of God to the world be discouraged and fainthearted? "If the world hate you, ye know that it hated me before it hated you." Ye "are not of the world, even as I am not of the world." They will "revile you, and persecute you, and . . . say all manner of evil against you falsely, for my sake." "Yea, the time cometh, that whosoever killeth you will think that he doeth God service. And these things will they do unto you, because they have not known the Father, nor me."

Satan's malignity reached its height when the Lord of Glory was crucified, and we may expect in our day that human hearts will be open to prejudice and to the falsehoods, wicked misrepresentations, and slander of those who love this kind of satanic work. It is a wisdom from beneath. It is hell-born, and its results will be as in Christ's day.—Manuscript 55, 1886.

January 24
CHRIST ONLY COULD MAKE ATONEMENT FOR SIN

◆ *Forasmuch as ye know that ye were not re-deemed with corruptible things . . . but with the precious blood of Christ, as of a lamb without blemish and without spot. 1 Peter 1:18, 19.*

*T*HE fall of humanity filled all heaven with sorrow. The world that God had made was blighted with the curse of sin and inhabited by beings doomed to misery and death. There appeared no escape for those who had transgressed the law. Angels ceased their songs of praise. Throughout the heavenly courts there was mourning for the ruin that sin had wrought.

The Son of God, heaven's glorious Commander, was touched with pity for the fallen race. His heart was moved with infinite compassion as the woes of the lost world rose up before Him. But divine love had conceived a plan whereby the lost might be redeemed. The broken law of God demanded the life of sinners. In all the universe there was but One who could, in behalf of humanity, satisfy its claims. Since the divine law is as sacred as God Himself, only one equal with God could make atonement for its transgression. None but Christ could redeem fallen humans from the curse of the law and bring them again into harmony with Heaven. Christ would take upon Himself the guilt and shame of sin—sin so offensive to a holy God that it must separate the Father and His Son. . . .

Before the Father [Christ] pleaded in the sinner's behalf, while the host of heaven awaited the result with an intensity of interest that words cannot express. Long continued was that mysterious communing—"the counsel of peace"—for the fallen human race. The plan of salvation had been laid before the creation of the earth, for Christ is "the Lamb slain from the foundation of the world." Yet it was a struggle, even with the King of the universe, to yield up His Son to die for the guilty race. . . . Oh, the mystery of redemption! The love of God for a world that did not love Him! Who can know the depths of that love that "passeth knowledge"? . . .

God was to be manifest in Christ, "reconciling the world unto himself." Human beings had become so degraded by sin that it was impossible for them, in themselves, to come into harmony with Him whose nature is purity and goodness. But Christ, after having redeemed them from the condemnation of the law, could impart divine power to unite with human effort. Thus by repentance toward God and faith in Christ the fallen children of Adam might once more become "sons of God."—*Patriarchs and Prophets,* pp. 63, 64.

January 25
ANGELS AMAZED AT GOD'S PLAN TO SAVE HUMANITY

◆ *Are they not all ministering spirits, sent forth to minister for them who shall be heirs of salvation? Hebrews 1:14.*

HE plan by which alone humanity's salvation could be secured involved all heaven in its infinite sacrifice. The angels could not rejoice as Christ opened before them the plan of redemption, for they saw that salvation of the human race must cost their loved Commander unutterable woe. In grief and wonder they listened to His words as He told them how He must descend from heaven's purity and peace, its joy and glory and immortal life, and come in contact with the degradation of earth, to endure its sorrow, shame, and death.

He was to stand between the sinner and the penalty of sin; yet few would receive Him as the Son of God. He would leave His high position as the Majesty of heaven, appear upon the earth and humble Himself as a man, and by His own experience become acquainted with the sorrows and temptations that humans would have to endure. All this would be necessary in order that He might be able to succor them that should be tempted.

When His mission as a teacher should be ended, He must be delivered into the hands of wicked men and be subjected to every insult and torture that Satan could inspire them to inflict. He must die the cruelest of deaths, lifted up between the heavens and the earth as a guilty sinner. He must pass long hours of agony so terrible that angels could not look upon it, but would veil their faces from the sight. He must endure anguish of soul, the hiding of His Father's face, while the guilt of transgression—the weight of the sins of the whole world—should be upon Him.

The angels prostrated themselves at the feet of their Commander and offered to become a sacrifice for lost humans. But an angel's life could not pay the debt; only He who created them had power to redeem them. Yet the angels were to have a part to act in the plan of redemption. Christ was to be made "a little lower than the angels for the suffering of death." As He should take human nature upon Him, His strength would not be equal to theirs, and they were to minister to Him, to strengthen and soothe Him under His sufferings. They were also to be ministering spirits, sent forth to minister for them who should be heirs of salvation. They would guard the subjects of grace from the power of evil angels and from the darkness constantly thrown around them by Satan. . . .

Christ assured the angels that by His death He would ransom many, and would destroy him who had the power of death.—*Patriarchs and Prophets*, pp. 64, 65.

January 26
FALLEN HUMANS CAN BECOME ONE WITH GOD

◆ *So if anyone is in Christ, there is a new creation: everything old has passed away; see, everything has become new! 2 Corinthians 5:17, NRSV.*

UMAN beings have severed their connection with God, and their souls have become palsied and strengthless by the deadly poison of sin. But there was a time when the proclamation sounded through the heavenly courts, "I have found a ransom! A divine life is given as humanity's ransom. One equal with the Father has become humanity's substitute.". . .

God gave His only begotten Son to the human race, that people might become partakers of the divine nature by accepting the remedy for sin and allowing the divine grace of Christ to work in their lives. . . . Fallen humans, by laying hold of the divine power brought within their reach, can become one with God. Everlasting life is the blessing that Christ came to give to the world.

"The angels which kept not their first estate," God declares, ". . . he hath reserved in everlasting chains under darkness unto the judgment of the great day." The element of evil introduced into heaven by the first angels that fell will never again be allowed to enter heaven. But just so long as we live on this earth, we shall have to meet evil and battle against it. A battle is being fought with every soul. All who choose their own will and way and refuse to be converted to the Lord's way, Satan will use in his service. The knowledge they have acquired in divine things is then united with the knowledge that Satan uses to strengthen his side of the controversy. . . .

Grace abounds with Christ, and those who take their position on the side of the Redeemer become new creatures. In character they become one with God. Herein is love! God places the virtues of His character upon those who receive Him. Through His infinite sacrifice He lifts the human race from its position of slavery to the will of Satan and makes men and women sons and daughters of the heavenly King. . . .

Christ came to suffer in behalf of the fallen race, for Satan made the boast that no one could withstand his devising and in this world live a spotless life. Clothed with human nature, the Redeemer subjected Himself to all the temptations with which human beings are beset; and He overcame on every point. The record of His life is given to the world, that no one need be in doubt as to the power of the grace of God. To every soul who strives for perfection of Christian character, this world becomes a battlefield on which is fought the controversy between good and evil. And everyone who trusts in Christ will gain the victory.—Letter 38, 1907.

January 27
**DON'T SEEK
THE KNOWLEDGE
OF FOOLS**

◆ *And the Lord God said, Behold, the man is become as one of us, to know good and evil. Genesis 3:22.*

GE after age the curiosity of people has led them to seek for the tree of knowledge, and often they think they are plucking fruit most essential, when, like Solomon's research, they find it altogether vanity and nothingness in comparison with that science of true holiness, which will open to them the gates of the city of God. The human ambition has been seeking for that kind of knowledge that will bring to them glory and self-exaltation and supremacy. Thus Adam and Eve were worked upon by Satan until God's restraint was snapped asunder, and their education under the teacher of lies began in order that they might have the knowledge that God had refused them—to know the consequence of transgression.

Human beings have had a practical knowledge of evil, but Christ came to the world to show them that He had planted for them the tree of life, the leaves of which were for the healing of the nations.

The whole probationary period is a time of test and trial, but by all who are obedient to Christ the words of the inspired John will be experienced: "As many as received him, to them gave he power to become the sons of God, even to them that believe on his name." The Lord Jesus came to strengthen every earnest seeker for truth, to reveal the Father. He allowed nothing to divert His mind from the great work of restoring to men and women the moral image of God. And every human agent must see that the great and important work for them in this life is to receive the divine likeness, to prepare a character for the future life. . . .

Satan has been constantly at work to obscure the vital truths that are essential for the well-being of the human family, making indistinct and unimportant the obedience that must be rendered to the commandments of God. But fallen humans are to return to their obedience to God and walk in communion with God, as did Enoch. This God will help every soul to do if they will learn their lessons out of the Word. . . .

[Satan] plans to crowd the mind so fully that no time can be given to consider what they propose to do with the knowledge they gain, or to the quality of their studies, or whether they are of such a character to give them an increased knowledge of God and of Jesus Christ, whom He has sent. If their education is according to the standard of the world, if they seek their knowledge in order that the world may call them great and learned, God calls them fools.—Manuscript 67, 1898.

January 28
**HOPE DELAYED,
BUT NOT
TERMINATED**

◆ *When the fullness of time had come, God sent his Son . . . to redeem those who were under the law, so that we might receive adoption as children. Galatians 4:4, 5, NRSV.*

HE Saviour's coming was foretold in Eden. When Adam and Eve first heard the promise, they looked for its speedy fulfillment. They joyfully welcomed their firstborn son, hoping that he might be the Deliverer. But the fulfillment of the promise tarried. Those who first received it died without the sight. From the days of Enoch the promise was repeated through patriarchs and prophets, keeping alive the hope of His appearing, and yet He came not. The prophecy of Daniel revealed the time of His advent, but not all rightly interpreted the message. . . . The hand of the oppressor was heavy upon Israel, and many were ready to exclaim, "The days are prolonged, and every vision faileth."

But like the stars in the vast circuit of their appointed path, God's purposes know no haste and no delay. Through the symbols of the great darkness and the smoking furnace, God had revealed to Abraham the bondage of Israel in Egypt, and had declared that the time of their sojourning should be four hundred years. "Afterward," He said, "shall they come out with great substance." Against that word, all the power of Pharaoh's proud empire battled in vain. On "the selfsame day" appointed in the divine promise, "it came to pass, that all the hosts of the Lord went out from the land of Egypt." So in heaven's council the hour for the coming of Christ had been determined. When the great clock of time pointed to that hour, Jesus was born in Bethlehem.

"When the fulness of the time was come, God sent forth his Son." Providence had directed the movements of nations, and the tide of human impulse and influence, until the world was ripe for the coming of the Deliverer. The nations were united under one government. One language was widely spoken and was everywhere recognized as the language of literature. From all lands the Jews of the dispersion gathered to Jerusalem to the annual feasts. As these returned to the places of their sojourn, they could spread throughout the world the tidings of the Messiah's coming. . . .

While few understood the nature of Christ's mission, there was a widespread expectation of a mighty prince who should establish his kingdom in Israel, and who should come as a deliverer to the nations.—*The Desire of Ages*, pp. 31-34.

January 29
FAITHFULNESS TO GOD EXCITES FURY OF WICKED

◆ *And the Lord had respect unto Abel and to his offering: but unto Cain and to his offering he had not respect. Genesis 4:4, 5.*

HE Lord gave Cain and Abel directions regarding the sacrifice they were to bring Him. Abel, a keeper of sheep, obeyed the Lord's command and brought a lamb as his offering. This lamb, as it was slain, represented the Lamb of God, who was to be slain for the sins of the world. Cain brought as an offering the fruit of the ground, his own produce. He was not willing to be dependent on Abel for an offering. He would not go to him for a lamb. He thought his own works perfect, and these he presented to God. . . .

Cain talked with Abel about their sacrifices and charged God with partiality. Abel interceded with his brother, repeating to him the very words of God's command to them both regarding the offerings He required. Cain was provoked because his younger brother should presume to teach him. He allowed envy and jealousy to fill his heart. He hated his brother because he was preferred before him.

As Cain pondered over the matter, he grew still more angry. He saw his mistake in offering only his own substance before the Lord, without the fitting sacrifice of a lamb, but he determined to vindicate himself and condemn Abel. Satan worked through him, inspiring him with a desire to slay his brother. . . .

By this history the Lord would teach everybody that His Word is to be implicitly obeyed. Cain and Abel represent two classes—the wicked and the righteous, those who follow their own way and those who conscientiously keep the way of the Lord to do justice and judgment. . . .

Abel did not try to force Cain to obey God's command. It was Cain, inspired by Satan and filled with wrath, who used force. Furious because he could not compel Abel to disobey God and because God had accepted Abel's offering and refused his, which did not recognize the Saviour, Cain killed his brother.

The two parties represented by Cain and Abel will exist till the close of this earth's history. The well-doer, the obedient, does not war against the transgressor of God's holy law. But those who do not respect the law of God oppress and persecute other people. They follow their leader, who is an accuser of God and of those who are made perfect through obedience. . . . The spirit that leads people to accuse, condemn, imprison, and put to death other people has waxed strong in our world. It is this spirit that always works in the children of disobedience.—Manuscript 136, 1899.

January 30
ABEL'S OFFERING REPRESENTED CHRIST'S SACRIFICE

◆ *Why art thou wroth? and why is thy countenance fallen? If thou doest well, shalt thou not be accepted? and if thou doest not well, sin lieth at the door. Genesis 4:6, 7.*

*I*N the working of God's people there are always times of test and trial, and God does not design that we shall shield men and women and youth from the liabilities that test the character. God will reveal His workings and will supply His attributes to the humble people who are seeking Him. Satan also will reveal his workings and will supply every soul he tempts with his attributes, his evil surmisings, his evil speaking and accusing of the brethren.

From this condition of things, the Lord cannot possibly shield those who place themselves on the enemy's side, for God does not compel the human mind. He gives His bright beams of light as a lamp to lead and guide all who will walk in the rays reflected from Him. That lamp, His Word, is a light unto our feet. But if people disregard the path lighted by the heavenly beams and choose a path suited to their own natural hearts, they will stumble on in darkness, not knowing where they stumble or why. They will accuse and hate the very ones who make straight paths for their feet.

The history of Cain and Abel will be repeated. Cain insisted on carrying out his own plans in his offering to the Lord. Abel was steadfast in carrying out the directions of the Lord. He would not be converted in Cain's way. Although the offering of Cain was a very acceptable one, that which made the offering required at all—the blood of the slain lamb—was left out. There could be no harmony between the two brothers, and contention must come. Abel could not concede to Cain without being guilty of disobedience to the special commands of God. . . .

The Lord preferred the offering of Abel because it was correct. His offering was of value because it prefigured the redemption plan of God in the costly offering of His only begotten Son as the hope and salvation of the fallen race.

Cain was very angry when God accepted the offering of Abel and gave no sign that He recognized the offering of Cain, because it left out the true figure, the representation of the world's Redeemer. But the Lord did not give up His way and will to conciliate Cain. He reasoned with him: "Why art thou wroth? and why is thy countenance fallen? If thou doest well, shalt thou not be accepted? and if thou doest not well, sin lieth at the door."— Letter 16, 1897.

January 31
**BITTERNESS
LEADS TO
DISLOYALTY**

◆ *And Cain was very wroth, and his countenance fell. Genesis 4:5.*

I beseech of all who engage in the work of murmuring and pitying themselves because something has been said or done that does not suit them, and that does not, as they think, give them due consideration, to remember that they are carrying on the very work Satan began in heaven. They are following in his track, sowing unbelief, discord, and disloyalty, for no one can entertain feelings of disaffection and keep it secret. They must tell others that they are not treated as they should be. Thus others are led to murmur and complain. This is the root of bitterness springing up, whereby many are defiled. . . .

Thus Satan works today through his evil angels. He confederates with people who claim to be in the faith, and those who are trying to carry forward the work of God with fidelity . . . will have just as severe trials brought against them as Satan can bring through those who claim to know the truth. Satan's success is proportionate to the light and knowledge these opposers have. The root of bitterness strikes down deep, and is communicated to others. Thus many are defiled. . . .

Satan must deceive in order to lead away. . . . Underhand work must be done, a deceiving influence must be exerted; false pretenses must be set forth as truth; suspicion must be lulled to sleep. Satan will clothe temptation and sin with the garments of righteousness, and by this deception he will win many to his side. Christ pronounced Satan a liar and a murderer. Oh, that unwary souls would learn wisdom from God. . . .

Test and trial will come to every soul that loves God. The Lord does not work a miracle to prevent this ordeal of trial, to shield His people from the temptations of Satan. If they are tempted severely, it is because circumstances have been so shaped by the apostasy of Satan that temptations are permitted in order that characters may be developed that will decide the fitness of the human family for the home in heaven, characters that will stand through all the pressure of unfavorable circumstances in private and public life.—Manuscript 57, 1896 (*Manuscript Releases,* vol. 18, pp. 363-365).

February 1
**GOD BEGINS
ANEW WITH SETH**

◆ *God . . . hath appointed me another seed
instead of Abel, whom Cain slew. . . . Adam
. . . begat a son in his own likeness, after
his image; and called his name Seth.
Genesis 4:25-5:3.*

*T*O Adam was given another son, to be the inheritor of
the divine promise, the heir of the spiritual birthright. The name Seth,
given to this son, signified "appointed," or "compensation," "for," said the
mother, "God . . . hath appointed me another seed instead of Abel, whom
Cain slew." Seth was of more noble stature than Cain or Abel, and resem-
bled Adam more closely than did his other sons. He was a worthy character, following in the steps of Abel. Yet he inherited no more natural
goodness than did Cain. Concerning the creation of Adam it is said, "In
the likeness of God made he him"; but Adam, after the Fall, "begat a son
in his own likeness, after his image." . . .

The Sabbath was honored by all the children of Adam that remained
loyal to God. But Cain and his descendants did not respect the day upon
which God had rested. They chose their own time for labor and for rest,
regardless of Jehovah's express command. . . .

For some time the two classes remained separate. The race of Cain,
spreading from the place of their first settlement, dispersed over the plains
and valleys where the children of Seth had dwelt; and the latter, in order
to escape from their contaminating influence, withdrew to the mountains,
and there made their home. . . . But in the lapse of time they ventured, little by little, to mingle with the inhabitants of the valleys. This association
was productive of the worst results. "The sons of God saw the daughters
of men that they were fair." The children of Seth, attracted by the beauty
of the daughters of Cain's descendants, displeased the Lord by intermar-
rying with them. Many of the worshipers of God were beguiled into sin by
the allurements that were now constantly before them, and they lost their
peculiar, holy character. . . .

For nearly a thousand years Adam lived among his descendants, a witness to the results of sin. Faithfully he sought to stem the tide of evil. . . .
He witnessed the wide-spreading corruption that was finally to cause the
destruction of the world by a flood; and though the sentence of death pronounced upon him by His Maker had at first appeared terrible, yet after
beholding for nearly a thousand years the results of sin, he felt that it was
merciful in God to bring to an end a life of suffering and sorrow.—
Patriarchs and Prophets, pp. 80-82.

February 2
SETH'S DESCENDANTS SETTLE FOR LESS THAN GOD'S PLAN

◆ *To Seth also a son was born, and he named him Enosh. At that time people began to invoke the name of the Lord. Genesis 4:26, NRSV.*

*A*FTER the translation of Enoch to heaven, the sons of men that were set against the worship of God were drawing away the sons of God. There were two parties in the world then, and there always will be. The worshipers of God called themselves the sons of God. The descendants of Seth went up into the mountains and there made themselves homes separate from the sons of Cain. Here in their mountainous homes they thought to preserve themselves from the prevailing wickedness and idolatry of the descendants of Cain. But after the exhortations and the influence of Enoch were removed from them, they commenced to unite with the descendants of Cain.

Here I wish to impress upon your minds that there are always two parties: those who stand as faithful sentinels for God, and those who are against God. God has a test and a trial for every living soul upon the face of the earth. There are always witnesses standing faithful to God, as representatives of God's righteousness, and those who are opposed to God, representatives of the government of Satan. It is the privilege of all who witness these two parties to choose which party they will be in. . . .

The descendants of Seth might have preserved their integrity before God, and they might have exerted a saving influence upon the inhabitants of the Noachic world, but in place of doing this they began to unite with the universal corruption that was prevailing in the valleys.

The Cain worshipers despised everything like the sacrificial offerings that represented the Lamb of God that was to take away the sins of the world. . . . Here we see the two parties standing right out in that degenerate age. It was not all corruption; it was not all fidelity. . . .

The law of God was trampled under the feet of the Cain worshipers—they were idolaters; they worshiped the creature instead of the Creator. The descendants of Seth acknowledged the power and government and right of the living God to govern. God had borne with the perversity and iniquity of that long-lived race until He declared that He would bear with them no longer. He sent His angels to Noah to tell him what His purpose was in regard to the inhabitants of the old world. That faithful creature of righteousness [Noah] declared the message to the inhabitants that one hundred twenty years would be the end of their probation.—Manuscript 86, 1886.

39

February 3
**A TIME OF RARE
SPIRITUAL
OPPORTUNITY**

◆ *When they knew God, they glorified him not as God, neither were thankful; but became vain in their imaginations, and their foolish heart was darkened. Romans 1:21.*

*N*OTWITHSTANDING the wickedness of the antediluvian world, that age was not, as has often been supposed, an era of ignorance and barbarism. The people were granted the opportunity of reaching a high standard of moral and intellectual attainment. They possessed great physical and mental strength, and their advantages for acquiring both religious and scientific knowledge were unrivaled. It is a mistake to suppose that because they lived to a great age their minds matured late; their mental powers were early developed, and those who cherished the fear of God and lived in harmony with His will continued to increase in knowledge and wisdom throughout their life. . . . As the years of human beings have decreased, and their physical strength has diminished, so their mental capacities have lessened. . . .

The antediluvians were without books, they had no written records; but with their great physical and mental vigor, they had strong memories, able to grasp and to retain that which was communicated to them, and in turn to transmit it unimpaired to their posterity. . . . Far from being an era of religious darkness, that was an age of great light. All the world had opportunity to receive instruction from Adam. . . .

Skepticism could not deny the existence of Eden while it stood just in sight, its entrance barred by watching angels. The order of creation, the object of the garden, the history of its two trees so closely connected with human destiny, were undisputed facts. And the existence and supreme authority of God, the obligation of His law, were truths that people were slow to question while Adam was among them.

Notwithstanding the prevailing iniquity, there was a line of holy men and women who, elevated and ennobled by communion with God, lived as in the companionship of heaven. They were people of massive intellect, of wonderful attainments. They had a great and holy mission—to develop a character of righteousness, to teach a lesson of godliness not only to the people of their time but for future generations. Only a few of the most prominent are mentioned in the Scriptures, but all through the ages God had faithful witnesses, truehearted worshipers.—*Patriarchs and Prophets,* pp. 82-84.

February 4
WITH WHOM ARE YOU WALKING?

◆ *Can two walk together, except they be agreed? Amos 3:3.*

$\mathcal{E}$VEN some who are striving for the mastery over the enemy develop a predisposition to do wrong. Evil prevails over good because they do not trust wholly in Christ. They do not abide in Him, and because of their lack of dependence on God, they show inconsistency of character. But no one is compelled to choose this class as familiar associates. The temptations of life are met everywhere, and those who complain of the church members' being cold, proud, haughty, un-Christlike, need not associate with this class. There are many who are warmhearted, self-denying, self-sacrificing, who would if necessary lay down their lives to save souls. Let none then become accusers of the church members, but let the tares grow together with the wheat, for thus Christ has said it should be. But we are not under the necessity of being tares ourselves, because the harvest is not all wheat.

Those who reject the life and character of Jesus, refusing to be like Him, declare themselves to be in controversy with God. "He that is not with me is against me," Christ declares, "and he that gathereth not with me scattereth abroad." Those who love God will not choose His enemies as their friends. The question is asked, "Shouldest thou help the ungodly, and love them which hate the Lord?" True Christians will not choose the society of non-Christians.

If the Lord gives them a special position in the world, as He gave Joseph and Daniel, He will keep them from being contaminated. We need to discern good from evil. We need all the help and instruction that comes from a true faith. We need to listen to the inculcation of Scripture doctrines, which are free from the sophistry and deception of the great deceiver. We need to live in as pure a religious atmosphere as possible, that we may bring solid timbers into our character-building.

By association with those who have no faith in God, wrong ideas are imperceptibly insinuated into mind and heart by the master worker of deception. These prove the ruin of many. Will you choose the association of the irreligious and the disloyal who are openly transgressing God's law? Will you separate yourselves by your own choice from those who love God? Will you place yourselves as far from the light as possible? This is the way of delusion. You will never be where you will find too much light, but woe to those who choose darkness rather than light.—Manuscript 49, 1893.

41

February 5
**ENOCH'S
EXPERIENCE
CAN BE OURS**

◆ *For the one who sanctifies and those who are sanctified all have one Father. For this reason Jesus is not ashamed to call them brothers and sisters. Hebrews 2:11, NRSV.*

F Enoch it is written that he lived sixty-five years, and begat a son. After that he walked with God three hundred years. During these earlier years Enoch had loved and feared God and had kept His commandments. . . . But after the birth of his first son, Enoch reached a higher experience; he was drawn into a closer relationship with God. He realized more fully his own obligations and responsibility as a son of God. . . .

What a blessed thing it is that we have an Enoch! . . . Notwithstanding the corruption that was so great around him, yet he walked with God, and his light shone out to that degenerate age. And if Enoch walked with God amid corruption then, why cannot men and women walk with God today, in this age of the world?

Many of us know something of this experience. We know that in sadness and grief we feel very frail, but we know that Jesus is right by our side to sympathize with us, and He will help us. We can commune with our best Friend; He is right by our side. We need not go into the heavens to bring Him down, for He is right by us to help us.

As we walk in the streets with those who care not for God or heaven or heavenly things, we can talk to them of Jesus. We have something more precious than they to look upon—it is Jesus. He is with us in the moral darkness of this age. We can tell Him of the afflictions of our soul and the wickedness in the world, and none of these things need hinder us. We can talk with Jesus. We can talk with Jesus as Enoch talked with God; he could tell his Lord all about his trials. . . .

Enoch formed a righteous character, and the result was that he was translated to heaven without seeing death. When the Lord shall come the second time, there will be some who will be translated without seeing death, and we want to know if we will be among that number. We want to know if we are wholly on the Lord's side—partakers of the divine nature, having escaped the corruption that is in the world through lust—not by trying to make a clear path for our feet where we shall have no trials or difficulties to meet, but by placing ourselves in right relation to God and letting Him take care of the consequences.—Manuscript 83, 1886.

February 6
**HOW DID
ENOCH WALK?**

◆ *Open thou mine eyes, that I may behold
wondrous things out of thy law. Psalm 119:18.*

COULD your eyes be opened, you would see not only good angels who are trying to impress hearts, but you would see also evil angels who are seeking to make of none effect the message of truth God has in mercy sent.

While we are in this world we are not safe unless our petitions are continually ascending to the God of heaven that He will keep us unspotted from the corruptions of the world. Our Saviour has told us what would be in these last days. Iniquity will abound, but the souls that are open to the influence of the Spirit of God will receive strength to withstand the corruptions of this degenerate age.

Enoch walked with God three hundred years previous to his translation to heaven, and the state of the world was not then more favorable for the perfection of Christian character than it is today. And how did Enoch walk with God? He educated his mind and heart to ever feel that he was in the presence of God, and when in perplexity his prayers would ascend to God to keep him. He refused to take any course that would offend his God. He kept the Lord continually before him. He would pray, "Teach me Thy way, that I may not err. What is Thy pleasure concerning me? What shall I do to honor Thee, my God?". . .

We want to pray with David, "Open thou mine eyes, that I may behold wondrous things out of thy law." Many close their eyes lest they shall see the truth. They do not want to see the defects in their life and character, and they are disturbed if you mention anything about God's law. In this they show that they have a human standard of their own, that their will is not the will of God. We want that you should not be deceived by Satan, the first great adversary of God's law. We want to bear in mind that God's law is the only standard by which He will judge us. . . .

In the beginning God said, "Let us make man in our image, after our likeness." But sin has almost obliterated the moral image of God in human beings. Jesus came down to our world that He might give us a living example, that we might know how to live and how to keep the way of the Lord. He was the image of the Father. His beautiful and spotless character is before us as an example for us to imitate. We must study and copy and follow Jesus Christ, then we shall bring His loveliness and beauty into our character. In doing this we are standing before God through faith, winning back by conflict with the powers of darkness the power of self-control, the love of God that Adam lost.—Manuscript 6a, 1886 (*Sermons and Talks*, vol. 1, pp. 31-34).

February 7
**ENOCH'S EXAMPLE
CHALLENGES
US TODAY**

◆ *Whereby are given unto us exceeding great and precious promises: that by these ye might be partakers of the divine nature, having escaped the corruption that is in the world through lust. 2 Peter 1:4.*

*I*T was no easier for Enoch to live a righteous life in his day than it is for us at the present time. The world in Enoch's time was no more favorable to a growth in grace and holiness than it is now, but Enoch devoted time to prayer and communion with God, and this enabled him to escape the corruption that is in the world through lust. It was his devotion to God that fitted him for translation.

We are living amid the perils of the last days, and we must receive our strength from the same source as did Enoch. We must walk with God. A separation from the world is required of us. We cannot remain free from this pollution unless we follow the example of faithful Enoch and walk with God. But how many are slaves to the lust of the flesh, and the lust of the eye, and the pride of life. This is the reason they are not partakers of the divine nature, and do not escape the corruption that is in the world through lust. They are serving and honoring self. Their constant study is: What shall I eat, what shall I drink, and wherewithal shall I be clothed?

Many talk of sacrifice, when they do not know what sacrifice is. They have not tasted its first draught. They talk of the cross of Christ, they profess the faith, but they have no experience in self-denial, lifting the cross and bearing it after their Lord.

If they were partakers of the divine nature, the same spirit that dwelt in their Lord would dwell in them. The same tenderness and love, the same pity and compassion, would be manifested in their lives. They would not then wait to have the needy and unfortunate come to them, and be entreated to feel their woes. It would be as natural for them to aid the needy and minister to their wants as it was for Christ to go about doing good.

Every man, woman, and youth who professes the religion of Christ should realize the responsibility resting upon them. All should feel that this is an individual work, an individual warfare, an individual preaching of Christ in the daily practice. If each would realize this, and take hold of the work, we should be mighty as an army with banners. The heavenly dove would hover over us. The Sun of Righteousness would shine upon us, and the light of the glory of God would no more be shut from us than it was from the devoted Enoch.—Manuscript 1, 1869 (*Sermons and Talks*, vol. 2, pp. 5, 6).

February 8
**CHANNELS OF
GOD'S GRACE**

◆ *Let your light shine before others, so that
they may see your good works and give glory to
your Father in heaven. Matthew 5:16, NRSV.*

HE Holy Spirit is waiting for channels through whom
to work. If all would do the work to which they were appointed, thousands
of people might be saved. Satan will not always triumph. The Spirit of God
will be poured out upon the church just as soon as the vessels are prepared
to receive it. . . . Why not exercise faith that the divine blessings of the Holy
Spirit shall increase in large measure and will intensify human agencies, so
that the glory of the Lord shall be revealed?

My son Edson,* the more humble you keep, the closer you draw to
God and show you trust Him as a little child trusts its parents, the more
securely you will walk. Your strength is wholly in God—in your simple,
entire trust in God. The churches of Seventh-day Adventists need to walk
more by faith and be less dependent upon feeling. . . .

The softening, subduing influence of the Spirit of God upon human
hearts and minds will make the true children of God sit together in heavenly places in Christ Jesus. . . . There will be a soft, subdued spirit in all
those who are looking unto Jesus. The love of Jesus always leads to
Christian courtesy, refinement of language, and purity of expression that
testify to the company we are with—that like Enoch we are walking with
God. There is no storming, no harshness, but a sweet fragrance in speech
and in spirit.

The Word is to be our study. Here is a mine of precious ore. Much of
it has been glimpsed, but there is digging to be done to secure more precious treasures. There have been many who have just rummaged over the
surface in a most careless, slovenly manner, when others are searching
more carefully, prayerfully, and perseveringly, and hidden, inestimable
treasures are found. . . .

Do not let anyone's speeches, or thoughts revealed in actions, affect
you. You want an abiding Christ. He loves you. He has drawn you by the
cords of His love. Let it be seen that your life is hid with Christ in God. Let
there be no hasty speech, no cheap words, no slang phrases. Let it be
demonstrated that you are conscious of a Companion whom you honor,
and that you will not make Him ashamed of you. Only think, dear children [Edson and his wife, Emma], we are representatives of Jesus Christ!
Then represent His character in words, in deportment, that others may see
and understand your good works and glorify God.—Letter 171, 1897.

---

* James and Ellen White's second son, James Edson White (1849-1928).

February 9
BLENDING PERSONAL PIETY WITH OUTREACH TO OTHERS

♦ *Keep yourselves in the love of God, look-ing for the mercy of our Lord Jesus Christ unto eternal life. Jude 21.*

W E are the Lord's family, His children, and by Him we are to be instructed in regard to what is and what will be in the future. Vigilant waiting and earnest looking are required in preparation for the solemn events soon to take place. Perfect men and women in Christ do not spend all their time in waiting, in meditation and contemplation. While we should have quiet, prayerful hours of meditation, when we leave the busy bustle and excitement to commune with God, to learn from Him His will concerning us, we are not to forget that we have a positive message of warning to bear to the world.

Enoch walked with God, and he bore a message of warning to the in-habitants of the old world. His words and actions, his example of piety, were a continual witness in favor of the truth. In an age no more favorable to the development of a pure, holy character than is the present age, he lived a life of obedience. So filled had the earth become with impurity that the Lord washed it by a flood. He turned the world upside down, as it were, to empty it of its corruption.

Enoch was holy because he walked with God in God's way. In him the world had an example of what those will be who, when Christ comes, are caught up in the clouds to meet Him in the air. As Enoch was, so are we to be. Personal piety is to be blended with the most earnest and energetic warnings and appeals. We are to point to what is, with what is to be fol-lowing fast after. We are instructed to be "not slothful in business; fervent in spirit; serving the Lord." We are to be earnest in our efforts to clear the King's highway, to prepare a people for the coming of the Lord. Fervency of spirit must be brought into our service for the Lord. The lamps of the soul must be kept filled and burning.

Service for God demands the whole being—heart, mind, soul, and strength. Without reservation we are to give ourselves to God, that we may bear the image of the heavenly instead of the image of the earthly. There must be a quickening of the sensibilities, that the mind may be fully awake to the work to be done for all classes, high and low, rich and poor, learned and ignorant. We are to reveal the tenderness shown by the great Shepherd as He gathers the lambs in His arms and carefully guards His flock from harm, leading it in safe paths. Christ's followers are to show His tenderness and sympathy, and they must also show His intensity of desire to impart the truths that mean eternal life to the receiver.—Letter 97, 1902 (*Manuscript Releases*, vol. 12, pp. 213, 214).

February 10
**WALK WITH
GOD ANYWHERE**

◆ *Thou hast a few names even in Sardis
which have not defiled their garments; and
they shall walk with me in white: for they are
worthy. Revelation 3:4.*

HE men and women who have the most to do have
the greatest need of keeping God ever before them. When Satan presses his
suggestions upon their minds, they may, if they cherish a "Thus saith the
Lord," be drawn into the secret pavilion of the Most High. His promises
will be their safeguard. Amid all the confusion and rush of business, they
will find a quiet resting place. If they will place their trust in God, He will
be their resting place.

Take God with you in every place. The door is open for every son and
daughter of God. The Lord is not far from the soul who seeks Him. The
reason so many are left to themselves in places of temptation is that they
do not set the Lord ever before them. It is in the places God is least thought
of that you need to carry the lamp of life. If God be left out of sight, if our
faith and communion with Him are broken, the soul is in positive danger.
Integrity will not be maintained.

The Lord is our helper, our defense. God has provided that no soul
that trusts in Him shall be overcome by the enemy. Christ is just as much
with His believing ones when they are compelled to be associated in any
sense with the world as when they meet in His house to worship Him.
Think of these words: "Thou hast a few names even in Sardis which have
not defiled their garments; and they shall walk with me in white: for they
are worthy. He that overcometh, the same shall be clothed in white raiment; and I will not blot out his name out of the book of life, but I will
confess his name before my Father, and before his angels."

These words are given for the people while they are in connection with
the world, subject to temptations and influences that are deceiving and deluding. While they stay their mind upon Him who is their sun and their
shield, the blackness and darkness that surround them will not leave one
spot or stain upon their garments. They will walk with Christ. They will
pray and believe and work to save the souls that are ready to perish. These
are trying to break the bands that Satan has fastened upon them, and they
will not be put to shame if by faith they will make Christ their companion.
Temptations and deceptions will be constantly brought up by the great deceiver to spoil the work of the human agents, but if they trust God, if they
are humble and meek and lowly of heart, keeping the way of the Lord,
heaven will rejoice, for they will gain the victory.—Manuscript 97, 1898.

February 11
**ENOCH'S FAITH
WAS ALWAYS
EVIDENT**

◆ *And Enoch also, the seventh from Adam, prophesied of these, saying, Behold, the Lord cometh with ten thousands of his saints, to execute judgment upon all. Jude 14.*

ENOCH was an active worker for God. He did not seek ease and comfort. Nor did he spend his time in idle meditation or in striving to gain happiness for himself. He did not participate in the festivities and amusements constantly engaging the attention of the pleasure lovers of the antediluvian world. In his day the minds of many were absorbed in worldly pleasures—pleasures that tempted them to go astray. But Enoch was terribly in earnest. He did not idly saunter along the streets or linger near places of amusement as if he were an indifferent worldling. He never engaged in common conversation with those who were corrupt, as if he were one of them. With the sinful and with the workers of iniquity he mingled only as God's messenger, to warn them to turn with abhorrence from their evil ways and to repent and seek God.

Enoch lived an active, zealous life of self-denial. He walked with God in a world so corrupt that the Lord afterward destroyed it by the Flood. And he walked with the ungodly as one *among* them, not as one *of* them, but as one whose purposes and works and hopes were based not only on time, but on eternity. He did not give the worldly-wise any reason to question his profession and his faith. By earnest words and decided actions he showed that he was separate from the world. After periods of retirement he would mingle with the ungodly to exhort them to abhor the evil and to choose the good. As a faithful worker for God he sought to save them. He warned the world. He preached faith in Christ, the Saviour of sinners, the sinner's only hope.

Enoch was an Adventist. He carried the minds of people forward to the great day of God, when Christ will come the second time, to judge everyone's work. . . .

Like Enoch, we must walk with God, bringing the will into submission to His will. We must be willing to go where Jesus leads, willing to suffer for His dear sake. In seeking to save the souls for whom Christ has died, in conquering difficulties, and in keeping ourselves unspotted from the world, we reveal the genuineness of our religion. Faithful Christians do not seek the easiest place, the lightest burdens. They are found where the work is hardest, where their help is most needed.—Manuscript 36, 1902.

February 12
**ALWAYS STRIVE
TO BE ON
VANTAGE
GROUND**

◆ *Remembering without ceasing your work of faith, and labour of love, and patience of hope in our Lord Jesus Christ, in the sight of God and our Father. 1 Thessalonians 1:3.*

ROM the instruction given us in the Old and New Testaments God desires us to learn that we are not to place ourselves, and those connected with us, in intimate connection with [those] who are corrupt in thought, word, and action. If workers of limited experience are placed in close connection with this class, there is danger that they will by beholding become changed into the same image, that the standard of holiness and truth will be lowered. There is danger that corruption will cease to appear in its vileness to those who are trying to bring about a reform, and that the truth will become confused with that which is common and low. . . .

The difference between a good person and a wicked person is not always caused by natural goodness of disposition. Goodness is the result of divine power transforming human nature. By believing in Christ, the fallen race that He has redeemed may obtain that faith that works by love and purifies the soul from all defilement. Then Christlike attributes appear, for by beholding Christ people become changed into the same image. . . .

People who are compelled by circumstances they cannot control—to be where wickedness, deep and pronounced, is all around them—may remember that God and the angels are with them. Their only safety is to keep looking to Jesus, the Author and Finisher of their faith. Their father, mother, brothers, and sisters may be on the side of the enemy, but they have the assurance that they are guarded by the Lord. It may cost them their lives to stand for the truth, yet they will be saved when the wicked are destroyed. . . .

He [Enoch] did not make his abode with the wicked. He did not locate in Sodom, thinking to save Sodom. He placed himself and his family where the atmosphere would be as pure as possible. Then at times he went forth to the inhabitants of the world with his God-given message. Every visit he made to the world was painful to him. He saw and understood something of the leprosy of sin. After proclaiming his message, he always took back with him to his place of retirement some who had received the warning. Some of these became overcomers and died before the Flood came. But some had lived so long in the corrupting influence of sin that they could not endure righteousness. They did not retain their purity of faith, but returned to their former customs and practices.—Manuscript 42, 1900.

February 13
JESUS IN
THE HEART

◆ *I in them, and thou in me, that they may be made perfect in one; and that the world may know that thou hast sent me, and hast loved them, as thou hast loved me. John 17:23.*

ENOCH not only meditated and prayed, and put on the armor of watchfulness, but he came forth from his pleadings with God to plead with unbelievers. He did not mask the truth to find favor with unbelievers, thus neglecting their souls. This close connection with God gave him courage to work the works of God. Enoch walked with God and had the testimony that his ways "pleased God." This is the privilege of every believer today. It is the believer dwelling with God, and God taking up His abode with the believer. "I in them, and thou in me," says Jesus. To walk with God and have the witness that their ways please Him is an experience not to be confined to Enoch, to Elijah, to patriarchs, to prophets, to apostles, and to martyrs. It is not only the privilege but the duty of every follower of Christ to have Jesus enshrined in the heart, to carry Him with them in their lives, and they will indeed be fruit-bearing trees. . . .

How many who have been entrusted with talents of influence and means have lost sight of the Pattern, and follow the standard of the world instead of the example of Christ. Men and women who have been blessed with an abundance of money, with houses and with lands, generally train their children to a life of idleness and selfish indulgence. Thus they are made useless for this life, and unfit for the future, immortal life. Christ in His life gave people an altogether different example. In His youth He worked with His father at the carpenter's trade; but the youth of today are educated to believe that it is the money that makes the person. The sure result of such education is seen in the pride, the vanity, the love of pleasure, the sinful practices that are so prevalent in this degenerate age.

Where there is an abundance of idleness, Satan works with his temptations to spoil life and character. If youth are not trained to useful labor, whether they be rich or poor, they are in peril, for Satan will find employment for them after his own order. The youth who are not barricaded with principle do not regard time as a precious treasure, a trust from God for which every human being must give an account. Money is also a trust from God. It is given to parents, not to use in an extravagant way to gratify pride to the ruin of themselves and their children, but that they may be the means of doing good to persons in need.—Manuscript 43, 1900.

February 14
**ENOCH KEPT
GOD'S LAW**

◆ *The Lord saw that the wickedness of
humankind was great in the earth, and that
every inclination of the thoughts of their hearts
was only evil continually. Genesis 6:5, NRSV.*

*G*OD had a church when Adam and Eve and Abel accepted and hailed with joy the good news that Jesus was their Redeemer. They realized as fully then as we realize now the promise and the presence of God in their midst. Wherever Enoch found one or two who were willing to hear the message he had for them, Jesus joined with them in their worship of God. In Enoch's day there were some among the wicked inhabitants of earth who believed. The Lord never yet has left His faithful few without His presence, nor the world without a witness.

Enoch was a public teacher of the truth in the age in which he lived. He taught the truth; he lived the truth; and the character of the teacher who walked with God was in every way harmonious with the greatness and sacredness of his mission. Enoch was a prophet who spake as he was moved by the Holy Ghost. He was a light amid the moral darkness, . . . a man who walked with God, being obedient to God's law—that law that Satan had refused to obey, that Adam had transgressed, and that Abel had obeyed and, because of his obedience, been murdered over. And now God would demonstrate to the universe the falsity of Satan's charge that human beings cannot keep God's law. He would demonstrate that though humans had sinned, they could so relate themselves to God that they would have the mind and spirit of God and would be representative symbols of Christ. This holy man was selected of God to denounce the wickedness of the world, and to evidence to the world that it is possible for a person to keep all the law of God. . . .

Enoch walked with God, while of the world around him sacred history records: "And God saw that the wickedness of man was great in the earth, and that every imagination of the thoughts of his heart was only evil continually." Enoch's righteous life was in marked contrast to the wicked people around him. His piety, his purity, his unswerving integrity, was the result of his walking with God, while the wickedness of the world was the result of their walking with the [great] deceiver. . . .

Enoch was a representative man, but he is not praised, he is not exalted; he simply did that which every son and daughter of Adam may do.—Manuscript 43, 1900.

February 15
**PRESSING
INTO CHRIST'S
PRESENCE**

◆ *For ye were sometimes darkness, but now
are ye light in the Lord: walk as children of
light. Ephesians 5:8.*

*W*HAT think ye of Christ?" What is He to you personally? Is your faith centered in Him as your Redeemer? Do you believe that He saves you from sin, that He imputes to you His righteousness?

"This is the condemnation, that light is come into the world, and [men and women] loved darkness rather than light." They will not come to the light for fear that their deeds will be reproved. This is the position taken by many. Their names are in the church books. They observe a round of ceremonies, but they do not love the truth. They have been satisfied to stand at the door. They do not press their way into Christ's presence, to share with Him the glory of His royal life. Their characters are not brought into harmony with the truth. They have not the faith that works by love and purifies the soul. Evil-speaking, evil-surmising, dishonest actions, cast a dark shadow athwart their pathway. Their faith sinks into this shadow of shame, and they feel that they are separated from Christ. There is a sting in the conscience, a condemnation in the life. They feel a desire to hide away from God. Light has come into the world, but they love darkness rather than light, because their deeds are evil. . . .

The time has come when it is for our eternal interest to believe in Christ. . . . He is the Lamb of God, which taketh away the sin of the world. He says, "I will . . . write [My law] in their hearts." He will create in those who come to Him in faith a divine principle of holiness, which shall rule in the soul, enlightening the understanding and captivating the affections. . . .

[Matthew 11:28-30 quoted.] What an invitation! It was this invitation that He gave to Enoch before the world was destroyed by the Flood. . . . Christ was as verily Enoch's Saviour as He is our Saviour, and in His power, notwithstanding the corruption of that degenerate age, Enoch perfected a Christian character.

The voice saying to us, "He that followeth me shall not walk in darkness," said the same words to Enoch, assuring him that if he followed the Saviour, he would not walk in the darkness of ignorance.

The Lord instructed Enoch and made him His watchman. He was a faithful witness for God. He warned the inhabitants of the old world not to follow the example of the Cain-worshipers, but to serve the living God.—Manuscript 13, 1899.

February 16
**WE NEED AN
EVER-INCREASING
FAITH**

◆ *Work out your own salvation with fear and trembling. For it is God which worketh in you both to will and to do of his good pleasure. Philippians 2:12, 13.*

*T*HE fact that human beings can please God is a wonderful incentive for us to make the most persevering, intense efforts, efforts which are proportionate to the value of the object that we are seeking to gain. "We are labourers together with God: ye are God's husbandry, ye are God's building." . . . Enoch walked with God. He was not satisfied with his own companionship. He walked with God. He pleased God. The Lord is not pleased when those whom He has created are sinners. We are ever to walk with God and learn of Jesus Christ, who has overcome every temptation wherewith we are beset. He was tempted in all points like as we are, yet without sin.

The Lord draws people close to His side, to walk with them, to work with them, to teach them how He overcame every temptation in humanity, and how, therefore, they may overcome through the provision the Lord has made. With every temptation there is a way of escape, by walking humbly with God. Without faith, ever increasing faith, it is impossible to please God. . . .

In their fallen nature people can do the very things God expects them to do through the help provided for them. They can walk and work and live by faith in the Son of God. God is not pleased with those who are satisfied with a mere animal life. He has formed human beings after the divine similitude. He designs that they shall possess the character of God by obeying His law, the expression of His divine character. The Lord has given them mind, intellect, and affections. These gifts are entrusted to them to be exercised and improved. God has given them a conscience that must be carefully cherished and appreciated. He has given them knowledge and virtue. These entrusted capabilities are to hold the supremacy that God has assigned to them.

The Lord expects every person to exercise the faculty of faith. It is the real, vital essence of Christianity to grasp the unseen by faith, reaching out constantly to lay hold of the spiritual efficiency found in Christ. If people do not constantly improve by exercising the gifts of God, it is not possible for them to have that faith that works by love and purifies the soul. To cultivate a few of God's entrusted talents is not enough. The conscience is to be in touch with the life and character of God. This is spiritual walking with Jesus Christ, partaking of the divine nature, having overcome the corruptions that are in the world through lust.—Letter 195, 1899.

February 17
THE VALUE OF A LIVING FAITH

◆ *If ye then, being evil, know how to give good gifts unto your children: how much more shall your heavenly Father give the Holy Spirit to them that ask him? Luke 11:13.*

E are assured that the greatest gift that can be given to us will not be withheld. Christ says, "If ye then, being evil, know how to give good gifts unto your children: how much more shall your heavenly Father give the Holy Spirit to them that ask him?" But ask in faith, nothing doubting. It is because of unbelief that so many of our church members are weak. Christ said to Martha at the grave of Lazarus, "If thou wouldest believe, thou shouldest see the glory of God."

This is the greatest blessing that can be bestowed upon God's believing children. But many do not have the virtue of a living faith. They think they have faith, but it is only the thought or action of a moment. They do not persevere in knocking at the door and keeping their request before the Lord. It is not a transient thought that is to be given to God. Our prayers are to be fervent and earnest as were the petitions of the needy friend who asked for the loaves at midnight. The more you ask, the firmer will be your spiritual union. You may come into that place where you will have increased blessings because you have increased faith.

While [you are] trusting in your heavenly Father for the help you need, He will not leave you. God has a heaven full of blessings that He wants to bestow on those who are earnestly seeking for that help that the Lord alone can give. It was in looking in faith to Jesus, in asking of Him, in believing that every word spoken would be verified, that Enoch walked with God. He kept close by the side of God, obeying His every word. And the record comes down along the line to our time, "Enoch walked with God." His was a wonderful life of oneness. Christ was his companion. He was in intimate fellowship with God.

Enoch prophesied in regard to the last days. He said, "Behold, the Lord cometh with ten thousands of his saints, to execute judgment upon all, and to convince all that are ungodly among them of all their ungodly deeds which they have ungodly committed, and of all their hard speeches which ungodly sinners have spoken against him."—Manuscript 111, 1898.

February 18
NOAH HAD GENUINE FAITH— WE CAN TOO

◆ *And the Lord said unto Noah, Come thou and all thy house into the ark; for thee have I seen righteous before me in this generation. Genesis 7:1.*

OAH was commanded to build an ark for the saving of himself and his house. It is stated, "Noah . . . have I found righteous before me in this generation." And it is also stated that "Noah walked with God." Noah did not stop to question, "What will the inhabitants of the old world think of me if I begin to build this boat upon dry land?" He believed just what God had told him, and he commenced to work upon the light and plan that God had given him. He had to employ many carpenters to help him in this great work of building, and there were many of these who were believers at that time. But the largest part of the Noachic world were unbelievers, and they made a great deal of sport of Noah. They ridiculed the idea of building a great boat on dry land.

The surface of the earth was very much as it was when God created it, although some changes had taken place. They looked at the lofty trees and the wonderful things that God had made in nature and said, "It is impossible that God shall destroy these things." The sight of their eyes and their senses made a greater impression upon the inhabitants of the Noachic world than the message from heaven, and Noah stood there in his faithful integrity as a witness to that generation.

Abel, Enoch, and Noah were representative men in that age to the inhabitants of the old world. Everyone had had their test upon the law of God. Would they obey God, would they do just as He told them to do, or would they disobey and realize the results? If Noah had been like many in our day who say, "Believe, believe; all you have to do is believe," then he would not have condemned the world. But Noah had that genuine faith, that faith that works. He testified by his faith and works to the inhabitants of the Noachic world that he believed God. Had he stood back and said, "I cannot build this ark; why, I will be considered crazy if I build this ark on dry land," then he would have had no influence for good upon them. But he believed just what God had said, and carried it out by his works.

They considered him insane; they laughed at him and mocked him, but still he kept at work building the ark according to God's directions. When the last message of Noah was given to that degenerate age, as he stood before the people giving his warning, they turned from him to ridicule him. They had listened to the prayers of Noah that had ascended day after day in their behalf, and with his heart drawn out for them he delivered his very last message to them.—Manuscript 86, 1886.

55

February 19
**ONLY TWO
CLASSES OF
PEOPLE; ONLY ONE
ARK OF SAFETY**

◆ *And God said unto Noah, The end of all flesh is come before me; for the earth is filled with violence through them; and, behold, I will destroy them with the earth. Genesis 6:13.*

IN the future there will be broken thrones and great distress of nations with perplexity. Satan will work with intense activity. The earth will be filled with the shrieks of suffering, expiring nations. There will be war. The places of the earth will be in confusion, as from its bowels pour forth its burning contents to destroy the inhabitants of the world who, in their wickedness, resemble the inhabitants of the antediluvian world.

In that time [before the Flood], as in this, there were two classes, the righteous and the wicked. Enoch and others walked with God in uprightness. But the great majority of the inhabitants of the earth were given over to iniquity, and their wickedness rose before God. . . .

God gave direction that an ark was to be built for those who desired to be saved from the coming destruction. He was about to speak in determined language against the wickedness that had grown to fearful proportions. He was about to clothe Himself with vengeance and execute His judgment against the transgressors of His law.—Manuscript 72, 1902 (*Manuscript Releases*, vol. 18, pp. 92, 93).

As Noah proclaimed his warning message, some listened and worked with him in building the ark. But they did not endure. Evil influences prevailed. They turned away from the truth to become scoffers.

Thus it will be in the last days of this earth's history. Those who today hear the message of truth, but do not believe, will fall amid the moral infidelity, even as in Noah's day those who were not firmly grounded failed to stand till the end of their probation. When the Lord rewards everyone according to his deeds, these people will understand that God is truth, and that His message would have been their life and salvation if they had accepted the evidence given and practiced the conditions laid down. Then they will see that they might have been saved had they not rejected the only means of salvation.

The trials of God's people may be long and severe, but the Lord never forgets them. Those who believe the truth and obey the commandments will find refuge in Christ. They will have the effectual protection of His ever-loving care as long as they take their position on the side of God and His law, which ever has governed, and ever will govern, His kingdom.—Manuscript 42, 1900.

February 20
WHEN WE ARE TESTED, WILL OUR FAITH ENDURE?

◆ *And Noah did according unto all that the Lord commanded him. Genesis 7:5.*

ND God said to Noah that he and his wife, and his sons and their wives, should come into the ark. You see how few there were who would believe the message of Heaven, the Word of God, and thus be saved from the waters of the Flood. The consequences of the transgression of God's law were evidenced upon the population and upon the earth. Violence and corruption were prevailing everywhere.

But the time came when there was a singular sight witnessed by the inhabitants of the Noachic world. Those who had laughed and scoffed and derided Noah now could see that something was taking place that was wonderful. There were seen coming, through the forest and from every quarter, animals, two by two, making their way to the ark. These animals were obedient to the commandments of God, but humans were disobedient. Then there was seen, like a dark cloud in the heavens, the fowls of the air flocking to that ark. At that moment this made an impression upon their minds. But as they spent time with one another, in their unbelief and corruption they put it away from their minds.

Then the commandment was given for Noah and his family to enter the ark. The probation for the inhabitants of the Noachic world was ended. Noah went into the ark and there was seen a bright light—an angel of heaven came and shut the massive door. . . . Noah and his family were shut into the ark and the unrighteous were shut out. The mercy of God was withdrawn from that polluted and corrupt generation. . . .

It was a tremendous test brought to bear upon Noah and his family; [they were] shut in that ark for seven days, and yet no rain came. The jeers and scoffs and triumphs of their enemies seemed complete. But as soon as the seven days were ended, there began to come in the dark and heavy clouds such as they had never seen before. The clouds increased in blackness, and the rain began to fall from them.

Up to this time there had never been any rain, but a mist had arisen and watered the earth. For this very reason the people had taken occasion to triumph. But the rain continued to fall, and then there were some serious thoughts. But in order to put these reflections away from them, they went still deeper into their iniquity, and they earnestly looked to see if there was not some evidence that the clouds were rolling back, but there was none. The rain increased until it came in torrents.—Manuscript 86, 1886.

February 21
**RESULTS OF
TRANSGRESSING
GOD'S LAW**

◆ *Hearken unto me, my people; and give ear unto me, O my nation: for a law shall proceed from me, and I will make my judgment to rest for a light of the people. Isaiah 51:4.*

*G*OD had concealed in the earth His weapons whereby He would purify the earth at that time. The jets of water began to come up from the depths of the earth, and as this water increased in force, it would throw up stones and uproot trees. Do you not think that there were some who would have been glad at that time to find refuge in the ark? There were some reaching toward the ark, and some entreaties, but it was too late. They began to move their families, and they climbed up to the highest points of land . . . and struggled for refuge there. They would climb into the highest trees, thinking to find refuge there, but these trees would be uprooted and they would be buried in the waters of the earth.

Thus the inhabitants of that long-lived race perished in the Flood, and even the beasts perished, except those that were in the ark. Christ said, "As it was in the days of Noe, so shall it be also in the days of the Son of man. They did eat, they drank, they married wives, they were given in marriage, until the day that Noe entered into the ark, and the flood came, and destroyed them all." Thus shall it be when Christ shall be revealed at His second coming.

The law of God was first transgressed by Satan in heaven. He has kept up his controversy upon that point till the present time, and will until the close of time. The test that was brought to bear upon the representative people in past ages will be brought to bear upon people in this age. Will men and women acknowledge the government of the God of the universe and honor that government? Did it make the inhabitants of the old world any better by trampling upon the law of Jehovah? Did it improve their condition to separate themselves from the law of their Creator? Will it make men and women any better in this age to put their feet upon God's holy law and transgress it?

The very same results that were seen in the transgression of God's law by the inhabitants of the Noachic world will be seen in the inhabitants of this generation. The rights and property, and even human life, were not respected then, but violated. The thoughts and imaginations of the heart were evil continually. They worshiped anything and everything but God. So it is in this age of the world—deception, infidelity, and idolatry prevail to an alarming extent.—Manuscript 86, 1886.

February 22
**VINDICATORS OF
GOD'S LAW**

◆ *But those who look into the perfect law, the
law of liberty, and persevere, being not hearers
who forget but doers who act—they will be
blessed in their doing. James 1:25, NRSV.*

*D*OES it make a nation happy to put away the laws of
God? The countries here [in Europe] have their laws, and the safety of the
inhabitants of these countries is due to their obedience to these laws, and
you know how strictly they require that these laws shall be observed. You
see an officer by the side of a man who wears shackles upon his hands and
feet, and you know that man has transgressed the laws of the land. He forfeited his liberty and was put in prison because he transgressed the laws of
the country.

And shall anybody advocate that the Lord of the universe has no law
to govern His kingdom? Is it the doctrine of Jesus Christ or of heaven that
the law of God has no binding claims upon the world's inhabitants? Why,
the law of ten commandments is the great moral standard of righteousness
in heaven and upon earth. This great law is the foundation of all laws, to
all nations, and to all families.

What a piece of workmanship of the devil it is to say that the law of
God is done away, and is no more binding upon the human race. We
know that the murderer, the adulterer, and the thief get in trouble with
this law at once. They are the ones that would like to have this law swept
away so they could have free license to all their imaginations and wickedness. We do not think as we see a man attended by an officer of justice that
he has been keeping the law but that he has been transgressing it.

Every soul of us living upon the face of the earth must have our test
and trials. Circumstances will occur in the providence of God when we
will be called to vindicate our faith. We shall give decided evidence which
side we are on. We shall either be decidedly the vindicators of God's holy
law, or on the side of the transgressors. We shall be tested as Noah was
tested. Because the corruption was nearly universal in his age, did he then
argue that it would not pay for him to stand separate and alone for God's
law? He took his position as God's nobleman on the side of right because
it was right.—Manuscript 86, 1886.

February 23
**MORE THAN
BELIEVING
IS NEEDED**

◆ *Thou believest that there is one God; thou doest well: the devils also believe, and tremble. James 2:19.*

*I*N the near future we shall understand something of what it is to be tested. There will be laws of the land that will interfere with our obedience to the laws of God, and then the test will come as to whose side we are on, on the side of God or the side of those who are against God. We want, every one of us, to be prepared for that which is coming upon our world. You cannot, any one of you, at once jump into the position to stand the test of God. It is by patient continuance in well-doing that you gain the element of character that will enable you to stand the test at last. It is by persevering integrity of soul day by day, and by calling upon God, that we get strength to stand the test.

There will be every influence that will lead us to make light of God's requirements. But if we are prepared to meet the Son of man when He shall come in the clouds of heaven, we must be getting ready for it now. . . . We want a living faith and a living religion. We want that our faith shall be made perfect by our works. And of those who are crying, "Only believe, only believe, and you shall be saved," we want to inquire, "What shall we believe? What is the testing faith for this time?" . . .

There was one in the parable that Christ gave us who begged that someone from the dead might go to his relatives and warn them that they might believe. But Christ told them, "They have Moses and the prophets. . . . If they hear not [them], neither will they be persuaded, though one rose from the dead." . . .

We read that the devil believed and trembled, but that faith did not save him. We want that faith that has the Bible foundation for it—that faith that grasps a living Saviour and a living God. . . . The blood of Christ alone can cleanse the sinner from every stain of sin. Had they acknowledged that law, it would have pointed out to them in the old world what sin was, and they would not have dared to sin. . . .

God is gathering out and binding up those who love and serve Him, and the wicked are being bound in bundles, ready for the fires of the last day. It depends wholly upon us which bundles we will be in, whether we will be with the good wheat or bound in bundles for the fires of the last day. . . .

The eternal reward is to be given to those who are faithful and obedient to God.—Manuscript 86, 1886.

February 24
**WILL WE LOOK
FOR SAFETY
AFTER IT IS
TOO LATE?**

◆ *The same day were all the fountains of the great deep broken up, and the windows of heaven were opened. Genesis 7:11.*

HE antediluvians were warned, but the record states that they knew not until the Flood came and took them all away. . . . They saw Noah and his wife and their sons and their wives passing into the ark; and the door was closed upon them. Only eight persons entered that refuge from the storm, and for a week they waited for the rain to come. . . . Daily the sun rose and set in a clear sky, and daily there came to Noah the temptation to doubt. But the Lord had said that the Flood was coming, and Noah rested in this word.

At the end of seven days clouds began to gather. This was a new sight, for the people had never seen clouds. . . . Thicker and thicker gathered the clouds, and soon rain began to fall. Still the people tried to think that this was nothing very alarming. But soon it seemed as if the windows of heaven had been opened, for the rain poured down in torrents. For a time the ground drank up the rain; but soon the water began to rise, and day by day it rose higher and higher. Each morning as the people found the rain still falling they looked at one another in despair, and each night they repeated the words "Raining still!" Thus it was, morning and evening.

For forty days and forty nights the rain poured down. The water entered the houses and drove the people to the temples that they had erected for their idolatrous worship. But the temples were swept away. The crust of the earth was broken, and the water that had been concealed in its bowels burst forth. Large stones were thrown into the air.

Everywhere could be seen human beings fleeing in search of a refuge. The time had come when they would have been only too glad to accept an invitation to enter the ark. Filled with anguish, they cried, "Oh, for a place of safety!" Some shrieked to Noah, pleading for admission into the ark. But amid the furious blast of the tempest their voices were unheard. Some clung to the ark till they were washed away by the dashing waves. God had shut in those who believed His word, and no others could enter.

Parents with their children sought the highest branches of the trees yet standing; but no sooner had they reached this refuge than the wind flung tree and people into the foaming, seething water. . . .

Where now was the ark and those at whom the people had jeered and mocked? Preserved by the power of God, the immense boat was riding safely upon the waters, and Noah and his family were safe inside.—*Signs of the Times*, Apr. 10, 1901.

February 25
**IN THE WORLD,
BUT NOT OF IT**

◆ *Wherefore come out from among them,
and be ye separate, saith the Lord, and touch
not the unclean thing; and I will receive you.
2 Corinthians 6:17.*

ECAUSE iniquity abounds, the love of many is growing cold, but shall we cover our light on account of this? The prevalence of greatest iniquity should be the time of the greatest earnestness of the people of God. As you see the love of many waxing cold, you should work to show Christ to the world.

The law and the gospel are interwoven as warp and woof. Here mercy and truth have met together, and righteousness and peace have kissed each other. We want to come to God's standard. He has a law governing human intelligences, and it is for our happiness to observe it. We are to love God. Love leading to disobedience is the inspiration of the devil; love leading to obedience is the inspiration of Heaven.

"Come out from among them, and be ye separate," says the Lord, and again, "Cleanse yourselves." But how are we to know that we have impurity? The law of God shows this. The first four commandments point out duty to God, and the last six allow no selfishness toward our friends and acquaintances. When I see that I fail, I flee to the Stronghold. I know that He pardons sins of ignorance. Jesus is a sin-pardoning Saviour. Jesus kept His Father's commandments, and He says, Blessed are they that do; they shall enter in.

When we obey we shall have happy families. Teach the children the commandments of God forever. This was important in Israel's time, and it is none the less so now. All your profession of keeping the commandments will not give you an entrance to the city. Bind them on your heart and carry them out in every act. . . .

Will you not from this very day try to represent Christ to the world? You will have a refuge. You will be sunny Christians. We have been gloomy long enough. Had we not better come out of the cave and stand with God? Then we will have Christ with us so that we can talk of redemption as did the disciples when they had been with Jesus and learned of Him. Carry the light of Jesus. Carry it to your neighbors.

When we bring Christ into our experience, there will be a loving of one another, there will be an unlocking of the hardest hearts. . . . If we humble ourselves and have His converting power every moment, His righteousness will be our covering.—Manuscript 27, 1891 (*Sermons and Talks,* vol. 2, pp. 97, 98).

February 26
**JESUS:
CHANGELESS
THROUGHOUT
ETERNITY**

◆ *Jesus Christ the same yesterday, and to-day, and for ever. Hebrews 13:8.*

*T*HE power of Christ, a crucified Saviour, to give eternal life should be presented to the people. We should show them that the Old Testament is as verily the gospel in types and shadows as the New Testament is in its unfolding power. The New Testament is not a new religion, and the Old Testament is not an old religion to be superseded by the New. The New Testament is only the advancement and unfolding of the Old. Abel was a believer in Christ and was as verily saved by His power as were Peter and Paul.

Enoch was a representative of Christ as surely as was the beloved disciple John. Enoch walked with God, and he was not, for God took him. To him was committed the message of the second coming of Christ. "And Enoch also, the seventh from Adam, prophesied of these, saying, Behold, the Lord cometh with ten thousands of his saints, to execute judgment upon all, and to convince all that are ungodly among them of their ungodly deeds which they have ungodly committed, and of all their hard speeches which ungodly sinners have spoken against him." The message preached by Enoch, and his translation to heaven, were a convincing argument to all who lived in Enoch's time. These things were an argument that Methuselah and Noah could use with power to show that the righteous would be translated.

That God who walked with Enoch was our Lord and Saviour, Jesus Christ. He was the light of the world then, just as He is today. Those living then were not without teachers to instruct them in the paths of life, for Noah and Enoch were Christians. The gospel is given in precept in Leviticus. Implicit obedience is required now, as then. How important it is that we understand the meaning of this word. Only two classes will be developed in the world—the obedient and the disobedient. This must be made apparent in all our labors. If we could only bear in mind that Christ, in disguise, is constantly by our side. "I am at your right hand to help you." We are to be His witnesses to convince the sinner of sin. None can be compelled against their will, but they can be convinced. Christ is the miracle-working power that can do this.—Letter 119, 1895.

February 27
SINGLENESS OF PURPOSE

◆ *The light of the body is the eye: if therefore thine eye be single, thy whole body shall be full of light. Matthew 6:22.*

*T*HIS says, "thine eye," not some other person's eye. The rich experience that it is our privilege to have, we lose when we expect someone else to do our seeing for us, and guide us in our spiritual experience as if we were blind. We must have a single eye to God's glory, a single and persistent purpose to leave self and the preferences of others out of the question, not asking, "If I take this course, shall I increase my personal possessions, or shall I decrease them?"

Great simplicity must be cherished by those who seek wisdom of God. Then their feet will not slide. "The path of the just is as the shining light, that shineth more and more unto the perfect day. The way of the wicked is as darkness: they know not at what they stumble." . . .

A person who truly loves and fears God, striving with singleness of purpose to do His will, will place body, mind, heart, soul, and strength under service to God. Thus it was with Enoch. He walked with God. His mind was not defiled by an impure, defective eyesight. Those who are determined to make the will of God their own must serve and please God in everything. Then the character will be harmonious and well-balanced, consistent, cheerful, and true.

"But if thine eye be evil," if you study selfish purposes, and work only to that end, the whole character is defective, the whole body is full of darkness. Such do not look to Jesus. They do not behold His character, and they are not changed into His image. The spiritual vision is defective, and the way from earth to heaven is darkened by the hellish shadow of Satan. So Satan is pleased to have it, for he can lead that person blindfolded to ruin.

"If therefore the light that is in thee be darkness, how great is that darkness!" The conscience is the regulative faculty, and if people allow their conscience to become perverted, they cannot serve God aright. Their object in life shows to the world whether they are Christians or in rebellion against God. Their whole life is a failure. It is distorted and double, and all the faculties are misdirected. The profession may be all right, but the faith is perverted, and this is revealed by the practice, which misleads others. "No man can serve two masters: for either he will hate the one, and love the other; or else he will hold to the one, and despise the other. Ye cannot serve God and mammon."—Letter 128, 1897 (*Manuscript Releases*, vol. 13, pp. 154, 155).

February 28
**MORE OF
HEAVEN—
LESS OF SELF**

◆ *These are they which came out of great
tribulation, and have washed their robes, and
made them white in the blood of the Lamb.
Revelation 7:14.*

wish that I could carry your minds to the future
glory, and could impress upon each the great sacrifice that had to be made
to redeem the human race. It rests with you whether you will enjoy this
glory. . . .

To each one God has given talents, and if we neglect to cultivate them,
we shall fail and lose eternal life. Everything has been done for us that
could be done to elevate us, and if we fail on our part, then the sacrifice
has been in vain so far as we are concerned. Shall we be weighed in the balances and found wanting? Or shall we be with the white-robed throng?
This will depend upon our course of action. If we are in the workshop of
God, He will beautify us and polish us, and we shall be fitted for the heavenly mansions.

Oh, the matchless charms of our loving Saviour! There is nothing in
earthly treasures; it is enough to look to Calvary. I want everyone to accept
the salvation offered. All have something to do, and if they come off vic-
tors they will cry, Worthy, worthy is the Lamb that was slain for us.

Will you have eternal life? If so, you must turn away from the pleasures of the world. The wickedness in this age is as great as it was in the days
of Noah. But one man was found that walked with God even in that
crooked and perverse generation. Enoch kept his mind stayed upon God,
and God did not leave him but finally took him from this sinful world.
This man was a representative of those who will be translated to heaven
when Christ comes to gather His people. Are we ready for the appearing
of Christ? Are we constantly seeking God for strength to stand against the
wiles of the enemy? Have we washed our robes and made them clean in
the blood of the Lamb?

God is in earnest with us and claims all the power of our being. We
need the Great Physician to heal us. We need more of heaven and less of
self. We must be partakers of the divine nature. Oh, what love has been
manifested for us! The divine Son of God left the throne of heaven and
gave His life for us, and for our sakes became poor. He clothed His divinity with humanity. Now in return are you willing to deny self and follow
your Saviour? Oh, do not trifle away the few moments left you by seeking
worldly honor and thus lose the precious boon of everlasting life!—
Manuscript 40, 1886.

February 29
CHRISTIANS ARE GOD'S AGENTS

◆ *Ho, every one that thirsteth, come ye to the waters, and he that hath no money; come ye, buy, and eat. Isaiah 55:1.*

*B*EFORE Christ clothed His divinity with humanity and came to our world, God sent this message through Noah, Enoch, Seth, and Methuselah. Lot bore the message in Sodom, and a race of messengers proclaimed the coming One. But at this time the message is to be proclaimed everywhere. . . .

The feast is now spread. The last invitation to be given is to go forth to all nations to the end of the world. This is our work. The messengers are now in a more special sense to call, "Hearken diligently." The message is to go forth from the lips of human intelligences. He who came to our world to proclaim the message was the Lord Himself. Then tell the people that Christ came in human form, that His humanity might touch humanity, and that His divinity might lay hold upon divinity. His servants are to be linked together. "Ye are labourers together with God," He says. "Ye are God's husbandry, ye are God's building." If His workers will be worked by the Holy Spirit, a great work can be done. "Compel them to come in" are the words addressed to the messengers, "that my house may be filled." The Lord means that we shall be in earnest. If we are wholly consecrated to God, the Holy Spirit will work with us.

Look at our world today, you who claim to be Christians. Are you awake to the situation as you see how the kindness and love of a long-forbearing God is treated with contempt and absolute rejection? Finite, fallen human beings in need of pardon and peace, and all are invited to come. The Lord Jesus, the Great Teacher, gives the invitation, but often it is met with frivolous excuses or turned from with jesting and contempt. All who will may come and respond to the gracious invitation. Why cannot people see the importance of accepting the call and making their peace with God?

The devil is not dead. He is working with all his attractive allurements to persuade people to close their ears that they shall not hear, and thousands who ought to be giving this testing message to the world are hiding their talents in the earth. They are making no use of their powers to draw souls to the bountifully spread table. Unfaithful, slothful servants! God will call you to account. But we thank God that there are some faithful voices heard, that there are some who feel their responsibility, and who are at work with every means in their power to compel them to come in.— Letter 89, 1898.

March 1
**CHARACTER
MAKES A
DIFFERENCE
IN LIFE**

◆ *The Lord knoweth the days of the upright:
and their inheritance shall be for ever. . . .
For such as be blessed of him shall inherit the
earth; and they that be cursed of him shall be
cut off. Psalm 37:18-22.*

*T*HE reverence manifested by Shem and Japheth for their father, and thus for the divine statutes, promised a brighter future for their descendants. Concerning these sons it was declared: "Blessed be Jehovah, God of Shem; and Canaan shall be his servant. God shall enlarge Japheth, and he shall dwell in the tents of Shem; and Canaan shall be his servant." The line of Shem was to be that of the chosen people, of God's covenant, of the promised Redeemer. Jehovah was the God of Shem. From him would descend Abraham, and the people of Israel, through whom Christ was to come. "Happy is that people, whose God is the Lord." And Japheth "shall dwell in the tents of Shem." In the blessings of the gospel the descendants of Japheth were especially to share. . . .

The prophecy of Noah was no arbitrary denunciation of wrath or declaration of favor. It did not fix the character and destiny of his sons. But it showed what would be the result of the course of life they had severally chosen and the character they had developed. It was an expression of God's purpose toward them and their posterity in view of their own character and conduct. As a rule, children inherit the dispositions and tendencies of their parents, and imitate their example; so that the sins of the parents are practiced by the children from generation to generation. Thus the vileness and irreverence of Ham were reproduced in his posterity, bringing a curse upon them for many generations. "One sinner destroyeth much good."

On the other hand, how richly rewarded was Shem's respect for his father; and what an illustrious line of holy people appears in his posterity! "The Lord knoweth the days of the upright," "and his seed is blessed." "Know therefore that the Lord thy God, he is God, the faithful God, which keepeth covenant and mercy with them that love him and keep his commandments to a thousand generations."—*Patriarchs and Prophets,* pp. 117, 118.

March 2
**AN EVIL
CHARACTER
LEADS TO
APOSTASY**

◆ *Cursed be Canaan; a servant of servants
shall he be unto his brethren. Genesis 9:25.*

O repeople the desolate earth, which the Flood had so lately swept from its moral corruption, God had preserved but one family, the household of Noah, to whom He had declared, "Thee have I seen righteous before me in this generation." Yet in the three sons of Noah was speedily developed the same great distinction seen in the world before the Flood. In Shem, Ham, and Japheth, who were to be the founders of the human race, was foreshadowed the character of their posterity.

Noah, speaking by divine inspiration, foretold the history of the three great races to spring from these fathers of the human race. Tracing the descendants of Ham, through the son rather than the father, he declared, "Cursed be Canaan; a servant of servants shall he be unto his brethren.". . . Evil characteristics were perpetuated in Canaan and his posterity, whose continued guilt called upon them the judgments of God. . . .

Though the prophetic curse had doomed them to slavery, the doom was withheld for centuries. God bore with their impiety and corruption until they passed the limits of divine forbearance. Then they were dispossessed, and became bondmen to the descendants of Shem and Japheth. . . .

For a time the descendants of Noah continued to dwell among the mountains where the ark had rested. As their numbers increased, apostasy soon led to division. Those who desired to forget their Creator and to cast off the restraint of His law felt a constant annoyance from the teaching and example of their God-fearing associates, and after a time they decided to separate from the worshipers of God. Accordingly they journeyed to the plain of Shinar, on the banks of the river Euphrates. They were attracted by the beauty of the situation and the fertility of the soil, and upon this plain they determined to make their home.

Here they decided to build a city, and in it a tower of such stupendous height as should render it the wonder of the world. These enterprises were designed to prevent the people from scattering abroad in colonies. God had directed men and women to disperse throughout the earth, to replenish and subdue it; but these Babel builders determined to keep their community united in one body, and to found a monarchy that should eventually embrace the whole earth. . . . The magnificent tower, reaching to the heavens, was intended to stand as a monument of the power and wisdom of its builders, perpetuating their fame to the latest generations.—
Patriarchs and Prophets, pp. 117-119.

March 3
**SOME GO TO
GREAT LENGTHS
TO AVOID GOD**

◆ *Let us build us a city and a tower, whose top may reach unto heaven; and let us make us a name, lest we be scattered abroad. Genesis 11:4.*

*S*OME of the descendants of Noah soon began to apostatize.... They journeyed a distance ... and selected a large plain wherein to dwell. There they built a city, and then conceived the idea of erecting a large tower to reach unto the clouds, that they might dwell together in the city and tower, and be no more scattered. They reasoned that they would secure themselves in case of another flood, for they would build their tower to a much greater height than the waters prevailed in the time of the Flood, and all the world would honor them.... Before the work of building was accomplished, people dwelt in the tower. Rooms gorgeously furnished and decorated were devoted to their idols.....—*Signs of the Times,* Mar. 20, 1879.

But among the people of Babel there were living some God-fearing persons who had been deceived by the pretensions of the ungodly and drawn into their schemes. These would not join this confederacy to thwart the purposes of God. They refused to be deceived by the wonderful representations and the grand outlook. For the sake of these faithful ones, the Lord delayed His judgments and gave the people time to reveal their true character....

This confederacy was born of rebellion against God. The dwellers on the plain of Shinar established their kingdom for self-exaltation, and not for the glory of God.... Determined individuals, inspired by the first great rebel, would have been urged on by him and would have permitted nothing to interfere with their plans or to stop them in their evil course. In the place of the divine precepts they would have substituted laws framed in accordance with the desires of their selfish hearts, in order that they might carry out their purposes.

But God never leaves the world without witnesses for Him. Those who loved and feared Him at the time of the first great apostasy after the Flood humbled themselves and cried unto Him. "O God," they pleaded, "interpose Thyself between Thy cause and the plans and methods of men." "And the Lord came down to see the city and the tower, which the children of men builded." ...

God bears long with the perversity of human beings, giving them ample opportunity for repentance, but He marks all their devices to resist the authority of His just and holy law. As an evidence of His displeasure over the building of this tower, He confounded the language of the builders, so that none could understand the words of fellow workers.—Manuscript 94, 1903 (*Manuscript Releases,* vol. 8, pp. 42, 43).

March 4
BABEL BUILDERS
STILL EXIST

♦ *The Lord bringeth the counsel of the hea-*
then to nought: he maketh the devices of the
people of none effect. The counsel of the Lord
standeth for ever, the thoughts of his heart to
all generations. Psalm 33:10, 11.

*T*HE schemes of the Babel builders ended in shame and defeat. The monument to their pride became the memorial of their folly. Yet people today are continually pursuing the same course—depending upon self, and rejecting God's law. It is the principle that Satan tried to carry out in heaven; the same that governed Cain in presenting his offering.

There are tower builders in our time. Infidels construct their theories from the supposed deductions of science and reject the revealed Word of God. They presume to pass sentence upon God's moral government; they despise His law and boast of the sufficiency of human reason. Then, "because sentence against an evil work is not executed speedily, therefore the heart of the sons of men is fully set in them to do evil."

In the professedly Christian world many turn away from the plain teachings of the Bible and build up a creed from human speculations and pleasing fables, and they point to their tower as a way to climb up to heaven. People hang with admiration upon the lips of eloquence while it teaches that the transgressor shall not die, that salvation may be secured without obedience to the law of God. If the professed followers of Christ would accept God's standard, it would bring them into unity; but so long as human wisdom is exalted above His Holy Word, there will be divisions and dissension.

The existing confusion of conflicting creeds and sects is fitly represented by the term "Babylon," which prophecy applies to the world-loving churches of the last days. Many seek to make a heaven for themselves by obtaining riches and power. They "speak wickedly concerning oppression: they speak loftily," trampling upon human rights and disregarding divine authority. The proud may be for a time in great power, and may see success in all that they undertake, but in the end they will find only disappointment and wretchedness.

The time of God's investigation is at hand. The Most High will come down to see that which rebel humans have builded. His sovereign power will be revealed; the works of human pride will be laid low. . . . "The Lord bringeth the counsel of the heathen to nought: he maketh the devices of the people of none effect. The counsel of the Lord standeth forever, the thoughts of his heart to all generations."—*Patriarchs and Prophets,* pp. 123, 124.

March 5
ABRAHAM'S
FAITH TESTED

◆ *I will make of thee a great nation, and I will bless thee, and make thy name great; and thou shalt be a blessing. Genesis 12:2.*

*I*T was not a small trial to Abraham to be called to leave his home and acquaintances and go into a land that he knew not. When he came into that land, he found that the Canaanites were there, and he would have all their idolatry to meet.

This was a severe trial to Abraham's faith. He could not see any possession that he could claim as his own. But in his perplexity the God of heaven condescended to preach the gospel to him and show him the possession that he should have for an eternal inheritance.

Abraham moved from place to place, as it seemed advisable for him, in order to obtain a support for his family, and his family was not small. His trained servants numbered more than four hundred. At every place where he pitched his tent, close beside it he erected an altar; so he worshiped God in every place where he was called to be. In thus doing he was training his family to love and fear God. . . .

All God's followers, wherever they shall go, should carry the true principles of their religion with them. If sin, forgetfulness of God, and idolatry exist in the places where they shall go, then is the time for them to show their true principles.

When we set ourselves where all is convenience and ease, we do not feel so much the necessity of depending moment by moment upon God. God in His providence brings us into positions where we shall feel our necessity of His help and strength. . . .

Now, the Lord has a controversy with His people, and He wants every one of us to come into obedience to His requirements. We are none of us, when duty is laid out before us, to question, "Is it convenient or will it please me to do this?" If God says it, it is enough. We are to take our Bibles; we are to study and see what the will of God is concerning us, and then to follow as Abraham did, in faith and confidence.

Now, you see, the first test was a very close test for Abraham—to leave everything and go into a land of strangers. . . . There were adverse circumstances that followed Abraham for a time that brought him into positions of trial and where he was proved of God. . . . When the Lord opened before him the view of immortal life, of this earth purified, which was to be his home, he was satisfied.—Manuscript 19, 1886 (see also *In Heavenly Places*, p. 112; *Manuscript Releases*, vol. 10, pp. 120, 121).

March 6
**THE EFFECT
OF CHOICES**

◆ *If thou wilt take the left hand, then I will
go to the right; or if thou depart to the right
hand, then I will go to the left. Genesis 13:9.*

ABRAHAM was tested to see whether he would hear
the voice of God and obey. The Lord saw that it was not for his best spiritual interest to remain in his country and among his relatives, where he could not exert that influence over them that would be a blessing. He told him to leave them. Abraham was a rich man, but in the greatest simplicity he obeyed God and went out, a sojourner into a strange country. As he left his home and his kindred, God assured him that he would have earthly greatness and prosperity in the land of Canaan.

Why did not Abraham make use of all his means to bring about this prosperity? Why did he not invest his means to enrich himself with wealth and influence above anyone with whom he was brought in contact? Abraham did not do anything to glorify himself. He did not aim at power. He did not aspire to greatness by building up cities and calling them by his name. He was content.

The record tells us that Abraham took Lot, his nephew, with him, and for a time they lived together. But their families were large, and there was a quarrel between the herdsmen of Abraham and the herdsmen of Lot over their cattle. "And Abraham said unto Lot, Let there be no strife, I pray thee, between me and thee, and between my herdmen and thy herdmen; for we be brethren. Is not the whole land before thee?". . .

Lot's choice was the land of Sodom. Abraham dwelt in the land of Canaan and Lot in the cities of the plain, and he pitched his tent toward Sodom. But the men of Sodom sinned before the Lord exceedingly.

Here is brought to view another separation. It makes a great difference when and how a separation takes place. It was Lot's privilege to inquire, to be very careful where he should go, very careful in regard to the society he chose for his family. But without reference to the inhabitants, he chose a land that was beautiful in situation, that promised great returns. Lot went in rich, and came forth with nothing as the result of his choice. It makes every difference whether people place themselves in positions where they will have the very best help of correct influences or whether they choose temporal advantages. There are many ways that lead to Sodom. We all need anointed eyesight, that we may discern the way that leads to God.—
Letter 109, 1899.

March 7
LOT'S EXPERIENCE SERVES AS A WARNING

◆ *Then Lot chose him all the plain of Jordan; and Lot journeyed east: and they separated themselves the one from the other. Genesis 13:11.*

*W*E see the marked traits in Abraham's character when the strife commenced between the herdsmen, and Abraham said, "Let there be no strife, I pray thee, between me and thee. . . . Separate thyself, I pray thee, from me: if thou wilt take the left hand, then I will go to the right; or if thou depart to the right hand, then I will go to the left."

Lot saw that the country near Sodom was most favorable for his worldly and temporal prosperity, and he chose that location. If Lot had manifested the same courtesy that Abraham had, he would have given him the choice. But Abraham did not take the position that he was superior to everyone around him; he took a humble position. It was the right of Abraham to make his choice, and to be first, but he chose to be courteous in this matter.

Lot, instead of inquiring whether this would be the most favorable for his morality and godliness, thought only of his worldly prosperity. But the time came when Lot was placed in a most trying position because of the wickedness of the inhabitants of Sodom. When Lot and his family were taken by those who came in to conquer Sodom and Gomorrah, Abraham went to deliver him from his captors. When the king of Sodom would have Abraham take some gifts of the spoils, he there again showed the true nobility of his character. He said he would not take so much as a thread or a shoe tie lest they should say, "I have made Abraham rich." God had given to Abraham the promise that he should have great riches, and he would not have anyone say that the wicked had given him the treasures he possessed. We see that every step with Abraham was one of faith.

We read [in Genesis 18] of visitors coming to Abraham as he was sitting in the door of his tent. . . . These were angels of God, and one of them was no less than the Son of God. When these guests came up to his tent, they were strangers, but he observed the rules of true courtesy toward them. The Word of God tells us to "be not forgetful to entertain strangers: for thereby some have entertained angels unawares." Abraham did this. And when the heavenly guests made themselves known to Abraham, they told him what their purpose was in regard to Sodom. . . . And while Abraham was not in Sodom, was not connected with Sodom, yet we see that he had an intense interest that Sodom should not be destroyed if God could spare it.—Manuscript 19, 1886.

March 8

IMPORTANCE OF CHOOSING OUR LOCATION CAREFULLY

◆ *And Lot lifted up his eyes, and beheld all the plain of Jordan, that it was well watered every where. Genesis 13:10.*

THE eyes of Abraham's understanding were not closed when he decided that the best thing he could do was to separate from Lot, although he had been to him as a father. But contention and strife he could not endure, even among the herdsmen. He could not have his peace of mind disturbed by unpleasant differences. Separation was painful to him, but it must be.

Abraham gave Lot the choice of where he would go so that afterward Lot should not be tempted to think that in the separation Abraham had his own interest in view. Lot chose a beautiful location near Sodom. The land of his choice possessed every natural advantage, but he failed to investigate the morals and religion of the Sodomites. We have on record his after-history. The time came when he had to flee from the corrupt city, which was dark with crime of every stripe and type. He was permitted to warn his daughters and sons-in-law, but they would not heed this warning any more than they had heeded his instruction. They mocked at his faith in God, and they perished in the destruction of Sodom.

This is a lesson for us all. We should move carefully in the selection of homes for our families. We should seek the help of the Lord in the training of our children and their choice of a lifework. Every family should constantly look to God, trusting in Him to guide aright. Sharp discrimination is necessary in order to avoid following a wrong course for the sake of worldly gain.

The Lord's will is to be our will. God must be made first and last and best in everything. We are to be as teachable as a little child, moving carefully and with entire trust in God. Our eternal interests are involved in the steps we take, whether we move heavenward toward the city whose maker and builder is God, or earthward toward Sodom's beautiful attractions.

God does not consult our opinions or preferences. He knows what human beings do not know—the future results of every movement—and therefore our eyes should be directed to Him and not to the worldly advantages presented by Satan.—Manuscript 50, 1893 (*Sermons and Talks,* vol. 1, pp. 219, 220).

March 9
GOD HEARS OUR INTERCESSORY PRAYERS

◆ *And Abraham drew near, and said, Wilt thou also destroy the righteous with the wicked? Genesis 18:23.*

WE are told that Abraham drew near and said: "Wilt thou also destroy the righteous with the wicked?" While Abraham had a true sense of humility that every child of God should possess, yet he had an intense interest in the souls of sinners. He is represented as drawing near. He steps close to those heavenly messengers and pleads with them as a child would plead with its parents. He remembers that Lot has made his home in Sodom and that Lot has connections all through Sodom by marriage. Therefore Abraham commences at fifty, and the Lord tells him that He will spare it for fifty; then he goes down to ten, and the Lord tells him that He will spare it for ten's sake. He does not make any further appeal, but he does hope that there will be found ten righteous [persons] in Sodom.

But when the angels came to Sodom, they could not find even five righteous ones in that splendid city, so we may reason that there may be the most splendid cities, having the greatest wealth, and yet there may not be found five righteous in them. As we are seeking for the future immortal life, every one of us should have everything connected with us as favorable as we can make it for the development of Christian character. God frequently calls us to break every tie that binds us to unholy influences and to come out from among them.

Here Abraham stands as one who is a representative for God, and his history is brought down along the line to our time. Abraham's interest and anxiety for Sodom is a lesson to us that we should have an intense interest for those around us. Although we should hate the sin, we should love the souls of those for whom Christ died. And then we should feel most grateful to God that we have One who is pleading in the heavens above in our behalf.

Jesus knows the worth of every soul because it is He who paid the price for everyone. When He was in His agony at the crucifixion, He prayed there for His enemies and He said, "Father, forgive them; for they know not what they do." And here, as we see in the case of Abraham, He pleads for the guilty as one person pleads for another. We should [offer] that [same] earnest prayer for those who are in darkness.—Manuscript 19, 1886.

March 10
**ANGELS ARE
LIMITED IN
WHAT THEY
CAN DO FOR US**

◆ *And there came two angels to Sodom at even: and Lot sat in the gate of Sodom: and Lot seeing them rose up to meet them; and he bowed himself with his face toward the ground. Genesis 19:1.*

*L*OT had been kept with Abraham's household, and he had become so molded that he had the same courteous spirit that Abraham manifested. These men [the angels] appeared just like other men when they came to Lot, and if a spirit of courtesy had not been cultivated by Lot, he might have perished with the rest of Sodom. The wickedness of the inhabitants of Sodom was so great that they would have abused the men who brought this message and were entertained by Lot. But angels of God protected Lot from being torn in pieces by the rabble that were outside his door. They smote them with blindness so that they could not find the door.

After this exhibition of wickedness the angels opened to Lot the object of their visit. They told Lot that if he had any sons or daughters in that place to bring them out of the city. Lot was permitted to go to his relatives and tell them that the city was to be destroyed and that they must flee from it. But all his entreaties and all his warnings were of no avail with them. They mocked at what they called his superstitious fears. Why, here was Sodom just as it had been, and there was no evidence in anything their eyes beheld that led them to think there was a destruction before them.

But the angel, as Lot returned, was in haste, and bade them flee out of Sodom. Lot was, as it were, stupefied at the thought that he must go without his property, and with only his wife and two children with him. The angels laid hold upon them and led them out of the city. . . . As soon as they were out of the city and on their way toward the mountain, the angel said to them, "Flee for your life, and tarry not in all the plain." The command was "Look not behind you." . . .

The wife of Lot turned her eyes toward the city, [looking] for what she had left there; the curse of God came upon her, and she was turned into a pillar of salt. . . . We can see that Lot made a mistake when he made his home in Sodom. Here he lost not only all his possessions; he lost all but two of his children. This is a lesson that we should take to heart. There may be very flattering openings for the children of God, but they must look on every side of the question before deciding. The very first question with every one of us should be "How will it be with my soul?"—Manuscript 19a, 1886.

March 11
**GIVE NOTHING
LESS THAN LOVING
OBEDIENCE
TO GOD**

◆ *Whoever says, "I have come to know him," but does not obey his commandments, is a liar, and in such a person the truth does not exist. 1 John 2:4, NRSV.*

I have been reported as saying you could not be saved unless you kept the Sabbath. Does it indeed seem meaningless, the requirement of the fourth commandment? Does not the habitual subjection to our heavenly Master's will lead the obedient to ask constantly and earnestly, not "What is pleasing?" not "What is the most convenient or agreeable to self or those around us?" but "What does my Lord require? What is the will of God concerning me?"

Is it anything strange that one should do this or that under the conviction of the Spirit of God, under a sense of the fact that a refusal or neglect to do so would endanger the soul's salvation? Is this a matter hard to comprehend, that obedience on our part to all God's law is absolutely essential to eternal life? Is this an unfathomable mystery to the Christian—to secure the soul's salvation at any cost to self or selfish interest? Does the Word of God give us any assurance that we can get to heaven just as well transgressing the law as obeying it? If so, the whole requirement of God as a condition of salvation is an entire mistake.

Were the inhabitants of the old world who perished in the Flood punished for their disobedience of God's requirements? Or were they washed by the waters of the deluge straight into glory because our merciful God is too good to execute the final penalty of transgressing His law? Were the Sodomites punished for their disobedience and only Lot saved? Or were the inhabitants of Sodom winged by the fire that fell from heaven straight into glory?

Has God commanded? Then we must obey—without hesitating and seeking to find some way to be saved without obedience; this would be climbing up some other way. "I am the way, the truth, and the life." "I have kept my Father's commandments," says the Majesty of heaven. . . .

We should not obey the commandments merely to secure heaven, but to please Him who died to save sinners from the penalty of the transgression of the Father's law. The sinner's salvation depends upon . . . ceasing to transgress and obedience to that transgressed law. No one should venture or presume upon the mercy of God, feeling at liberty to sin as much as they dare. . . . It is a sad resolve to follow Christ as far off as possible, venturing as near the verge of perdition as possible without falling in.—Letter 35b, 1877.

March 12
**SEEK BIBLE
TRUTH AT
ANY COST**

◆ *For this is the love of God, that we keep
his commandments: and his commandments
are not grievous. 1 John 5:3.*

*I*T was a great sacrifice Christ made for us in dying for us upon the cross. What are we willing to sacrifice for His love? Jesus says, "If ye love me, keep my commandments"—not to select out one or two or nine, but the whole ten. All His commandments must be kept. John tells us of those who pretend to love but do not obey God's requirements. "He that saith, I know him, and keepeth not his commandments, is a liar, and the truth is not in him." "For this is the love of God, that we keep his commandments: and his commandments are not grievous."

You may say, So you believe that all the learned world is wrong and that a poor company, greatly in the minority, looked upon as ignorant, common people, are all that will be saved? I answer, Jesus was among the lowly of the earth. He did not take His position by the side of the learned rabbis or the rulers. He was not found among the potentates of earth, but among the lowly ones. The truth was never found among the majority. It was ever found among the minority.

The angels from heaven did not come to the school of the prophets and sing their anthems over the Temple or synagogues, but they went to those who were humble enough to receive the message. They sang the glad tidings of a Saviour over Bethlehem's plains while the great, the rulers, and the honorable were left in darkness because they were perfectly satisfied with their position and felt no need of a piety greater than that which they possessed. Teachers in the schools of the prophets, the scribes and priests and rulers, were the worst persecutors of Christ. Those who made the highest pretensions to spiritual light were the very ones who slighted and rejected and crucified Christ.

Great men and women and professedly very good people may do terrible deeds in their bigotry and self-exalted position, and flatter themselves that they are doing God service. It will not do to rely upon them. Truth, Bible truth, you and I want at any cost. Like the noble Bereans we want to search the Scriptures daily with earnest prayer, to know what is truth, and then obey the truth at any cost to ourselves, without reference to prominent people or good people. If truth is in the Bible, we can find it there as well as the good and great ones of earth. God help us to be wise unto salvation is my prayer.—Letter 35b, 1877.

March 13
DO NOT RESIST SALVATION'S INVITATION

◆ *To day if ye will hear his voice, harden not your hearts. Hebrews 3:15.*

*W*HO will describe to you the lamentations that will arise when, at the boundary line that parts time and eternity, the righteous Judge will lift up His voice and declare, "It is too late." Long have the wide gates of heaven stood open, and the heavenly messengers have invited and entreated: "Whosoever will, let him take the water of life freely." "To day if ye will hear his voice, harden not your hearts." But at length the mandate goes forth: "He that is unjust, let him be unjust still: and he which is filthy, let him be filthy still: and he that is righteous, let him be righteous still: and he that is holy, let him be holy still."

The heavenly gate closes, the invitation of salvation ceases. In heaven it is said, "It is done." Such a time is not far distant. I plead with you to make sure work for eternity, to lay hold on the hope set before you in the gospel. Strive to enter in at the strait gate, for if you merely seek, you will not be able.

The world is loaded down with the curse that sin brings. It is literally deluged with sin, with violence and corruption, as in the days of Noah. And yet at this fearful period of our world's history many are asleep. They cease to make efforts to become Christians. Self-gratification and carnal security still imperil the eternal welfare. Is not this foolhardy? Satan's followers may call it honorable, praiseworthy, to manifest that independence of mind that will lead you to regard with indifference your former instructions and make you think you have found a better way. As you listen to these suggestions, you are becoming hardened through the deceitfulness of sin. . . .

What shall worldly pleasures avail you when all the world shall be overwhelmed as was Sodom and destroyed like Gomorrah? These cities are set forth as examples to other sinners that they may know that their day is coming.

Too late will sinners realize that they have sold their birthright. The crown that they might have had shines upon the brow of another. The inheritance that they might have had is lost. Beware how you trifle with temptation. Beware how you boast of your strength. Christ is your everlasting strength; confide in God, lay hold of His strength, and He will bring you off conqueror and you will wear the crown of victory.—Letter 21, 1867 (see also *In Heavenly Places*, p. 362).

March 14
STRIVE FOR A HEAVENLY INHERITANCE

◆ *If the mighty works, which have been done in thee, had been done in Sodom, it would have remained until this day. Matthew 11:23.*

GOD promised to Abraham, and his seed after him, that they should have possessions and lands, and yet they were only strangers and sojourners. The inheritance and lands that are to be given not only to Abraham but to the children of Abraham will not be until after this earth is purified. Abraham will then receive the title to his farm, his possessions; and the children of Abraham will have a title to their possessions. Every one of us should constantly bear in mind that this earth is not our dwelling place, but that we are to have an inheritance in the earth made new. The destruction of Sodom and Gomorrah symbolizes to us how this world will be destroyed by fire. It is not safe for any one of us to build our hopes in this life. We want first to seek the kingdom of God and His righteousness. . . .

Sodom and Gomorrah were like the Garden of Eden. The Lord had lavished His blessings upon that portion of the earth. Everything was beautiful; everything was lovely; and yet it did not lead people to honor the Giver. When the Lord rained the fire and brimstone from heaven to consume Sodom and Gomorrah, what a desolation! How easily could the blast of God make that beautiful situation an unsightly place.

There is a lesson in this destruction of Sodom to those who lived in Christ's day, and the message comes down the lines to our time. [Matthew 11:20-24 quoted.] We can see that their guilt was measured according to the proportion of light that shone upon them. And this is a lesson to every one of us before whom God has opened the precious light of truth. . . .

You may feel that you have accepted the truth, that you understand it, and you may stop there and go no further. It is one thing to accept and hold the truth, and another thing to have the truth as it is in Jesus. While you are engaged in labor, while your hands and minds are employed in doing useful work, there is a necessity for meditation and reflection and earnest prayer. You want this light that comes down from heaven to do something for you. You want that faith that is represented as gold. You want to cultivate the love of Jesus in your heart, and you want to bear in mind that the very angels that appeared to Abraham and to Lot may be in your midst, though you may not see them.—Manuscript 19a, 1886.

March 15
GUARD AGAINST LOSING COMMUNION WITH GOD

◆ *I know him, that he will command his children and his household after him, and they shall keep the way of the Lord, to do justice and judgment. Genesis 18:19.*

*T*HERE is hope for every one of us, but only in one way—by fastening ourselves to Christ and exerting every energy to attain to the perfection of His character. This goody-goody religion that makes light of sin, and that is forever dwelling upon the love of God to the sinner, encourages sinners to believe that God will save them while they continue in sin and know it to be sin. This is the way that many are doing who profess to believe present truth. The truth is kept apart from their life, and that is the reason it has no more power to convict and convert the soul. There must be a straining of every nerve and spirit and muscle to leave the world, its customs, its practices, and its fashions. . . .

The lives of many show that they have no living connection with God. They are drifting into the channel of the world. In reality they have no part or lot with Christ. They love amusement and are filled with selfish plans, hopes, and ambitions. They serve the enemy under the pretense of serving God. They are in bondage to a taskmaster, and this bondage they choose, making themselves willing slaves of Satan. . . .

Are there not reasons the Spirit of God does not work with His people? Truth is kept in the outer court. Communion with God is forfeited to please worldly relations and friends whose hearts are constantly in opposition to the truth. . . .

God's blessing was upon Abraham because he would cultivate home religion. He who blesses the habitation of the righteous says, "I know him, that he will command his . . . household after him." There will be no betraying of the truth on his part. . . .

If you want the blessing of God, parents, do as did Abraham. Repress the evil, and encourage the good. Some commanding may be necessary in the place of consulting the inclination and pleasure of the children. Blind affection will not be the rule of the house. Indulgence, which is the veriest cruelty, will not be practiced. . . . Bring your children with you into the house of God. . . . Satan will surely take possession of them if you are not on your guard. Do not encourage their association with the ungodly. Draw them away. Come out from among them yourselves, and show them that you will be on the Lord's side.—Letter 53, 1887.

March 16
ABRAHAM'S FAILURE OF FAITH CAN SERVE AS A WARNING TO US

◆ *And Abraham . . . took bread, and a bottle of water, and gave it unto Hagar, putting it on her shoulder, and the child, and sent her away. Genesis 21:14.*

*A*BRAHAM had accepted without question the promise of a son, but he did not wait for God to fulfill His word in His own time and way. A delay was permitted, to test his faith in the power of God; but he failed to endure the trial. Thinking it impossible that a child should be given her in her old age, Sarah suggested, as a plan by which the divine purpose might be fulfilled, that one of her handmaidens should be taken by Abraham as a secondary wife. Polygamy had become so widespread that it had ceased to be regarded as a sin, but it was no less a violation of the law of God, and was fatal to the sacredness and peace of the family relation. . . .

Though it was at Sarah's earnest entreaty that he had married Hagar, she now reproached him as the one at fault. She desired to banish her rival; but Abraham refused to permit this; for Hagar was to be the mother of his child, as he fondly hoped, the son of promise. . . . "When Sarai dealt hardly with her, she fled from her face."

She made her way to the desert, and as she rested beside a fountain, lonely and friendless, an angel of the Lord, in human form, appeared to her. . . . He bade her, "Return to thy mistress, and submit thyself under her hands." . . . As a perpetual reminder of His mercy, she was bidden to call her child Ishmael, "God shall hear."

When Abraham was nearly one hundred years old, the promise of a son was repeated to him, with the assurance that the future heir should be the child of Sarah. But Abraham did not yet understand the promise. . . .

The birth of Isaac, bringing, after a lifelong waiting, the fulfillment of their dearest hopes, filled the tents of Abraham and Sarah with gladness. But to Hagar this event was the overthrow of her fondly cherished ambitions. Ishmael, now a youth, had been regarded by all in the encampment as the heir of Abraham's wealth and the inheritor of the blessings promised to his descendants. Now he was suddenly set aside; and in their disappointment, mother and son hated the child of Sarah. . . .

The general rejoicing increased their jealousy, until Ishmael dared openly to mock the heir of God's promise. Sarah saw in Ishmael's turbulent disposition a perpetual source of discord, and she appealed to Abraham, urging that Hagar and Ishmael be sent away from the encampment. . . .

The instruction given to Abraham touching the sacredness of the marriage relation was to be a lesson for all ages.—*Patriarchs and Prophets,* pp. 145-147.

March 17
THE SUPREME TEST OF ABRAHAM'S FAITH

◆ *Take now thy son, thine only son Isaac, whom thou lovest, and get thee into the land of Moriah; and offer him there for a burnt offering upon one of the mountains which I will tell thee of. Genesis 22:2.*

*I*N a vision of the night, in his home in Beer-sheba, when he was one hundred and twenty years old, Abraham received the startling command, "Take now thy son, thine only son Isaac, whom thou lovest; and get thee into the land of Moriah; and offer him there for a burnt offering upon one of the mountains which I will tell thee of." His son, his only son, the son of promise, to be sacrificed. There was no more sleep for Abraham that night. . . . God had promised him that his name was to be perpetuated in Isaac, but here was a severe trial of his faith. Abraham had clung to the promise of a son from his own wife Sarah, and God had fulfilled His promise. . . . He left Ishmael out of the question, saying, "Thine only son, Isaac.". . .

God had already told him that through Isaac his seed should be as the sand of the sea for multitude. As he stepped out into the night, he seemed to hear the divine voice that called him out of Chaldea fifty years before and said to him, "Look now toward heaven, and tell the stars, if thou be able to number them. . . . So shall thy seed be." Can it be the same voice that commands him to slay his son? He remembered the promise, "I will make thy seed as the dust of the earth: so that if a man can number the dust of the earth, then shall thy seed also be numbered." Is it not the voice of a stranger that commands him to offer his son as a sacrifice? Can God contradict Himself? Shall He cut off the only hope of the fulfillment of the promise? Must he become childless?

But Abraham does not reason; he obeys. His only hope is that the God who can do all things will raise his son from the dead. The knife was raised, but it did not fall. God spoke, "It is enough." The faith of the father and the submission of the son were fully tested. "Now I know that thou fearest God, seeing that thou hast not withheld thy son, thine only son from me."

Abraham's test was the most severe that could ever come to a human being. Had he then turned from God, he would never have been registered as the father of the faithful. Had he deviated from God's command, the world would have lost this rich example of faith in God and victory over unbelief. . . .

Nothing is too precious to give to God. Confidence in the divine Word will lead to a doing of that Word.—Letter 110, 1897.

March 18
CHARACTERS OF JACOB AND ESAU CONTRASTED

◆ *One people shall be stronger than the other people; and the elder shall serve the younger. Genesis 25:23.*

ESAU grew up loving self-gratification and centering all his interest in the present. Impatient of restraint, he delighted in the wild freedom of the chase, and early chose the life of a hunter. Yet he was the father's favorite. The quiet, peace-loving shepherd was attracted by the daring and vigor of this elder son, who fearlessly ranged over mountain and desert, returning home with game for his father and with exciting accounts of his adventurous life.

Jacob, thoughtful, diligent, and care-taking, ever thinking more of the future than the present, was content to dwell at home, occupied in the care of the flocks and the tillage of the soil. His patient perseverance, thrift, and foresight were valued by the mother. His affections were deep and strong, and his gentle, unremitting attentions added far more to her happiness than did the boisterous and occasional kindnesses of Esau. To Rebekah, Jacob was the dearer son. . . .

Esau had no love for devotion, no inclination to a religious life. The requirements that accompanied the spiritual birthright were an unwelcome and even hateful restraint to him. The law of God . . . was regarded by Esau as a yoke of bondage. Bent on self-indulgence, he desired nothing so much as liberty to do as he pleased. To him power and riches, feasting and reveling, were happiness. He gloried in the unrestrained freedom of his wild, roving life. . . .

Jacob had learned from his mother of the divine intimation that the birthright should fall to him, and he was filled with an unspeakable desire for the privileges that it would confer. . . . The spiritual birthright was the object of his longing. To commune with God as did righteous Abraham, to offer the sacrifice of atonement for his family, to be the progenitor of the chosen people and of the promised Messiah, and to inherit the immortal possessions embraced in the blessings of the covenant—here were the privileges and honors that kindled his most ardent desires. . . .

He carefully treasured what he had learned from his mother. Day and night the subject occupied his thoughts, until it became the absorbing interest of his life. . . . He believed that the promise concerning himself could not be fulfilled so long as Esau retained the rights of the firstborn, and he constantly studied to devise some way whereby he might secure the blessing that his brother held so lightly, but that was so precious to himself.—*Patriarchs and Prophets*, pp. 177-179.

March 19
NEVER SACRIFICE INTEGRITY, NOR DESPISE YOUR BIRTHRIGHT

◆ *And Esau said to Jacob, Feed me, I pray thee, with that same red pottage; for I am faint: . . . And Jacob said, Sell me this day thy birthright. . . . And he sold his birthright unto Jacob. Genesis 25:30-34.*

*T*HERE is too much yielding to desire and inclination for present enjoyment. There is not that earnest soul hunger for spiritual strength and heavenly wisdom. Temptations are yielded to, the appetite is gratified, and there is a separation from God. . . .

You remember the case of Esau. He passed the crisis of his life without knowing it. What he regarded as a matter worthy of scarcely a thought was the act that revealed the prevailing traits of his character. It showed his choice, showed his true estimate of that which was sacred and which should have been sacredly cherished. He sold his birthright for a small indulgence to meet his present wants, and this determined the after course of his life. To Esau, a morsel of meat was more than the service of his Master.—Letter 5, 1877.

Oh, that the people of God would consider that by one wrong action on their part a blot is made in the history and experience that nothing but the blood of Christ can wash away. Every action of the life should be carefully considered, for it is sending forth to the world, as from an open fountain, streams of blessing or streams of evil. Let those who know their Bibles live the life of Christ. All should consider that they are doing work that will be as lasting as eternity. . . .

No one in our world can do a selfish act but that they are in danger of selling their birthright for a mess of pottage. Let them remember that Esau was controlled by his desires; appetite and inclination ruled the man, and he sold his soul for the gratification of appetite. Are there any doing this who know the present truth? . . .

"Lest there be any fornicator, or profane person, as Esau, who for one morsel of meat sold his birthright." How many whose names are registered on the church books will, for the sake of some selfish advantage, sacrifice integrity and risk the consequences. In order to gratify their own carnal desires, they will walk unguarded into Satan's snares. For selfish influences they sell their peace, they sell their souls.

After his desire was gratified, Esau regretted what he had done. "For ye know how that afterward, when he would have inherited the blessing, he was rejected: for he found no place of repentance, though he sought it carefully with tears." May the Lord grant that everyone who has named the name of Christ shall depart from all iniquity!—Letter 47, 1894.

March 20
WHEN ALL SEEMS HOPELESS, LOOK FOR HEAVEN'S LADDER

◆ *And Jacob awaked out of his sleep, and he said, Surely the Lord is in this place; and I knew it not. Genesis 28:16.*

HE angels of God were ascending and descending upon this mystic ladder, and when he [Jacob] awoke he said, "Surely the Lord is in this place; and I knew it not." Thus it is with us. If our eyes could be opened, we would see the angels of God all around us, and the evil angels are here also, trying to destroy us, but the good angels are pressing them back.

Jacob thought to gain a right to the birthright through deception, but he found himself disappointed. He thought he had lost everything, his connection with God, his home and all; and there he was a disappointed fugitive. But what did God do? He looked upon him in his hopeless condition, He saw his disappointment, and He saw there was material there that would render back glory to God. No sooner does He see his condition than He presents the mystic ladder, which represents Jesus Christ. Here is a man who had lost all connection with God, and the God of heaven looks upon him and consents that Christ shall bridge the gulf that sin has made.

We might have looked and said, I long for heaven, but how can I reach it? I see no way. That is what Jacob thought, and so God shows him the vision of the ladder, and that ladder connects earth with heaven, with Jesus Christ. A person can climb it, for the base rests upon the earth and the topmost round reaches into heaven. Then the soul climbs right away from the customs, practices, and fashions of earth right towards heaven. The light and glory of God are upon every round of this mystic ladder, and men and women climb upon whom? Jesus Christ. Cling to what? Jesus Christ. Made one with whom? Jesus Christ. . . .

Now we find that the battlements can be reached, that God is above the ladder and is waiting with arms outstretched to help every soul who will come into the everlasting kingdom of our God. Praise His holy name! Ye inhabitants of the earth, praise Him! And why? Because through Jesus Christ—whose long human arm encircles the race while with His divine arm He grasps the throne of the Almighty—the gulf is bridged with His own body; and this atom of a world, which was separated from the continent of heaven by sin and became an island, is again reinstated because Christ bridged the gulf—Christ has bridged it!

Here is a soul in danger; well, God stands ready to help that soul. All the heavenly angels will be sent to assist that soul.—Manuscript 5, 1891.

March 21
TRUTH MOVES US
TOWARD HEAVEN

◆ *Whoever enters by me will be saved, and*
will come in and go out and find pasture.
John 10:9, NRSV.

RUTH is an active, working principle, molding heart and life so that there is a constant upward movement, climbing the ladder Jacob saw, to the Lord above the ladder. In every step of climbing, the will is obtaining a new spring of action. . . . The glory of God revealed above the ladder can be appreciated only by the progressive climber, who is ever attracted higher, to nobler aims that Christ reveals. All the faculties of mind and body must be enlisted. . . .

To make our calling and election sure requires far greater diligence than many are giving to this important matter. "For if ye do these things"—live on the plan of addition, growing in grace and the knowledge of our Lord Jesus Christ—ye shall mount up, step by step, the ladder Jacob saw, and "ye shall never fall." . . .

Let us consider this ladder that was presented to Jacob. The human race was cut off from intercourse [communication] with God. They might look at a paradise lost but could see no means of entering it and holding communion with heaven. The sin of Adam cut off all intercourse between heaven and earth. Up to the moment Adam and Eve transgressed God's law there had been free communion between earth and heaven. They were connected by a path Deity could traverse. But the transgression of God's law broke up this path, and the human race was separated from God.

As soon as Satan seduced our first parents to disobedience of God's holy law, every link that bound earth to heaven and the human race to the infinite God seemed broken. Humans might look to heaven, but how could they attain it? But joy to the world! The Son of God, the Sinless One, the One perfect in obedience, becomes the channel through which the lost communion may be renewed, the way through which the lost paradise may be regained. Through Christ, our substitute and surety, we may keep the commandments of God. We may return to our allegiance, and God will accept us.

Christ is the ladder. . . . This is the ladder, the base of it resting upon the earth, the top reaching to the highest heavens. The broken links have been repaired. A highway has been thrown up along which the weary and heavy laden may pass. They may enter heaven and find rest.—Manuscript 13, 1884 (*Manuscript Releases*, vol. 19, pp. 341-353).

March 22
CHRIST IS OUR ONLY LADDER TO HEAVEN

◆ *And he dreamed, and behold a ladder set up on the earth, and the top of it reached to heaven . . . And, behold, the Lord stood above it, and said . . . the land whereon thou liest, to thee will I give it, and to thy seed. Genesis 28:12, 13.*

*T*HE ladder is the medium of communication between God and the human race. Through the mystic ladder the gospel was preached to Jacob. As the ladder stretched from earth, reaching to the highest heavens, and the glory of God was seen above the ladder, so Christ in His divine nature reached immensity and was one with the Father. As the ladder, though its top penetrated into heaven, had its base upon the earth, so Christ, though [He was] God, clothed His divinity with humanity and was in the world "found in fashion as a man." The ladder would be useless if it rested not on the earth or if it reached not to the heavens.

God appeared in glory above the ladder, looking down with compassion on erring, sinful Jacob, addressing to him words of encouragement. It is through Christ that the Father beholds sinful human beings. The ministering angels were communicating to the inhabitants of the earth through the medium of the ladder. The only way that people can be saved is by clinging to Christ.

We ascend to heaven by climbing the ladder—the whole height of Christ's work—step by step. There must be a holding fast to Christ, a climbing up by the merits of Christ. To let go is to cease to climb, to fall, to perish. . . .

The question with men and women gazing heavenward is How can I obtain the mansions for the blessed? It is by being a partaker of the divine nature. It is by escaping the "corruption that is in the world through lust." It is by entering into the holiest by the blood of Jesus, laying hold of the hope set before you in the gospel. . . . It is by being in Christ and yet led by Christ, by believing and working—trusting in Jesus, yet working upon the plan of addition, holding on to Christ and constantly mounting upward toward God. . . .

We point you to the mansions Christ is preparing for all those who love Him. We point you to that city that hath foundations, whose builder and maker is God. . . . Climb step by step, and you will reach God above the ladder and the Holy City of God. None who will resolutely mount up on the ladder will fail of everlasting life. "For so an entrance shall be ministered unto you abundantly into the everlasting kingdom of our Lord and Saviour Jesus Christ."—Manuscript 13, 1884 (*Manuscript Releases,* vol. 19, pp. 353-355).

March 23
VALUABLE LESSONS IN JACOB'S EXPERIENCE

◆ *And he said, Let me go, for the day breaketh. And he said, I will not let thee go, except thou bless me. Genesis 32:26.*

O tell tempted souls of their guilt in no way inspires them with a determination to do better. . . . Hold up before them the possibilities that are theirs. Point them to the heights to which they may attain. Help them to take hold upon the mercy of the Lord, to trust in His forgiving power. Jesus is waiting to clasp them by the hand, waiting to give them power to live a noble, virtuous life.

God often brings people to a crisis to show them their own weakness and to point them to the Source of strength. If they pray and watch unto prayer, fighting bravely, their weak points will become their strong points. Jacob's experience contains many valuable lessons for us. God taught Jacob that in his own strength he could never gain the victory, that he must wrestle with God for strength from above.

All night Jacob wrestled with the Angel. Finally the strong wrestler was weakened by a touch on his thigh. He was now disabled and suffering the keenest pain, but he would not loose his hold. All penitent and broken, he clung to the Angel, . . . pleading for a blessing. He must have the assurance that his sin was pardoned. His determination grew stronger, his faith more earnest and persevering, until the very last. The Angel tried to release Himself; He urged, "Let me go, for the day breaketh," but Jacob answered, "I will not let thee go, except thou bless me."

Had this been a boastful, presumptuous confidence, Jacob would have been instantly destroyed; but his was the assurance of one who confesses his own unworthiness, yet trusts to the faithfulness of a covenant-keeping God. . . . Through humiliation, repentance, and self-surrender this sinful, erring mortal prevailed with the Majesty of heaven. He had fastened his trembling grasp on the promises of God, and the heart of infinite love could not turn away the sinner's plea.

As an evidence that Jacob had been forgiven, his name was changed from one that was a reminder of his sin to one that commemorated his victory. "Thy name," said the Angel, "shall be called no more Jacob, but Israel: for as a prince hast thou power with God and with men, and hast prevailed."

Shall we obtain strength from God, and win victory after victory, or shall we try in our own strength, and at last fall back defeated, worn out by vain efforts? Let us, by unreserved surrender to God, obtain the power that everyone must have who conquers in the battle against evil.—Manuscript 2, 1903.

March 24
LOVE FOR GOD
LEADS US TO
SECURITY IN HIM

◆ *Though an host should encamp against me, my heart shall not fear: though war should rise against me, in this will I be confident. Psalm 27:3.*

*Y*OU should be willing for all to know that you are not your own but His who bought you with an infinite price, and that you are not only bound but are determined to glorify Him in your body and in your spirit, which are God's. May the love of so great magnitude constrain you to confess Christ not only with the mouth but with the life, to bear fruit to the glory of God.

We are passing through an enemy's land. Foes are upon every side to hinder our advancement. They hate God and all who follow after Him and bear His name. But those who are our enemies are the Lord's enemies, and although they are strong and artful, yet the Captain of our salvation who leadeth us can vanquish them. As the sun disperses the clouds from its path, so will the Sun of Righteousness remove the obstacles to our progress. We may cheer our souls by looking at the things unseen that will cheer and animate us in our journey.

We may indeed say, "Thy presence is our security, our treasure, our glory, our joy.". . . Do we pray that Christ will go where we go and dwell where we dwell? If we can live without Christ in this world, He will live without us in the better world. But if we cling to Him by living faith, saying with Jacob, "I will not let thee go"; if we entreat, "Cast me not away from thy presence; and take not thy holy spirit from me," the promise is to us "I will never leave thee, nor forsake thee."

We cannot afford to live in neglect of the great salvation offered to us upon such liberal terms. The knowledge of the claims of God as our Father will keep us from offending Him. This will make us anxious to please Him. As His children we must walk in the light, walk worthy of God, who hath called us unto glory and His immortal kingdom.

We have read an account of a noble prince who carried the picture of his father always near his heart, and on important occasions, when there was danger of forgetting him, he would take out the likeness and view it, and say, "Let me do nothing unbecoming so excellent a father." God has claims upon us as Christians that we should never, never lose sight of for a moment. . . .

God's people are called a crown, a diadem. Satan would eagerly seize the Lord's treasure, but God has secured it so that Satan cannot obtain it. . . . We are secure, perfectly secure, from the enemy's subtlety while we have unwavering trust in God.—Letter 8, 1873.

March 25
OUR CHARACTER OFTEN REVEALED IN OUR CHILDREN

◆ *Now Israel loved Joseph more than all his children, because he was the son of his old age: and he made him a coat of many colours. Genesis 37:3.*

*J*ACOB had chosen the inheritance of faith. He had endeavored to obtain it by craft, treachery, and falsehood; but God had permitted his sin to work out its correction. . . . The sin of Jacob, and the train of events to which it led, had not failed to exert an influence for evil—an influence that revealed its bitter fruit in the character and life of his sons. . . .

There was one, however, of a widely different character—the elder son of Rachel, Joseph, whose rare personal beauty seemed but to reflect an inward beauty of mind and heart. . . . He listened to his father's instructions, and loved to obey God. . . . His mother being dead, his affections clung the more closely to the father, and Jacob's heart was bound up in this child of his old age. . . .

But even this affection was to become a cause of trouble and sorrow. Jacob unwisely manifested his preference for Joseph, and this excited the jealousy of his other sons. . . . The father's injudicious gift to Joseph of a costly coat, or tunic, such as was usually worn by persons of distinction, seemed to them another evidence of his partiality. . . . Their malice was still further increased as the boy one day told them of a dream that he had had. . . .

As the lad stood before his brothers, his beautiful countenance lighted up with the Spirit of Inspiration, they could not withhold their admiration; but they did not choose to renounce their evil ways, and they hated the purity that reproved their sins. . . .

The brothers were obliged to move from place to place to secure pasturage for their flocks. . . . Some time passed, bringing no tidings from them, and the father began to fear for their safety. . . . He therefore sent Joseph to find them, and bring him word as to their welfare. . . .

Joseph came on, unsuspicious of danger . . . ; but instead of the expected greeting, he was terrified by the angry and revengeful glances he met. . . . He was seized and his coat stripped from him. . . . Rudely dragging him to a deep pit, they thrust him in, and having made sure that there was no possibility of his escape, they left him there to perish from hunger, while they "sat down to eat bread."

But some of them were ill at ease; they did not feel the satisfaction they had anticipated from their revenge. Soon a company of travelers was seen approaching.—*Patriarchs and Prophets,* pp. 208-211.

March 26
REACTION TO CIRCUMSTANCES REVEALS TRUE CHARACTER

◆ *And Judah said unto his brethren, What profit is it if we slay our brother, and conceal his blood? Come, and let us sell him to the Ishmeelites, and let not our hand be upon him; for he is our brother. Genesis 37:26, 27.*

JUDAH now proposed to sell their brother to these heathen traders [Ishmaelites] instead of leaving him to die. While he would be effectually put out of their way, they would remain clear of his blood; "for," he urged, "he is our brother and our flesh." To this proposition all agreed, and Joseph was quickly drawn out of the pit.

As he saw the merchants the dreadful truth flashed upon him. To become a slave was a fate more to be feared than death. In an agony of terror he appealed to one and another of his brothers, but in vain. Some were moved with pity, but fear of derision kept them silent; all felt that they had now gone too far to retreat. If Joseph were spared, he would doubtless report them to the father, who would not overlook their cruelty toward his favorite son. Steeling their hearts against his entreaties, they delivered him into the hands of the heathen traders. The caravan moved on, and was soon lost to view. . . .

As the caravan journeyed southward toward the borders of Canaan, the boy could discern in the distance the hills among which lay his father's tents. Bitterly he wept at thought of that loving father in his loneliness and affliction. . . . With a trembling heart he looked forward to the future. What a change in situation—from the tenderly cherished son to the despised and helpless slave! . . .

But, in the providence of God, even this experience was to be a blessing to him. He had learned in a few hours that which years might not otherwise have taught him. His father, strong and tender as his love had been, had done him wrong by his partiality and indulgence. . . . Faults had been encouraged that were now to be corrected. He was becoming self-sufficient and exacting. . . .

Then his thoughts turned to his father's God. . . . He had been told of the Lord's promises to Jacob, and how they had been fulfilled. . . . His soul thrilled with the high resolve to prove himself true to God—under all circumstances to act as became a subject of the King of heaven. He would serve the Lord with undivided heart; he would meet the trials of his lot with fortitude and perform every duty with fidelity. One day's experience had been the turning point in Joseph's life. Its terrible calamity had transformed him from a petted child to a man, thoughtful, courageous, and self-possessed.—*Patriarchs and Prophets*, pp. 211-214.

March 27
TRUTH WILL GAIN VICTORY EVENTUALLY

◆ *The sceptre shall not depart from Judah, nor a lawgiver from between his feet, until Shiloh come; and unto him shall the gathering of the people be. Genesis 49:10.*

HE great controversy between the Prince of life and the prince of darkness has been going forward, strengthening with each successive generation. Severe indeed has been the conflict waged between right and wrong, between truth and error, between the kingdom of light and the kingdom of darkness. Truth has fought against error and error against truth. The conflict has existed for thousands of years. . . .

The truth as it is in Jesus will gain the victory that the prophecy assured to it; but to all human appearance, error will overwhelm truth. The larger number of the human race will be swept into idolatry. They will lift up that which Christ has not lifted up and strive to tear down God's great standard of righteousness. . . .

Satan is referred to as the originator of sin. "For this purpose the Son of God was manifested, that he might destroy the works of the devil." Satan's first manifest defeat was his failure to overcome Christ in the wilderness of temptation. . . .

"The sceptre shall not depart from Judah, nor a lawgiver from between his feet, until Shiloh come; and unto him shall the gathering of the people be." This prophecy was uttered by the dying Jacob, and addressed to his sons. But it bore with weight upon future generations. . . . The scepter is a rod carried in the hands of chiefs and rulers as a badge of authority. . . . "The sceptre shall not depart from Judah." The ensign of his tribeship shall remain. Judah shall not cease to be a distinct tribe until Shiloh come. . . . And the tribe of Judah did maintain its supremacy through all its adversities till Christ's first advent. It remained a distinct tribe till Shiloh came.

Nearly seventeen hundred years before the death of Christ the dying Jacob uttered this prophecy. Christ Himself threw back the veil, that with prophetic eye Jacob could trace the history of his descendants. . . . He saw a wonderful Counsellor arise in the midst of this tribe. It was the promised Seed, Shiloh, the Sent of God, who was to set up a spiritual kingdom. Jacob saw the time when the scepter would no longer be in the hands of Judah. The nations would be gathered under the banner of Christ. When the Jews appeared before Pilate to secure Christ, they said, "We have no king but Caesar." By this they confessed that the scepter had indeed departed from Judah.—Manuscript 110, 1897.

March 28
GOODNESS IS
TRUE GREATNESS

◆ *And his master saw that the Lord was with him. . . . And Joseph found grace in his sight, and he served him: and he made him overseer over his house, and all that he had he put into his hand. Genesis 39:3, 4.*

OD can make the humblest followers of Christ more precious than fine gold, even than the golden wedge of Ophir, if they yield themselves to His transforming hand. They should be determined to make the noblest use of every faculty and opportunity. The Word of God should be their study and their guide in deciding what is the highest and best in all cases. The one faultless character, the perfect Pattern set before them in the gospel, should be studied with deepest interest. The one lesson essential to learn is that goodness alone is true greatness. . . .

The weakest follower of Christ has entered into an alliance with Infinite Power. In many cases God can do little with men and women of learning, because they feel no need of leaning upon Him who is the source of all wisdom. . . .

If you trust in your own strength and wisdom, you will surely fail. God calls for complete and entire consecration, and anything short of this He will not accept. The more difficult your position, the more you need Jesus. The love and fear of God kept Joseph pure and untarnished in the king's court. . . .

It is impossible to stand upon a lofty height without danger. The tempest leaves unharmed the modest flower of the valley, while it wrestles with the lofty tree upon the mountain height. There are many people whom God could have used in poverty—He could have made them useful there, and crowned them with glory hereafter—but prosperity ruined them. They were dragged down to the pit, because they forgot to be humble—forgot that God was their strength—and became independent and self-sufficient.

Joseph bore the test of character in adversity, and the gold was undimmed by prosperity. He showed the same sacred regard for God's will when he stood next to the throne as when in the prisoner's cell. Joseph carried his religion everywhere, and this was the secret of his unwavering fidelity. As a representative of Christ, you must have the all-pervading power of godliness. You must be hid in Jesus. You are not safe unless you hold the hand of Christ. You must guard against everything like presumption and cherish that spirit that would rather suffer than sin. No victory you can gain will be so precious as that gained over self. Selfish ambition, desire for supremacy, will die when Christ takes possession of the affections.—Manuscript 14, 1889.

March 29
CIRCUMSTANCES NEED NOT CONTROL US

◆ *The Lord blessed the Egyptian's house for Joseph's sake. . . . Joseph was a goodly person, and well favoured. Genesis 39:5, 6.*

ANY blame their circumstances and plead, as an excuse for their condition, that they are unfavorably situated, being thrown into the society of the irreligious and self-indulgent and intemperate. But do not let yourself be deceived. You can shape your surroundings in the place of bending and being molded in character by circumstances. Godliness will stand the test, because it has a living root to sustain it, a wellspring from which it draws its nourishment.

The corruption of the human heart is that which leads it to love the society of the careless and unholy. The true secret of all true followers of Jesus, and their continued, unsullied integrity, is that they love truth, they love righteousness. Their moral taste is not depraved, and although they are surrounded by evil the deep work of the truth wrought in their hearts keeps them true and steadfast to God even in very bad circumstances. This is the fruit that grows on the Christian tree, the faith that realizes the presence and help of God at all times. There is a constant dread of incurring the displeasure of God, whom they reverence and whom they love. It was this principle that preserved Joseph amid temptation. You must cultivate real faith in God, in His gracious goodness, faith in His presence. You must pray as you have never prayed before.

Albert [a friend] is no help to you and you are no help to him, because you do not exercise the power of influence for good. Your influence is to strengthen the temptations of Satan, to lead each other away from truth, purity, and holiness. Angels blush over your words and your actions. You have become tempters to one another. You both need to greatly humble your souls at the foot of the cross and learn meekness and lowliness of heart. It is genuine godliness woven into the character that will make young men a light in the world. . . .

Fearing God—how little of it there is! . . . There are those who will be like the men and women who helped to build the ark. They hear the truth; they have every advantage to become people of moral worth, yet they will not choose the good society, but the corrupt. If there is an influence that is not heavenly, they will gather to their side and unite with them, and although they act a part in the preparation of the truth that is to fit a people to stand in the day of the Lord, they will perish in the general ruin like Noah's carpenters who helped to build the ark. God help you that you may not be of that class.—Letter 36, 1887 (*Manuscript Releases,* vol. 18, pp. 260-262).

March 30
**INNER
CHARACTER
REVELED IN
ACTIONS**

◆ *His master's wife cast her eyes upon Joseph; and she said, Lie with me. But he refused, and said unto his master's wife . . . : how then can I do this great wickedness, and sin against God? Genesis 39:7-9.*

OSEPH, in the providence of God, was deprived of his happy home and the teachings and example of his God-fearing father, and his lot was cast in a family of dark heathen. There his virtue was severely tested. It is always a critical period in a young man's life when he is separated from home influences and wise counsels and enters upon new scenes and trying tests. . . .

God was with Joseph in his new home. He was in the path of duty, suffering wrong but not doing wrong. He therefore had the love and protection of God, for he carried his religious principles into everything he undertook. What a difference there was in Joseph's case and the case of young people who apparently force their way into the very field of the enemy, exposing themselves to the fierce assaults of Satan. Joseph suffered for righteousness' sake, while the trials of others are of their own procuring. Joseph did not conceal his religion or manly piety to avoid persecution.

The Lord prospered Joseph, but in the midst of his prosperity came the darkest adversity. The wife of his master was a licentious woman, one who urged his steps to take hold on hell. Would Joseph yield his moral gold of character to the seductions of a corrupt woman? Would he remember that the eye of God was upon him?

Few temptations are more dangerous or more fatal to young men than the temptation of sensuality, and none, if yielded to, will prove so decidedly ruinous to soul and body for time and eternity. The welfare of his entire future was suspended upon the decision of a moment. Joseph calmly cast his eyes to heaven for help, slipped off his loose outer garment, leaving it in the hand of his tempter, and while his eye was lighted with determined resolve in the place of unholy passion, he exclaimed, "How can I do this great wickedness and sin against God?". . .

True religion extends to all the thoughts of the mind, penetrating to all the secret thoughts of the heart, to all the motives of action, to the object and direction of the affections, to the whole framework of our lives. "Thou God seest me" will be the watchword, the guard of the life. . . .

But Joseph was a Christian. . . . He entered into the troubles of his fellow prisoners. He was cheerful, for he was a Christian gentleman. God was preparing him under this discipline for a situation of great responsibility, honor, and usefulness, and he was willing to learn . . . the lessons the Lord would teach him.—Letter 3, 1879 (*Manuscript Releases*, vol. 4, pp. 220-223).

March 31
**VICE DOES
NOT TRIUMPH
OVER VIRTUE**

◆ *And Joseph's master took him, and put him into the prison. . . . But the Lord was with Joseph, and shewed him mercy, and gave him favour in the sight of the keeper of the prison. Genesis 39:20, 21.*

HEREVER you may be placed, you must be forti-fied by firm principle. Enter life determined by the help of God to cleave close to whatsoever things are honest, true, lovely, and of good report. The fear of God, united with the love of that which is noble, pure, and elevating, will guard you from a dishonest action. . . . How pleasant, how satisfactory, will be the recollection all through life that though exposed to many and fierce temptations, your hands were unstained by dishonesty, and your heart undefiled by cherishing temptation. . . .

What a lesson for all youth we have in the history of Joseph. Here moral integrity was preserved under the strongest temptations. How fierce and seductive was the assault upon his virtue! Coming from such a source and in such a form, it was the most likely to corrupt a youthful mind. Joseph was saved by his religious principles, which led him promptly and firmly to resist the device of Satan. His tempter, defeated in her purpose, wickedly sought to ruin the youth whose virtues she could not corrupt, and accused Joseph of the very crime he would not commit. . . . God made the imprisonment of this faithful youth the means of his elevation. Had it not been for this wicked act of Potiphar's wife, Joseph would never have become prime minister of Egypt.

Although vice seemed to triumph while virtue was trampled in the dust, Joseph did not make his lot worse by repining. He possessed genuine religion. . . . God was teaching Joseph important lessons. He was preparing him for a position of trust, honor, and usefulness. Joseph learned to govern by first learning to obey. He humbled himself, and God exalted him. The religion of the Bible never degrades the receiver; on the contrary, it elevates and ennobles all who accept and obey its teachings. The fear of God is a strong defense for the youth. With this shield they may pass through the most corrupting scenes uncontaminated.

My dear son [Edson], do not get above the simplicity of a humble Christian life. Let the character of Joseph be your character; let his strength to resist temptation be your strength. Your efforts will be successful if you make them in the strength of God. Jesus is a present help. May the blessing of Jesus ever rest upon you is the prayer of your mother.—Letter 20, 1868.

April 1
**WE CAN
GROW IN FAITH
AS DID MOSES**

◆ *By faith Moses, when he had come to years,
refused to be called the son of Pharaoh's daughter; choosing rather to suffer affliction with the
people of God, than to enjoy the pleasures of sin
for a season. Hebrews 11:24, 25.*

GYPT, in that age the greatest kingdom of the
world, offered its highest position of honor to Moses. But he did not accept
the alluring temptation, "for he endured, as seeing him who is invisible.". . .

The strength of Moses was his connection with the Source of all
power, the Lord God of hosts. He rises grandly above every earthly inducement, and trusts himself wholly to God. He considered that he was
the Lord's. While he was connected with the official interests of the king
of Egypt, he was constantly studying the laws of God's government, and
thus his faith grew. That faith was of value to him. It was deeply rooted in
the soil of his earliest teachings, and the culture of his life was to prepare
him for the great work of delivering Israel from bondage. . . .

After slaying the Egyptian, he saw that he had not understood God's
plan, and he fled from Egypt and became a shepherd. He was no longer
planning to do a great work, but he became very humble; the mists that
were beclouding his mind were expelled, and he disciplined his mind to
seek after God as his refuge. He recognized the presence of God in his surroundings. All nature seemed to be filled with the presence of the Unseen
One. He knew God as a personal God, and as he meditated upon His character, he grasped more and more the sense of His presence. He found
refuge in the everlasting arms. God talked with Moses face-to-face, as a
man speaketh with his friend. The bright beams of the Sun of
Righteousness shone into his heart and into the chambers of his mind.
God was his refuge; God was his dwelling place, his home. . . .

By faith you, like Moses, may endure as seeing Him who is invisible.
The Lord desires to give you a precious experience. God has a work for
you to do. You may seek after a higher sense of eternal things. God is nigh
unto all them that call upon Him with the whole heart. What are the advantages and honors that the world proffers you when compared with the
privileges of the sons of God? . . .

The shades of darkness will soon pass away; the morning cometh; the
conflict is well-nigh ended. There is a crown of life laid up for everyone
who has been a partaker with Christ in His suffering.—Letter 21a, 1893
(*Manuscript Releases,* vol. 14, pp. 14-16).

April 2

GOD'S METHODS OF TRAINING DIFFERENT FROM MAN'S

◆ *Moses fled from the face of Pharaoh, and dwelt in the land of Midian. Exodus 2:15.*

OSES spent forty years as a shepherd of flocks to prepare him to understand himself, and to purify himself by emptying himself so that the Lord could accomplish His will in him. The Lord does not take for His workers mere machines in intellect or feelings. Both are essential to do the work, but these human elements of character must be purged from defects, not by talking of the will of God, but by doing His will. If any will do His will, they shall know of the doctrine. Moses was under training to God. He endured a long process of mental training to fit him to be leader of the armies of Israel.

Inspiration will come to people of God's appointment, but not to those who retain a high idea of their own mental superiority. Every person whom God will use to do His will must have humble ideas of self and must seek, in persevering earnestness, for light. God will not require any person to become a novice and to sink down into a voluntary humility, and become more and more incapacitated. God calls upon everyone with whom He works to do the very highest kind of thinking and praying and hoping and believing.

Many have, as had Moses, very much to unlearn in order to learn the very lessons that they need to learn. Moses had need to be self-trained by severest mental and moral discipline, and God wrought with him before he could be fitted to train others in mind and heart. He had been instructed in the Egyptian courts. Nothing was left as unnecessary to train him to become a general of armies. The false theories of the idolatrous Egyptians had been instilled into his mind, and the influences surrounding him, and the things his eyes looked upon, could not be easily shaken off or corrected.

Thus it is with many who have had a false training in any line. All the idolatrous rubbish of heathen lore must be removed—bit by bit, item by item—from Moses' mind. Jethro helped him in many things to a correct faith, as far as he himself understood. He was working upward toward the light where he could see God in singleness of heart. God Jehovah was revealed to him. This thorough intellectual training in Egypt, and as a shepherd among the mountains, in the pure air, made him a strong thinker and a strong doer of the Word of God.—Manuscript 45, 1890 (*Manuscript Releases*, vol. 2, pp. 324-326).

April 3
**WE NEED
ALWAYS TO
LEAN UPON GOD**

◆ *By faith he [Moses] forsook Egypt, not fearing the wrath of the king: for he endured, as seeing him who is invisible. Hebrews 11:27.*

*M*OSES was a child of God, chosen for a special work. Having been adopted by Pharaoh's daughter, he was greatly honored by those in the king's court. As the king's intended grandson, everyone was intensely desirous of exalting him. They looked upon him as the successor to the throne.

Moses was a man of intelligence, and God in His providence placed him where he could acquire knowledge and fitness for a great work. He was thoroughly educated as a general. When he went out to meet the enemy, he was successful; and on his return from the battle, his praises were sung by the whole army.

Notwithstanding this, Moses constantly kept in mind the fact that by his hand God would deliver the children of Israel. But although learned among the Egyptians, he received in the service of Pharaoh a certain mold that disqualified him for the wonderful work he was to do. This weakness was manifested when he visited his brethren and "spied an Egyptian smiting an Hebrew." Moses took the case in hand and privately "slew the Egyptian, and hid him in the sand.". . .

In order that Moses might be fitted for his appointed work, the God of heaven separated him from his former surroundings. He was to enter another school—the school of Providence. What a change here took place in the life and employment of Moses! . . .

Looking at this experience from a human standpoint, observers would pronounce it a splendid failure on the part of Moses. Instead of allowing this learned general, who was regarded as fully prepared to do his appointed work, to go ahead and accomplish that which it had been foretold he should do, the Lord sent him into the mountains to obtain an education that would fit him to stand as the general of Israel. . . .

God designed that Moses should stand out alone, leaning upon His strong arm, that he should learn to pray and to believe. . . . Everyone should have an individual experience. We should ever be learning the lessons that Providence designs us to learn. . . . If we place ourselves where we look to others to brace us and support us, if we depend on finite help, we do not really know our own strength because we do not stand alone, making God our helper. When thrust out where we have to stand alone, the taproot of our faith fastens upon the only sure support—the infinite God.—Manuscript 36, 1885.

April 4
**WE MUST
LABOR FOR TIME
AND ETERNITY**

◆ *He smote the Egyptians, and delivered our houses. Exodus 12:27.*

ETERNAL interests are at stake with every one of us. We shall all be tried and tempted. Many act as though there were no devil, no tempter, no conflict between good and evil. Unless you realize that you have something to contend against, your feet will slip from under you. Someone will come to our churches with a message, and you will be unable to discern light from darkness, and will be just as likely to accept the darkness as the light.

"Remember therefore how thou hast received and heard, and hold fast, and repent. If therefore thou shalt not watch, I will come on thee as a thief, and thou shalt not know what hour I will come upon thee" (Rev. 3:3).

Many are bringing themselves into close affinity to the world. Many have not heeded the light that has called us to place our children under the best influences, where they will hear the truth. Many have not heeded the instruction of the Lord to take their children from the public schools and place them in schools where they can learn the truths of the Word of God, line upon line, and precept upon precept. Their education should be made preparatory to the education that is to be continued in the higher school above.

When the judgments of God were about to fall upon the land of Egypt, Christ gave instructions through Moses that the children of Israel were to call their children in and keep them under their own roof. If any should be found in the houses of the Egyptians, they would not escape the plagues. Keep your children close to you and, so far as possible, away from worldly and evil influences. The Lord wants you to prepare your children for the future, immortal life. Unless we are more careful, our children will imbibe the same spirit of unbelief that was revealed among the Israelites of old, by reason of which God could not bring them into the Promised Land.

Let us put on the whole armor of God and act like people who are waiting for their Lord to come in the clouds of heaven. When you do this, souls will be converted. Your ministers will not labor month after month and bring no one into the truth. We are to hunt and fish for souls. Sometimes you will catch fish and sometimes you will not, but we are to persevere in the work of God, knowing that He has given us a message to unbelievers, a message that will win its way to many hearts.—Manuscript 161, 1904.

April 5
GOD'S OUTWARD SEAL SIGNIFIES INWARD FAITH

◆ *When your children shall say unto you, What mean ye by this service? That ye shall say, It is the sacrifice of the Lord's passover, who passed over the houses of the children of Israel in Egypt. Exodus 12:26, 27.*

*E*VERY human agent is merging his or her character under one of two heads—the Prince of Life or the prince of darkness. . . . If we serve sin we shall meet the reward of the transgressor of the law of Jehovah before the judgment seat of Christ. . . . All the invitations given by a gracious God—given, but slighted and refused and rejected—will be presented to every individual, and the sentence that will fix the destiny of the soul in eternal bliss or to be punished with the fiery element of the wrath of God, which will close the history of the wicked forever.

The condition given to the Hebrews in Egypt on that night when the firstborn were slain was that every family should manifest that faith in the message given them of God that would lead them to act in perfect obedience to the directions given them of God. Every member of the family was to be gathered into the dwelling place of the Hebrews. They were to eat the Passover with their preparations all made for their departure, even with their staffs in their hands. God was about to do His work in judgment, and this was to bring Pharaoh to understand that the Lord, He was God, and beside Him there was none else.

The angel of God was to pass over the houses of the Hebrews with the blood sprinkled on the lintels and doorposts. This sign was to be respected.

But suppose that the inmates of the house were careless and did not gather their children with them in the house. Or suppose the children who had been born and brought up in Egypt thought this only a whim, and altogether unnecessary, and should refuse the entreaties of their parents, making some excuse as did those called to the marriage supper. Then the judgment of God would not spare, but the stroke would as surely come upon the firstborn of the Hebrews as the firstborn of the Egyptians.

What is the condition of those who keep the commandments of God and have the faith of Jesus? If in families there are those who are refusing obedience to the Lord in keeping His Sabbath, then the seal cannot be placed upon them. The sealing is a pledge from God of perfect security to His chosen ones. Sealing indicates you are God's chosen. He has appropriated you to Himself. As the sealed of God we are Christ's purchased possession, and no one shall pluck us out of His hands.—Manuscript 59, 1895 (*Manuscript Releases*, vol. 15, pp. 223-225).

April 6
**RESULTS OF
HARDENING
THE HEART
AGAINST GOD**

◆ *And the Lord hardened the heart of
Pharaoh king of Egypt, and he pursued after
the children of Israel. Exodus 14:8.*

HEN light from God, strong and convincing, came
to make known the great I AM, Pharaoh was compelled to yield. But as
soon as the pressure was removed, his unbelief returned and counteracted
the great light God had given. When he refused the evidence of the first
miracle, he sowed the seed of infidelity, which, left to its natural course,
produced a harvest after its own kind. Afterward the king would not be
convinced by any working of God's power. The monarch hardened his
heart, and went on from one step to another of unbelief, until throughout
the vast realm of Egypt the firstborn, the pride of every household, had
been laid low. After this he hurried with his army after Israel. He sought
to bring back a people delivered by the arm of Omnipotence. But he was
fighting against a Power greater than any human power, and with his host
he perished in the waters of the Red Sea.

The despisers of God's law are practicing the same sin that Pharaoh practiced. They are hardening their hearts. The voice of God is rejected for human
theories, for satanic suggestions and delusions. The Holy Spirit is resisted and
set aside. The iniquities of the fathers are visited upon the children. . . .

The Spirit of God keeps evil under the control of conscience. When
people exalt themselves above the influence of the Spirit, they reap a harvest of iniquity. . . . Warnings have less and less power over them. They
gradually lose their fear of God. They sow to the flesh; they will reap corruption. The harvest of the seed that they themselves have sown is ripen-
ing. . . . Their heart of flesh becomes a heart of stone. Resistance to truth
confirms them in iniquity. . . . All should be intelligent in regard to the
agency by which the soul is destroyed. It is not because of any decree that
God has sent out against men or women. He does not make them spiritu-
ally blind. God gives sufficient light and evidence to enable them to distinguish truth from error. But He does not force them to receive truth. He
leaves them free to choose the good or to choose the evil. If people resist
evidence that is sufficient to guide their judgment in the right direction
and choose evil once, they will do this more readily the second time. The
third time they will still more eagerly withdraw from God and choose to
stand on the side of Satan. And in this course they will continue until they
are confirmed in evil and believe the lie they have cherished as truth.—
Manuscript 126, 1901 (*Sermons and Talks,* vol. 2, pp. 183, 184).

April 7
**GOD'S
PROTECTIVE
CLOUD IN
THE DESERT**

◆ *Because there were no graves in Egypt, hast thou taken us away to die in the wilderness? wherefore hast thou dealt thus with us?* Exodus 14:11.

*T*HERE is a lesson of the greatest importance for us in the experience of the children of Israel as they left Egypt. More than a million people had been led out of the right course, as many of them thought, into a valley hemmed in by mountains. Before them lay the Red Sea, and behind them, following fast after in pursuit, was Pharaoh's host.

In the beginning of their march the children of Israel had been guided by a cloud. Ignorant and superstitious because of their long years of bondage in a land of superstition, the people looked upon this cloud with wonder. Some regarded it with fear, while others declared that it was a favorable omen. As the people were encamped beside the sea, they saw in the distance the flashing armor and moving chariots of Pharaoh's host. Terror filled their hearts. Some cried unto the Lord, but by far the greater part hastened to Moses with their complaints. . . .

Moses was greatly troubled that his people should manifest so little faith in God, notwithstanding they had repeatedly witnessed the manifestation of His power in their behalf. . . . True, there was no possibility of deliverance unless God Himself should interpose for their release, but having been brought into this position in obedience to the divine direction, Moses felt no fear of the consequences. His calm and assuring reply to the people was "Fear ye not, stand still, and see the salvation of the Lord.". . .

It was not an easy thing to hold the hosts of Israel in waiting before the Lord. Lacking discipline and self-control, they became violent and unreasonable. . . . The wonderful pillar of cloud had been followed as the signal of God to go forward; but now they questioned if it might not foreshadow some great calamity, for had it not led them on the wrong side of the mountain, into an impassable way? . . .

But now, as the Egyptian host approached them, expecting to make them an easy prey, the cloudy column arose majestically, passed over the Israelites, and descended between them and the armies of Egypt. A wall of darkness interposed between the pursued and their pursuers. The Egyptians could no longer discern the camp of the Hebrews and were forced to halt. But as the darkness of night deepened, the wall of cloud became a great light to the Hebrews, flooding the entire encampment with the radiance of day. That which had been a terror to the people had become their protection.—Manuscript 6a, 1903.

April 8
GOD DELIVERS HIS PEOPLE FROM THE ENEMY

◆ *And the Lord caused the sea to go back by a strong east wind all that night, and made the sea dry land, and the waters were divided. And the children of Israel went into the midst of the sea. Exodus 14:21, 22.*

"GO forward" was the word given by Moses, and it was echoed by the captains of the different divisions. In obedience the host of Israel stepped into the path so strangely and so wonderfully prepared for them. The light from God's pillar of fire shone upon the foam-capped billows and lighted the road that was cut like a mighty furrow through the waters of the sea.

As the cloud moved slowly on, the Egyptian sentinels discovered that the Israelites had moved their encampment, and at once the mighty army was set in readiness for motion. They heard the sound of the marching of the Hebrews, but they could see nothing, for the cloud that gave light to Israel was to the Egyptians a wall of darkness. Guided by the sound, they followed on into the miraculous path God had prepared for His people. All night they followed, but they moved slowly, for their chariots drove heavily. Yet still they moved on, expecting soon to break through the cloud and overtake the fugitives.

At last the shadows of the night passed away, the morning dawned, and the pursuing army was almost within reach of the fleeing Hebrews. . . . Before their astonished eyes the mysterious cloud changed to a pillar of fire reaching from earth to heaven. The thunders pealed and the lightnings flashed. "The clouds poured out water: the skies sent out a sound: thine arrows also went abroad. The voice of thy thunder was in the heaven: the lightnings lightened the world: the earth trembled and shook."

The Egyptians were seized with confusion and dismay. Amid the wrath of the elements, in which they heard the voice of an angry God, they endeavored to retrace their steps and to flee to the shore they had quitted. But Moses stretched out his rod, and the piled-up waters, hissing, roaring, and eager for their prey, rushed together and swallowed the Egyptian army in their black depths.

As morning broke, it revealed to the multitudes of Israel all that remained of their mighty foe—the mail-clad bodies cast upon the shore. From the most terrible peril one night had brought deliverance. . . . Jehovah alone had brought them deliverance, and to Him their hearts were turned in gratitude and faith. Their emotions found utterance in songs of praise.—Manuscript 6a, 1903.

April 9
IN THE END
GOD'S ENEMIES
WILL PERISH

◆ *And the Lord overthrew the Egyptians in the midst of the sea. Exodus 14:27.*

*I*N the whole territory of the world He has created, there is not a kingdom that is independent of God. And when men and women in an earthly kingdom or community understand the laws made to govern the subjects of the Ruler of the universe but still refuse obedience, they bring themselves under condemnation of the law that God, our Supreme Ruler, has established from the foundation of the world. . . .

Because of the stubbornness of Pharaoh, it was decided that the voice of God, in words of command, must demand that the Israelites be set free from their life of slavery. Pharaoh refused, and the Lord punished the kingdom because the earthly ruler would not let God's people go to become a kingdom under divine rulership. Pharaoh's refusal brought many plagues upon Egypt, until the stubborn king was impelled to concede to God's plan. And then he again hardened his heart in rebellion against God and sent his immense army to bring the Israelites back to continual service for the Egyptian ruler.

The Lord wrought wonderfully for the salvation of His people. He made a way of escape in the midst of the Red Sea. The waters were piled up as a strong wall, and a path of deliverance was made for the hosts of Israel following the leadership of Moses.

In pursuit of Israel the vast armies of Egypt ventured to traverse the sea by the same path. A dark cloud was before them, and yet they pressed on. When the whole army—"all Pharaoh's horses, his chariots, and his horsemen"—were in the very bed of the sea, the Lord said unto Moses, "Stretch out thine hand over the sea." Israel had passed over on dry land, but they heard the shouting of the armies in pursuit. As Moses stretched out his rod over the sea, the embanked waters that had stood as a great wall rolled on in their natural course. Of all the men of Egypt in that vast army, not one escaped. All perished in their determination to have their own way and to refuse God's way. That occasion was the end of their probation.

Thus it will be with every class who choose to refuse the light God gives, and persist in following a course of action that makes void the law of Him who is Supreme Ruler over all kings—over all human powers that oppose themselves to the law of the Supreme Ruler of the universe, and set themselves in array against the expressed will of the great I AM.—Manuscript 35, 1906 (*Manuscript Releases*, vol. 21, pp. 64, 65).

April 10
ONLY GENUINE FAITH SURVIVES WHEN TESTED

◆ *And Israel saw the great work which the Lord did upon the Egyptians: and the people feared the Lord, and believed the Lord, and his servant Moses. Exodus 14:31.*

*T*HE voices of the people rang out over the waters of the Red Sea in glorious triumph.

But soon their faith was tested. The Lord would know how much He could depend on His people to be true and loyal to Him. They went three days' journey into the wilderness and found no water. "And when they came to Marah, they could not drink of the waters of Marah, for they were bitter.". . . "The people murmured against Moses, saying, What shall we drink?" Instead of trusting and fearing the Lord, believing in Him under apparently discouraging circumstances, they cast reflections upon their leader.

So people act in this generation. Satan's plan of temptation is always the same. While everything moves prosperously, people think that they have faith. But when suffering, disaster, or disappointment comes, they lose heart. A faith that is dependent on circumstances or surroundings, that lives only when everything goes smoothly, is not a genuine faith.

In his trouble Moses cried to the Lord. This is what the children of Israel, so recently delivered, ought to have done. The Lord heard the cry of His servant, against whom the people had said so many bitter things. He showed Moses a tree, "which when he had cast into the waters, the waters were made sweet." It was not the virtue of the tree that turned the bitter water to sweet; it was the power of Him who was enshrouded in the pillar of cloud, the One who can do all things. . . .

Did the people then appreciate and acknowledge God's blessings? Were their hearts filled with gratitude and thanksgiving to Him? Did they have a praise service, as when they stood on the banks of the Red Sea? We have no evidence that their faith was strengthened by God's mercy and grace and love toward them. . . .

When trial comes to prove us, when we cannot see an increase of prosperity and comfort before us, but a probable lessening of these things, when there is a pressure necessitating sacrifice on the part of all, how shall we receive Satan's insinuations that we are going to have a hard time, that everything is going to pieces, that there is sore trouble ahead of us? . . . We ought to gather up the fragments of heaven's blessings and tokens for good, saying, Lord, I believe in Thee, in Thy servants, and in Thy work. I will trust in Thee.—Letter 49a, 1896.

April 11
**THE SIN OF
UNBELIEF LEADS
AWAY FROM GOD**

◆ *In all their affliction he was afflicted, and the angel of his presence saved them: in his love and in his pity he redeemed them; and he bare them, and carried them all the days of old. But they rebelled, and vexed his holy Spirit. Isaiah 63:9.*

ROM the beginning of sin Christ was with His people to dispute the authority of Satan, for He saw that the conflict must be carried on here in the earth. Satan withstood the Son of God in every effort to redeem His people. Enshrouded in the pillar of cloud by day and in the pillar of fire by night, Christ directed, guided, counseled the children of Israel in their journeyings from Egypt to Canaan. But how unwilling were the children of Israel to be led, how unwilling to be controlled by the voice of the Angel of the Lord! How eager they were in vindicating their own course, in justifying themselves in their rebellious feelings, and in following their own ideas and plans!

It was the mighty Counselor who was enshrouded in the pillar of cloud and fire, and who was beholding the encampment of His people. It was He who corrected them in their evil ways, and encouraged them to trust in the living God to lead them safely to the Land of Promise. They were continually under the eye that never slumbers nor sleeps, and yet they murmured against Moses, the man whom God had appointed as their visible leader, and to whom Jesus Christ talked face-to-face, as a man talketh with his friend. Notwithstanding the fact that the Lord wrought through His servant Moses, yet when the enemy tempted them to evil surmising, jealousy, and faultfinding, they did not resist his temptations and stand firmly for principle.

But their failure is explained by the Inspired Word, and a warning given to us upon whom the ends of the world are come, lest we also fall after the same example of unbelief. . . . The children of Israel fell under the power of the enemy by cherishing an evil heart of unbelief in departing from the living God, and when once they were found on the enemy's side, he pressed his advantage, and made them his allies to the utmost extent. The sin of unbelief, by which their confidence in the Son of God was destroyed, led Israel far astray. At the very time when they should have been praising God and magnifying the name of the Lord, talking of His goodness, telling of His power, they were found in unbelief, and full of murmuring and complaint. The deceiver was seeking through every means possible to sow discord among them, to create envy and hatred in their hearts against Moses, and to stir up rebellion against God. By listening to the voice of the great deceiver they were led into affliction, trial, and destruction.—Manuscript 65, 1895 (*Signs of the Times,* Apr. 25, 1895).

April 12
"HOW LONG WILL YOU REFUSE TO KEEP MY COMMANDMENTS?"

◆ *And it shall come to pass, that on the sixth day they shall prepare that which they bring in; and it shall be twice as much as they gather daily. Exodus 16:5.*

HE Lord suffered His people Israel to go into bondage in Egypt because they did not walk in His ways but dishonored Him by their continual transgressions. Here, subjected to oppression and hard servitude, they could not keep God's Sabbath, and by their long mingling with a nation of idolaters their faith became confused and corrupted. Association with the ungodly and unbelieving will have the same influence upon those who believe the present truth unless they keep the Lord ever before them so that His Spirit shall be their shield. . . .

Pharaoh saw the mighty working of the Spirit of God; he saw the miracles the Lord performed by His servant; but he refused obedience to God's command. The rebellious king had proudly inquired, "Who is the Lord, that I should obey his voice to let Israel go? I know not the Lord, neither will I let Israel go." And as the judgments of God fell more and more heavily upon him, he persisted in stubborn resistance. By rejecting light from heaven, he became hard and unimpressible. . . . Those who exalt their own ideas above the plainly specified will of God are saying, as did Pharaoh, "Who is the Lord, that I should obey his voice?" Every rejection of light hardens the heart and darkens the understanding; and thus people find it more and more difficult to distinguish between right and wrong, and they become bolder in resisting the will of God.

The Lord brought Israel from Egypt, that they might keep His Sabbath, and He gave them special directions how to keep it. The instructions given to Moses were recorded for the benefit of all who should live upon the earth to the close of time. God has spoken; let us listen to His words and obey them.

When the manna was given, the people were tested upon God's law. Then said the Lord to the children of Israel through Moses, "I will rain bread from heaven for you; and the people shall go out and gather a certain rate every day, that I may prove them, whether they will walk in my law, or no.". . .

Notwithstanding this special direction of God, some did go out to gather manna on the seventh day, but they found none; and the Lord said unto Moses, "How long refuse ye to keep my commandments and my laws?" That there might be no mistake in the matter, the Father and the Son descended upon Mount Sinai, and there the precepts of His law were spoken in awful grandeur in the hearing of all Israel.—Manuscript 3, 1885.

April 13
ISRAEL'S EXPERI-ENCE REMINDS US OF SABBATH IMPORTANCE

◆ *See! The Lord has given you the sabbath, therefore on the sixth day he gives you food for two days; each of you stay where you are; do not leave your place on the seventh day. So the people rested on the seventh day. Exodus 16:29, 30, NRSV.*

*B*EFORE the law was given from Sinai, God wrought a miracle each week to impress the people with the sanctity of the Sabbath. He rained manna from heaven for their food, and each day they gathered this manna, but on the sixth day they gathered twice as much as usual, according to the directions of Moses. . . .

"And the children of Israel did eat manna forty years, until they came to a land inhabited; they did eat manna, until they came unto the borders of the land of Canaan." Thus for forty years God worked a miracle before His people each week, to show them that His Sabbath was a sacred day.

God directed that a tabernacle should be built where the Israelites, during their wilderness journeying, could worship Him. Orders from heaven were given that this tabernacle should be built without delay. Because of the sacredness of the work and the need for haste, some argued that the work on the tabernacle should be carried forward on the Sabbath, as well as on other days of the week. Christ heard these suggestions, and saw that the people were in great danger of being ensnared by concluding that they would be justified in working on the Sabbath so that the tabernacle might be completed as quickly as possible.

The word came to them, "Verily my sabbaths ye shall keep." Though the work on the tabernacle must be carried forward with expedition, the Sabbath must not be employed as a working day. Even the work on the Lord's house must give way to the sacred observance of the Lord's rest day. Thus God is jealous for the honor of His memorial of creation.

The Sabbath is a token between God and His people. It is a holy day, given by the Creator to us as a day upon which to rest, and reflect upon sacred things. God designed it to be observed through every age as a perpetual covenant. . . .

As we refrain from labor on the seventh day, we testify to the world that we are on God's side and are striving to live in perfect conformity to His commandments. Thus we recognize as our Sovereign the God who made the world in six days and rested on the seventh. . . . The true Sabbath is to be restored to its rightful position as God's rest day.—Manuscript 77, 1900 (*Review and Herald*, Oct. 28, 1902).

April 14
**WARNINGS
AGAINST A
DEPRAVED
APPETITE**

◆ *Would to God we had died by the hand of the Lord in the land of Egypt, when we sat by the flesh pots, and when we did eat bread to the full; for ye have brought us forth . . . to kill this whole assembly with hunger. Exodus 16:3.*

GOD designed to bestow great blessings upon His people. He purposed to bring them to a good land, which for its richness and fertility was called a land flowing with milk and honey. God designed to establish them there as a healthful, strong, and mighty people if they would submit to His requirements. The people of Israel had lived upon rich and luxurious food in Egypt, not the most healthful for them, and God would bring them through the wilderness to the good land He had promised them. In their travels [He] would remove from them flesh meats and give them a simple yet healthful quality of food and establish them in the good land of Canaan, a powerful people with not a feeble man, woman, or child in all their tribes. . . .

Since the fall of Eve in Eden through intemperate desire to gratify the taste, this has been the prevailing sin of the human family. Eve, after her transgression, prevailed upon her husband to eat also. Adam was not deceived as was Eve, but he was influenced by her to do as she had done—eat and risk the consequences since no harm, she said, had come to her. Adam yielded to the temptations of his wife. He could not endure to be separated from her. He ate and fell from his integrity. Since this lamentable occurrence—which has introduced sin into our world—intemperate, lustful appetite, and the power of influence that one in the wrong exerts over another, have brought an accumulation of misery that it is not possible for language to describe. In no other way has Satan come with his temptations to fallen humankind as successfully as through the appetite.

In their journeyings through the wilderness, rebellion and insurrection were continually arising in the armies of Israel because their depraved appetites would not be indulged. Moses was brought into the greatest perplexity and his heart made sad through the continual murmurings of the children of Israel because God, for their own good, withheld from them flesh meats.

They were continually imagining trouble and anticipating evil. They were jealous of Moses, thinking that he might have selfish motives in leading them from Egypt, that it might be his desire to lead them into the wilderness so that they might perish there, and he enrich himself with their possessions.—Manuscript 32, 1885.

111

April 15
CHRISTIAN LIFE IS NOT ALWAYS GREEN PASTURES

◆ *Behold, I will stand before thee there upon the rock in Horeb; and thou shalt smite the rock, and there shall come water out of it, that the people may drink. Exodus 17:6.*

*T*HOUGH the way may be rough, we must exercise implicit faith in the power of the Lord to guide us. The experience of the children of Israel when journeying through the wilderness is a lesson for us on this point. "All the congregation of the children of Israel journeyed from the wilderness of Sin . . . according to the commandments of the Lord, and pitched in Rephidim: and there was no water for the people to drink.". . . .

He who was enshrouded in the pillar of cloud was leading them, and it was by His express command that they were encamped at this place. The General of the armies of heaven knew of the lack of water at Rephidim, and He brought His people hither to test their faith. But how poorly they proved themselves to be a people whom He could trust. Again and again He had manifested Himself to His chosen people. He had slain the first-born of all families of Egypt to accomplish their deliverance, and had brought them out of the land of their captivity with a high hand. He had fed them with angels' food, and had covenanted to bring them into the Promised Land. But now, when brought into difficulty, they broke into rebellion, distrusted God, and complained that Moses had brought them and their children out of Egypt only that they might die of thirst in the wilderness. By their murmurings and lack of faith they dishonored God and placed themselves where they could not appreciate His mercies.

Many today think that when they begin their Christian life they will find freedom from all want and difficulty. But all who take up their cross to follow Christ come to a Rephidim in their experience. Life is not all made up of green pastures and cooling streams. Disappointment overtakes us, privations come, circumstances occur that bring us into difficult places. As we follow in the narrow way, doing our best as we think, we find that grievous trials come to us. We think that we must have walked by our own wisdom far away from God. Conscience-stricken, we reason that if we had walked with God we would not have suffered so. . . .

But of old the Lord led His people to Rephidim, and He may choose to bring us there also in order to test our faithfulness and loyalty to Him. In mercy to us He does not always place us in the easiest places, for if He did, in our self-sufficiency we would forget that the Lord is our helper in time of necessity.—Letter 24, 1896.

April 16
**CLEANLINESS
SHOULD MARK
THE LIFE OF
A CHRISTIAN**

◆ *And the Lord said unto Moses, Go unto the people, and sanctify them today and tomorrow, and let them wash their clothes. Exodus 19:10.*

*I*NCORRECT personal habits are among the most prolific causes of disease. Order and cleanliness are laws of heaven. The directions given to Moses when the Lord was about to declare His law upon Mount Sinai were very strict in this respect. . . . They were directed to do this, lest there should be impurity about them as they should come before God. He is a God of order, and He requires order and cleanliness in His people.

On no occasion were the children of Israel to allow impurities to remain upon their clothing or their persons. Those who had any uncleanness were to be shut out of the camp until the evening and then were required to cleanse themselves and their clothing before they could return. They were also commanded to carry all their refuse to a distance from the camp. . . .

The Lord requires no less of His people now than He did anciently. If cleanliness was so necessary to those journeying in the wilderness, who were in the open air nearly all the time, it is no less necessary to us, who live in close houses, where impurities are more observable and have a more unhealthful influence.

The moral law, spoken from Sinai, cannot have a place in the hearts of persons of disorderly, filthy habits. If the children of Israel could not so much as listen to the proclamation of that holy law without cleanliness of person and clothing, how can its pure precepts be written upon the hearts of those who are untidy in their persons and their homes? . . .

Violent epidemics of fever have occurred in villages and cities that were considered perfectly healthful, and these have resulted in death or broken constitutions. In many instances the premises of the very ones who fell victims to these epidemics contained the agents of destruction, which sent forth deadly poison into the atmosphere to be inhaled by the family and the neighborhood. . . .

When Lord Palmerston was premier of England, he was at one time petitioned by the Scottish clergy to appoint a day of fasting and prayer to avert the cholera. He replied, "Cleanse and disinfect your streets and houses, promote cleanliness and health among the poor, and see that they are plentifully supplied with good food and raiment, and employ right sanitary measures generally, and you will have no occasion to fast and pray. Nor will the Lord hear your prayers while these, His preventatives, remain unheeded."—Manuscript 58, 1890.

April 17
GOD'S LAW NOT GIVEN FOR ISRAEL ONLY

◆ *If ye will obey my voice indeed, and keep my covenant, then ye shall be a peculiar treasure unto me above all people: for all the earth is mine: And ye shall be unto me a kingdom of priests, and a holy nation. Exodus 19:5, 6.*

*G*OD purposed to make the occasion of speaking His law a scene of awful grandeur, in keeping with its exalted character. . . . Preparations were made according to the command; and in obedience to a further injunction, Moses directed that a barrier be placed about the mount, that neither man nor beast might intrude upon the sacred precinct. . . .

On the morning of the third day, as the eyes of all the people were turned toward the mount, its summit was covered with a thick cloud, which grew more black and dense, sweeping downward until the entire mountain was wrapped in darkness and awful mystery. Then a sound as of a trumpet was heard, summoning the people to meet with God; and Moses led them forth to the base of the mountain. From the thick darkness flashed vivid lightnings, while peals of thunder echoed and re-echoed among the surrounding heights. . . .

The thunders ceased; the trumpet was no longer heard; the earth was still. There was a period of solemn silence, and then the voice of God was heard. Speaking out of the thick darkness that enshrouded Him, as He stood upon the mount, surrounded by a retinue of angels, the Lord made known His law. . . .

Jehovah revealed Himself, not alone in the awful majesty of the judge and lawgiver, but as the compassionate guardian of His people: "I am the Lord thy God, which have brought thee out of the land of Egypt, out of the house of bondage." He whom they had already known as their guide and deliverer, who had brought them forth from Egypt, making a way for them through the sea, and overthrowing Pharaoh and his hosts, who had thus shown Himself to be above all the gods of Egypt—He it was who now spoke His law.

The law was not spoken at this time exclusively for the benefit of the Hebrews. God honored them by making them the guardians and keepers of His law, but it was to be held as a sacred trust for the whole world. The precepts of the Decalogue are adapted to all humankind, and they were given for the instruction and government of all. Ten precepts, brief, comprehensive, and authoritative, cover the duty of human beings to God and to other humans; and all based upon the great fundamental principle of love.—*Patriarchs and Prophets*, pp. 303-305.

April 18
SETTLED
REBELLION
IS INCURABLE

◆ *The people gathered themselves together unto Aaron, and said unto him, Up, make us gods, which shall go before us; for as for this Moses, . . . we wot not what is become of him. Exodus 32:1.*

*A*LL are at liberty to choose and take their position with the rebellious or take their stand with those who are on the side of God and the truth—those who have labored earnestly, faithfully, and unselfishly in this great cause, and who have endured trial, reproach, and fought with courage the battles of the Lord.

Settled rebellion is incurable. It first originated in heaven with the angel next highest in order to Jesus Christ. This exalted angel had sympathizers who joined him in his rebellion. He, Satan, the great rebel, was turned out of heaven, and all his rebel sympathizers shared his fate. Since then it has been his special work to excite to rebellion all he can gain control over.

Said the angel, "Rebellion will occur up to the time of the closing of the work of the third angel's message. Marvel not, neither be discouraged. He who conquered the leader in rebellion stands at the head of this great work. Although Satan may exult and seem for a time to triumph, the first great Conqueror has His eyes upon him, and he can go no farther than He permits. He is permitted to have power for a time to reveal the true-hearted, to prove the faithful, to develop the spurious and separate them from the pure in heart. Rebels will be purged out from among the loyal and true in due time, for the truth has gathered of every kind."

I was then shown the travels of the children of Israel. Rebellion was common among ancient Israel. Moses was gone from them only forty days, but the time was long enough for there to be enacted one of the greatest apostasies from God, who had shown to them such special favors and whose voice they had recently heard from Mount Sinai. In awful grandeur He spoke the Ten Commandments in the hearing of the people, which led them to exceedingly fear and tremble and plead with Moses that the great Jehovah should not speak to them any more, but that he should receive the words and speak to them. They wrought out a calf and turned from God to the lowest idolatry, that of worshiping the work of their own hands.—Manuscript 1, 1865.

April 19
MOSES WAS AN EXAMPLE OF GENUINE HUMILITY

◆ *If thou wilt forgive their sin—and if not, blot me, I pray thee, out of thy book which thou hast written. Exodus 32:32.*

*A*FTER the children of Israel had listened at Sinai to the giving of the Ten Commandments, they fell into idolatry, and the Lord was angry with them. He said to Moses, "Let me alone . . . that I may consume them: and I will make of thee a great nation." But no; the man who had learned to seek after the lost sheep in the wilderness, who had endured cold and storm rather than leave one sheep to perish, could not give up the people placed in his care. He pleaded with God not to give them up, but to forgive their transgression. . . .

Moses declared, "If thy presence go not with me, carry us not up hence." He no longer had any confidence in himself. His watchword was The God of Israel is my Strength and my Leader. He received no adoration as did the kings of other nations. Repeatedly he told the children of Israel that he was only what the God of Israel had made him. In all the battles in which they obtained the victory, he told them that they were not to claim the honor, for it was the God of Israel who gained the victory in their behalf.

When the Lord told Moses, "My presence shall go with thee," we might think that this mighty man of God would have been satisfied. But he was not. He still urged his petition. "He said, I beseech thee, shew me thy glory." Was Moses rebuked for his presumption? . . . He [God] took that mighty man of faith, and put him into a cleft in the rock, and there revealed to him His glory. . . .

When Moses returned to the people, they could not look upon his countenance, for he had been talking with God, and his face reflected the glory of God, which had been revealed to him. "The skin of his face shone." When talking with the people, he was obliged to cover his face with a veil.

Not the pompous, boastful, unbelieving person, but the humble, faithful one is mighty in the sight of God. In order that He may answer their prayers, the Lord desires His people to obtain an individual experience. The nearer they come to Jesus Christ, the closer their view of His loveliness and life, the more humble will be their opinion of themselves. The lower their estimate of self, the more distinct will be their views of the glory and majesty of God. When individuals claim that they are sanctified and holy, no clearer evidence is needed to show that they are not holy.—Manuscript 36, 1885.

April 20
**GOD INVITES
HOLY BOLDNESS
AS WE
APPROACH HIM**

◆ *And he said, I beseech thee, shew me thy glory. Exodus 33:18.*

*A*LL who have responsible positions must realize that they must first have power with God, in order that they may have power with the people. . . . God listens to the appeal of His self-denying workers who labor to advance His cause. He has even condescended to talk face-to-face with feeble mortals. He listens not only with patience but with approval to the importunate prayers of those who really long for His help.

His servant Moses felt his insufficiency for the great work before him and pleaded, with an earnestness that seemed almost presumption, for the presence of God to be with him. But instead of receiving a reproof, the earnest pleader receives the reply "My presence shall go with thee, and I will give thee rest"—an assurance that all his burdens may be rested upon God. But the mind of Moses is so burdened with the tremendous weight of the responsibilities resting upon him that he approaches still nearer to God, and his request is pressed still further. The answer from God is "I will do this thing also that thou hast spoken; for thou hast found grace in my sight, and I know thee by name."

Encouraged by his success, Moses ventures still further—a holy boldness he possesses, until it reaches a point that is incomprehensible to poor, finite human beings. The servant of God has been, through prayer, approaching nearer and nearer to God, and now [makes] a request such as no mortal human had ever dared to make—"I beseech thee, shew me thy glory." Will God thrust aside His servant now for his apparent presumption? The third time the answer comes, "I will make all my goodness pass before thee." . . .

Oh, what condescension on the part of God! That hand that made the worlds takes the mighty man of faith and puts him in a cleft of the rock, that He may show him His glory, and make all His goodness to pass before him. . . .

The most brilliant intellect, the most earnest study, the highest eloquence, can never be substituted for the wisdom and power of God in those who are bearing the responsibilities connected with His cause. . . . God has made every provision for workers to have the help that He alone can give. If they allow their work to hurry, drive, and confuse, so that they will have no time for devotional thought or for prayer, they will make mistakes. If a standard is not lifted up by Jesus Christ against Satan, he will overcome those who are engaged in the important work for this time.—Manuscript 6, 1879.

April 21
**HEAVENLY
OBSERVERS
WITNESS EVERY
WORD SPOKEN**

◆ *And they said, Hath the Lord indeed spoken only by Moses? hath he not spoken also by us? And the Lord heard it. Numbers 12:2.*

ARON and Miriam became displeased with Moses because of his marriage. . . . They thought Moses regarded himself as superior to them, and they must ever stand as second. This state of feeling was just what Satan desired to bring about. It was in his lines to carry forward the work he began in heaven. . . . Satan could not touch the head, the reasoning faculties, the eyes of the mind; but he could make things that the outward eye looked upon appear in accordance with his subtle working. . . . Aaron and Miriam became one in mind. They communicated with one another and they said, "Hath the Lord indeed spoken only by Moses? hath he not spoken also by us?" Mark that which follows: "And the Lord heard it."

The Lord hears many things human beings say, and He understands the current of evil started into intense activity by words spoken in secret. If persons could always consider that there is a Witness present to hear every word they speak, even in the secret chamber, there would be fewer private communications coming from human lips to leaven the minds of others by their ideas and evil suggestions that are voicing the temptations of the great deceiver. . . .

There was One who could vindicate Moses. Hear His testimony; the words come sounding down along the lines to our time, evidencing that the mind of God is not in agreement with the thoughts of unsanctified humans. "(Now the man Moses was very meek, above all the men which were upon the face of the earth.) . . . And the Lord came down in the pillar of the cloud, and stood in the door of the tabernacle, and called Aaron and Miriam: and they both came forth.

"And he said, Hear now my words: If there be a prophet among you, I the Lord will make myself known unto him in a vision, and will speak unto him in a dream. My servant Moses is not so, who is faithful in all mine house. With him will I speak mouth to mouth. . . . And the cloud departed from off the tabernacle; and, behold, Miriam became leprous, white as snow.". . .

Because Aaron and Miriam were honored with a part in the work, they thought they were equal to Moses, and were indeed a very essential part of the great whole. They felt that credit should be given to them and that Moses should not have all the honor. Let the human agent consider that in any position where God has placed him or her, he or she must put entire confidence in God.—Letter 7, 1894.

April 22
**BE CAREFUL
OF GIVING A
FALSE REPORT**

◆ *We be not able to go up against the
people; for they are stronger than we.*
Numbers 13:31.

*Y*OUNG people are needed in the work—those who will undertake the work interestedly and will carry it forward zealously and strongly. But the Lord is, and ever will be, with the old, steadfast leaders who have held fast to the truth in times of peril. When the foundation of the faith of the younger leaders seems to be swept away and their houses falling, the testimony, like that of Caleb, will be heard from the old warriors, "Let us go up at once, and possess it; for we are well able to overcome it." Then the voice of unbelief was heard. "We be not able to go up against the people; for they are stronger than we." One word of unbelief prepares the way for more. Satan does not easily let alone any person whom he can tempt to dishonor God by expressing unbelief. . . .

What effect did this report have upon the congregation? . . . "And all the children of Israel murmured against Moses and against Aaron: and the whole congregation said unto them, Would God that we had died in the land of Egypt! or would God we had died in this wilderness!". . . .

Let all read carefully the fourteenth chapter of Numbers, and let them understand that people can make false reports as did these who had been sent on an errand that concerned the movements of more than a million people. . . .

Those who bore the discouraging report and brought discouragement to the whole camp of Israel, when opposed because of their unfaithful witness, served the satanic powers in complete rebellion. And they carried the disappointed congregation with them, in that they believed their interpretation of the land. The congregation took the wrong side, and, inspired by satanic agencies, they cried out against the faithful spies, and bade them stone Joshua and Caleb, who dared to bear the truthful representation in regard to the land.

But there is always a defense provided for those who have borne witness for the truth. What was it that saved the lives of Joshua and Caleb? "And the glory of the Lord appeared in the tabernacle of the congregation before all the children of Israel.". . . .

We have here a positive evidence that the anger of the Lord was awakened against the rebellious people—those who had been blessed with great light and precious opportunities to know the will of God, which was communicated to them by Christ Himself, their invisible Leader, enshrouded in the pillar of cloud by day and the pillar of fire by night.—Letter 106, 1897 (*Manuscript Releases,* vol. 15, pp. 289-291).

April 23
**SPEAK NO WORDS
OF UNBELIEF**

◆ *We came unto the land whither thou
sentest us, and surely it floweth with milk
and honey; and this is the fruit of it.*
Numbers 13:27.

*T*HUS far [the spies'] words had been spoken in faith;
but see what followed. After describing the beauty and fertility of the land,
all but two of the spies enlarged upon the difficulties and dangers that lay
before the Israelites should they undertake the conquest of Canaan. . . .

Their unbelief cast a gloomy shadow over the congregation. A wail of
agony arose and mingled with the confused murmur of voices. Caleb
comprehended the situation and did all in his power to counteract the evil
influence of his unfaithful associates. He did not contradict what had been
said. The walls were high and the Canaanites strong. But God had promised the land to Israel.

"Let us go up at once, and possess it," urged Caleb, "for we are well
able to overcome it." But the ten, interrupting him, pictured the obstacles
in darker colors than at first. "We be not able to go up against the people,"
they declared, "for they are stronger than we. . . . And all the people that
we saw in it are men of a great stature. And there we saw the giants, the
sons of Anak, which come of the giants: and we were in our own sight as
grasshoppers, and so we were in their sight."

It is right that human beings should be considered as grasshoppers
when compared with the Lord God of Israel. But it showed a lack of faith
for the spies to speak of the Israelites thus in comparison with the people
they had seen in Canaan. The children of Israel had on their side the mighty
powers of heaven. The One who, enshrouded in the pillar of cloud, had led
them through the wilderness was fighting for them. They had seen His
power displayed at the Red Sea, when at His word the waters parted, leaving a plain path for them through the sea. Nevertheless, when the spies saw
the walled cities in the Promised Land, they allowed unbelief to enter their
hearts, and they returned to the congregation with a faithless report. . . .

This shows us to what desperation unbelief will bring people. My
brethren and sisters, when thoughts of unbelief and distrust come to you,
remember that silence is eloquence. Speak no words of unbelief, for such
words are as seeds that will spring up and bear fruit. There is among us altogether too much talking and too little praying. We think and speak of
the difficulties that exist, and forget to trust the Lord. God's Spirit would
work mightily in behalf of His people if we would give Him opportunity.
—Manuscript 10, 1903.

April 24
**LEARNING TO
TRUST AND OBEY**

◆ *Now if thou shalt kill all this people as one man, then the nations . . . will speak, saying, Because the Lord was not able to bring this people into the land . . . therefore he hath slain them in the wilderness. Numbers 14:15, 16.*

HE Lord had fulfilled the word that He spoke to Abraham when He declared that after the children of Israel had been in bondage four hundred years, He would deliver them. . . . Yet here, on the border of the Promised Land, they dishonored Him by giving way to unbelief.

We shall be brought into strait places, but we do not want to wait until then before we learn to trust and obey. Now, just now, is our day of opportunity and privilege. When the light of truth is shining upon us, we are to learn the lesson. Let us plead with God to give us a true conception of His character and a willingness to obey Him.

We are to stand in the strength and power of Israel's God. Shall we do it, brethren and sisters? Or shall we murmur and complain, looking at the obstacles in the way and making a mountain out of a molehill? Today God gives His people, to confirm their faith, evidences of His power such as He gave to Israel. Will they make these evidences of no effect? Will they act as if God had not wrought in their behalf? The Lord wants us to acknowledge His power and His grace and His great salvation, which He has brought us at an infinite cost—in the death of His only-begotten Son.

We are living in a day of trial, a day of probation, a day of test. God is proving His people, to see whether He can work in their behalf. He cannot work for them if they open their hearts to the impulses of the enemy. He cannot cooperate with them if they trust in human beings in the place of looking to Jesus, and rejoicing in His goodness and His love. He wants to make of us a people through whom He can reveal His grace, and He will do this if we will only give Him opportunity, if we will open the windows of the soul heavenward and close them earthward against human rabble, against murmuring, complaining, and faultfinding. . . .

Those who today murmur against God's appointed agencies, weakening the confidence of the people in them, are doing the same work that the children of Israel did. The Lord hears every murmuring word. He hears every word that detracts from the influence of those whom He is using to proclaim the truth that is to prepare a people to stand in the last days.—Manuscript 10, 1903 (*General Conference Bulletin*, Mar. 30, 1903).

April 25
CALEBS STILL NEEDED TODAY

◆ *And Caleb stilled the people before Moses, and said, Let us go up at once, and possess it; for we are well able to overcome it. Numbers 13:30.*

ALEBS have been greatly needed in different periods of the history of our work. Today we need workers of thorough fidelity, workers who follow the Lord fully, workers who are not disposed to be silent when they ought to speak, who are as true as steel to principle, who do not seek to make a pretentious show, but who walk humbly with God—patient, kind, obliging, courteous workers, who understand that the science of prayer is to exercise faith and show works that will tell to the glory of God and the good of His people. . . .

God will have no leaders in His work who offer divided service. His servants are to take the position that they will not sanction any evil work. To follow Jesus requires wholehearted conversion at the start, and a repetition of this conversion every day.

There have been times when a crisis has determined character. . . . There are workers who have put out their spiritual eyesight. They cannot distinguish between the sacred and the common. Their voice is the loudest when they are in the enemy's service. It will be greatly to their credit to keep still. This is their strength. Silence is their eloquence. It means very much to every person whether he or she is on the Lord's side of the question or on Satan's side.

God's people today have far greater light than had ancient Israel. They have not only the increased light that has been shining upon them, but the instruction given by God to Moses, to be given to the people. God specified the difference between the sacred and the common, and declared that this difference must be strictly observed. . . .

The Lord has given His people great light and precious instruction. What sorrow, what shame, what agony of soul, has been felt by God's faithful servants who have stood, as did Joshua and Caleb, to hear Israel cast off their leader . . . and choose one of their rebellious number to lead them back to Egypt. In their complaints the Israelites blasphemed God. God had signified that the defense of the land of Canaan had departed, and that now was the opportune time for them to enter it.

Caleb declared the truth for that and every time: "The land, which we passed through to search it, is an exceeding good land. If the Lord delight in us, then he will bring us into this land, and give it us; a land which floweth with milk and honey. Only rebel not ye against the Lord, neither fear ye the people of the land; for they are bread for us: their defense is departed from them, and the Lord is with us: fear them not."—Letter 39, 1899.

April 26
WHEN WE FACE DIFFICULTIES AND TESTS

◆ *Surely they shall not see the land which I sware unto their fathers. Numbers 14:23.*

*W*HEN difficulties arise in any branch of the cause—as they surely will, for the church militant is not the church triumphant—all heaven is watching to see what will be the course of those who are entrusted with sacred responsibilities. Some will stumble; some will give heed to seducing spirits; some will choose darkness rather than light because they are not true to God. Like their Master, those who are abiding in Christ will not fail nor be discouraged. . . .

The Lord requires our undivided affections. If people are not wholehearted, they will fail in the day of test and proving and trial. When the enemy shall put his forces in array against them, and the battle seems to go hard, at the very time when all the strength of intellect and capability, all the tact of wise generalship, is needed to repulse the enemy, those who are halfhearted will turn their weapons against their own soldiers; they weaken the hands that should be strong for warfare.

God is testing all who have a knowledge of the truth to see if they can be depended on to fight the battles of the Lord when hard pressed by principalities and powers, and the rulers of the darkness of this world, and wicked spirits in high places. Perilous times are before us, and our only safety is in having the converting power of God every day, yielding ourselves fully to Him to do His will and walk in the light of His countenance. (See 1 Peter 2:9.)

Now when we are just on the borders of the Promised Land, let none repeat the sin of the unfaithful spies. . . . They made it appear as folly and presumption to think of going up to possess the land. Thus they leavened the whole congregation with their unbelief. . . .

While the people were cherishing doubts and believing the unfaithful spies, the golden opportunity for Israel passed by. The inhabitants of the land were aroused to make a determined resistance, and the work that the Lord had prepared to do for them to manifest His greatness and His favor to His people could not be done because of their wicked unbelief and rebellion. . . .

Shall it be then in these last days, just before we enter into the heavenly Canaan, that God's people shall indulge the spirit that was revealed by ancient Israel? Men and women full of doubts and criticisms and complaints can sow seeds of unbelief and distrust that will yield an abundant harvest.—Manuscript 6, 1892.

April 27
TRUE MORAL AND INTELLECTUAL POWER ORIGINATES WITH GOD

◆ *My servant Caleb, because he had another spirit with him, and hath followed me fully, him will I bring into the land whereinto he went; and his seed shall possess it. Numbers 14:24.*

HE whole of the Christian world is involved in the great conflict of faith and unbelief. All will take sides. Some apparently may not engage in the conflict on either side. They may not appear to take sides against the truth, but they do not come out boldly for Christ through fear of losing property or suffering reproach; all such are numbered with the enemies of God.

Morality cannot be separated from religion. Not all conservative tradition received from educated persons and from the writings of outstanding people of the past are a safe guide for us in these last days, for the great struggle before us is such as the world has never seen. . . .

We are not one of us safe, even with past experience, unless we live as seeing Him who is invisible. Daily, hourly, we must be actuated by the principles of Bible truth—righteousness, mercy, and the love of God. Any person who would have moral and intellectual power must draw from the Divine Source.

At every point and decision inquire, Is this the way of the Lord? With your Bibles open before you, consult sanctified reason and a good conscience. Your heart must be moved, your soul touched, your reason and intellect awakened by the Spirit of God. The holy principles laid down in His Word will give light to the soul. I tell you . . . our true source of wisdom and virtue and power is in the cross of Calvary. Christ is the Author and Finisher of our faith. He says, "Without me ye can do nothing." Jesus is the only sure guarantee for intellectual success and advancement.

We need to practice temperance in all things so that the taste may be elevated, the appetite controlled, the passions subdued. The Lord Jesus can supply every grace. Love, joy, peace, long-suffering, gentleness, goodness, faith, meekness, temperance—these are the fruits borne by the Christian tree. . . .

If you would have divine enlightenment, go to the throne of grace, and you will be answered from the seat of mercy. A compact was entered into by the Father and the Son to save the world through Christ, who would give Himself that whosoever believeth in Him should not perish, but have eternal life. No human power or angelic power could make such a covenant.—Manuscript 16, 1890.

April 28
ACKNOWLEDGE CORRECTION AND PROFIT FROM IT

◆ *Ye take too much upon you, seeing all the congregation are holy. Numbers 16:3.*

*W*HILE some under correction will acknowledge that they have been an injury to the cause, there are others who will charge with having an unkind spirit the one who has manifested true friendship by pointing out their wrongs, and will either be impudent or disrespectful to the reprover or will put on the disguise of injured innocence. This martyr-like appearance is a specious hypocrisy and is calculated to deceive those who are easily blinded, who are always ready to sympathize with the wrongdoer. . . .

[Korah, Dathan, and Abiram] complained and influenced the people to stand with them in rebellion, and even after God stretched forth His hand and swallowed up the wrongdoers and the people fled to their tents in horror, their rebellion was not cured.

The depth of their disaffection was made manifest even under the judgment of the Lord. The morning after the destruction of Korah, Dathan, and Abiram and their confederates, the people came to Moses and Aaron saying, "Ye have killed the people of the Lord." For this false charge on the servants of God thousands more were killed, for there was in them sin, exultation, and presumptuous wickedness.

Shall the example presented in the history of the children of Israel have any weight with us? Shall those who claim to believe the truth be influenced to judge from their human feelings as did Israel? When the servants of God are called upon to do the disagreeable duty of correcting the erring, let not those upon whom the Lord has not laid this burden stand between the offender and God. If you cannot see matters in the light in which they have been presented, hold your peace; let the arrows of the Almighty fall just where He has directed they shall fall. . . .

Reproof and rebuke may, and will, come closer home to individuals than they dream of. God has His work in hand, and declarations will be made that will test the faith and loyalty of the people of God. There are those who have had great light, who are far from God, who in heart are apostates. . . .

But we may still rejoice in the fact that it is not yet too late for wrongs to be righted. Jesus is a risen, living Saviour, our Advocate in the courts of heaven. "And if any man sin, we have an advocate with the Father, Jesus Christ the righteous." As soon as sinners see their sins in the light of God's Word, repent, and seek pardon with contrition of soul, confessing their sins, the Lord hears and answers.—Letter 12a, 1893.

April 29
TO GOD, NOT SELF, BE THE GLORY

◆ *With his rod he smote the rock twice: and the water came out abundantly. . . . And the Lord spake unto Moses and Aaron, Because ye believed me not, ye shall not bring this congregation into the land. Numbers 20:10-12.*

*I*T would be the greatest folly in the world for any of us to take credit to ourselves for any success we may have. The more humbly we walk with God, the more will He manifest Himself to us to help us. The Lord never designed to send out His servants to do a work for Him, with all the opposition of Satan and evil angels against them, unless He gives them divine help. The reason that we do not have greater success in the work is that we depend on our own efforts rather than upon the help God will give us. . . . Consider how Satan rules his agents and works through them to do his work of darkness and deception. It is your privilege to believe that Jesus will work more earnestly for you so that you can do His work. . . .

All heaven is interested in the work of those who are to be saved in the kingdom of God. "Without me," says Christ, "ye can do nothing." Therefore there is not one iota of glory that we can take to ourselves. Notwithstanding you may feel your weakness, yet you may link yourself to the mighty God. I know that I am nothing, but Jesus is mighty to save. I can do nothing, but Jesus can do great things. God wants me in the work, but my efforts will be useless without His help.

The constant cry of Israel was "It is Moses that has done this," and they did not keep God in view. God had a lesson to teach His people, and when Moses ventured to take the glory to himself, God showed the people that it was not Moses but God who had done the work. At last came the word to Moses, "Thou shalt not go into the holy land." The Lord demonstrated to the Israelitish host whose hand it was that was leading them.

When we feel our utter nothingness, it is then that Christ sees it is time for Him to give us His Spirit. He will clothe us with His salvation when we give the whole credit and glory of the work to Him. The Lord help us, my dear brethren and sisters, to learn the precious lessons in the school of Christ. These lessons are meekness and lowliness of heart. Some never learn these lessons. They work and work in themselves, and they do not understand who is the Source of their strength and power.—Manuscript 8, 1886.

April 30
**UNBELIEF AND
MURMURING
EXALT SATAN**

◆ *And the Lord said unto Moses, Make thee
a fiery serpent, and set it upon a pole: and it
shall come to pass, that every one that is bitten, when he looketh upon it, shall live.
Numbers 21:8.*

*T*HE same lesson that Christ bade Moses give to the
children of Israel in the wilderness is for all such souls suffering under the
plague spot of sin. From the billowy cloud Christ spoke to Moses and told
him to make a brazen serpent and place it upon a pole, and then bid all
that were bitten with the fiery serpents to look and live. What if, in the
place of looking as Christ commanded them, they had said, "I do not believe it will do me the least bit of good to look. I am too great a sufferer
from the sting of the poisonous serpent." Obedience was the object to be
gained, implicit and blind obedience, without stopping to inquire the reason or the science of the matter. . . .

Looking at self will give you neither light nor hope nor peace. The
longer you look and ponder over these things, the more dark and discouraged will you become. You please the enemy of God and of the
human race by keeping in the cave of darkness where there is not a ray of
the Light of life. . . .

If men and women could only see and realize how their unbelief and
mournful murmurings exalt Satan and give him honor, while they rob
Jesus Christ of His glory in the work of saving them, wholly and entirely,
from all sin! . . . He broke the fetters of the tomb and came forth to take
again His life that He laid down for us. He ascended on high, having led
captivity captive and received gifts for us. All this suffering He endured for
us. . . . He will be our helper, and He will be our refuge in every time of
need. He should be revealed in our Christian experience as all-sufficient, a
present Saviour.

Only look and live. We dishonor God when we do not go forth from the
dark cellar of doubts into the upper chamber of hope and faith. When the
Light shineth in all its brightness, let us take hold on Jesus Christ by the
mighty hand of faith. No longer cultivate your doubts by expressing them
and pouring them into other minds, and thus becoming an agent of Satan to
sow the seeds of doubt. Talk faith, live faith, cultivate love to God; evidence
to the world all that Jesus is to you. Magnify His holy name. Tell of His goodness; talk of His mercy; and tell of His power.—Manuscript 42, 1890.

May 1

IN VISION MOSES VIEWED THE PROMISED LAND

◆ *Thou shalt see the land before thee; but thou shalt not go thither unto the land which I give the children of Israel. Deuteronomy 32:52.*

S he [Moses] looked back upon his experience as a leader of God's people, one wrong act marred the record. If that transgression could be blotted out, he felt that he would not shrink from death. He was assured that repentance, and faith in the promised Sacrifice, were all that God required, and again Moses confessed his sin and implored pardon in the name of Jesus.

And now a panoramic view of the Land of Promise was presented to him. Every part of the country was spread out before him, not faint and uncertain in the dim distance, but standing out clear, distinct, and beautiful to his delighted vision. In this scene it was presented, not as it then appeared, but as it would become, with God's blessing upon it, in the possession of Israel. He seemed to be looking upon a second Eden. There were mountains clothed with cedars of Lebanon, hills gray with olives and fragrant with the odor of the vine, wide green plains bright with flowers and rich in fruitfulness, here the palm trees of the tropics, there waving fields of wheat and barley, sunny valleys musical with the ripple of brooks and the song of birds, goodly cities and fair gardens, lakes rich in "the abundance of the seas," grazing flocks upon the hillsides, and even amid the rocks the wild bee's hoarded treasures. . . .

Moses saw the chosen people established in Canaan, each of the tribes in its own possession. He had a view of their history after the settlement of the Promised Land; the long, sad story of their apostasy and its punishment was spread out before him. He saw them, because of their sins, dispersed among the heathen, the glory departed from Israel, her beautiful city in ruins, and her people captives in strange lands. He saw them restored to the land of their fathers, and at last brought under the dominion of Rome.

He was permitted to look down the stream of time and behold the first advent of our Saviour. He saw Jesus as a babe in Bethlehem. . . . He followed the Saviour to Gethsemane, and beheld the agony in the garden, the betrayal, the mockery and scourging—the crucifixion. . . .

Still another scene opens to his view—the earth freed from the curse, lovelier than the fair Land of Promise so lately spread out before him. There is no sin, and death cannot enter. There the nations of the saved find their eternal home.—*Patriarchs and Prophets*, pp. 472-477.

May 2
THE GRAVE CANNOT HOLD GOD'S SLEEPING SAINTS

◆ *So Moses the servant of the Lord died there in the land of Moab, according to the word of the Lord. Deuteronomy 34:5.*

FTER sin entered the world Eden had been caught up from the earth, for God would not suffer it to feel the marks of the curse. . . . As Moses beheld that lovely garden [in vision], an expression of joy came over his countenance. But the servant of God was carried still farther. He saw the earth purified by fire and cleansed from every vestige of sin, every mark of the curse, and renovated and given to the saints to possess forever and ever. He saw the kingdoms of the earth given to the saints of the Most High. . . .

In the new earth the prophecies that the Jews applied to the first advent of Christ will be fulfilled. The saints will then be redeemed and made immortal. Upon their heads will be crowns of immortality, and joy and glory will be pictured on their countenances, which will reflect the image of their Redeemer.

Moses saw the land of Canaan as it will appear when it becomes the home of the saints. John the revelator was given a view of this same land, of which he writes: "I saw a new heaven and a new earth: for the first heaven and the first earth were passed away; and there was no more sea. And I John saw the holy city, new Jerusalem, coming down from God out of heaven, prepared as a bride adorned for her husband. And I heard a great voice out of heaven saying, Behold, the tabernacle of God is with men, and he will dwell with them, and they shall be his people, and God himself shall be with them, and be their God.". . .

As Moses beheld this scene, joy and triumph were expressed in his countenance. He could understand the force of all that the angels revealed to him. He took in the whole scene as it was presented before him. His mind was firm, his intellect clear. His strength was unabated, his eye was undimmed. Then he closed his eyes in death and the angels of God buried him in the mount. And there he slept.

But it was not long before Christ came to raise Moses to life. As He stood by the grave and bade him come forth, Satan stood by His side, saying, "I have control over him. I tempted him and he yielded. Even Moses was not able to keep God's law. He has transgressed and has placed himself on my side of the controversy. He appropriated to himself the glory that belonged to God. He is my property, for by his sin he has placed himself in my dominion and in my power."—Manuscript 69, 1912 (*Manuscript Releases,* vol. 10, pp. 158, 159).

May 3
**MOSES'
RESURRECTION
CERTIFIES
SATAN'S DEFEAT**

◆ *Yet Michael the archangel, when contending with the devil he disputed about the body
of Moses, durst not bring against him a railing accusation, but said, The Lord rebuke
thee. Jude 9.*

ATAN contended earnestly for the body of Moses.
Again he sought to enter into controversy with Christ in regard to the in-
justice of God's law, and with deceiving power reiterated his false statements about not being fairly treated. His accusations were such that Christ
did not bring against him the record of the cruel work he had done in
heaven by deceptive misrepresentation, the falsehoods he had told in Eden
that led to Adam's transgression, and the stirring up of the worst passions
of the hosts of Israel to incite them to murmur and rebel until Moses lost
command of himself. . . . Christ did not retaliate in answer to Satan. He
brought no railing accusation against him, but raised Moses from the dead
and took him to heaven.

Here for the first time the power of Christ was exercised to break the
power of Satan and give life to the dead. Here began His work of making
alive that which was dead. Thus He testified that He was indeed the
Resurrection and the Life, that He had power to ransom those whom
Satan had made his captives, that although people die they will live again.
The question had been asked, "If a man die, shall he live again?" (Job
14:14). The question was now answered.

This act was a great victory over the powers of darkness. This display
of power was an incontrovertible testimony to the supremacy of the Son
of God. Satan had not expected that the body would be raised to life after
death. He had concluded that the sentence "Dust thou art, and unto dust
shalt thou return" gave him undisputed possession of the bodies of the
dead. Now he saw that he would be despoiled of his prey, that mortals
would live again after death.

After Moses was raised to life, the heavenly gates of Paradise were
opened, and Jesus passed in with His captive. No longer was Moses the
captive of Satan. In consequence of his sin Moses merited the penalty of
transgression and became subject to death. When he was raised to life he
held his title in another name—the name of Jesus his Head.

The day of exile is nearly ended. The time is at hand when all who are
sleeping in their graves will hear His voice and come forth, some to everlasting life, and some to final destruction. Christ will raise all His saints,
glorify them with an immortal body, and open to them the gates of the city
of God.—Manuscript 69, 1912 (*Manuscript Releases,* vol. 10, pp. 159, 160).

May 4
WE SHOULD CONVEY THE TRUTH IN TACTFUL WORDS

◆ *Blessed is anyone who endures temptation. Such a one has stood the test and will receive the crown of life that the Lord has promised to those who love him. James 1:12, NRSV.*

*S*TRONG statements often are made by our workers who bear the message of mercy and warning to our world that would better be repressed. Every statement should be carefully considered. Not one word should be spoken that will give the opposers of our faith advantage over us. Let nothing be said in a spirit of retaliation, nothing that will bear even the appearance of railing accusation. Let everyone read and ponder the signification of the scripture that relates how Christ, when contending with Satan about the body of Moses, dared not bring against him a railing accusation.

Truth will bear the test of all opposition. Let it be put strongly, as in Jesus, and let the characteristics of the worker be hidden in Christ. Let not one word be expressed to stir up the spirit of retaliation in opposers of the truth. Let nothing be done to arouse the dragon-like spirit, for it will reveal itself soon enough, and in all its dragon character, against those who keep the commandments of God and have the faith of Jesus. There are hereditary tendencies and natural dispositions that will wrestle for exhibition, but self must be lost in Jesus. The truth must appear in its beautiful, solemn character, dignified, uplifting, and ennobling. Let souls that are ready to perish receive from the teacher of truth only such impressions as are not perishable, but enduring as eternity. Give opportunity for the Holy Spirit to place the acceptable mold upon the souls that are turning from error to truth, from darkness to light. . . .

Guard every word, control every emotion, giving no occasion for Satan to triumph over the believers. The time will come when we shall be called to stand before kings and rulers, magistrates and powers, in vindication of the truth. Then it will be a surprise to those witnesses to learn that their positions, their words, the very expressions made in a careless manner or thoughtless way when attacking error or advancing truth—expressions that they had not thought would be remembered—will be reproduced, and they will be confronted with them, and their enemies will have the advantage, putting their own construction on these words that were spoken unadvisedly.

Satanic agencies in disguise are on the track of every true worker for the Master. Let this be borne in mind: all who strive for the faith must strive lawfully, then when brought into strait places they will not be confused and confounded at meeting their own careless assertions, and words spoken from impulse.—Letter 66, 1894.

May 5
GOD PERFORMS MIRACLES FOR A REASON

◆ *And the priests that bare the ark of the covenant of the Lord stood firm on dry ground in the midst of Jordan, and all the Israelites passed over on dry ground, until all the people were passed clean over Jordan. Joshua 3:17.*

AT this time of the year—in the spring season—the melting snows of the mountains had so raised the Jordan that the river over-flowed its banks, making it impossible to cross at the usual fording places. God willed that the passage of Israel over Jordan should be miraculous. . . .

At the appointed time began the onward movement, the ark, borne upon the shoulders of the priests, leading the van. . . . All watched with deep interest as the priests advanced down the bank of the Jordan. They saw them with the sacred ark move steadily forward toward the angry, surging stream, till the feet of the bearers were dipped into the waters. Then suddenly the tide above was swept back, while the current below flowed on, and the bed of the river was laid bare. . . .

When the people had all passed over, the ark itself was borne to the western shore. No sooner had it reached a place of security, and "the soles of the priests' feet were lifted up unto the dry land," than the imprisoned waters, being set free, rushed down, a resistless flood, in the natural chan-nel of the stream.

Coming generations were not to be without a witness to this great miracle. While the priests bearing the ark were still in the midst of Jordan, twelve men previously chosen, one from each tribe, took up each a stone from the riverbed where the priests were standing, and carried it over to the western side. These stones were set up as a monument in the first camping place beyond the river. . . .

The influence of this miracle, both upon the Hebrews and upon their enemies, was of great importance. It was an assurance to Israel of God's continued presence and protection—an evidence that He would work for them through Joshua as He had wrought through Moses. . . .

This exercise of divine power in behalf of Israel was designed also to in-crease the fear with which they were regarded by the surrounding nations, and thus prepare the way for their easier and complete triumph. . . . To the Canaanites, to all Israel, and to Joshua himself, unmistakable evidence had been given that the living God, the King of heaven and earth, was among His people, and that He would not fail them nor forsake them.—*Patriarchs and Prophets*, pp. 483-485.

May 6
WE CAN FOLLOW THE LORD WITH CONFIDENCE

◆ *And Joshua went unto him, and said unto him, Art thou for us, or for our adversaries? And he said, Nay; but as captain of the host of the Lord am I now come. Joshua 5:13, 14.*

*A*FTER the death of Moses the reins of government were placed in the hands of Joshua. As the servant of the Lord he was given a special work to do. His office carried with it great honor and responsibility, and the instruction given to Moses was transferred to him in a marked manner. "Now therefore," the Lord said, "arise, go over this Jordan, thou, and all this people, unto the land which I do give to them, even to the children of Israel. Every place that the sole of your foot shall tread upon, that have I given unto you, as I said unto Moses.". . .

As Joshua viewed the city of Jericho, and viewed its fortifications, he lifted up his heart in prayer to God, for appearances seemed against him. "And, behold, there stood a man over against him with his sword drawn in his hand." This was no vision, but Christ in person, His glory hidden by the garb of humanity. . . .

Had the eyes of Joshua been opened he would have seen the heavenly host present to take down the walls of Jericho and place the city in the hands of God's people. Now with all confidence Joshua could follow the instruction and leave his burden, so great and perplexing, with the Lord! . . .

The Lord favored His chosen people with prosperity. . . . God declared this people to be a holy people unto Himself, and He promised that if they would keep their covenant with Him, He would supply them with every necessity for their happiness.

Very definite was the instruction that Christ gave when He made known to Moses the terms of their prosperity, and their freedom from disease. "The Lord thy God hath chosen thee to be a special people unto himself," He said, "above all people that are upon the face of the earth. The Lord did not set his love upon you, nor choose you, because ye were more in number than any people; for ye were the fewest of all people: but because the Lord loved you, and because he would keep the oath which he had sworn unto your fathers, hath the Lord brought you out with a mighty hand, and redeemed you out of the house of bondmen, from the hand of Pharaoh king of Egypt.". . .

This assurance comes to the people of God through their earthly pilgrimage to the heavenly Canaan, where an abundant inheritance is prepared for all who love God and keep His commandments.—Manuscript 134, 1899.

May 7

**VICTORIES
ARE WON BY
GOD'S POWER,
NOT OURS**

◆ *And it came to pass, when . . . the people shouted with a great shout, that the wall fell down flat, so that the people went up into the city . . . and they took the city. Joshua 6:20.*

N obedience to the divine command Joshua marshaled the armies of Israel. No assault was to be made. They were simply to make the circuit of the city, bearing the ark of God and blowing upon trumpets. First came the warriors, a body of chosen men, not now to conquer by their own skill and prowess, but by obedience to the directions given them from God. Seven priests with trumpets followed. Then the ark of God, surrounded by a halo of divine glory, was borne by priests clad in the dress denoting their sacred office. The army of Israel followed, each tribe under its standard. . . . No sound was heard but the tread of that mighty host and the solemn peal of the trumpets, echoing among the hills and resounding through the streets of Jericho. . . .

For six days the host of Israel made the circuit of the city. The seventh day came, and with the first dawn of light, Joshua marshaled the armies of the Lord. Now they were directed to march seven times around Jericho, and at a mighty peal from the trumpets to shout with a loud voice, for God had given them the city. . . .

As the seventh circuit was completed, the long procession paused. The trumpets, which for an interval had been silent, now broke forth in a blast that shook the very earth. The walls of solid stone, with their massive towers and battlements, tottered and heaved from their foundations, and with a crash fell in ruin to the earth. The inhabitants of Jericho were paralyzed with terror, and the hosts of Israel marched in and took possession of the city.

The Israelites had not gained the victory by their own power; the conquest had been wholly the Lord's; and as the firstfruits of the land, the city, with all that it contained, was to be devoted as a sacrifice to God. . . . Only faithful Rahab, with her household, was spared, in fulfillment of the promise of the spies. . . .

The utter destruction of the people of Jericho was but a fulfillment of the commands previously given through Moses concerning the inhabitants of Canaan: "Thou shalt smite them, and utterly destroy them.". . . . To many these commands seem to be contrary to the spirit of love and mercy enjoined in other portions of the Bible, but they were in truth the dictates of infinite wisdom and goodness. . . . The Canaanites had abandoned themselves to the foulest and most debasing heathenism, and it was necessary that the land should be cleared of what would so surely prevent the fulfillment of God's gracious purposes.—*Patriarchs and Prophets*, pp. 488-492.

May 8
OUR EYES MUST BE FIXED ON JESUS

◆ *I press toward the mark for the prize of the high calling of God in Christ Jesus. Philippians 3:14.*

*T*HROUGHOUT life we will have our conflicts with the powers of darkness and will be obtaining precious victories. Our eyes must be kept fixed upon the mark of the prize. When Joshua went up from the Jordan to take Jericho, he met a majestic Being, and at once challenged Him: "Art thou for us, or for our adversaries?" The answer was "As captain of the host of the Lord am I now come. . . . Loose thy shoe from off thy foot; for the place whereon thou standest is holy." Not Joshua, the leader of Israel, but Christ Himself, accomplished the work of taking Jericho.

These were the lessons continually given the children of Israel. By directing their attention to the God of heaven, Christ taught them not to take the glory to themselves. Let us not cherish self-exaltation. When we begin to think we are something, let us remember that we have nothing different from or better than other mortals, except what God has given us.

When in need, bear in mind our relation to the children of Israel. Their history is clearly traced by the pen of inspiration. We are not to imitate their example of murmuring and repining. God placed upon the lips of Moses no words of condemnation. In this respect they were separate and distinct from other nations.

In accepting the religion of Jesus Christ, many seem to think that they are taking a downward step. These are in need of stepping down from their self-esteem and self-righteousness, and humbling themselves before God. But those who place themselves in connection with the living God, as His sons and daughters, are taking steps upward. . . .

We are to talk of heaven and heavenly things, keeping ourselves in a position of supplication before God. It is not safe for any of us to feel that we are where our feet cannot slip, but we should feel that the ground whereon we stand is holy. Cleanse the soul temple of its defilement, that Christ may come in and reign supreme. By beholding Jesus Christ, we shall grow up into His likeness. The more closely we are connected with Him, the more clearly we shall see our imperfections. . . . In order to know the power and strength of true godliness, we must hide in Jesus, dedicating ourselves to Him without reserve. . . . Fully dedicate your strength, your mind, all your abilities, to God. Wherever He places you, however humble may be your position, work with fidelity.—Manuscript 36, 1885.

May 9
FAITH AND TRUST IN CHRIST ASSURES TRUE SUCCESS

◆ *In the world ye shall have tribulation: but be of good cheer; I have overcome the world. John 16:33.*

UR Lord is cognizant of the conflict of His people in these last days with the satanic agencies combined with evil people who neglect and refuse this great salvation. With the greatest simplicity and candor, our Saviour, the mighty General of the armies of heaven, does not conceal the stern conflict that they will experience. He points out the dangers, He shows us the plan of the battle and the hard and hazardous work to be done, and then lifts His voice before entering the conflict, [telling us] to count the cost while at the same time [encouraging] all to take up the weapons of their warfare and expect the heavenly host to compose the armies to war in defense of truth and righteousness.

Human weakness shall find supernatural strength and help in every stern conflict to do the deeds of Omnipotence, and perseverance in faith and perfect trust in God will ensure success. While the past confederacy of evil is arrayed against His people He bids them to be brave and strong and fight valiantly, for they have a heaven to win, and they have more than an angel in their ranks—the mighty General of armies leads on the armies of heaven. As on the occasion of the taking of Jericho, not one of the armies of Israel could boast of exercising their finite strength to overthrow the walls of this city, but the Captain of the Lord's host planned that battle in the greatest simplicity, that the Lord God alone should receive the glory and mortals should not be exalted. God has promised us all power.

It is not great talent that we want now, it is humble hearts and direct, consecrated, personal effort, watching, praying, working with all perseverance. . . . Christ has sent His representative, the Holy Spirit, surrounding His living agents who are employed to pierce the ignorance with the bright beams of the Sun of Righteousness. His voice will give assurance, "Lo I am with you alway, even unto the end of the world." The fact is to be ever kept before us that we are carrying forward the warfare in the presence of an invisible world.

We are all to calmly depend upon God as we look upon the obstacles and stubborn unbelief and consider all the risks that must be ventured, and then listen to the voice of Jesus: "Be of good cheer; I have overcome the world." Yes, Christ is conqueror. He is our Leader, our Captain, and we can advance to the victory. Because He lives, we shall live also.—Letter 51, 1895.

May 10
**GOD'S VIEW
OF A SUPPOSED
"SMALL" SIN**

◆ *There is an accursed thing in the midst of thee, O Israel: thou canst not stand before thine enemies, until ye take away the accursed thing from among you. Joshua 7:13.*

HOSE who make a profession of Christianity and yet fail to have true piety are false lights, false signboards pointing in a wrong direction. . . . They fail to bring the principles of the truth they profess to believe into their life practices, and regard their sins and errors as trifling things. When Achan stole the golden wedge and the Babylonish garment, he also thought it was a trifling matter. . . .

Because of this one man's sin, the presence of the Lord was withdrawn from the armies of Israel. The Lord would not serve with their sins. When the children of Israel went up against Ai, they were defeated. . . .

When they came back in disgrace, overcome by the enemy, "Joshua rent his clothes, and fell to the earth upon his face before the ark of the Lord until the eventide, he and the elders of Israel, and put dust upon their heads. And Joshua said, Alas, O Lord God, wherefore hast thou at all brought this people over Jordan, to deliver us into the hand of the Amorites, to destroy us? would to God we had been content, and dwelt on the other side Jordan! O Lord, what shall I say, when Israel turneth their backs before their enemies! For the Canaanites and all the inhabitants of the land shall hear of it, and shall environ us round, and cut off our name from the earth: and what wilt thou do unto thy great name?"

You can see by the prayer of Joshua, if you have spiritual discernment, that that which was esteemed by Achan as a very little thing was the cause of great anguish and sorrow to the responsible men of Israel. . . . Achan, the guilty party, did not feel the burden. He took it very coolly. . . .

Before the people had gone to take Jericho, they had been instructed what course to pursue. Joshua had said, "The city shall be accursed, even it, and all that are therein.". . . Achan had heard all this charge, but he coveted the accursed thing of Jericho, appointed to destruction. He was even ready to steal the gold and silver that were to be consecrated to God and put them into the treasury of his house. . . .

Hear the words from the lips of Jesus Christ, who was enshrouded in the cloudy pillar: "Neither will I be with you any more, except ye destroy the accursed from among you."—Letter 13, 1893 (*Youth's Instructor*, Jan. 25, 1894).

May 11
NO SIN
CAN BE HIDDEN
FROM GOD

♦ *And it shall be, that he that is taken with the accursed thing shall be burnt with fire, he and all that he hath: because he hath transgressed the covenant of the Lord, and because he hath wrought folly in Israel. Joshua 7:15.*

HE Lord did not specify who was the guilty party, but He gave directions as to what was to be done. He said, "In the morning therefore ye shall be brought according to your tribes: and it shall be, that the tribe which the Lord taketh shall come according to the families thereof; and the family which the Lord shall take shall come . . . man by man.". . .

In thus sifting the matter to the bottom, the Lord reveals the fact that He is acquainted with the hidden things of dishonesty, however people may think that they are hidden. In all the transaction, Achan manifested a determination not to acknowledge his sin; but now the Lord fastened his sin upon him. Had Joshua declared Achan's sin, many might have sympathized with the guilty one as he protested that he was innocent, and they might, in their human judgment, have thought he was misused and maltreated. It is thus that many do today when people are reproved for sin, for they drop God out of their reckoning. This is the reason that Joshua addressed Achan as he did. He said, "My son, give, I pray thee, glory to the Lord God of Israel, and make confession unto him; and tell me now what thou hast done; hide it not from me."

The Lord had told Joshua just what Achan had done, but so many are led by human sympathy, and the wrongdoer is so often excused, that the Lord meant to give Israel a lesson that should also be of benefit to us in our day. Therefore Joshua entreated the young man to tell him what he had done. . . .

Had punishment come upon Achan before he had with his own lips made confession of his wrong, the people, who were naturally ready to rebel, would have charged Joshua with dealing harshly with the young man, and would have denounced him as unmerciful in apportioning so dreadful a punishment. . . .

Achan confessed, and said, "Indeed I have sinned against the Lord God of Israel, and thus and thus have I done: When I saw among the spoils a goodly Babylonish garment, and two hundred shekels of silver, and a wedge of gold of fifty shekels weight, then I coveted them . . . and, behold, they are hid in the earth in the midst of my tent, and the silver under it.". . .

"And all Israel stoned him with stones, and burned them with fire, after they had stoned them with stones."—Letter 13, 1893 (*Youth's Instructor,* Jan. 25, 1894; Feb. 1, 1894).

May 12
GOD FAITHFULLY FULFILLS HIS PROMISES

◆ *Ye have seen all that the Lord your God hath done unto all these nations because of you; for the Lord your God is he that hath fought for you. Joshua 23:3.*

HE wars of conquest ended, Joshua had withdrawn to the peaceful retirement of his home at Timnath-serah. . . . The Lord had impressed His faithful servant to do as Moses had done before him—to recapitulate the history of the people, and call to mind the terms that the Lord had made with them when He gave them His vineyard.

Several years had passed since the people had settled in their possessions, and already could be seen cropping out the same evils that had heretofore brought judgments upon Israel. As Joshua felt the infirmities of age stealing upon him, he was filled with anxiety for the future of his people. It was with more than a father's interest that he addressed them, as they gathered once more about him. . . . Although the Canaanites had been subdued, they still possessed a considerable portion of the land promised to Israel, and Joshua exhorted the people not to settle down at ease and forget the Lord's commands to utterly dispossess these idolatrous nations. . . .

Joshua appealed to the people themselves as witnesses that, so far as they had complied with the conditions, God had faithfully fulfilled His promises to them. . . . Satan deceives many with the plausible theory that since God's love for His people is so great, He will excuse sin in them; that while the threatenings of God's Word are to serve a certain purpose in His moral government, they are never to be literally fulfilled. But in His dealings with His creatures, God has maintained the principles of righteousness by revealing sin in its true character—by demonstrating that its sure result is misery and death. The unconditional pardon of sin never has been and never will be. Such pardon would show the abandonment of the principles of righteousness that are the very foundation of the government of God. . . .

God has faithfully pointed out the results of sin, and if these warnings are not true, how can we be sure that His promises will be fulfilled? That so-called benevolence, which would set aside justice, is not benevolence, but weakness. . . .

After presenting the goodness of God toward Israel, Joshua called upon the people, in the name of Jehovah, to choose whom they would serve. . . . Joshua desired to lead them to serve God, not by compulsion, but willingly. Love to God is the very foundation of religion. To engage in His service merely from the hope of reward or the fear of punishment would avail nothing. Open apostasy would not be more offensive to God than hypocrisy and mere formal worship.—Manuscript 135, 1899 (*Youth's Instructor*, June 13, 1901; June 20, 1901).

May 13
**NEVER FORGET
GOD'S LEADING
IN THE PAST**

◆ *Choose you this day whom ye will serve; . . .
but as for me and my house, we will serve the
Lord. Joshua 24:15.*

*I*F those who are still on the stage of action, who have had an experience in the dealings of God in the rise and progress of the work, would stand as did Joshua to strengthen the faith of the people of God by reviewing past blessings and mercies, they themselves would be blessed and they would prove a blessing to those who have not had this experience. If they would recount the sacrifices made by those who led out in the work, and would keep before the people the simplicity of the early workers and the power of God that was manifested to keep the work free from error, delusion, and extravagance, they would have a molding influence upon the workers at this time.

When we lose sight of what the Lord has done in the past for His people, we lose sight of His present working in their behalf. Those who enter the work now know comparatively nothing of the self-denial and self-sacrifice of those upon whom the Lord laid the burden of the work at its commencement. This should be told them again and again. . . .

A stern conflict is in progress between the Prince of life and the prince of darkness, and this battle calls for constant vigilance on the part of devoted workers. . . . If men and women refuse to accept the ways of the Lord, if they resist for any cause the light sent them by heaven, they will be found among the workers of iniquity. . . . When these see the error they have made and realize that they have not had a right spirit, that they have tried to kill that which the Lord would have live, let them honestly and frankly acknowledge their error. . . . When they humble their hearts before God as did David, confessing that they have erred, they have the sure Word of God that they will find pardon. . . .

Satan has been encouraged in his special work for this time. Those who have erred in the past, and have not humbled themselves to fully confess their wrongs and make them right, will continue to move in their own spirit. They will call truth error and error truth. These workers will eventually be found on Satan's side of the controversy. . . .

As God is faithful in His promise, so also will He be faithful in His threatenings. Brethren and sisters, I may be silent in the grave before these warnings from God may have the desired effect upon your minds and hearts; but in the words of Paul I say to you, "Knowing therefore the terror of the Lord, we persuade men" everywhere to repent.—Manuscript 23, 1899.

May 14
**UNSANCTIFIED
DESIRES ARE
SOMETIMES
GRANTED**

◆ *And the Lord said unto Samuel, Hearken
unto the voice of the people in all that they
say unto thee: for they have not rejected thee,
but they have rejected me, that I should not
reign over them. 1 Samuel 8:7.*

E have a living Head, and every person in office
where sacred responsibilities are involved must inquire at every step, "Is
this the way of the Lord?" All must look constantly and continuously to
Jesus for His guidance and maintain principle at any cost. It is not what finite human beings can do, but what God can do through finite people
who are teachable, humble, unselfish, and sanctified. We cannot put the
least confidence in human ability unless the divine power cooperates with
the human. . . .

God has given minds and talents to mortals only in trust, on trial, to
test and prove them to see if they will work in His way and do His will and
put not confidence in themselves alone. . . .

When Israel demanded a king to "judge us like all the nations," "the
thing displeased Samuel." "And Samuel prayed unto the Lord. And the
Lord said unto Samuel, Hearken unto the voice of the people in all that
they say unto thee: for they have not rejected thee, but they have rejected
me, that I should not reign over them.". . . Israel had become tired of pious
rulers who kept God's purposes and God's will and God's honor ever before them according to God's instructions. They wanted a reformed religion that they might by external, flattering prosperity be esteemed great in
the eyes of the surrounding nations. As they at one time hankered after the
leeks and onions of Egypt, and murmured because they did not have
everything to gratify their appetites, and declared their choice to go back
into bondage rather than deny their appetites, so they now insulted God
to His face in throwing off His wise rule. They were hankering after riches
and splendor like those of other nations around them. . . .

Satan's mind was imbuing the hearts of people that Israel should follow his own satanic counsel. They were bewitched by the devil to carry out
their own purposes even in the face of the solemn protestations from their
aged prophet, whom they had every reason to respect and to believe spoke
to them the words that God Himself had told him to speak.—Manuscript
40, 1890.

May 15

GOD WANTS TO LEAD HIS PEOPLE —IF THEY WILL ONLY LET HIM

◆ *Nevertheless the people refused to obey the voice of Samuel; and they said, Nay; but we will have a king over us. 1 Samuel 8:19.*

HE Lord told Samuel further to grant their [the people's] request, but to bear a strong testimony against them in regard to their sin in choosing a temporal ruler rather than a divine ruler. . . . To have a king was not after God's arrangement but after the order of the nations who did not know and acknowledge God.

After this plain statement they still persisted in having their own way, and Samuel consented. The people still were determined to have a king. They decided that Samuel did not understand the situation. If he only knew all the circumstances, the motives, and the designs, and understood as well as themselves the great advantages, he would be as ready as they to have a king to go in and out before them, that the nations should not look down upon them and despise them. They did not, in their spiritual blindness, look beyond Samuel and discern that it was the word of God that they were hearing through His servant.

God was leading and guiding and working for His people in many ways unseen. Their enemies could not distinguish the source of their wisdom and power and who was to be glorified for their wonderful deliverance and marvelous success. God wrought through Gideon. But the manner of their deliverance was of that character that no human being could take the glory, and in recounting the wonderful victory, they could not extol any mortal's wisdom. . . . The power, the wisdom, and the might were in heaven, but they wanted it upon the earth. It was of God, their mighty King, but they wanted it visibly embodied in a person. In this light God accounted the sin of Israel a rejection of Himself. If they had cherished a sacred, reverent fear of God as their Supreme Ruler, they would never have invested authority in human power, to be controlled by it.

Yet the Lord would not leave Saul to be placed in a position of trust without divine enlightenment. He was to have a new calling, and the Spirit of the Lord came upon him. The effect was that he was changed into a new man. The Lord gave Saul a new spirit, other thoughts, other aims and desires, than he had previously had. This enlightenment, with the spiritual knowledge of God, was to bind his will to the will of Jehovah.

Knowing the will of God, which had been plainly stated to him, did Saul bear the test, did he show reverence for God? When brought into a strait place, he did not heed and obey the express command of God, but he ventured to transgress.—Letter 12a, 1888.

May 16
DISOBEDIENCE TO GOD BRINGS ABOUT POOR EXCUSES

◆ *Hath the Lord as great delight in burnt offerings and sacrifices, as in obeying the voice of the Lord? Behold, to obey is better than sacrifice, and to hearken than the fat of rams. 1 Samuel 15:22.*

*T*HE last days are upon us, and Satan is working with all his hellish arts to deceive and destroy souls. Reproofs by testimony are met almost universally, by the ones corrected and reproved, with "I believe the testimonies, but I do not understand them." The Lord has corrected their wrong ways in order to save them from unhappiness, deception, and ruin; but they pass on the same as if light and warnings had never come to them. If they were in harmony with God, they would not be departing from Him. It is because they are so far departed from God that they do not hear His voice as He calls to them, "Return unto me, and I will return unto you," "and I will heal your backslidings."

Saul, after he had disobeyed the requirement of God to destroy the Amalekites, met Samuel and said, "Blessed be thou of the Lord: I have performed the commandment of the Lord. And Samuel said, What meaneth then this bleating of the sheep in mine ears?". . . The answer was the same that we have heard in similar cases—an excuse, a falsehood: "The people spared the best of the sheep and of the oxen, to sacrifice unto the Lord thy God." Saul did not say "my" or "our," but "thy" God. Many who profess to be serving God are in the same position as Saul—covering over ambitious projects, pride of display, with a garment of pretended righteousness. . . .

Samuel looked upon Saul with indignation, yet with deep pity and undisguised grief for the sinful course of one he loved sincerely; but this love must not close his lips. . . . Samuel then spake the cutting words of the Lord. . . . "Because thou hast rejected the word of the Lord, he hath also rejected thee from being king.". . .

Oh, how few can know the sadness of heart that Samuel bore back to Ramah! God had laid upon him the burden of Saul and the burden of this terrible message that he must bear to the monarch.

Sinners seldom feel right in regard to reproof. They blame the ones who open their lips to speak the words of warning, as though it were a personal matter. In their blindness they fail to see that they are flinging from them, in their stubborn resistance, the last offer of light and mercy. —Manuscript 1a, 1890.

May 17
**KINDNESS
OVERCOMES
SELFISHNESS**

◆ *And she said unto her servants, Go on before me; behold, I come after you. But she told not her husband Nabal. 1 Samuel 25:19.*

*T*HE Lord would have the wife render respect unto her husband, but always as it is fit in the Lord. In the character of Abigail, the wife of Nabal, we have an illustration of womanhood after the order of Christ, while her husband illustrates what a man may become who yields himself to the control of Satan. When David was a fugitive from the face of Saul, he had camped near the possessions of Nabal and had protected the flocks and the shepherds of this man from all depredation while in Carmel. In a time of need David sent messengers to Nabal with a courteous message, asking for food for himself and his men, and Nabal answered with insolence, returning evil for good and refusing to share his abundance with his neighbors. . . .

Nabal accused David and his men falsely in order to justify himself in his selfishness, and represented David and his followers as runaway slaves. . . . One of the young men in the employ of Nabal, fearing that evil results would follow Nabal's insolence, came and stated the case to Nabal's wife, knowing that she had a different spirit from her husband and was a woman of great discretion. He set forth the true character of Nabal as he presented the difficulties to her, saying, "Now therefore know and consider what thou wilt do; for evil is determined against our master, and against all his household: for he is such a son of Belial, that a man cannot speak to him."

Abigail saw that something must be done to avert the result of Nabal's fault, and that she must take the responsibility of acting immediately, without the counsel of her husband. She knew that it would be useless to speak to him, for he would receive her proposition only with abuse and contempt. He would remind her that he was the lord of his household, that she was his wife and therefore in subjection to him and must do as he should dictate. . . . She gathered together such stores as she thought best to conciliate the wrath of David, for she knew he was determined to avenge himself for the insult he had received. . . .

Abigail's course in this matter was one that God approved, and the circumstance revealed in her a noble spirit and character. . . . Abigail met David with respect, showing him honor and deference, and pleaded her cause eloquently and successfully. While not excusing her husband's insolence, she still pleaded for his life. She also revealed the fact that she was not only a discreet woman, but a godly woman, acquainted with the works and ways of God in David.—Manuscript 17, 1891 (*Manuscript Releases*, vol. 21, pp. 213, 214).

May 18
THE FRUITS OF A SOFT ANSWER

◆ *A soft answer turneth away wrath: but grievous words stir up anger. Proverbs 15:1.*

ABIGAIL'S manner and conciliatory gifts softened the spirit of David. He declared that it had been his intention to destroy Nabal and his household, but that now he would refrain from vengeance, for he believed that she had been sent by the Lord to prevent him from doing so great an evil. He promised that her request should be ever remembered, even when he should sit as ruler over Israel, and he would never seek retaliation for the insult of Nabal.

Although Nabal had refused the needy company of David and his men, yet that very night he made an extravagant feast for himself and his riotous friends, and indulged in eating and drinking till he sank in drunken stupor. The next day after the effects of his drunken debauch had somewhat passed away, his wife told him of how near he had been to death, and of how the calamity had been averted. . . . Palsied with horror, he sat down and never recovered from the shock.

From this history we can see that there are circumstances under which it is proper for a woman to act promptly and independently, moving with decision in the way she knows to be the way of the Lord. The wife is to stand by the side of the husband as his equal, sharing all the responsibilities of life, rendering due respect to him who has selected her for his lifelong companion. "For the husband is the head of the wife, even as Christ is the head of the church: and he [referring to Christ] is the saviour of the body," or church. . . . When the Spirit of Christ controls the husband, the wife's subjection will result only in rest and benefit, for he will require from her only that which will result in good, and in the same way that Christ requires submission from the church. . . .

When the husband has the nobility of character, purity of heart, and elevation of mind that every true Christian must possess, it will be made manifest in the marriage relation. If he has the mind of Christ he will not be a destroyer of the body, but will be full of tender love, seeking to reach the highest standard in Christ. He will seek to keep his wife in health and courage. . . .

The Lord Jesus has not been correctly represented in His relation to the church by many husbands in their relation to their wives, for they do not keep the way of the Lord. . . . It was not the design of God that the husband should have control, as head of the house, when he himself does not submit to Christ.—Manuscript 17, 1891 (*Manuscript Releases*, vol. 21, pp. 214, 215).

May 19
INSTRUCTION OF GOD TO BE CAREFULLY CHERISHED

◆ *How long wilt thou mourn for Saul, seeing I have rejected him from reigning over Israel? fill thine horn with oil, and go, I will send thee to Jesse the Beth-lehemite: for I have provided me a king among his sons. 1 Samuel 16:1.*

WHEN God called David from his father's sheepfold to anoint him king of Israel, He saw in him one to whom He could impart His Spirit. David was susceptible to the influence of the Holy Spirit, and the Lord in His providence trained him for His service, preparing him to carry out His purposes. . . .

How joyfully David triumphs in God and his relation to Him. "Who is a rock save our God? . . . The Lord liveth; and blessed be my rock; and let the God of my salvation be exalted." He is my strength, my power. He is the source and foundation of all my blessings. He is to be as the shadow of a great rock in a weary land. He is my strength, my support. He it is who keeps me safe. In Him will I trust. . . .

After David had been made king of Israel, God did not compliment him on his exalted position or his dignity and the extent of his power, but instructed him in regard to the obligations resting on him. This instruction was to be carefully cherished as the Word of the Lord for all who should follow David as rulers of the people. They were to be often repeated as lessons of counsel to future generations. . . .

The heavier the responsibilities that people bear, the more humble should they be and the more jealous of themselves, lest they withdraw their confidence from God and become haughty, overbearing, presumptuous, and self-exalted. This is the danger threatening those who have been especially favored by God. Unless they become wise in the wisdom of God, and strive constantly to reveal the attributes of God, they are in danger of thinking themselves sufficient for all things. . . .

Those placed in positions of responsibility should be men and women who fear God, who realize that they are humans only, not God. They should be people who will rule under God and for Him. Will they give expression to the will of God for His people? Do they allow selfishness to tarnish word and action? Do they, after obtaining the confidence of the people as leaders of wisdom who fear God and keep His commandments, belittle the exalted position that the people of God should occupy in these days of peril? Will they through self-confidence become false guideposts, pointing the way to friendship with the world instead of the way to heaven?—Manuscript 163, 1902.

May 20
ONE SIN OFTEN
FORCES ANOTHER

♦ *And David's anger was greatly kindled against the man; and he said to Nathan, As the Lord liveth, the man that hath done this thing shall surely die. 2 Samuel 12:5.*

*T*HE Bible has little to say in praise of mortals. Little space is given to recounting the virtues of even the best men and women who have ever lived. This silence is not without purpose; it is not without a lesson. All the good qualities that people possess are the gift of God; their good deeds are performed by the grace of God through Christ. . . .

It was the spirit of self-confidence and self-exaltation that prepared the way for David's fall. . . . According to the customs prevailing among Eastern rulers, crimes not to be tolerated in subjects were uncondemned in the king; the monarch was not under obligation to exercise the same self-restraint as the subject. All this tended to lessen David's sense of the exceeding sinfulness of sin. . . . As soon as Satan can separate the soul from God, the only Source of strength, he will seek to arouse the unholy desires of humanity's carnal nature. . . .

When in ease and self-security he let go his hold upon God, David yielded to Satan and brought upon his soul the stain of guilt. . . . Bathsheba, whose fatal beauty had proved a snare to the king, was the wife of Uriah the Hittite, one of David's bravest and most faithful officers. . . . Every effort that David made to conceal his guilt proved unavailing. He had betrayed himself into the power of Satan. . . . There appeared but one way of escape, and in his desperation he was hurried on to add murder to adultery. . . .

Nathan the prophet was bidden to bear a message of reproof to David. It was a message terrible in its severity. To few sovereigns could such a reproof be given but at the price of certain death to the reprover. . . . Appealing to David as the divinely appointed guardian of his people's rights, the prophet repeated a story of wrong and oppression that demanded redress. . . .

Nathan fixed his eyes upon the king; then, lifting his right hand to heaven, he solemnly declared, "Thou art the man." "Wherefore," he continued, "hast thou despised the commandment of the Lord, to do evil in his sight?" The guilty may attempt, as David had done, to conceal their crime . . . ; they may seek to bury the evil deed forever from human sight or knowledge; but "all things are naked and opened unto the eyes of him with whom we have to do." . . .

The prophet's rebuke touched the heart of David; conscience was aroused; his guilt appeared in all its enormity. His soul was bowed in penitence before God. With trembling lips he said, "I have sinned against the Lord."—*Patriarchs and Prophets*, pp. 717-722.

147

May 21
IN ADVERSITY
THE CHARACTER
IS REVEALED

◆ *And David said unto all his servants that were with him at Jerusalem, Arise, and let us flee; for we shall not else escape from Absalom. 2 Samuel 15:14.*

AVID was never more worthy of admiration than in his hour of adversity. Never was this cedar of God truly greater than when wrestling with the storm and tempest. . . . With spirits broken and in tearful emotion, but without one expression of repining, he turns his back upon the scenes of his glory and also of his crime, and pursues his flight for his life.

Shimei comes forth as David passes and, with a storm of curses, hurls against him invectives, throwing stones and dirt. Said one of David's faithful men, "Let me go over, I pray thee, and take off his head." David in his sorrow and humility says, "Let him curse, because the Lord hath said unto him, Curse David.". . .

When the march of the procession is arrested by Zadok and Abiathar with the Levites who come bearing the ark of God, the symbol of God's presence, David for a moment sees the star of hope amid the clouds, for with this precious token with him, he may greatly improve his situation. . . .

But how unselfish, how noble, is the man David! In his overwhelming affliction, David's resolution is taken. He, like the tall cedar of Lebanon, looks toward heaven. The royal command is "Carry back the ark of God into the city.". . . His reverence and respect for the ark of God would not allow him to consent that it should be imperiled by his vicissitudes in his hasty flight. . . .

To rob the city of that symbol that gives it the name of the "Mount of Holiness," he could not consent. Had he possessed selfish motives and a high opinion of himself, he would gladly have gathered everything that would build up his sinking fortunes and give him power to secure his safety. But he sends back to its place the sacred chest and will make no advancement until he sees the priests returning with the hallowed burden, to place it in the tabernacle of Zion. . . .

The voice of conscience, more terrible than Shimei, was bringing his sins to his mind. Uriah was continually before his eyes. His great crime was the sin of adultery. . . . Although he did not with his own hand kill Uriah, he knew that the guilt of his death rested upon him. . . .

He recalled how ofttimes God had worked for him, and thought, "If He accepts my repentance, He may yet give me His favor and turn my mourning to joy. . . . On the other hand, if He has no delight in me, if He has forgotten me, if He will leave me to exile or to perish, I will not murmur. I deserve His judgments and will submit to it all."—Letter 6, 1880.

May 22
DAVID'S REMORSE WAS AS GREAT AS WAS HIS GUILT

◆ *I dwell in the high and holy place, and also with those who are contrite and humble in spirit, to revive the spirit of the humble, and to revive the heart of the contrite. Isaiah 57:15, NRSV.*

*S*INNERS seldom feel right in regard to reproof. . . . How little sympathy they feel for the one who has carried the heavy load the Lord has laid upon him! They assume the role of a martyr and think they deserve great pity, because they are reproved and counseled contrary to their own ideas and feelings. They may admit some things, but with dogged persistency they hold fast to their errors, their own ideas. "For rebellion is as the sin of witchcraft, and stubbornness is as iniquity and idolatry." To all intents and purposes the Word of God is rejected. . . .

How different was the character of David! Though he had sinned, when God sent him sharp rebukes he always bowed under the chastisement of the Lord. David was beloved of God, not because he was a perfect man, but because he did not cherish stubborn resistance to God's expressed will. His spirit did not rise up in rebellion against reproof. . . .

David erred greatly, but he was just as greatly humbled and his contrition was as profound as his guilt. There was never a person more humble than David under a sense of his sin. He showed himself a strong man, not in always resisting temptation, but in the contrition of soul and sincere penitence manifested. He never lost his confidence in God, who put the stern rebuke in the mouth of His prophet. He had no hatred for the prophet of God. He was beloved, also, because he relied upon the mercy of a God whom he had loved and served and honored.

To whom much is forgiven, the same loveth much. David did not take counsel of associates who were sinning against God. This is where many fail. They are left in midnight darkness because they choose to counsel with those who walk not in the counsel of the Lord. They will excuse sin in the sinner when it is not repented of, and pass over wrongs when God has not forgiven them. David trusted in God more than in humans. The decision of God was accepted as just and merciful. Oh, how many are walking in blindness and leading others in the same path, where both must perish because they will not heed the reproofs of the Spirit of God!—Manuscript 1a, 1890.

May 23
TO RECEIVE GOD'S PARDON IS TO RECEIVE HIS JUSTIFICATION

◆ *Happy are those whose transgression is forgiven, whose sin is covered. Happy are those to whom the Lord imputes no iniquity, and in whose spirit there is no deceit. Psalm 32:1, 2, NRSV.*

ANY commit the error of trying to define minutely the fine points of distinction between justification and sanctification. Into the definitions of these two terms they often bring their own ideas and speculations. Why try to be more minute than is Inspiration on the vital question of righteousness by faith? Why try to work out every minute point, as if the salvation of the soul depended upon all having exactly your understanding of this matter? All cannot see in the same line of vision. You are in danger of making a world of an atom, and an atom of a world.

As penitent sinners, contrite before God, discern Christ's atonement in their behalf, and accept this atonement as their only hope in this life and the future life, their sins are pardoned. This is justification by faith. Every believing soul is to conform his or her will entirely to God's will, and keep in a state of repentance and contrition, exercising faith in the atoning merits of the Redeemer, and advancing from strength to strength, from glory to glory. Pardon and justification are one and the same thing. . . .

Justification is the opposite of condemnation. God's boundless mercy is exercised toward those who are wholly undeserving. He forgives transgressions and sins for the sake of Jesus, who has become the propitiation for our sins. Through faith in Christ the guilty transgressor is brought into favor with God and into the strong hope of life eternal. . . .

David was pardoned of his transgression because he humbled his heart before God in repentance and contrition of soul and believed that God's promise to forgive would be fulfilled. He confessed his sin, repented, and was reconverted. In the rapture of the assurance of forgiveness he exclaimed, "Blessed is he whose transgression is forgiven, whose sin is covered. Blessed is the man unto whom the Lord imputeth not iniquity, and in whose spirit there is no guile." The blessing comes because of pardon; pardon comes through faith that the sin, confessed and repented of, is borne by the great Sin-bearer. Thus from Christ cometh all our blessings. His death is an atoning sacrifice for our sins. He is the great medium through whom we receive the mercy and favor of God. He, then, is indeed the Originator, the Author, as well as the Finisher, of our faith.—Manuscript 21, 1891 (*Manuscript Releases*, vol. 9, pp. 300, 301).

May 24
**DAVID'S
EXPERIENCES
WERE LIKE OURS**

◆ *Unto thee will I cry, O Lord my rock; be not silent to me: lest, if thou be silent to me, I become like them that go down into the pit. Psalm 28:1.*

AVID was a representative human being. His history is of interest to every soul who is striving for eternal victories. In his life two powers struggled for the mastery. Unbelief marshaled its forces, and tried to eclipse the light shining upon him from the throne of God. Day by day the battle went on in his heart, Satan disputing every step of advance made by the forces of righteousness. David understood what it meant to fight against principalities and powers, against the rulers of the darkness of this world. At times it seemed that the enemy must gain the victory. But in the end, faith conquered, and David rejoiced in the saving power of Jehovah.

The struggle that David went through, every other follower of Christ must go through. Satan has come down with great power, knowing that his time is short. The controversy is being waged in full view of the heavenly universe, and angels stand ready to lift up for God's hard-pressed soldiers a standard against the enemy, and to put into their lips songs of victory and rejoicing.—Manuscript 38, 1905 (*The Seventh-day Adventist Bible Commentary,* Ellen G. White Comments, vol. 3, pp. 1142, 1143).

Wherever the will of God is violated by nations or by individuals a day of retribution comes. Many set aside the wisdom of God and prefer the wisdom of worldly people and adopt some human invention or device. David placed the Word of God beside him on his throne. He was then immovable. But forsaking its doctrines he sullied one of the fairest reputations. . . .

We must bring our religion to the Bible standard. We must not place ourselves where we claim wisdom to welcome or reject God's words at pleasure. Never let the world think that the Christian and the world are the same in mind and judgment. There is a line drawn between the eternal God and the church on one side and the world on the other. There is no unity between the two. One chooses the way of the Lord, the other the ways of Satan. There will always be found a necessity to contend for the faith once delivered to the saints. . . .

People of the world hate the Bible because it will not let them sin just as they please and carry along with them their hereditary and cultivated traits of character. They want their own ideas to be cherished as the mind of God. They oppose the Word of God for the same reason that the Jews cried "Away with Christ!"—because He rebuked their sins and laid bare their iniquities.—Letter 16, 1888 (*Manuscript Releases,* vol. 21, p. 169).

May 25

GOD'S PUNISH-MENTS—PREFER-ABLE TO THOSE OF MORTALS?

◆ *Then David said to Gad, "I am in great distress: let us fall into the hand of the Lord, for his mercy is great; but let me not fall into human hands." 2 Samuel 24:14, NRSV.*

*I*T was an insult to God when David numbered Israel. God's rebuke rested upon him, for he made himself as God, as though he could tell the strength of the armies of Israel by their numbers. "This is the word of the Lord unto Zerubbabel, saying, Not by might, nor by power, but by my spirit, saith the Lord of hosts." God looks not on the numbers of Israel for the success of His work. His armies number thousands of thousands, and ten thousand times ten thousand. These cooperate with the people who will connect with God to be channels of light.— Manuscript 17, 1898.

The soul that is conscious of sincere and honest intentions finds less to fear from God than from people who have hearts of steel. The soul wrenched with human agony turns away from the misjudgment and condemnation of people who cannot read the heart, yet have taken it upon them to judge their associates. He turns to One who is without a shadow of misapprehension, One who knows all the impulses of the heart, who is acquainted with all the circumstances of temptation. God knows every deed of the past life, and yet in consideration of all this, the troubled soul is ready to trust his or her case with God, knowing that He is a God of mercy and compassion.

When David was bidden to choose the punishment for his sin, he said, "Let us fall now into the hand of the Lord; for his mercies are great: and let me not fall into the hand of man." He felt that God knew the struggle and anguish of the soul. When people are enabled to catch a glimpse of the character of God, they see not in Him the heartless, vindictive spirit manifested by human agents; they see that affliction and trial are God's appointed means of disciplining His children, and teaching them His way, that they may lay hold of His grace. . . . As poor backsliding souls are led to the river of God's love, they exclaim, When He hath tried me, I shall come forth as gold purified. Suffering souls are made patient, trustful, triumphant in God under adverse circumstances. . . .

When finite, erring human beings give evidence that they regard themselves as of greater importance than God, when they think themselves righteous, yet do not manifest the tenderness of spirit that characterized the life of our Lord Jesus, we may know that unless they repent, the candlestick will quickly be removed out of its place.—Manuscript 7, 1895 (*Testimonies to Ministers,* pp. 354-356).

May 26
OUR IDEAS OF GOD ARE BASED ON OUR EXPERIENCES

◆ *I will remember the works of the Lord: surely I will remember thy wonders of old. I will meditate also of all thy work, and talk of thy doings. Psalm 77:11, 12.*

E careful how you interpret Scripture. Read it with a heart opened to the entrance of God's Word, and it will express Heaven's light, giving understanding unto the simple. This does not mean the weak-minded but those who do not stretch themselves beyond their measure and ability in trying to be original and independent in reaching after knowledge above that which constitutes true knowledge. . . .

The psalmist David in his experience had many changes of mind. At times as he obtained views of God's will and ways, he was highly exalted. Then as he caught sight of the reverse of God's mercy and changeless love, everything seemed to be shrouded in a cloud of darkness. . . . When he meditated upon the difficulties and dangers of life, they looked so forbidding that he thought himself abandoned by God because of his sins. He viewed his sin in such a strong light that he exclaimed, "Will the Lord cast off for ever? and will he be favourable no more?"

As he wept and prayed, he obtained a clearer view of the character and attributes of God, and being educated by heavenly agencies, he decided that his ideas of God's justice and severity were exaggerated. . . . As David considered His [God's] pledges and promises to them [Israel], knowing they were for all who need them as much as for Israel, he appropriated them to himself. . . .

As David appropriated these promises and privileges to himself, he decided that he would no longer be hasty in judgment, becoming discouraged and casting himself down in helpless despair. His soul took courage as he contemplated the general character of God as displayed in His teaching, His forbearance, His surpassing greatness and mercy, and he saw that the works and wonders of God are to have no confined application.

But again David's experience changed. As he saw that transgressors and sinners were allowed to receive blessings and favors, while those who really loved God were compassed with difficulties and perplexities that the open sinner did not have, he thought that God's ways were not equal. . . . "For I was envious at the foolish, when I saw the prosperity of the wicked. . . . They are not in trouble as other men."

David could not understand this till he went into the sanctuary of God, and then, he says, "Understood I their end." "Surely thou didst set them in slippery places: thou castedst them down into destruction. . . . It is good for me to draw near to God."—Manuscript 4, 1896.

May 27
CHURCHES
TO BE BUILT TO
GOD'S GLORY

◆ *Thus Solomon finished the house of the Lord . . . and all that came into Solomon's heart to make in the house of the Lord, and in his own house, he prosperously effected.*
2 Chronicles 7:11.

NEARLY three thousand years ago by divine appointment the temple was built in Jerusalem. The nation of God's choice had been greatly favored; they dwelt in costly houses while they still worshiped God in the curtained tabernacle. Here the Shekinah, the visible emblem of God's presence, dwelt between the cherubim, and out of the perfection of beauty God shined. . . .

There have been times when it seemed necessary to worship God in very humble places; but the Lord did not withhold His Spirit nor refuse His presence because of this. It was the best His people could do at the time, and if they worshiped Him in Spirit and in truth, He never reproved or condemned their efforts. . . .

The Lord reminded David of the lowly position he was in when He called him and entrusted him with great responsibilities, and He would have him ever bear in mind that his prosperity and success came through the blessing of God and not through any inherited goodness that he possessed. Although God did not allow him to carry out the wish of his heart, He granted him the next highest honor, that of entrusting the work to his son.

Solomon received special wisdom from God. Yet Solomon did not find among the workers of his nation and religion those qualifications, that fine skill, that he deemed essential to carry forward the work of building a temple for the God of heaven. He was therefore obliged to send away for artisans, people who would do justice to the responsible work entrusted to them. . . .

We have no command from God to erect a building that will compare for richness and splendor with the temple. But we are to build a humble house of worship, plain and simple, neat and perfect in its design. Then let those who have means look to it that they are as liberal and tasteful in erecting a temple wherein we may worship God as they have been in locating and building and furnishing their own houses. Let them manifest a willingness and a desire to show greater honor to God than themselves. Let them build with nicety, but not with extravagance. Let the house be built conveniently and thoroughly so that when it is presented to God He can accept it and let His Spirit rest upon the worshipers who have an eye single to His glory. . . . Let everyone, old and young, bring gifts and donations to help in building a house for God.—Manuscript 23, 1886.

May 28
CHURCHES SHOULD BE SUITABLE DWELLING PLACES FOR GOD

◆ *The king [David] said unto Nathan the prophet, See now, I dwell in an house of cedar, but the ark of God dwelleth within curtains. 2 Samuel 7:2.*

AVID, while dwelling in his palace of cedar, felt disturbed in his conscience as he considered that there was no suitable dwelling place for the ark of God, which symbolized His presence. It still rested in the tabernacle which had been constructed in the wilderness, and borne all the way from Horeb to Jerusalem in a pilgrimage of nearly forty years. But now the nation had ended their pilgrimage and obtained a permanent location. David looked around him upon the costly buildings of cedar, the homes of the inhabitants settled in the goodly land of Canaan, and conceived the idea that a temple should be built, more worthy for the residence of God. The site of the building was indicated and the most complete instructions were given, and Solomon entered upon the great work. . . .

The people that built the temple were many and the house that they built was large and grand; and the Lord God of heaven honored them because they had built Him a sanctuary where they could meet to worship Him. Those that worshiped Him sincerely had His blessing.

The first tabernacle, built according to God's directions, was indeed blessed of Him. The people thus were preparing themselves to worship in the temple not made with hands—a temple in the heavens. The stones of the temple built by Solomon were all prepared at the quarry and then brought to the temple site. They came together without the sound of ax or hammer. The timbers were also fitted in the forest. The furniture was likewise brought to this house all prepared for use.

Even so, the mighty cleaver of truth has taken out a people from the quarry of the world and is fitting this people, who profess to be the children of God, for a place in His heavenly temple. We want the cleaver of truth to do its work for us. . . . We are here as probationers, and we must pass under the hand of God. All rough edges and rough surfaces must be removed, and we must be stones fitted for the building. We are brought into church capacity with defects of character, but we must not retain them. We must be fitted and squared for the building. We must be "labourers together with God," for we are "God's husbandry," we are "God's building." In view of this we must see that the temple is not defiled with sin. We should be lively stones, not dead ones, but live ones that will reflect the image of Christ. We must be worshipers in spirit and in truth.—Manuscript 49, 1886 (*Manuscript Releases,* vol. 3, pp. 230-232).

May 29
LEADERS WITH VARIOUS TALENTS ARE NEEDED IN GOD'S CHURCH

◆ *Keep and seek for all the commandments of the Lord your God: that ye may possess this good land, and leave it for an inheritance for your children after you for ever.*
1 Chronicles 28:8.

*T*HE last great work of David in his official position was to call the attention of the people once more to their solemn relation to God as subjects of His theocracy. . . .

Fidelity to God is required for the reception of the blessings that He has promised to impart to all who obey His instruction. All who are accepted in His service are required to do His commandments. If with heart and mind and soul they do His holy will, they become representatives of His kingdom.

David's solemn charge should be kept in mind by those who are in positions of trust today, for it is as verily binding upon these people as it was upon Solomon at the time it was given. In this our day of probation God's people are being tested and tried as surely as they were in the days of Solomon.

This whole chapter [1 Chronicles 28] is of importance to all the people of God living in this age. . . . God's service is not committed to one person's judgment and option, but is divided among those who are willing to labor interestedly and self-sacrificingly. Thus all, according to the skill and ability God has given them, bear the responsibilities that He has appointed to them. The important interests of a great nation were entrusted to leaders whose talents fitted them to handle these responsibilities. Some were chosen to direct the business affairs; others were chosen to look after spiritual matters connected with the worship of God. All the religious service and every branch of the business was to bear the signature of heaven. "Holiness Unto the Lord" was to be the motto of the laborers in every department. It was regarded as essential that everything be conducted with regularity, propriety, fidelity, and dispatch.

To all who are engaged in His service, the Lord gives wisdom. The tabernacle to be borne in the wilderness, and the temple at Jerusalem, were built in accordance with special directions from God. In the very beginning He was particular as to the design and the accomplishment of His work. In this age of the world He has given His people much light and instruction in regard to how His work is to be carried forward—on an elevated, refined, ennobling basis.—Manuscript 81, 1900.

May 30
**EXERCISE CARE
IN FORMING
FRIENDSHIPS**

◆ *If any of you is lacking in wisdom,
ask God, who gives to all generously and
ungrudgingly, and it will be given you.
James 1:5, NRSV.*

LL the wisdom that people possess is God's gift, and He can and will impart wisdom to every person who asks it of Him in faith. Solomon sought wisdom from God, and it was given him in large measure. But how did the universe of heaven look upon him when he perverted that wisdom and employed God's great and holy gift to exalt himself? God chose him to build the temple, but how he perverted the sacred trust! He leagued himself with idolatrous nations. Thus he, who at the dedication of the temple had prayed that their hearts might be undividedly given to the Lord, himself began to separate his heart from God. He imperiled his soul's interest by the formation of friendships with the Lord's enemies.

What carefulness should be exercised in the formation of friendship! Companionship with the world will surely lower the standard of religious principle. Solomon's heathen wives turned away his heart from God. His finer sensibilities were blunted, and he became hardhearted, for he lost his sympathy for humankind and his love for God. His conscience was seared, and his rule became tyranny.

Solomon prepared the way for his own ruin when he sought for wise artisans from other nations to build the temple. God had been the educator of His people, and He designed that they should stand in His wisdom, and with His imparted talents they should be second to none. If they had the clean hands, the pure heart, and the noble, sanctified purpose, the Lord would communicate to them His grace. But Solomon looked to worldlings instead of God, and he found his supposed strength to be weakness. He brought to Jerusalem the leaven of the evil influences that were perpetuated in polygamy and idolatry. It was no question as to who made Israel to sin.

Although Solomon afterward repented, his repentance could not abolish the idolatrous practices that he had brought into the nation. We shall individually transmit an inheritance of either good or evil. The silver of Tarshish and the gold of Ophir were obtained by Solomon at a terrible expense, even the betrayal of sacred trusts. The evil communications with heathen nations corrupted good manners. When the Lord's people turn from the God of all wisdom, and look to people who love not God, in order to obtain wisdom and arrive at decisions, the Lord will allow them to follow that wisdom that is not from above but from beneath.— Manuscript 44, 1894 (*General Conference Bulletin,* Feb. 25, 1895).

May 31
DEPARTURE FROM INTEGRITY MAY IMPERIL THE SOUL

◆ *And the Lord magnified Solomon exceedingly in the sight of all Israel, and bestowed upon him such royal majesty as had not been on any king before him in Israel. 1 Chronicles 29:25.*

SOLOMON, who had once solemnly charged the people at the dedication of the temple, "Let your heart therefore be perfect with the Lord our God," chose his own way and in his heart separated from God. He might have linked himself with God and have received more and still more of the knowledge of God, but he betrayed his trust and wandered farther and farther from God. . . .

Looking upon this picture, we see what human beings become when they separate from God. One false step prepares the way for a second and a third, and every step is taken more easily than the last. Let us beware of imperiling the soul by departing from the principles of integrity. There is no safety in tampering with the divine safeguards of peace and righteousness.

Did the Lord make a mistake in placing Solomon in a position of so great responsibility? Nay; God prepared him to bear these responsibilities and promised him grace and strength on condition of obedience. "Then shalt thou prosper," David said to him, "if thou takest heed to fulfil the statutes and judgments which the Lord charged Moses with concerning Israel: be strong, and of good courage; dread not, nor be dismayed."

The Lord sets people in responsible places, not to act out their own wills, but His will. So long as they cherish His pure principles of government, He will bless and strengthen them, recognizing them as His instrumentalities. God never forsakes the one who is true to principle.

Let those in positions of responsibility remember that we are approaching the perils of the last days. The whole world is passing in review before God. . . . Let none make erring, finite beings their guide. God is the one who stands behind mortals, the one from whom all receive the wisdom and knowledge that enable them to do anything good. And God is willing to help everyone. He is no respecter of persons.

Let those upon whom the Lord bestows rich gifts be guarded, lest pride and self-sufficiency obtain the control. The person who exerts a wide influence, the one that people are willing to follow, needs to be constantly prayed for and admonished by other workers. Let them pray that he or she may be kept from pride and self-exaltation.—Manuscript 164, 1902.

June 1
PROSPERITY SOMETIMES CAUSES SPIRITUAL DOWNFALL

◆ *Then I looked on all the works that my hands had wrought, and on the labour that I had laboured to do: and, behold, all was vanity and vexation of spirit, and there was no profit under the sun. Ecclesiastes 2:11.*

*S*OLOMON wrote the book of Proverbs, but after a time his wisdom became mingled with chaff. Whence came the chaff? After a manhood of such glorious promise, a change came in Solomon's history. He did not continue true to his purity and allegiance to God. He broke through the barriers that God had erected to preserve His people from idolatry. The Lord had singled out Israel as a nation, making them the depositories of sacred truth to be given to the world. But Solomon cherished pride of political powers. He encouraged alliances with pagan kingdoms. . . .

In the early part of his reign, Solomon was visited by the queen of Sheba. She came to see and hear his wisdom, and after she had heard him she said that the half had not been told her. But his wise and strictly just reign changed. He who had known God and the truth made a great outlay of means to please his godless wives. He made expensive gardens. God's money, which should have been held sacred to help the poor among the people, as God directed, was absorbed by the king's ambitious projects. It was diverted from its original channel. . . . The suffering ones were not given houses and food and clothing as God had specified they should be given. By his extravagant outlay of means Solomon sought to please his wives and glorify himself. Thus he used the means that had been abundant and brought a heavy taxation upon the poor. . . .

His moral efficiency was gone, as the power is gone from a paralytic. He made an effort to incorporate light with darkness, to serve God and mammon. He felt at liberty to experiment in wild license. But Belial and purity could not mingle, and the course the king pursued brought its own penalty. He separated from God, and the knowledge of God departed from him. . . .

People who have the use of money are to learn a lesson from the history of Solomon. Those who have a competence are in continual danger of thinking that money and position will ensure them respect and they need not be so particular. But self-exaltation is but a bubble. By misusing the talents given him, Solomon apostatized from God. When God gives people prosperity, they are to beware of following the imaginations of their own hearts, lest they endanger the simplicity of their faith and deteriorate in religious experience.—Manuscript 40, 1898.

June 2
SATAN ARRANGES OVERPOWERING TEMPTATIONS

◆ *Those to whom God gives wealth, posses-sions, and honor, so that they lack nothing of all that they desire, yet God does not enable them to enjoy these things, but a stranger enjoys them. Ecclesiastes 6:2, NRSV.*

HE life of Solomon is full of warning, not only to youth but to those of mature years, and to the aged, those who are descending the hill of life and facing the western sun. We see and hear of unsteadiness in youth, the young wavering between right and wrong and the current of evil passions proving too strong for them. But we do not look for unsteadiness and unfaithfulness in those of mature years; we expect the character to be es-tablished, the principles to be firmly rooted. In many cases this is so, but there are exceptions, as with Solomon. . . . When his strength should have been the firmest, he was found the weakest of men. . . .

We need to inquire at every step, "Is this the way of the Lord?" As long as life shall last there is need of guarding the affections and the passions with a firm purpose. There is inward corruption; there are outward temp-tations, and wherever the work of God shall be advanced, Satan plans to arrange circumstances so that temptation shall come with overpowering force upon the soul. As long as life shall last, there is need of guarding the affections and the passions with a firm purpose. . . .

Many have closed their eyes to danger and have gone on in their own way, infatuated, deluded by Satan until they fall under his temptations. Then they abandon themselves to despair. This was the history of Solomon. But even for him there was help. He truly repented of his course of sin and found help. Let none venture into sin as he did, in the hope that they too may recover themselves. Sin can be indulged only at the peril of infinite loss. But none who have fallen need give themselves up to despair. . . .

The misapplication of noble talents in Solomon's case should be a warning to all. Goodness alone is true greatness. Everyone will transmit a heritage of good or of evil. On the southern eminence of the Mount of Olives were the memorial stones of Solomon's apostasy. . . . Josiah, the youthful reformer, in his religious zeal destroyed these images of Ashtoreth and Chemosh and Moloch, but the broken fragments and masses of ruins remained opposite Mount Moriah, where stood the temple of God. As strangers in after generations asked, "What mean these ruins confronting the temple of the Lord?" they were answered, "There is Solomon's Mount of Offense, where he built altars for idol worship to please his heathen wives."—Letter 8b, 1891.

June 3

BEWARE OF THOSE WHO CONTRADICT GOD'S COMMANDS

◆ *Jeroboam stood by the altar to burn incense. . . . The altar also was rent, and the ashes poured out from the altar, according to the sign which the man of God had given by the word of the Lord. 1 Kings 13:1-5.*

HEN Jeroboam [king of ten tribes of Israel after Solomon] saw the altar rent and the ashes from it poured out on the ground, he cried out in wrath, "Lay hold on him." "And his hand, which he put forth against him, dried up, so that he could not pull it in again to him." In alarm he said to the prophet, "Entreat now the face of the Lord thy God, and pray for me, that my hand may be restored me again. And the man of God besought the Lord, and the king's hand . . . became as it was before."

"And the king said unto the man of God, Come home with me, and refresh thyself, and I will give thee a reward. And the man of God said unto the king, If thou wilt give me half thine house, I will not go in with thee . . . for so was it charged me by the word of the Lord, saying, Eat no bread, nor drink water, nor turn again by the same way that thou camest."

The prophet refused to receive anything from Jeroboam, but he fell under the temptation of an aged prophet living at Bethel. . . . To him he said, "Come home with me, and eat bread." But the man of God answered him as he had answered Jeroboam. . . . The old prophet then lied to him, saying, "I am a prophet also as thou art; and an angel spake unto me by the word of the Lord, saying, Bring him back with thee into thine house, that he may eat bread and drink water." He declared that the Lord had spoken through him, when He had not. . . .

The man of God had been fearless in delivering his message of rebuke. He had not hesitated to denounce the king's false system of worship. And he had refused Jeroboam's invitation, even though promised a reward. But he allowed himself to be overpersuaded by the one who claimed to have a message from heaven.

When the Lord gives a person a command such as He gave this messenger, He Himself must countermand the order. Upon those who turn from the voice of God to listen to counterorders, the threatened evil will come. Because this messenger obeyed false orders, God permitted him to be destroyed. . . .

The rent altar, the palsied arm, the fearful result of the prophet's disobedience—these were evidences that should have led the king to turn from his evil ways and serve the Lord. But we read, "After this thing Jeroboam returned not from his evil way."—Manuscript 1, 1912.

June 4
ANGER AT GOD'S MESSENGERS

◆ *Ahab said unto him, Art thou he that troubleth Israel? And he answered, I have not troubled Israel; but thou, and thy father's house, in that ye have forsaken the commandments of the Lord. 1 Kings 18:17, 18.*

*G*OD would have been with Ahab if he had walked in the counsel of heaven. But Ahab did not do this. He married a woman given to idolatry. Jezebel had more power over the king than God had. She led him into idolatry, and with him the people. God sent Elijah to Israel with messages of warning, but neither king nor people would heed his words. They looked upon him as a messenger of evil. At last God sent a drought upon the land.

Did the people discern and acknowledge the object of this judgment and humble their hearts before Him? No; Jezebel said that the prophets of Jehovah had brought this calamity upon them. She said that all Israel was suffering because of their reproofs, and that there would be no rest or prosperity in the land until these prophets were put to death. Thus a feeling of anger was aroused against the men whom God had sent to entreat the people to repent of their wickedness. Many holy men died for their testimony. Elijah was preserved by a miracle of divine power, to proclaim before the king and queen the warnings and threatenings of God.

"Go, shew thyself unto Ahab," God said to Elijah. When the king and the prophet met, Ahab said, "Art thou he that troubleth Israel?". . . But Elijah said, "I have not troubled Israel; but thou, and thy father's house, in that ye have forsaken the commandments of the Lord, and thou hast followed Baalim."

He told Ahab to gather the prophets of Baal together; and then came a wonderful manifestation of the power of God. All day long the false prophets called upon Baal, but received no response. When Elijah appealed to the God of heaven, the answer was at once given. The prophets of Baal had prayed wildly and incoherently. Elijah prayed simply and fervently, asking God to show His superiority over Baal that Israel might be led to turn to Him. As his prayer ascended, the answer came. Fire descended from heaven and consumed the sacrifice and the water with which it had been drenched.

Seeing this wonderful manifestation of power, Israel cried, "The Lord, he is the God." While their hearts were touched and softened by the miracle they had witnessed, Elijah took this opportune time to slay the false prophets.—Manuscript 29, 1911.

June 5
SPIRITUAL HIGHS WILL NOT PREVENT SPIRITUAL LOWS

◆ *Then Jezebel sent a messenger unto Elijah, saying, So let the gods do to me, and more also, if I make not thy life as the life of one of them by to-morrow about this time. 1 Kings 19:2.*

OWEVER bold and successful and courageous the people of God may have been in doing a special work, unless they constantly look to God and continue to have confidence in the work He has given them, they will lose their courage. After God has given them a wonderful revelation of His power, bracing them up to do His work, circumstances will arise to test their faith, and they will fail unless they trust implicitly in the Lord.

Thus it was with Elijah. He had by the help of God defeated the prophets of Baal. But he was disappointed as to the results of the manifestation of God. Under the threats of the wicked queen he lost his courage and his faith. He lost sight of Him in whose keeping he was, and without being sent he fled for his life. He was terribly depressed, for he had hoped for much from the miracle wrought before the people.

Had Elijah, knowing he had done the divine will, maintained his confidence in God, had he made God his refuge and strength, standing steadfast and immovable for the truth, the impression made upon the king and the people would have wrought a reformation. Elijah had been braced for trial under the inspiration of God, but when Jezebel's threatening message was brought to him and shouted in his ear, awakening from a deep sleep, he lost his hold on God. . . .

This was the time when he should have had courage in the Lord, showing a living, active faith. He should not have fled from his post of duty. God had given him a wonderful manifestation of His power to assure him that He would not forsake him, that His power was wholly sufficient to sustain him, for He was the Lord of the powers of heaven and earth.

But Elijah forgot God and fled. . . . "And as he lay and slept under a juniper tree, behold, then an angel touched him, and said unto him, Arise and eat. And he looked, and, behold, there was a cake baken on the coals, and a cruse of water at his head. . . . And the angel of the Lord came again the second time, and touched him, and said, Arise and eat; because the journey is too great for thee."

My heart melts within me as I read the words of Holy Writ, and see the interest that the heavenly family has in the faithful servants of the Most High. "And he arose, and did eat and drink, and went in the strength of that meat forty days and forty nights unto Horeb the mount of God."—Letter 62, 1900.

June 6
WHEN SORELY TEMPTED, LOOK TO JESUS

◆ *And he requested for himself that he might die; and said, It is enough; now, O Lord, take away my life; for I am not better than my fathers. 1 Kings 19:4.*

*I*N all our afflictions, Jesus was afflicted. The Captain of our salvation was made perfect through suffering. In this life we shall be proved whether we bear the test of God. When Satan's temptations come, we shall have a trial. Shall we be overcome by the bewitching power of Satan or shall we overcome Satan's temptations as Christ overcame them? Shall we have the mind stored with the heavenly treasures of truth, that we may be enabled to meet the adversary of souls with "It is written" as did Christ, and not with any of our impetuous speeches? Satan understands more of what "is written" than many a professed Christian, for he is a diligent student of the Scriptures, and his work is to pervert the truth of God, to lead people to disobedience and to neglect the searching of God's Word. . . .

It is a great mistake to dictate to God. Elijah knew not what he said when he told God that he had enough of life and asked to die. The Lord did not take him at his word, for he had a work to do before he would be exalted and translated to heaven. Have we forgotten that Jesus, the Majesty of heaven, suffered being tempted? Jesus did not allow the enemy to pull Him into the mire of unbelief, or crowd Him into the mire of despondency and despair. . . .

God hates sin. Satan's work is to allure to works of evil. How adroitly Satan worked with his bewitching power to fascinate the mind to choose sin rather than righteousness. The influence of one person on another had become dangerous because of Satan's leading and controlling the mind and pressing this influence of one over another in his own service. But the Lord Jesus, by the agency of His Holy Spirit, changes the order of things and takes the sins and guilt of the human race upon Himself, and draws people to Himself, and sanctifies and employs the human agent as His instrumentality to engage his powers to do an entirely opposite work than Satan advised. . . .

"Resist the devil, and he will flee from you. Draw nigh to God, and he will draw nigh to you." How precious to the tempted soul is this positive promise. If those in trouble and temptation keep their eyes fixed on Jesus and draw nigh to God, talking of His goodness and mercy, Jesus draws nigh to them, and the annoyances that they thought almost unbearable vanish. . . .

Troublous times are before us, but this is not to worry us. To be worried is to be unbelieving, but Christ invites you saying, "Come unto me, all ye that labour and are heavy laden, and I will give you rest."—Letter 43, 1892.

June 7
LARGEST IS NOT NECESSARILY BEST

◆ *Yet I have left me seven thousand in Israel, all the knees which have not bowed unto Baal. 1 Kings 19:18.*

ND he [Elijah] came thither [to Mount Horeb] unto a cave, and lodged there; and, behold, the word of the Lord came to him, and he said unto him, What doest thou here, Elijah? And he said, I have been very jealous for the Lord God of hosts: for the children of Israel have forsaken thy covenant, thrown down thine altars, and slain thy prophets with the sword; and I, even I only, am left; and they seek my life, to take it away.

"And he said, Go forth, and stand upon the mount before the Lord. And, behold, the Lord passed by, and a great and strong wind rent the mountains, and brake in pieces the rocks before the Lord; but the Lord was not in the wind: and after the wind an earthquake; but the Lord was not in the earthquake: and after the earthquake a fire; but the Lord was not in the fire: and after the fire a still small voice. And it was so, when Elijah heard it, that he wrapped his face in his mantle, and went out, and stood in the entering in of the cave."

His petulance was silenced. The Lord desired him to understand that boisterous, noisy elements are not always producers of the best results. The still small voice could subdue and soften and accomplish great things.

The Lord convinced Elijah that the wrongdoers would not always go unpunished. He told him to go to the land of Horeb and appoint three persons who were to fulfill the Lord's purpose in punishing idolatrous Israel. All working in different ways, these three were to avenge the controversy God had with Israel.

Then He who knows every heart corrected the impression held by Elijah that he was the only one left who was true to the worship of God. "I have left me," God said, "seven thousand in Israel, all the knees which have not bowed unto Baal, and every mouth which hath not kissed him."

The Lord desired to teach His servant that it is not the thing that makes the greatest show, the most powerful representation, that is the most successful in doing His work. It is not always the most powerful presentation by pen or voice that accomplishes the most good.—Letter 62, 1900.

June 8
LEARNING TO LEAD THROUGH SERVING

◆ *Elisha the son of Shaphat of Abelmeholah shalt thou anoint to be prophet in thy room.*
1 Kings 19:16.

E would do well to consider the case of Elisha when [he was] chosen for his work. Elisha was of a family who had kept the ancient true faith of Israel. He did not live in the thickly populated cities. His father was a tiller of the soil, a farmer. Even during the captivity there were souls who had not degenerated and gone into apostasy, and this family was included in the seven thousand who had not bowed the knee to Baal.

Elijah was about to close his earthly labors. Another was to be chosen to carry forward the work to be done for that time. In his course of travel, Elijah was directed northward. . . . Now everything seems to be springing up as if to redeem the time of famine and dearth. The plenteous rains had done more for the earth than for the hearts of humanity; it was better prepared for labor than were the hearts of apostate Israel.

Wherever Elijah looked, the land he saw was owned by one man—a man who had not bowed the knee to Baal, whose heart had remained undivided in the service of God. The owner of this land was Shaphat. Busy activity was seen among the husbandry. While the flocks were enjoying the green pastures, the busy hands of his servants were sowing the seed for a harvest.

The attention of Elijah was attracted to Elisha, the son of Shaphat. . . . Far from city and court dissipation, Elisha had received his education. He had been trained in habits of simplicity, of obedience to his parents and to God. . . . But though of a meek and quiet spirit, Elisha had no changeable character. Integrity and fidelity and the love and fear of God were his. He had the characteristics of a ruler, but with it all was the meekness of one who would serve. His mind had been exercised to be faithful in the little things, to be faithful in whatever he should do, so that if God should call him to act more directly for Him, he would be prepared to hear His voice. . . .

His surroundings at home were those of wealth, but he realized that in order to obtain an all-around education, he must be a constant worker in any line of work that needed to be done. He would not consent to be in any respect less informed than his father's servants. He would learn how to serve first, that he might know how to lead and instruct and command. While doing all that he possibly could do with his God-entrusted capabilities in cooperating with his father in the home firm, he was doing God service.—Letter 12, 1897.

June 9
WHEN GOD CALLS, HOW DO WE RESPOND?

♦ *So he . . . found Elisha the son of Shaphat, who was plowing with twelve yoke of oxen before him . . . and Elijah passed by him, and cast his mantle upon him. 1 Kings 19:19.*

WHEN Elijah saw Elisha in the field with the servants, plowing with his twelve yoke of oxen, he went to the field of labor, and while passing by he unfastened his mantle and threw it upon the shoulders of Elisha. During the three and a half years of barrenness and famine, the family of Shaphat became familiar with the work and mission of Elijah the prophet. The Spirit of God impressed the heart of Elisha in regard to the meaning of this action. This was his signal that God had called him to be the successor of Elijah. It was similar to the commission of Christ to the young ruler to leave all—houses, lands, friends, riches, comforts, and ease, "and come and follow me."

Elijah passed on as if that were the end of the matter. But he knew that Elisha had understood the significance of the action, and he left him, without speaking a word, to decide whether he would accept the call or reject it. Elisha hastened after the prophet and, overtaking him, asked permission to take leave of his parents, and bid farewell to his family.

The answer of Elijah was "Go back again: for what have I done unto thee?" This was not a repulse, but a test, a trial. If his heart clung to his home and its advantages, he was at liberty to remain there. But Elisha was prepared to hear the call of God. He had not been disorderly, running before the call had come, and when he was called he revealed that he would not hesitate, nor relent, nor draw back. . . .

Had Elisha asked Elijah what was expected of him, what would be his work, he would have answered, God knows; He will make it known to you. If you wait upon the Lord He will answer your every question. You may come with me if you have evidence that God has called you; if not, forbear. Come not simply because I called you. Know for yourself that God stands back of me, and that it is His voice you hear. If you can count everything but dross that you may win the favor of God, Come.

Let all bear in mind that the Lord will not accept halfhearted service. Those who love to do the will of God can do perfect service. . . . If we follow on to know the Lord, willingly, gladly, we shall know that "his going forth is prepared as the morning." . . .

Elisha immediately left all to commence his ministry.—Letter 12, 1897.

June 10
**HUMBLE TASKS
PREPARE FOR
HIGHER SERVICE**

◆ *Here is Elisha the son of Shaphat, which poured water on the hands of Elijah.*
2 Kings 3:11.

*H*IS [Elisha's] leave-taking was not with mourning and bitter regrets. They made a feast in his home in commemoration of the honor conferred upon one of the family. And what was the first work of Elisha? It was to take up the little things, and do them with heartiness. He is spoken of as pouring water on the hands of Elijah his master. He was the prophet's personal attendant.

Any work, however small it may appear, that is done for the Master with a thorough surrender of self, is as acceptable to Him as the highest service. . . . Humble, willing service is before everyone who claims to be a child of God.

After Elisha had been some time in the service of Elijah, he was called to take his place in the first rank. No one in that time was to be greater than he. He had worked under Elijah as a learner, and the time came when the head manager was removed, and the one under him came to the front; and as in Elijah there was a preparedness to be translated, so Elisha was prepared to take his place as the successor of the prophet. . . .

"And the sons of the prophets that were at Jericho came to Elisha, and said unto him, Knowest thou that the Lord will take away thy master from thy head today? And he answered, Yea, I know it. . . . And Elijah said unto him, Tarry, I pray thee, here; for the Lord hath sent me to Jordan. And he said, As the Lord liveth, and as thy soul liveth, I will not leave thee." So they came to Jericho. . . . "And they two stood by Jordan. And Elijah took his mantle, and wrapped it together, and smote the waters, and they were divided hither and thither, so that they two went over on dry ground. . . . And it came to pass, as they still went on, and talked, that, behold, there appeared a chariot of fire, and horses of fire, and parted them both asunder; and Elijah went up by a whirlwind into heaven.

"And Elisha saw it. . . . He took the mantle of Elijah that fell from him, and smote the waters, and said, Where is the Lord God of Elijah? and when he also had smitten the waters, they parted hither and thither: and Elisha went over." . . .

By plowing in the field, Elisha had learned the lesson of not allowing failure or discouragement to be entertained. He had now set his hand to the plow in another line of work, and he would not fail nor be discouraged. Every time the invitation to turn back was given, he declared, "As the Lord liveth, and as thy soul liveth, I will not leave thee."—Letter 12, 1897.

June 11
EVERYDAY DUTIES OF LIFE ARE IMPORTANT

◆ *Whoever is faithful in a very little is faithful also in much. Luke 16:10, NRSV.*

HEN Elisha followed Elijah, and traveled with him, he was first given the position of a servant; he had to perform the humble duty of pouring water on the hands of Elijah. Yet he kept at the humble work until the last journey. There it was to be revealed to him that Elijah was to be translated. Called as Elisha was from the twelve yoke of oxen and the plow, he followed Elijah without complaint, leaving a wealthy home where he was beloved, to attend the prophet in his uncertain life. He willingly fulfilled the very humblest duties. His connection with Elijah revealed that he had traits of character that would endure test and trial, that he was a valuable young man with precious traits of character. Trials and temptations he had in abundance, but he relied upon God in trying circumstances. His surroundings of wealth and comfort were a temptation. In his home he was fully capable of ruling, but in the service of Elijah he must obtain an experience, he must learn how to serve under a ruler, that he might learn to serve God.

Many errors are entertained by people in their vocations. They overestimate their capabilities, and in test and trial reveal that they need a different kind of experience than they have had in order to be a laborer together with Christ. Persons who do not see their need of serving God in little things, doing humble work, give unmistakable evidence that they are not fitted to serve in larger things. In overlooking the humble service as nonessential, they bear testimony that they cannot be trusted with larger responsibilities.

The idea that prevails in some minds, and that is difficult to change, an idea they have permitted to be unconsciously woven into their experience, is that a certain position of gentility and dignity must be maintained or else their influence will be marred in their work of preaching. But when these learn to minister, they will know that humble, active service means to interest themselves in the duties of everyday life, and to obtain the education essential to do the ordinary duties of life in any small vocation—it may be in tilling the soil, in following the plow, in sowing or in reaping. . . .

There is to be no neglect or low estimate of the lowly, everyday duties of life. True conversion to God will act as leaven in every phase of duty in the relationships of life. Then, if the Lord sees us faithful in that which is least, diligent and persevering in the use of our physical powers, doing with our hands that which someone must do, He will say, "Come up higher. You may be entrusted with greater responsibilities."—Letter 64, 1897.

June 12
**ANGER CAN
CAUSE US TO MISS
GOD'S BLESSINGS**

◆ *And his servants came near, and spake unto him, and said, My father, if the prophet had bid thee do some great thing, wouldest thou not have done it? how much rather then, when he saith to thee, Wash, and be clean? 2 Kings 5:13.*

*O*ften think of the case of Naaman. He wished a great blessing, even cleansing from leprosy. Hearing of the power of Elisha the prophet, he went to him, to know what he might do to be healed. And Elisha sent him the message "Go and wash in Jordan seven times, and thy flesh shall come again to thee, and thou shalt be clean.

"But Naaman was wroth, and went away, and said, Behold, I thought, He will surely come out to me, and stand, and call on the name of the Lord his God, and strike his hand over the place, and recover the leper. Are not Abana and Pharpar, rivers of Damascus, better than all the waters of Israel? may I not wash in them, and be clean? So he turned and went away in a rage.

"And his servants came near, and spake unto him, and said, My father, if the prophet had bid thee do some great thing, wouldest thou not have done it? how much rather then, when he saith to thee, Wash, and be clean?

"Then went he down, and dipped himself in Jordan seven times, according to the saying of the man of God: and his flesh came again like unto the flesh of a little child, and he was clean."

Each soul inherits certain un-Christlike traits of character. It is the grand and noble work of a lifetime to keep under control these tendencies to wrong. It is the little things that cross our path that are likely to cause us to lose our power of self-control.

The Lord will honor those who in this life have been faithful in the little things. . . . They will not be found wanting when the greater tests come to them. Those who honor God in the smaller duties of the daily life will develop into men and women of sound judgment. Whatever trial may come to them, they will stand firm for the right.

God will understand you as you open your heart to Him. He knows what discipline each one needs. If you ask Him, He will surely give you power to resist evil. Your faith will be increased, and you will give evidence to others of the keeping power of God.—Letter 123, 1904.

June 13
THE TANGLED
WEB OF SINNING

◆ *But Gehazi, the servant of Elisha the man of God, said . . . I will run after him, and take somewhat of him. 2 Kings 5:20.*

$\mathcal{I}$T is seldom that one sin will stand alone or be restricted in the range of transgression to one precept or one prohibition of the moral law. There is ever a complication of disobedience, which leads the perverted conscience to a greater length of entanglement by entering to greater temptations and sinning more and more. . . .

The heart not given entirely to the control of Jesus Christ has a door open for Satan to enter, and the archdeceiver weaves about the soul ingenious apologies in performing its hidden purposes of evil. All these excuses and pretensions are seen of God, and are as spiderwebs in the eyes of Him who never slumbers or sleeps. Oh, how readily will the human soul find poor and wretched excuses to deceive and cover up its own course of evil, which it pursues. There is an exact judge who weigheth actions. He cannot be deceived, neither can He be mocked. He will one day strike off the covering, unveil the conscience, and sweep away these excuses as smoke.

The Lord God hath a witness to every transaction. Elisha's reproof to Gehazi when he denied having left to follow Naaman was: "Whence comest thou, Gehazi?" The answer is "Thy servant went no whither." Then the stern reproof came that showed he knew all. "Went not mine heart with thee, when the man turned again from his chariot to meet thee? Is it a time to receive money, and to receive garments, and oliveyards, and vineyards, and sheep, and oxen, and menservants, and maidservants? The leprosy therefore of Naaman shall cleave unto thee, and unto thy seed for ever." The Lord had revealed the whole matter. The interview with Naaman, the minutest incidents of the scene, were accurately presented before him. Oh, the workings of the powers of darkness are so deceiving!

Elisha revealed to Gehazi the very thoughts of his heart, and that he would enrich himself with the earthly treasure from Naaman. There was a man who should have been a standard-bearer in the army of the Lord, [but] through Satan's temptations his course of action was a stumbling block to Naaman, upon whose mind a wonderful light had broken and he was favorably disposed toward truth, to serve the living God. Gehazi went from his presence a leper. The Lord calls upon you to seek His counsel, to be true to your own soul and to God, and to seek most earnestly to recover yourself and your children from Satan's snares.—Letter 22, 1893.

June 14
THE VALUE OF SOULS VERSUS ONE'S REPUTATION

◆ *Arise, go to Nineveh, that great city, and cry against it; for their wickedness is come up before me. Jonah 1:2.*

HEN the people of Nineveh humbled themselves before God, and cried to Him for mercy, He heard their cry. "God saw their works, that they turned from their evil way; and God repented of the evil, that he had said that he would do unto them; and he did it not."

But Jonah revealed that he did not value the souls in that wretched city. He valued his reputation, lest they should say he was a false prophet. . . . Now when he sees the Lord exercise His compassionate attributes and spare the city that had corrupted its ways before Him, Jonah does not cooperate with God in His merciful design. He has not the people's interests in view. It does not grieve him that so large a number must perish who have not been educated to do right. Listen to his complaint:

"Therefore now, O Lord, take, I beseech thee, my life from me; for it is better for me to die than to live. Then said the Lord, Doest thou well to be angry? So Jonah went out of the city, and sat on the east side of the city, and there made him a booth, and sat under it in the shadow, till he might see what would become of the city. And the Lord prepared a gourd, and made it to come up over Jonah, that it might be a shadow over his head, to deliver him from his grief. So Jonah was exceeding glad of the gourd."

Then the Lord gave Jonah an object lesson. He "prepared a worm when the morning rose the next day, and it smote the gourd that it withered. And it came to pass, when the sun did arise, that God prepared a vehement east wind; and the sun beat upon the head of Jonah, that he fainted, and wished in himself to die, and said, It is better for me to die than to live.". . . "Then said the Lord, Thou hast had pity on the gourd, for the which thou hast not laboured, neither madest it grow; which came up in a night, and perished in a night: And should I not spare Nineveh, that great city, wherein are more than sixscore thousand persons that cannot discern between their right hand and their left hand; and also much cattle?"

In the history of Nineveh there is a lesson that you should study carefully. . . . You must know your duty to your fellow beings who are ignorant and defiled, and who need your help.—Manuscript 164, 1897.

June 15
STAND FOR PRINCIPLE

◆ *But Daniel purposed in his heart that he would not defile himself with the portion of the king's meat, nor with the wine which he drank: therefore he requested of the prince of the eunuchs that he might not defile himself. Daniel 1:8.*

ANIEL was but a youth when carried away captive into Babylon. He was about fifteen or sixteen years old, for he is called a child, which means that he was in his youth. Why did Daniel refuse to eat at the king's luxurious table? Why did he refuse the use of wine as his beverage, when it was at the king's command that it was placed before him? He knew that, by use, wine would become to him a pleasant thing, and would be preferred before water.

Daniel could have argued that at the royal table and at the king's command, there was no other course for him to pursue. But he and his fellows had a council together. . . . The wine of itself, they decided, was a snare. They were acquainted with the history of Nadab and Abihu that had come to them in parchments. In these men the use of wine had encouraged their love for it. They drank wine before their sacred services in the sanctuary. Their senses were confused. They could not distinguish the difference between the sacred and the common fire. In their brain-benumbed state they did that which the Lord had charged all who served in holy office not to do. . . .

The instruction given to the people was carefully treasured up, and often composed into song and taught to their children, that through song they might become familiar with the truths. . . .

A second consideration of these youthful captives was that the king always asked a blessing before his meals, and addressed his idols as deity. . . . This act, according to their religious instruction, consecrated the whole to the heathen god. To sit at the table where such idolatry was practiced, Daniel and his three brethren deemed, would be a dishonor to the God of heaven. . . .

There was much involved in this decision. They were regarded as slaves, but were particularly favored because of their apparent intelligence and comeliness of person. But they decided that any pretense, even to sit at the table of the king and eat of the food or accept of the wine, even if they did not drink it, would be a denial of their religious faith. . . . They did not choose to be singular but they must be, else they would corrupt their ways in the courts of Babylon and be exposed to every kind of temptation in eating and drinking. The corrupting influences would remove their safeguard, and they would dishonor God and ruin their own characters.—Manuscript 122, 1897.

June 16
GOD'S WORD, THE FOUNDATION FOR CHARACTER BUILDING

◆ *Prove thy servants, I beseech thee, ten days; and let them give us pulse to eat, and water to drink . . . and as thou seest, deal with thy servants. Daniel 1:12, 13.*

*D*ANIEL placed himself in right relation to God and to his outward circumstances and opportunities. He was taken as a captive to Babylon, and with others was placed under training, to be prepared for a place in the king's court. His food and drink were appointed him, but we read that he determined that he would not defile himself with the king's meat nor with the wine which he drank.

In taking this step, Daniel did not act rashly. . . . Daniel said to Melzar, who had been given charge of him and his companions, "Prove thy servants. . . . And at the end of ten days their countenances appeared fairer and fatter in flesh than all the children which did eat of the portion of the king's meat." . . .

Having done this, Daniel and his companions did still more. They did not choose as friends those who were agents of the prince of darkness. They did not go with a multitude to do evil. They secured Melzar as their friend, and there was no friction between him and them. They went to him for advice, and at the same time educated him by the wisdom of their deportment.

It was God's purpose that these youth should become channels of light in the kingdom of Babylon. Satan was determined to defeat this purpose. He worked upon the minds of the youth who had refused to be God's representatives, causing them to be jealous of Daniel and his companions. At Satan's suggestion they laid plans to entrap those who were making such steady, rapid advancement in knowledge. . . .

Satan was trying to compass their destruction. . . . They made a faithful study of the Word of God, that they might know the divine will. By faith they believed that the One whom they served would communicate to them His will, and in answer to their faith God opened His Word to them. . . . They made the Word of God their textbook, looking upon it as the foundation upon which they must build character. They had only the Old Testament. . . .

Satan often cast his shadow across their pathway to obscure their view of divine light and darken their faith and confidence in God. But they would not yield, and the Lord gave them wisdom and power to prevail with Him in prayer.—Letter 34, 1900.

June 17
WRONG CHOICES IN FRIENDS PRODUCE EVIL CONSEQUENCES

◆ *As for these four children, God gave them knowledge and skill in all learning and wisdom: and Daniel had understanding in all visions and dreams. Daniel 1:17.*

*Y*OU will go through this world but once. Then do not choose as companions young men or young women who will lead you in wrong paths. Turn away from these tempters, for they are Satan's helping hand, used by him to beguile souls to dishonor God. . . . Do not give the enemy any advantage. Study the history of Daniel and his fellows. Though living where they were met on every side by the temptation to indulge self, Daniel and his companions honored and glorified God in their daily life. They determined to avoid all evil, to refuse to place themselves in the enemy's path. And with rich blessings God rewarded their steadfast loyalty.

Each one of us is making his or her future. All who desire the life that measures with the life of God must take a firm stand against the depravity that is spreading its loathsome disease over the world. They must reject the wrong and choose the right, bravely resisting temptation in every line. They must overcome small temptations; then they will be strengthened to overcome large ones.

There are those who say, You need not be so particular about little matters. In such, conscience accommodates itself to the suggestion of evil until they are educated to do the work that places them in Satan's army. From small wrongs they are led to large wrongs. . . . The lower passions bear sway, holding the entire being in the tyranny of satanic power. The high, noble purposes that might have controlled the life are swept away by self-indulgence. . . .

Unite with one another in being true to virtue, true to God. Be studious. Reach upward for the highest attainments. The Lord commends earnest, determined effort to gain that knowledge and understanding that will enable you to take your place in the higher grade in the courts above. He looks with approval on watchful, diligent students. . . .

Pray as did Daniel—three times a day, alone with God. Confess every sin you have committed, every mistake you have made. . . . God says, "Confess your faults one to another, and pray for one another, that ye may be healed." Thus you have built barriers between yourself and sin. You are walking in harmony with God. He has avouched Himself as one who will hear and answer your sincere prayers. He has assured you that He will pardon and accept you. How powerful you may be in this assurance! The Lord is near to all who call upon Him—near to answer and to bless.—Letter 134, 1901.

June 18
ALWAYS CREDIT
GOD FOR
IDEAS HE GIVES

◆ *Then was the secret revealed unto Daniel in a night vision. Then Daniel blessed the God of heaven. Daniel 2:19.*

*D*ANIEL sought the Lord when the decree went forth to slay all the wise men of the kingdom of Babylon because they could not relate or interpret a dream that had gone from the king's mind. He demanded not only the interpretation of the dream, but the relation of the dream itself. . . .

The magicians were full of fear and trembling. They declared that the request of the king was something unreasonable, and a test beyond that which had ever been required of anyone. The king became furious and acted like all persons who have great power and uncontrollable passions. He decided that every one of them should be put to death, and as Daniel and his fellows were numbered with the wise men, they also were to share their fate. . . .

Daniel came before the king and pleaded for time to bring this matter before the supreme court of the universe, from whose decision there could be no appeal. When his request was granted, Daniel laid the whole matter before his companions who were united with him in worshiping the true God. The matter was carefully considered, and on their bended knees, they pleaded that God would give them the power and wisdom that alone would avail them in their great necessity. . . . With contrition of heart they submitted their case to the great Judge of the earth. It was all that they could do. . . .

Daniel prayed, "I thank thee, and praise thee, O thou God of my fathers, who hast given me wisdom and might, and hast made known unto me now what we desired of thee: for thou hast now made known unto us the king's matter." . . .

Daniel was imbued with the Spirit of Jesus Christ, and he pleaded that the wise men of Babylon should not be destroyed. The followers of Christ do not possess the attributes of Satan, which make it a pleasure to grieve and afflict the creatures of God. They have the spirit of their Master, who said, I am "come to seek and to save that which was lost." . . .

"Then Arioch brought in Daniel before the king in haste, and said thus unto him, I have found a man of the captives of Judah, that will make known unto the king the interpretation." . . . Then in all humility of mind he [Daniel] acknowledges that the wisdom is not in him, but in the God of heaven, and that the vision has been revealed to him for the sake of God's servants, and that the king might know the thought of his heart.— Letter 90, 1894.

June 19
STANDING FOR GOD IN TIMES OF CRISIS

◆ *Our God whom we serve is able to deliver us from the burning fiery furnace, and he will deliver us out of thine hand, O king. But if not, . . . we will not serve thy gods, nor worship the golden image which thou hast set up. Daniel 3:17, 18.*

EBUCHADNEZZAR'S wonderful dream caused a marked change in his ideas and opinions, and for a little time he was influenced by the fear of God; but his heart was not yet cleansed from its pride, its worldly ambition, its desire for self-exaltation. After the first impression wore away, he thought only of his own greatness, and studied how the dream might be turned to his own honor.

The words "Thou art this head of gold" made the deepest impression upon Nebuchadnezzar's mind. He determined to make an image that should excel the original. This image was not to deteriorate in value from the head to the feet, like the one he had been shown, but was to be composed throughout of the most precious metal. Thus the whole image would represent the greatness of Babylon, and he determined that by the splendor of this image the prophecy concerning the kingdoms that were to follow should be effaced from his mind and from the minds of others who had heard the dream and its interpretation. From the treasures obtained in war, Nebuchadnezzar "made an image of gold". . . . and issued a proclamation, calling upon all the officers of the kingdom to assemble at the dedication of this image, and at the sound of musical instruments, to bow and worship it. . . .

The appointed day came, and at the sound of entrancing music the vast company "fell down and worshipped the golden image." But the three Hebrew youth, Shadrach, Meshach, and Abednego (we have no record of Daniel's being present), did not dishonor the God of heaven by paying homage to this idol. Their action was reported to the king. Angered, he called them before him and by threats endeavored to induce them to unite with the multitude in worshiping the image. Courteously yet firmly they declared their allegiance to the God of heaven and their faith in His power to deliver them in the hour of trial.

The king's wrath knew no bounds. He commanded that the furnace be heated seven times hotter than it was wont. And without delay the Hebrew exiles were cast in. So furious were the flames that the men who cast the Hebrews in were burned to death.—Manuscript 110, 1904.

June 20
IN EVERY TEST, GOD IS WITH US

◆ *And the princes, governors, and captains, and the king's counsellors, being gathered together, saw these men, upon whose bodies the fire had no power, nor was an hair of their head singed. Daniel 3:27.*

*S*UDDENLY the countenance of the king paled with terror. He looked intently upon the glowing flames and, turning to his lords, in tones of alarm, inquired, "Did not we cast three men bound into the midst of the fire?" The answer was "True, O king." His voice trembling with excitement, the monarch exclaimed, "Lo, I see four men loose, walking in the midst of the fire, and they have no hurt; and the form of the fourth is like the Son of God."

The Hebrew captives had told Nebuchadnezzar of Christ, the Redeemer that was to come, and from the description thus given the king recognized the form of the fourth in the fiery furnace as the Son of God. Hastening to the furnace, Nebuchadnezzar cried, "Ye servants of the most high God, come forth." And they obeyed, before that vast multitude showing themselves unhurt, not even the smell of fire being on their garments. True to duty, they had been proof against the flames. Only their fetters had been burned.

Tests will come to every one of us. We know not how many will be placed in peculiar positions where we shall have opportunity of showing forth the glory of God. We are to keep in view the honor of our heavenly Father. . . .

History will repeat itself. In this age the great test will be upon the point of Sabbath observance. . . . A rival sabbath is exalted, as was the great golden image in the plain of Dura. Leaders claiming to be Christians will call upon the world to observe the spurious sabbath that they have made. All who refuse will be put under oppressive laws. This is the mystery of iniquity, the devising of satanic agencies, carried into effect by the man of sin. . . .

We are to warn men and women against the worship of the beast and his image—against the worship of the idol Sunday. But in doing this work, we need not begin a warfare against unbelievers. We are simply to present the Word of the Lord, in its true dignity and purity, before the minds of those who are ignorant or indifferent regarding its teachings. . . . We need not tell them that they will go to hell unless they keep the Sabbath of the fourth commandment. The truth itself, accompanied by the power of the Holy Spirit, will convict and convert hearts.—Manuscript 110, 1904.

June 21
GOD WARNS AGAINST SELF-CENTERED PRIDE

◆ *They shall drive thee from men, and thy dwelling shall be with the beasts of the field, . . . and seven times shall pass over thee, till thou know that the most High ruleth in the kingdom of men. Daniel 4:22-25.*

THE faithful Daniel stood before the king, not to flatter, not to misinterpret in order to secure favor. A solemn duty rested upon him, to tell the king of Babylon the truth. He said, "My lord, the dream be to them that hate thee, and the interpretation thereof to thine enemies. The tree that thou sawest, . . . it is thou, O king."

Do we regard the kingdom of Babylon as of more importance in the estimation of God than are the instrumentalities and responsibilities He has entrusted to His chosen people, upon whom the ends of the world are come? We have here the workings of the great I AM to change even the heart of a heathen king. There is a Watcher just as really taking cognizance of all the works of human beings, but in a special sense of those who are to represent God by receiving His sacred truth into the heart and revealing it to the world. . . .

In the dream of Nebuchadnezzar, the true object of government is beautifully represented by the great tree "whose leaves were fair, and the fruit thereof much, and in it was meat for all; under which the beasts of the field dwelt, and upon whose branches the fowls of the heaven had their habitation."—Manuscript 29, 1895.

The prophet Daniel interpreted the dream to the king, and he added the solemn admonition "Wherefore, O king, let my counsel be acceptable unto thee, and break off thy sins by righteousness, and thy iniquities by shewing mercy to the poor; if it may be a lengthening of thy tranquillity." . . . For twelve months the king was tested and proved. During this time his actions were weighed in the balances of the sanctuary in heaven.

One morning as he walked in his palace, "the king spake, and said, Is not this great Babylon, that I have built for the house of the kingdom by the might of my power, and for the honour of my majesty?" While the king was swelling with self-importance, even "while the word was in the king's mouth, there fell a voice from heaven, saying, O king Nebuchadnezzar, to thee it is spoken; The kingdom is departed from thee."—Letter 71, 1894.

June 22
WE DECIDE OUR ETERNAL DESTINY

◆ *Now I Nebuchadnezzar praise and extol and honour the King of heaven, all whose works are truth, and his ways judgment: and those that walk in pride he is able to abase. Daniel 4:37.*

*T*HE strength of nations and of individuals is not found in the opportunities and facilities that appear to make them invincible; it is not found in their boasted greatness. That alone which can make them great and strong is the power and purpose of God. They themselves, by their attitude toward His purpose, decide their own destiny. Human histories relate people's achievements, their victories in battle, their success in climbing to worldly greatness. God's history describes men and women as heaven views them. . . .

The prophet Daniel described the kingdoms that would rise and fall. Interpreting to the king of Babylon the dream of the great image, he declared to Nebuchadnezzar that his kingdom would be superseded. His greatness and power in God's world would have its day, and a second kingdom would arise that also would have its period of test and trial as to whether the people would exalt the one Ruler, the only true God. Not doing this, they and their glory would fade away, and a third kingdom would occupy their place. Proved by obedience or disobedience, this also would pass away, and a fourth, strong as iron, was to subdue the nations of the world. This Word, opened by the infinite God to finite human beings, recorded on the prophetic page, and traced on the pages of history, declares that God is the ruling power. . . .

The voice of God, heard in past ages, is sounding down along the line from century to century, through generations that have come on the stage of action and passed away. . . . History and prophecy testify that the God of the whole earth revealeth secrets through His chosen light bearers to the world. . . . Nebuchadnezzar, through his terrible humiliation in the loss of his reason, was brought to see his own weakness, and to acknowledge the supremacy of the living God. . . .

To every person, God has assigned a place in His great plan. By truth or falsehood, by folly or wisdom, each is fulfilling a purpose, bringing about certain results. And each, according as he or she chooses obedience or disobedience, is deciding his or her own eternal destiny. To everyone is given freedom to act, and upon everyone rests the responsibility of their own actions. . . .

We are not to say God was, but God is. . . . Though kings shall be cast down, and nations removed, the souls that through faith link themselves with God's purposes shall abide forever.—Manuscript 36, 1896.

June 23
GOD STILL NEEDS PEOPLE WHO CANNOT BE CORRUPTED

◆ *The former governors that had been before me were chargeable unto the people, and had taken of them bread and wine, beside forty shekels of silver; yea, even their servants bare rule over the people. Nehemiah 5:15.*

HE children of Israel were taken captive to Babylon because they separated from God, and no longer felt that it was their duty to maintain principles unadulterated by the sentiments of the nations around them. Because of their separation from God, the Lord humbled them. He could not work for their prosperity, He could not fulfill His covenant with them while they were untrue to the principles He had given them to zealously maintain, that they might be kept from the methods and practices of the heathen nations who dishonored God. . . . He left them to their own ways, and the innocent suffered with the sinners in Zion.

But among the children of Israel there were Christian patriots, who were as true as steel to principle, and upon these loyal and true men the Lord looked with great pleasure. . . . They had to suffer with the guilty, but in the providence of God this captivity was the means of bringing them to the front. Their example of untarnished integrity, while captives at Babylon, shines with heaven's luster.

Many of the Lord's chosen people had proved themselves untrustworthy. They separated from God and became selfish, scheming, and dishonorable. The part acted by Daniel and his fellows, and by Ezra and Nehemiah, was in marked contrast to this, and the Lord specially blessed these men for standing firmly for the right.

Nehemiah was chosen by God because he was willing to cooperate with God as a restorer. . . . He would not be led and corrupted by the devices of unprincipled men who had been hired to do an evil work. He would not allow them to intimidate him into following a cowardly course. When he saw wrong principles being acted upon, he did not stand by as an onlooker and by his silence give consent. He did not leave the people to conclude that he would stand on the wrong side. He took a firm, unyielding stand for the right. He would not lend one jot of influence to the perversion of the principles that God had established. Whatever course others might pursue, he could say, "So did not I, because of the fear of God."—Manuscript 121, 1898.

June 24
POSITION DOES NOT PRECLUDE THE NEED FOR PRAYER

◆ *Let now thine ear be attentive to the prayer of thy servant, who desire to fear thy name: and prosper, I pray thee, thy servant this day, and grant him mercy in the sight of this man. Nehemiah 1:11.*

EHEMIAH, the Hebrew exile, occupied a position of influence and honor in the Persian court. As cupbearer of the king, he was admitted to the royal presence, and by virtue of this intimacy and his own high abilities and tried fidelity, he became the monarch's counselor. He was a man of high principle, unbending integrity, and great sagacity.

In that heathen land, surrounded by royal pomp and splendor, Nehemiah did not forget the God of his fathers or the people who had been entrusted with the holy oracles. The dignity of his position did not rob him of his piety or his love for his brethren. . . . He was not ashamed to own his relationship to them and to the truth. He felt that he must honor the truth in all places. He did not make apology for holding a faith distinct from the faith of those in the Persian court. . . .

Days of peculiar trial and affliction had come to the chosen city. Messengers from Judah described to Nehemiah its condition. The second temple had been reared, and portions of the city rebuilt, but its prosperity was impeded, the temple service disturbed, and the people kept in constant alarm by the fact that its walls were still in ruins and its gates burned with fire. The capital of Judah was fast becoming a desolate place, and the few inhabitants remaining were deeply embittered by the taunts of their idolatrous assailants, "Where is your God?"

The soul of the Hebrew patriot was overwhelmed by these evil tidings. So great was his sorrow that he could not eat or drink; he "wept, and mourned certain days, and fasted." But when the first outburst of his grief was over, he turned in his affliction to the sure Helper. The record says that he "prayed before the God of heaven." He unburdened his heart to God. He knew that the affliction that had come upon Israel was the result of her transgression, and with deep humiliation he came before God to ask for pardon and a renewal of the divine favor. Faithfully he makes confession of his sins and the sins of his people.

Taking hold by faith of the divine promise, Nehemiah lays down at the footstool of heavenly mercy his petition that God would maintain the cause of his penitent people, restore their strength, and build up their waste places.—Manuscript 58, 1903.

June 25
FAITH AND WORKS SHOULD BE COMBINED

◆ *And I said unto the king, If it please the king, and if thy servant have found favour in thy sight, that thou wouldest send me unto Judah, unto the city of my fathers' sepulchres, that I may build it. Nehemiah 2:5.*

T last the sorrow that burdened Nehemiah's heart could no longer be concealed. Sleepless nights devoted to earnest prayer, care-filled days, dark with the shadow of hope deferred, leave their trace upon his countenance. The keen eye of the monarch, accustomed jealously to guard his own safety, is accustomed to read countenances and to penetrate disguises. Seeing that some secret trouble is preying upon his servant, he suddenly inquires, "Why is thy countenance sad, seeing thou art not sick? this is nothing else but sorrow of heart."

The question fills the listener with apprehension. Will not the king be angry to hear that while outwardly engaged in his service, the courtier's thoughts have been far away with his afflicted people? Will not the offender's life be forfeited? And his cherished plan for restoring Jerusalem— is it not about to be overthrown? "Then," he says, "I was very sore afraid." With trembling lips and tearful eyes he reveals the cause of his sorrow— the city, which is the place of his father's sepulchre, lying waste, and its gates consumed with fire. The touching recital awakens the sympathy of the monarch without arousing his idolatrous prejudices; another question gives the opportunity for which Nehemiah has long sought: "For what dost thou make request?"

But the man of God does not reply until he has first asked the support of One higher than Artaxerxes. "I prayed," he says, "to the God of heaven." The silent petition then sent to God was the same that he had offered for many weeks—that God would prosper his request. And now, taking courage at the thought that he has a Friend, omniscient and all-powerful, to work in his behalf, the man of God calmly makes known to the king his desire to be released for a time from his office at the court and be authorized to build up the waste places of Jerusalem, and to make it once more a strong and defensed city. Momentous results to the Jewish city and nation hang upon this request. "And," says Nehemiah, "the king granted me, according to the good hand of my God upon me."

While Nehemiah implored the help of God, he did not fold his own hands, feeling that he had no more care or responsibility in the matter. With admirable prudence and forethought, he proceeded to make all the arrangements necessary to ensure the success of the enterprise.— Manuscript 58, 1903.

June 26
**CAREFUL
PLANNING
NECESSARY IN
GOD'S WORK**

◆ *Let letters be given me to the governors
beyond the river, that they may convey me
over till I come into Judah; and a letter unto
Asaph . . . that he may give me timber . . . for
the wall of the city. Nehemiah 2:7, 8.*

S his [Nehemiah's] request to the king had been so favorably received, he was encouraged to ask for such assistance as was necessary to carry out his plans. To give dignity and authority to his mission, as well as to provide protection on the journey, he secured a military escort. He obtained royal letters to the governors of the provinces beyond the Euphrates, the territory through which he must pass on his way to Judea; he obtained also a letter to the keeper of the king's forest in the mountains of Lebanon, directing him to furnish such timber as was needed for the wall of Jerusalem and such buildings as Nehemiah proposed to erect.

The example of this holy man should be a lesson to all the people of God, that they are not only to pray in faith but to work with wise diligence and fidelity. How many difficulties we encounter, and how we hinder the working of Providence on our behalf, because prudence, forethought, and painstaking are regarded as having little to do with religion. . . . Careful consideration and well-matured plans are as essential to the success of sacred enterprises today as in the time of Nehemiah. . . .

Nehemiah does not depend upon uncertainties. The means that he has not he solicits from those who are able to bestow. All the world, with its riches and treasures, belongs to God, although it is now in the possession of wicked people. If His servants take a wise and prudent course, so that the good hand of the Lord may be with them, they can obtain the means that they need to advance His cause.

Nehemiah's experience in connection with the rebuilding of Jerusalem teaches lessons that will be needed by God's people as long as time shall last. The times call for men and women of strength and decision of character. Paul says, "Finally, my brethren, be strong in the Lord, and in the power of his might. Put on the whole armour of God, that ye may be able to stand against the wiles of the devil." The enemy will mingle his evil with every good work that is done if the workers are not on guard. Thus he seeks to spoil God's purposes.—Manuscript 58, 1903.

June 27
OUR WORDS AND ACTS CARRY A POWERFUL INFLUENCE

♦ *Ezra had prepared his heart to seek the law of the Lord, and to do it, and to teach in Israel statutes and judgments. Ezra 7:10.*

ZRA was of the sons of Aaron, a priest whom God chose to be an instrument of good unto Israel, that He might put honor upon the priesthood, the glory of which had been greatly eclipsed during the captivity. Ezra was a man of great piety and holy zeal. He was also a man of learning and a ready scribe in the law of Moses. These qualifications made him an eminent man.

Ezra was impressed by the Spirit of God to search the historical and poetical books of the Bible, and by this means he became familiar with the sense and understanding of the law. During the captivity the knowledge of God's will had to some extent been lost. Ezra gathered all the copies of the law that he could find. He published copies of these among God's people and became a teacher of the law and the prophecies in the schools of the prophets. The pure Word, thus diligently taught by Ezra, gave knowledge that was invaluable at that time. . . .

Some of the prophecies were about to be fulfilled; he would search diligently for the light that had been obscured. He sought this knowledge that he might educate the people how to bring into their practical life the principles of the Word of God. . . .

That which Ezra knew he desired to teach others, and thus he became a mouthpiece for God, educating those about him in the holy principles that govern in heaven. . . . Teaching thus, he educated others in the knowledge of truth that would live through eternal ages. . . .

As Ezra labored to communicate what he had learned, his capabilities for labor increased and developed. He became the Lord's witness to the world of what Bible truth is when revealed in the daily life of the receiver.

Ezra's example, in words and deeds, carried with it a weight of influence, for the Spirit of God was with him. . . . He diligently prepared his heart to do the work that he believed was appointed to him. He searched out the words that had been written concerning the duties of God's denominated people, and he found a solemn pledge that God's people had given that they would obey the words of God and the pledge of God's blessing to the obedient. . . .

We each have an appointed work to do, and this can be accomplished only by consecrated effort. Shall we let the example of Ezra address itself to us individually, and teach us the use we should make of our knowledge of the Scriptures?—Letter 100, 1907.

June 28
JESUS RECEIVES AND DEFENDS REPENTANT SOULS

◆ *And the Lord said unto Satan, The Lord rebuke thee, O Satan; even the Lord that hath chosen Jerusalem rebuke thee: is not this a brand plucked out of the fire? Zechariah 3:2.*

ATAN claims a right to have those who once stood under his black banner, but who have turned from sin to the living God and have cast their helpless souls upon Jesus. All who take hold of the merits of Christ by faith have the pledged word of God that they shall make peace with Him. . . .

Trials are permitted to come upon the chosen people of God. The expressions are used, "God tempted Abraham," "God tempted the children of Israel." This means that the Lord permitted Satan to tempt them in order that their faith might be found unto honor and glory when the judgment shall sit, and when every person shall be judged according to the deeds done in the body. God knows every heart, every motive, every thought in the heart; but He permits Satan to try and tempt and test His believing ones in order that their trust and confidence in God may be revealed. . . .

The Lord hates sin; but He loves and forgives the repentant, believing sinner, and takes everyone under His guardianship and control. Satan is on the track of every soul, but with every temptation that is permitted to come upon the children of God's pardoning love, He makes a way of escape in order that they shall not be tempted above that which they are able to bear. . . .

"And he shewed me Joshua the high priest standing before the angel of the Lord, and Satan standing at his right hand to resist him." The work of Satan is plainly defined as that of resisting the meritorious work of Christ. . . . When Christ steps in between the tempted souls and Satan, the adversary is angry and opens up with a tirade of abuse and accusation, declaring that Christ is unfair in protecting these souls, and in lifting up a standard against him. . . .

In the presence of the unfallen worlds, in the presence of the universe of heaven, in the presence of the angry adversary who has painted them in robes of blackness and moral defilement, urging that they be given into his hands, Jesus answered Satan's malignant charge whereby he accused them before God day and night. To those who stood before Him, earnestly watching the controversy and marking the determination of Satan to destroy the righteous, Jesus spoke, saying, "Take away the filthy garments from him. And unto him he said, Behold, I have caused thine iniquity to pass from thee, and I will clothe thee with change of raiment."—Manuscript 27, 1894.

June 29
**ALL HEAVEN
HEARS OUR PRAISE
AND THANKS-
GIVING TO GOD**

◆ *Then they that feared the Lord spake often one to another: and the Lord hearkened, and heard it, and a book of remembrance was written before him for them that feared the Lord, and that thought upon his name. Malachi 3:16.*

WO classes of witnesses are presented in the prophet's [Malachi's] words. Of the first class it is written, "Your words have been stout against me, saith the Lord. . . . Ye have said, It is vain to serve God: and what profit is it that we have kept his ordinance, and that we have walked mournfully before the Lord of hosts?" These words describe those who ought to have better represented the precious truth, who ought to have been an example to those newly come to the faith. For all who follow Him the Lord has prepared a rich feast of heavenly things. He has ordained that those who follow Him shall not walk in darkness, but shall have the light of life. . . . The Lord does not call upon His believing, obedient followers to cover the altar with tears, but to walk cheerfully and happily along. . . .

Malachi turns away from the dark picture that Satan presents to these professed followers of Jesus Christ, for it is a libel on the paternal character of God. Satan has framed this picture for the contemplation of poor, unbelieving, mourning souls, and they have hung it up in memory's hall where they can gaze upon it. But the Lord has presented another picture for the contemplation of every believer. "Then they that feared the Lord spake often one to another: and the Lord hearkened." . . .

Do the believers who meet in their small assemblies in humble churches or in private houses often look upon this picture framed by the Lord of hosts? . . . What a hope-inspiring picture is this where the Lord is represented as bending down and hearkening to the testimonies borne by His witnesses! What inspiration it should give us to consider the fact that all the heavenly universe is represented as listening with pleasure to the words that are spoken exalting the name of God in the earth. . . .

The words to which God and the angels listen with delight are words of appreciation for the great Gift that has been made to the world in the only begotten Son of God. Every word of praise for the blessing of the light of truth that has come in messages of warning, and that has dispelled the darkness of error, is written in the heavenly records.—Manuscript 32, 1894.

June 30
**LEARNING THE
LESSONS OF
SACRED HISTORY**

◆ *Now all these things happened unto them for ensamples: and they are written for our admonition, upon whom the ends of the world are come. 1 Corinthians 10:11.*

HE instruction given in the Old Testament Scriptures is as verily the word of Christ as the instruction in the New Testament. Christ was as verily humanity's Redeemer in the days when the Old Testament was written as He was when He appeared in the form of a man. He gave those of ancient Israel just as favorable an opportunity of working out their own salvation as He did those who listened to His words.

A character formed after the divine likeness is the only treasure that people can take from this world to the next. The character as formed in this world determines one's destiny for eternity. The element of value in one's life in this world will be of value in the world to come. A person's future is determined by the way one allows himself or herself to be influenced. If one cherishes and cultivates hereditary tendencies for wrong, indulging fleshly inclinations, appetites, and passions, that individual can never enter the kingdom of God. But the person who strives to repress evil inclinations, who is willing to be governed by the Spirit of Jesus Christ, is transformed. . . .

Christ's character was exemplified in Abel, Noah, Seth, Enoch, Abraham, Joseph, Moses, Joshua, Samuel, David, and all the host of those recorded as having characters that God could approve. [As examples], we are also given Cain and all who form characters opposite to truth, fidelity, obedience, and righteousness. All had an opportunity to show themselves members of the Cain family, or as members of the royal family. . . . Purity and holiness come only through Christ. . . .

We are to listen to the voice of Christ speaking in the creation of the world and from the pillar of cloud, for our eternal welfare depends upon our obedience to the voice of God. Let all move guardedly. Let us not pass by anything that Christ has given through the holy people of old for the benefit of every generation.

All that God's mind has planned, that His hand has touched, are lessons written for our admonition upon whom the ends of the world are come. Those things that have been will be. Christ's words of approval or disapproval come sounding down along the line of our time. Our spiritual and eternal interests are involved in the facts stated. The Lord means what He says, and says what He means.—Letter 34, 1899.

July 1
CONSTANT PRAYER NEEDED TO RESIST SATAN'S CUNNING

◆ *And Jesus being full of the Holy Ghost returned from Jordan, and was led by the Spirit into the wilderness. Luke 4:1.*

*W*HY was it that at the beginning of His public ministry Christ was led into the wilderness to be tempted? It was the Spirit that led Him thence, and He went, not in His own behalf, but in our behalf, to overcome for us. There was no compulsion about it. He was led by the Spirit, His humanity to be proved, as one who had undertaken to stand at the head of the fallen race.

Christ had been, and was then, in perfect harmony with the Father. He was to be tried and tested as a representative of the race. He was led by the Spirit into the wilderness to meet the foe in personal encounter, to overthrow him who claimed to be the head of the kingdoms of the world.

While in the wilderness Christ fasted, but He was insensible to hunger. Engaged in constant prayer to His Father for a preparation to resist the adversary, Christ did not feel the pangs of hunger. He spent the time in earnest prayer, shut in with God. It was as if He were in the presence of His Father. He sought for strength to meet the foe, for the assurance that He would receive grace to carry out all that He had undertaken in behalf of humanity. The thought of the warfare before Him made Him oblivious to all else, and His soul was fed with the bread of life, just as today those tempted souls will be fed who go to God for aid. He ate of the truth that He was to give to the people as having power to deliver them from Satan's temptations. He saw the breaking of Satan's power over fallen and tempted ones. He saw Himself healing the sick, comforting the hopeless, cheering the desponding, and preaching the gospel to the poor—doing the work that God had outlined for Him; and He did not realize any sense of hunger until the forty days of His fast were ended. . . .

Christ is in the wilderness, the wild beasts His only companions, and everything around Him tending to make Him realize His humanity. Suddenly an angel appears before Him, apparently one of the angels that He saw not long since, and addresses Him with the words "If thou be the Son of God, command that these stones be made bread." "If thou be the Son of God"—here is the insinuation of distrust. The words rankle with the bitterness in his [Satan's] mind. In the tones of his voice is an expression of utter incredulity.—Letter 159, 1903 (*Manuscript Releases,* vol. 21, pp. 8, 9).

July 2
CHRIST REFUSED TO ARGUE WITH SATAN

◆ *When a strong man armed keepeth his palace, his goods are in peace. Luke 11:21.*

E [Satan] ridiculed the idea of Christ, the Majesty of heaven, being left in the wilderness to suffer from hunger. Would God treat His own Son thus? Would He leave Him in the desert with wild beasts, without food, without companions, without comfort? He insinuates that God never meant His Son to be in such a state as this. . . .

The words from heaven, "This is my beloved Son, in whom I am well pleased," were still sounding in the ears of Satan. But he was determined to make Christ disbelieve this testimony. The word of God was Christ's assurance of His divine mission. . . . It was Satan's purpose to make Him doubt this word. If Christ's confidence in God could be shaken, Satan knew that victory in the whole conflict would be his. He could overcome Jesus. He hoped that under the force of despondency and extreme hunger, Christ would lose faith in His Father and work a miracle in His own behalf. Had He done this, the plan of salvation would have been broken.

And Christ, the Son of God, answering said, "It is written, Man shall not live by bread alone, but by every word that proceedeth out of the mouth of God." Christ had been warned not to enter into argument with Satan. And though He recognized him from the beginning, He was not provoked to enter into controversy with him. Strengthened with the memory of the voice from heaven, He rested in His Father's love. He would not parley with temptation.

Satan tempted the first Adam in Eden, and Adam reasoned with the enemy, thus giving him the advantage. Satan exercised his power of hypnotism over Adam and Eve, and this power he strove to exercise over Christ. But after the word of Scripture was quoted, Satan knew that he had no chance of triumphing.

Satan came to Christ hoping to gain the victory. He thought that he had every advantage over Him. But he was conquered by the Saviour's meekness and humility, and by His reliance on the Word of God. Meek and lowly, and seemingly helpless, Christ was stronger than the strong man armed. Oh, how Satan strove to make Him sin against God! But all his efforts failed to make Christ swerve from His allegiance.

Our Saviour could receive the heavenly revelation without becoming self-exalted. . . . The enemy is subtle and very daring, but he is not invincible. He is a strong man armed, but if we keep close to the Captain of our salvation, using the weapon that He has given us, we shall be victorious.— Letter 159, 1903 (*Manuscript Releases*, vol. 21, pp. 9, 10).

July 3
NO TEMPTATION COULD INDUCE THE SAVIOUR TO SIN

◆ *But unto the Son he saith, Thy throne, O God, is for ever and ever: a sceptre of righteousness is the sceptre of thy kingdom. Hebrews 1:8.*

*I*N the wilderness Christ endured trials human beings cannot comprehend. Here Christ was brought face-to-face with the subtle power of Satan, the fallen angel. The enemy pursued the same course with the Saviour that he did with Adam and Eve in Eden. He began by disputing the sovereignty of Christ. If you are the Son of God, he said, give me evidence that You are. . . .

Well did Satan know who Christ was, for when the Saviour went to Gadara, the evil spirits in the two madmen there cried out, "What have we to do with thee, Jesus, thou Son of God? Art thou come hither to torment us before the time?" As Christ passed through the test of the second Adam, His beauty of character shone out through His disguise. Satan could see through His humanity the glory and purity of the Holy One with whom he had been associated in the heavenly courts. As he looked upon Christ, there rose before his mind a picture of what he himself was then. At the time he had beauty and holiness. Self-exaltation led him to strive for a place above Christ. But he had failed. Could he now carry out his design upon the enfeebled humanity of Christ? He knew that if he could induce Christ to yield one jot in His allegiance to His Father, he would have the world entirely in his power, and would be able to rule as only he in his changed spiritual nature could rule. But the One Satan was trying to overcome was the Lord of heaven, and all the efforts of the tempter were without avail. As Satan saw that he could not obtain the victory, he was aroused to malignant hatred. . . .

Then Satan took Christ to the pinnacle of the temple, and told Him to cast Himself down. . . . Thus he tried to lead Him to commit the sin of presumption. He reminded Him of the ministration of angels. But no temptation could make the Saviour accept the challenge of the tempter. . . .

The adversary seemed to have power to take Christ where he pleased, for he next took Him to an exceeding high mountain, and there presented before Him all the kingdoms of the world and the glory of them. . . . Then it was that divinity flashed through humanity, and the fallen angels saw Jesus glorified before them as He said, "Get thee behind me, Satan.". . .

As the Commander in the heavenly courts, Christ was accustomed to receive the attendance of angels. And at any time during His life on this earth He could have called to His Father for twelve legions of angels. But no bribe, no temptation to lead Him to manifest His divine prerogatives, could induce Him to deviate from the path of God's appointment.—Letter 7, 1900.

July 4
**CHRIST PROVED
THAT WE CAN
KEEP THE
COMMANDMENTS**

◆ *If thou be the Son of God, command that these stones be made bread. Matthew 4:3.*

*I*F His divine nature had not been clothed with the garb of humanity, Christ could not have associated with the fallen race and have become their Redeemer. It was necessary for Him to know the power of all our temptations, to pass through all the trials and afflictions that we are called to pass through, in order to be indeed a Saviour. . . . Satan, the powerful foe who had been turned out of heaven, had long claimed to have dominion on the earth, and Christ came to conquer this foe, in order that we might, through divine grace, also obtain the victory over the enemy of our souls. Standing at the head of humanity, Christ by His perfect obedience demonstrated to the universe that human beings could keep the commandments of God.

Under all circumstances—whether in prosperity or in adversity, whether received or rejected, whether at the marriage feast or suffering the pangs of hunger—Christ remained faithful to every precept of God's law, and wrought out for our example a perfect life. He has endured every hardship that comes to the poor and afflicted. Without sin He has suffered weariness and hunger. He understands every inconvenience to which we may be put. From childhood to manhood He stood the test of obedience.

When Jesus was led into the wilderness to be tempted, He was led by the Spirit of God. He did not invite temptation. He went into the wilderness to be alone, to contemplate His mission and work. By fasting and prayer He was to brace Himself for the bloodstained path He must travel. But Satan knew that the Saviour had gone into the wilderness, and he thought this was the best time to approach Him. Weak and emaciated from hunger, worn and haggard with mental agony, Christ's "visage was so marred more than any man, and his form more than the sons of men." Now was Satan's opportunity. Now he supposed that he could overcome Christ.

The first temptation was on the point of appetite. There came to the Saviour, as if in answer to His prayers, one in the guise of an angel from heaven. He claimed to have a commission from God to declare that Christ's fast was at an end. The Saviour was faint from hunger; He was craving for food when Satan came suddenly upon Him. Pointing to the stones that strewed the desert, and that had the appearance of loaves of bread, the tempter said, "If thou be the Son of God, command that these stones be made bread."—Manuscript 155, 1902 (*Sermons and Talks*, vol. 2, pp. 217, 218).

July 5
**CHRIST MET
TEMPTATION
WITH SCRIPTURE**

◆ *It is written, "One does not live by bread alone, but by every word that comes from the mouth of God." Matthew 4:4, NRSV.*

HOUGH he [Satan] appears as an angel of light, these first words betray his character: "If thou be the Son of God." Here is the insinuation of distrust. Should Jesus do that which Satan suggests, it would be an acceptance of the doubt. If Christ's confidence in God could be shaken, Satan knew that the victory in the whole controversy would be his. He hoped that under the force of despondency and extreme hunger, Christ would lose faith in His Father and work a miracle in His own behalf.

Not without a struggle could Jesus listen in silence to the archdeceiver. But the Son of God was not to prove His divinity to Satan. He met the tempter with the words of Scripture. "It is written," He said, "Man shall not live by bread alone, but by every word that proceedeth out of the mouth of God." In every temptation the weapon of His warfare was the Word of God.

When Christ said to the tempter, "Man shall not live by bread alone, but by every word that proceedeth out of the mouth of God," He repeated the words that more than fourteen hundred years before, He had spoken to Israel. And the same words are written for our admonition. We are to commune with the One who gives us life, the One who keeps the heart in motion and the pulse beating. God is giving the breath of life to every member of His great family here below. He deserves your sincere reverence, your earnest devotion. When you consider what He has done for you, how can you help loving Him? He has given His Son as a propitiation for sin, in order that you might stand on vantage ground with God.

If the world should recognize the claims of God upon them, we would not see and hear of the awful sins that are now so common; we would not read of the murders, the wickedness, and the tyranny daily chronicled in the newspapers. Like the antediluvians, the inhabitants of the world have almost entirely forgotten God and His law.—Manuscript 155, 1902 (*Sermons and Talks*, vol. 2, p. 218).

When Satan can bring his craftiness to bear on human minds, deceptive influences are received [as] from heaven. If his deceptions are allowed to enter, many souls will be ensnared by them before it is seen that they are not from God, but from the enemy of all righteousness.—Manuscript 37, 1903 (*The Upward Look*, p. 135).

July 6
CHRIST'S MISSION FULFILLED ONLY THROUGH SUFFERING

◆ *If thou be the Son of God, cast thyself down: for it is written, He shall give his angels charge concerning thee: and in their hands they shall bear thee up, lest at any time thou dash thy foot against a stone. Matthew 4:6.*

*T*HE second temptation was on the point of presumption. . . . Satan now supposes that he has met Jesus on His own ground. The wily foe himself presents words that proceeded from the mouth of God. He makes it evident that he is acquainted with the Scriptures. But when he quoted the promise "He shall give his angels charge over thee," he omitted the words "to keep thee in all thy ways," that is, in all the ways of God's choosing. Jesus refused to go outside the path of obedience. He would not force Providence to come to His rescue, and thus fail of giving us an example of trust and submission. Never did He work a miracle in His own behalf. His wonderful works were all for the good of others. Jesus declared to Satan, "It is written again, Thou shalt not tempt the Lord thy God." God will preserve all who walk in the path of obedience, but to depart from it is to venture on Satan's ground. There we are sure to fall. . . .

Jesus was victor in the second temptation, and now Satan manifests himself in his true character, claiming to be the god of this world. Placing Jesus upon a high mountain, Satan caused the kingdoms of the world, in all their glory, to pass in panoramic view before Him. The eyes of Jesus, so lately greeted by gloom and desolation, now gazed upon a scene of unsurpassed loveliness and prosperity. Then the tempter's voice was heard, "All this power will I give thee, and the glory of them: for that is delivered unto me; and to whomsoever I will give it. If thou therefore wilt worship me, all shall be thine."

Christ's mission could be fulfilled only through suffering. Before Him was a life of sorrow, hardship, and conflict, and an ignominious death. But now Christ might deliver Himself from the dreadful future by acknowledging the supremacy of Satan. But to do this was to yield the victory in the great controversy. Christ declared to the tempter, "Get thee behind me, Satan: for it is written, Thou shalt worship the Lord thy God, and him only shalt thou serve." Christ's divinity flashed through suffering humanity. Satan had no power to resist the command to depart. Humiliated and enraged, he was forced to withdraw from the presence of the world's Redeemer.—Manuscript 155, 1902 (*Sermons and Talks*, vol. 2, pp. 218, 219).

July 7
THE REDEEMER COMFORTED AFTER ENDURING THE TEST

◆ *Then the devil leaveth him, and, behold, angels came and ministered unto him.* Matthew 4:11.

FTER the foe had departed, Jesus fell exhausted to the earth. He had endured the test, but He now was fainting on the field of battle. What hand was there to be put beneath His head? How was He to be given care and nourishment so that He might regain His strength? Was He to be left to perish after gaining the victory? Oh, no; the angels of heaven had watched the conflict with intense interest, and they now came and ministered to the Son of God as He lay like one dying. He was strengthened with food, comforted with the message of His Father's love and the assurance that all heaven triumphed in His victory. He returned from the wilderness to proclaim with power His message of mercy and salvation.

What if Satan had gained the victory? What hope would we have had? Christ came to reveal to worlds unfallen, to angels, and to the human race that in God's law there is no restriction that we cannot obey. He came to represent God in humanity. He met every requirement that we are asked to meet.—Manuscript 155, 1902 (*Sermons and Talks*, vol. 2, pp. 219, 220).

In their conflicts with Satan, the human family has all the help that Christ had. They need not be overcome. They may be more than conquerors through Him who has loved them and given His life for them. . . . The Son of God in His humanity wrestled with the very same fierce, apparently overwhelming, temptations that assail us—temptations to indulgence of appetite, to presumptuous venturing where God has not led them, and to the worship of the god of this world, to sacrifice an eternity of bliss for the fascinating pleasures of this life. Everyone will be tempted, but the Word declares that we shall not be tempted above our ability to bear. We may resist and defeat the wily foe.

Every soul has a heaven to win and a hell to shun. And the angelic agencies are all ready to come to the help of the tried and tempted soul. He, the Son of the infinite God, endured the test and trial in our behalf. The cross of Calvary stands vividly before every soul. When the cases of all are judged, and they are delivered to suffer for their contempt for God and their disregard of His honor in their disobedience, not one will have an excuse, not one will need to have perished. It was left to their own choice who should be their prince, Christ or Satan. All the help Christ received, every person may receive in the great trial.—Letter 116, 1899.

July 8
ANGELS INVOLVED IN TIMES OF TEMPTATION

◆ *For he shall give his angels charge over thee, to keep thee in all thy ways. They shall bear thee up in their hands, lest thou dash thy foot against a stone. Psalm 91:11, 12.*

*I*T is expressly stated that Satan works in the children of disobedience, not merely having access to their minds, but working through their influence, conscious and unconscious, to draw others into the same disobedience. If evil angels have such power over human beings in their disobedience, how much greater power the good angels have over those who are striving to be obedient. When we put our trust in Jesus Christ, working obedience unto righteousness, angels of God work in our hearts unto righteousness. . . .

Angels came and ministered to our Lord in the wilderness of temptation. Heavenly angels were with Him during all the period in which He was exposed to the assaults of satanic agencies. These assaults were more severe than any of us have ever passed through. Everything was at stake in behalf of the human family. In this conflict Christ did not frame His words even. He depended upon "It is written." In this conflict the humanity of Christ was taxed as none of us will ever know.

The Prince of life and the prince of darkness met in terrible conflict, but Satan was unable to gain the least advantage in word or in action. These were real temptations, no pretense. Christ "suffered being tempted." Angels of heaven were on the scene on that occasion, and kept the standard uplifted, that Satan could not exceed his bounds and overpower the human nature of Christ. In the last temptation Satan presented to Christ the prospect of gaining the whole world with all its glory if He would only worship him who claimed to be sent of God. Christ must then issue His command. He must then exercise authority above all satanic agencies.

Divinity flashed through humanity, and Satan was peremptorily repulsed. "Get thee hence, Satan," Christ said. . . . It was enough. Satan could go no further. Angels ministered to the Saviour. Angels brought Him food. The severity of this conflict no human mind can compass. The welfare of the whole human family and of Christ Himself was at stake. One admission from Christ, one word of concession, and the world would be claimed by Satan as his; and he, the prince of the power of darkness would, he supposed, commence his rule. There appeared unto Christ an angel from heaven, for the conflict ended. Human power was ready to fail. But all heaven sang the song of eternal victory.—Letter 116, 1899 (*Selected Messages*, book 1, pp. 94, 95).

July 9
POWER OF GOD AVAILABLE TO GIVE US VICTORY

◆ *His divine power hath given unto us all things that pertain unto life and godliness, through the knowledge of him that hath called us to glory and virtue. 2 Peter 1:3.*

$\mathcal{W}$E are to be partakers of knowledge. As I have seen pictures representing Satan's coming to Christ in the wilderness of temptation in the form of a hideous monster, I have thought, How little the artists knew of the Bible! Before his fall Satan was next to Christ, the highest angel in heaven. How foolish then to suppose that he approached Christ in the wilderness in any such form as is given him in the illustration *The Game of Life.* Some have seen that picture. After the Saviour had fasted forty days and forty nights, "he was afterward an hungered." Then it was that Satan appeared to Him. He came as a beautiful angel from heaven, claiming that he had a commission from God to declare the Saviour's fast at an end. "If thou be the Son of God," he said, "command that these stones be made bread." But in Satan's insinuation of distrust, Christ recognized the enemy whose power He had come to the earth to resist. He would not accept the challenge, nor be moved by the temptation. . . .

Christ stood by every word of God, and He prevailed. If we would always take such a position as this when tempted, refusing to dally with temptation or argue with the enemy, the same experience would be ours. It is when we stop to reason with the devil that we are overcome. It is for us to know individually that we are right in the warfare, to take the affirmative in the sight of God, and there to stand. It is thus that we obtain the divine power promised, through which we obtain "all things that pertain unto life and godliness, through the knowledge of him that hath called us to glory and virtue."

There is such a thing as being partakers of the divine nature. We shall be tempted in a variety of ways, but when we are tempted we need to remember that a provision has been made whereby we may overcome. . . . Those who truly believe in Christ are made partakers of the divine nature and have power that they can appropriate under every temptation. They will not fall under temptation and be left to defeat. In time of trial they will claim the promises and by these escape the corruptions that are in the world through lust.

We think it costs us something to stand in this position before the world; and so it does. But what has our salvation cost the heavenly universe? To make us partakers of the divine nature, heaven gave its most costly treasure. The Son of God laid aside His royal robe and kingly crown and came to our earth as a little child.—Manuscript 9a, 1908.

July 10
**EVERY TEMP-
TATION RESISTED
IS A PRECIOUS
VICTORY**

◆ *Blessed is every one that feareth the Lord;
that walketh in his ways. For thou shalt eat the
labour of thine hands: happy shalt thou be,
and it shall be well with thee. Psalm 128:1, 2.*

*Y*OU are to show to the world your purpose to be a citizen of Paradise. Let no careless, irreverent expression come from your lips. What you say in the world will be marked with special consequence if it corresponds with what you say in the church. Your attitude, your words, your spirit, are constantly making an impression upon those with whom you associate. . . .

Satan is offering to every soul the kingdoms of this world in return for the carrying out of his will. This was the great inducement he presented to Christ in the wilderness of temptation. And so he says to Christ's followers, If you will follow my business methods, I will reward you with wealth. Every Christian is at some time brought to the test that will reveal any weak points of character. If the temptation is resisted, one has gained precious victories. . . . In Satan's last bold attempt to overcome Christ, the Saviour met him with the words "Get thee hence, Satan: for it is written, Thou shalt worship the Lord thy God, and him only shalt thou serve." Hitherto the Saviour's response to his temptations had been in the affirmative; now He commands the tempter to depart, and Satan leaves Him—defeated where he had hoped for victory. . . .

Those who purchase success at the fearful price of submission to the will of Satan will find that they have made a hard bargain. Everything in Satan's trade is secured at a high price. The advantages he presents are a fearful, deceptive mirage. The promised high hopes he holds out are secured at the loss of things that are good and holy and pure. Let Satan always be confounded with the words "It is written.". . . .

I speak these words to all who love and fear God. People who stand prepared to do the works of righteousness will not be deceived by the allurements of the enemy. The angels of God are by their side restraining them if they will be restrained. Their actions will be guided by an exalted sense of right. They will be enabled to distinguish between right and wrong, between truth—exalted truth—and error. Those who enter the kingdom of heaven will be those who have reached the highest standard of moral obligation, those who have not sought to hide the truth or to deceive, those by whom God has been exalted and His Word defended, those by whom principle has not been misapplied to vindicate the wiles of Satan.—Letter 188, 1905.

July 11
**JESUS HAS
POWER TO SAVE
EVERY SOUL**

◆ *That the trial of your faith, being much
more precious than of gold that perisheth,
though it be tried with fire, might be found
unto praise and honour and glory at the
appearing of Jesus Christ. 1 Peter 1:7.*

E are not kept by our intelligence, by our words, or
by our riches. In these we find no safety. We are kept only by the power of
God through faith unto salvation. We are living in a period of time during
which we must by faith be allied with an infinite God or else we cannot
overcome the strong powers of darkness seeking to destroy us. . . .

Temptations will come. But when Satan throws his hellish shadow before us, we should reach in faith through the shadow to the Light of life—
to Him who has not only created us but who by His own blood has
redeemed us. We are Christ's cherished heritage. In living faith we must
cooperate with Him in working out our own salvation. Amid trials and
temptations His hand upholds and sustains us. . . .

Those who hold fast their faith unto the end will come forth from the
furnace of trial as fine gold seven times purified. . . . When in trouble, remember that faith tried in the furnace of affliction is more precious than
gold tried with fire. . . .

Do you suppose that after Christ gave His precious life to redeem the
beings He created He would fail to give them sufficient power to enable
them to overcome by the blood of the Lamb and the word of their testimony? He has power to save every individual. At the time of His ascension
He said, "All power is given unto me in heaven and in earth." For our redemption all power is given to Him who stood at the head of humanity.
For nearly six weeks the Sinless One fought a battle with the powers of
darkness in the wilderness of temptation, overcoming not on *His* account,
but on *our* account, thus making it possible for every son and daughter of
Adam to overcome through the merit of His sinlessness. . . .

Only those who practice holiness in this life will see the King in His
beauty. Put away all vain, trifling talk, and everything of a frivolous and
sensational nature. Do not engross your mind with thoughts of worldly
entertainments and pleasures. Engage in the work of saving your soul. If
you should lose your soul, it would have been better for you never to have
been born. But you need not lose your soul. You may use every moment
of this God-given life to His name's glory. Strengthen yourself to resist the
powers of darkness, that they shall not obtain a victory over you.—
Manuscript 110, 1901 *(Sermons and Talks,* vol. 2, pp. 174-176).

July 12

**BE ALERT
TO SATAN'S
PERVERSION
OF SCRIPTURE**

◆ *The salvation of the righteous is of the Lord: he is their strength in the time of trouble. And the Lord shall help them, and deliver them: he shall deliver them from the wicked, and save them, because they trust in him. Psalm 37:39, 40.*

HE wilderness temptation Christ endured was a personal conflict with the wicked one who had shown himself to be the author of sin. Satan was once a covering cherub in the heavenly courts, the angel next in power to Christ Himself. But he lifted himself up against God and induced some of the angels to join him in rebellion. There was war in heaven, and Satan and his followers were cast out. Expelled from heaven, Satan determined to set up a kingdom on this earth and win the human race to his side. But Christ pledged His word that if humans were overcome by temptation, He, the Son of God, would be their surety.

Christ came to our world to stand where Adam stood, to endure the temptations Adam failed to endure. . . . After His baptism, He went forth to the wilderness, and there He was tempted by the enemy. For forty days and forty nights He fasted; then, when He was an hungered, Satan came to Him as though he were a messenger from the heavenly courts, and tempted Him. . . .

The enemy knew well the power of God's word. He knew that this word had supplied bread for the Israelites in their journeyings through the wilderness, and that the same word could now supply the necessities of Christ. But this was not God's plan. He designed that Christ should be treated as human beings are treated. He was not to exercise miraculous power in His own behalf, for if He did, Satan would say that His test had not been a fair one, because He had made use of supernatural power; and that He could not require human beings to keep all His requirements if the effort to keep them would destroy life. . . .

Satan desired Christ to make Himself guilty of the sin of presumption by needlessly exposing His life. He did not repeat the whole of the quotation, but left out the words "in all thy ways," that is, in the path of duty. If Christ had presumed on God's mercy by risking His life to give Satan evidence of His Messiahship, He would not have been in the path of duty.

All should become familiar with God's Word, because Satan perverts and misquotes Scripture, and people follow his example by presenting part of God's Word to those whom they wish to lead in false paths, withholding the part that would spoil their plans.—Manuscript 153, 1899.

July 13
JESUS GIVES US POWER TO BECOME GOD'S CHILDREN

◆ *But to all who received him, who believed in his name, he gave power to become children of God. John 1:12, NRSV.*

E are the Lord's property. Christ has paid a sum for our ransom that in no way can be computed. He gave Himself a living offering to God. He bore the sins of the transgressor, that God might be just and yet be the justifier of the repenting, believing sinner. In the wilderness of temptation He overcame every temptation on the point of appetite. He fasted forty days and forty nights, and in His weak condition Satan assailed Him. But He answered not with His own words, for Satan was ready to enter into controversy had He done this. . . . The insinuating temptation was presented, "If thou be the Son of God, command that this stone be made bread." But the "if " was not accepted, and there was no ground for controversy. . . .

In His human nature Jesus gave evidence that in every temptation wherewith Satan shall assail fallen human beings, there is help for them in God if they will take hold of His strength, and through obedience make peace with Him. . . .

All heaven was watching the working of the enemy against Christ when tempted in behalf of the fallen race. And all heaven is watching the strivings of every individual soul under every temptation by which men and women shall be beset. If they will resist the temptation, if they will not yield on any point, Satan cannot have the victory. In the books of heaven will stand registered against your name that on such a day Satan sought to overthrow and ensnare one of My redeemed ones, but the tempted one looked to Me, the conqueror, and I gave him or her angels to press back the powerful foe. . . .

And what will those answer who have turned away from light and from knowledge and lived a careless, self-indulgent life? The amount of evidence people have had presented before them, the number of talents they have received, the returns made to the Master—these will determine their destiny for eternity.

Those who have had privileges and opportunities and light upon light will find themselves brought into comparison with those whose religious advantages have been limited, but who have made diligent, persevering effort to lay hold on eternal life. Over such the Lord rejoices with singing.—Manuscript 49, 1897.

July 14
WE CAN ALWAYS RELY UPON "THUS SAITH THE LORD"

◆ *If thou be the Son of God, command this stone that it may be made bread. . . . If thou be the Son of God, cast thyself down from hence. Luke 4:3-9.*

*I*N the wilderness of temptation the riches of the world was the bribe presented to our Lord. Satan did not come to Him with his temptations until the human nature was weakened and was crying out its necessity. . . .

Christ's humanity would have shrunk from that which awaited Him in the desert. But He came to the world so that by coming into close contact with him [Satan], He might wrest from the hands of the usurper the Lord's human heritage. . . .

Satan knew that the personal controversy between the Prince of life and the prince of darkness had commenced, and he sought to overcome Christ in His physical weakness. The proof that Satan required was for Christ to accept the doubt and act upon it, thus showing that He entertained the doubt by giving the evidence that Satan desired. Had Christ complied with this suggestion of the enemy, his satanic majesty would still have said, Show me a sign, that I may believe you to be the Son of God. But not one of the signs specified was Christ to give. By working a miracle in His own behalf He would show that He questioned God. That sign that is greater than all miracles, a firm reliance upon a "Thus saith the Lord," was a sign that could not be controverted. . . .

How artfully had Satan approached Eve in Eden! "Yea, hath God said, Ye shall not eat of every tree of the garden?" Thus far every word that Satan spoke was truth, but his manner of saying them was a disguised contempt for the words of God. There was in his words of truth a covert negative, a denial, a doubt of the divine truthfulness. He sought to instill into her mind the thought that God would not do as He had said, that the withholding of such beautiful fruit was a contradiction of His love and compassion for them.

And now he seeks to inspire Christ with his own sentiments. "If thou be the Son of God." Thus he sought to imbue Christ with his doubts. . . . Would God treat His own Son thus? . . .

Temptations will arise [among some] to cause distrust of God and to question His love. . . . They become traitors, rebels against God, and accept the temptations of him whom they choose as their leader. They become a medium for Satan, a channel through which he communicates to other minds the doubts and infidelity with which he has imbued them.—Letter 3, 1897.

July 15
**FERVENT, IMPOR-
TUNATE PRAYER
WILL BRING
DIVINE HELP**

◆ *Strive to enter in at the strait gate: for
many, I say unto you, will seek to enter in,
and shall not be able. Luke 13:24.*

CHRIST resisted the manifold temptations of Satan on
our behalf, and through His name made it possible for us to overcome
Satan on our own behalf. When we are burdened, when we are pressed with
temptation, when the feelings and desires of the natural heart are contending for the victory, we should offer up fervent, importunate prayer to our
heavenly Father in the name of Christ; and this will bring Jesus to our help,
so that, through His all-powerful and efficacious name, we may gain the
victory and banish Satan from our side. But we should not flatter ourselves
that we are safe while we make but feeble efforts in our own behalf. . . .

Our danger does not arise from the opposition of the world, but it is
found in the liability of our being in friendship with the world, and imi-
tating the example of those who love not God or His truth. The loss of
earthly things for the truth's sake, the suffering of great inconvenience for
loyalty to principle, does not place us in danger of losing our faith and
hope, but we are in danger of suffering loss because of being deceived and
overcome by the temptations of Satan. Trials will work for our good if we
receive and bear them without murmuring, and will tend to separate us
from the love of the world, and will lead us to trust more fully in God.

There is help for us only in God. We should not flatter ourselves that
we have any strength or wisdom of our own, for our strength is weakness,
our judgment foolishness. Christ conquered the foe in our behalf, because
He pitied our weakness and knew that we would be overcome and would
perish if He did not come to our help. . . .

The merits of Christ elevate and ennoble humanity, and through the
name and grace of Christ it is possible for us to overcome the degradation
caused by the Fall, and, through the exalted, divine nature of Christ, to be
linked to the Infinite. It is dangerous for us to think that by any easy or
common effort we may win the eternal reward. Let us consider how much
it cost our Saviour in the wilderness of temptation to carry on in our behalf
the conflict with the wily, malignant foe. Satan knew that everything depended upon his success or failure in his attempt to overcome Christ with
his manifold temptations. Satan knew that the plan of salvation would be
carried out to its fulfillment, that his power would be taken away, that his
destruction would be certain, if Christ bore the test that Adam failed to
endure.—Manuscript 65, 1894 (*Review and Herald,* Feb. 5, 1895).

July 16
VICTORY OBTAINED IN THE NAME OF JESUS

◆ *To the one who conquers I will give a place with me on my throne, just as I myself conquered and sat down with my Father on his throne. Revelation 3:21, NRSV.*

THE temptations of Satan were most effective in degrading human nature, for human beings could not stand against their powerful influence; but Christ in our behalf, as our representative, resting wholly upon the power of God, endured the severe conflict in order that He might be a perfect example to us. . . .

Christ suffered on our account beyond our comprehension, and we should welcome trial and suffering on our own account for Christ's sake, that we may overcome as Christ also overcame, and be exalted to the throne of our Redeemer. Let us consider the life and suffering of our precious Saviour in our behalf, and remember that if we are not willing to endure trial, toil, and conflict, if we are not willing to be partakers with Christ of His sufferings, we shall be found unworthy of a seat upon His throne.

We have everything to gain in the conflict with our mighty foe, and we dare not for a moment yield to his temptations. We know that in our own strength it is not possible for us to succeed; but as Christ humbled Himself and took upon Himself our nature, He is acquainted with our necessities, and has Himself borne the heaviest temptations that human beings will have to bear, has conquered the enemy in resisting his suggestions, in order that we may learn how to be conquerors. . . .

Christ is our pattern, the perfect and holy example that has been given us to follow. We can never equal the pattern, but we may imitate and resemble it according to our ability. . . . When we surrender all we have and are to God, and are placed in trying and dangerous positions, coming in contact with Satan, we should remember that we shall have victory in meeting the enemy in the name and power of the Conqueror. Every angel would be commissioned to come to our rescue when we thus depend upon Christ, rather than that we should be permitted to be overcome. But we need not expect to get the victory without suffering, for Jesus suffered in conquering for us. . . .

The Christian life is a life of warfare, of continual conflict. It is a battle and a march. But every act of obedience to Christ, every act of self-denial for His sake, every trial well endured, every victory gained over temptation, is a step in the march to the glory of final victory.—Manuscript 65, 1894 (*Review and Herald,* Feb. 5, 1895).

July 17
CHRIST IS WITH US ALWAYS

◆ *While we look not at the things which are seen, but at the things which are not seen: for the things which are seen are temporal; but the things which are not seen are eternal.*
2 Corinthians 4:18.

OR forty days and nights He [Christ] fasted in the wilderness of temptation, and there Satan came to Him with great power, hoping to overcome Him in His weakness. The temptations then brought upon Christ were in every way greater than those brought upon Adam, but the Redeemer did not swerve a hairsbreadth from His allegiance to God. . . .

Although it may seem that you are alone, yet you are not alone, for Christ is with you; you are in blessed company. And you have the words sounding down along the line from the prophets and apostles to encourage you in steadfastness. Many of these holy people lost their lives because of their faithfulness to God. If you suffer for the truth's sake, remember that this is no more than others have done before you. What trials and afflictions Paul endured, and yet he says, "Our light affliction, which is but for a moment, worketh for us a far more exceeding and eternal weight of glory.". . .

When difficulties arise, as they will, remember that Jesus is by your side, a very present help in time of need. To meet trial bravely is part of the Christian warfare, and in this warfare all heaven is interested. Christ knows what temptations you will meet. He knows that when one accepts the truth he or she will have a cross to lift, and He is ready to give the needed help.

Let the light of truth shine forth in your life. Do you say, How shall I let it shine? If before you accepted the truth, you were impatient and fretful, let your life now show to those around you that the truth has had a sanctifying influence upon your heart and character, that instead of being fretful and impatient, you are now cheerful and uncomplaining. Thus you reveal Christ to the world. . . .

At the moment when you are offering your prayer for help, you may not feel all the joy and blessing that you would like to feel; but if you believe that Christ will hear and answer your petition, the peace of Christ will come.—Manuscript 8, 1885.

July 18
SALVATION PLACED WITHIN REACH OF EVERY HUMAN BEING

◆ *Give diligence to make your calling and election sure: for if ye do these things, ye shall never fall. 2 Peter 1:11.*

ERE is our life assurance policy [2 Peter 1:10]. Here we have the directions laid down as to how we shall secure the life that measures with the life of God. . . . Many profess the religion of Jesus Christ, but they do not live it. What is their profession good for? They might just as well trace their name in the sand—and how long would it stand?

The religion of Jesus Christ makes us better men and better women. . . . Christ came to our world to reshape the deformed character of humanity. It was a very crooked character. God wants us to be His sons and His daughters. He wants us, during the hours of probation here, to be fitted up with all these graces that He has presented "according as his divine power hath given unto us all things." Nothing is withheld that pertains unto life and godliness, through the knowledge of Him that hath called us to glory and virtue. Then the rich promise is that we shall be partakers of the divine nature. This means everything to us, to be a partaker of the divine nature.

What victories should we gain in this lifetime if Christ had not overcome point after point for us in the wilderness of temptation? Here the enemy met Him with the three great leading temptations wherewith we are beset. . . . Christ had instituted and framed the plan Himself that with humanity upon Him, He was to bear every temptation wherewith men and women are beset.

He was not to work a miracle so as to avoid suffering Himself, but He was to stand the test upon every point of appetite that could be brought to the human family. . . . If Adam had depended on the words of God in place of the words of a stranger, he would not have transgressed the law of Jehovah. Temptation will come to every one of us as it came to Jesus Christ, and what is our hope? We may be pressed sore with temptations, but we may overcome, because Christ has brought moral power within our reach.

Everything that pertains to godliness, everything that pertains to the salvation of the human soul, is to be placed within the reach of every human being upon the face of the earth. There is no excuse for one of us to falter and fail in any respect in the work of overcoming, for Christ has said, "To him that overcometh will I grant to sit with me in my throne, even as I also overcame, and am set down with my Father in his throne."—Manuscript 49, 1894.

July 19
ALL MAY BECOME CONQUERORS THROUGH CHRIST

◆ *Can the Ethiopian change his skin, or the leopard his spots? then may ye also do good, that are accustomed to do evil. Jeremiah 13:23.*

E know that intemperance is in our world everywhere. There is no sin in eating and drinking to sustain us physically, and in doing that which is for our spiritual good. But when we lose eternity out of our reckoning, and carry these necessary things to excess, that is when the sin comes in. We see on every side such crime, such iniquity. Is it not time that we shall begin to study for ourselves? . . .

Satan is represented by the serpent. The tempter is everywhere, on every side, and when God says ye shall not, what is the result? In many instances in the place of obeying the voice of warning, people listen to the tempter. And in the place of all the attractions that Satan presents they have woe and misery. . . .

When Christ came into our world as a babe in Bethlehem, the angels sang out, "Glory to God in the highest, and on earth peace, good will toward men.". . . Satan with all his synagogue—for Satan claims to be religious—determined that Christ should not carry out the counsels of heaven. After Christ was baptized, He bowed on the banks of Jordan, and never before had heaven listened to such a prayer as came from His divine lips. . . . The glory of God, in the form of a dove of burnished gold, rested upon Him, and from the infinite glory was heard these words, "This is my beloved Son, in whom I am well pleased." The human race is encircled by the human arm of Christ, while with His divine arm He grasps the throne of the Infinite One. The prayer of Christ cleaved right through the darkness and entered where God is. To each of us it means that heaven is open before us. It means that the gates are ajar, that the glory is imparted to the Son of God and all who believe in His name. . . .

Christ entered into the wilderness with the Spirit of God upon Him, to be tempted of the devil. . . . Satan left the field as a conquered foe. Our Saviour passed over the ground and was victor. . . .

What has He done for the human family? He has elevated us in the scale of moral value. We may become conquerors through our Sufficiency. There is hope for the most hopeless, in Christ. . . . What did Christ come here for? To represent the Father. What a heart of love and sympathy! . . . When God gave His Son, He gave all heaven. He could give no more.—Manuscript 27, 1893 (*Temperance,* pp. 283-287).

July 20
IN CHRIST WE MAY HAVE PERFECT HUMANITY

◆ *Abide in me, and I in you. As the branch cannot bear fruit of itself, except it abide in the vine; no more can ye, except ye abide in me. John 15:4.*

ATAN wished to change the government of God, to fix his own seal to the rules of God's kingdom. Christ would not be brought into this desire, and here the warfare against Christ commenced and waxed strong. Working in secrecy but known to God, Lucifer became a deceiving character. He told falsehood for truth.

He was expelled from heaven, and apparently Christ was alone with him in the wilderness of temptation. Yet He was not alone, for angels were round Him just as angels of God are commissioned to minister unto those who are under the fearful assaults of the enemy. Christ was in the wilderness with the one with whom there was war in heaven, and the one whom He overcame; and Satan was defeated.

Now Satan meets Him under different circumstances, as the glory that was round about Him is no longer visible. He has humbled Himself, taken upon Himself our nature. . . . What mental anguish Christ passed through! What grief! What torture of mind! He was face-to-face not with a hideous monster, as is represented with bat's wings and cloven feet, but a beautiful angel of light, apparently just from the presence of God. . . .

It is impossible to take in the depth and the force of these temptations unless the Lord shall bring us where He can open these scenes before us by a revelation of the matter, and then it can only be but partially comprehended. . . . Our Lord's trial and test and proving shows that He could yield to these temptations, else the battle was all a farce. But He did not yield to the solicitude of the enemy, thus evidencing that human nature, united with the divine nature by faith, may be strong and withstand Satan's temptations.

Christ's perfect humanity is the same that we may have through connection with Christ. As God, Christ could not be tempted any more than He was not tempted from His allegiance in heaven. But as Christ humbled Himself to our nature, He could be tempted. He had not taken on Him even the nature of the angels, but humanity, perfectly identical with our own nature, except without the taint of sin. . . .

Here the test to Christ was far greater than that of Adam and Eve, for Christ took our nature, fallen but not corrupted, and would not be corrupted unless He received the words of Satan in the place of the words of God.—Manuscript 57, 1890 (*Manuscript Releases,* vol. 16, pp. 180-183).

July 21
**ALL CALLED TO
BE CHILDREN
OF GOD**

◆ *Beloved, we are God's children now; what
we will be has not yet been revealed. What we
do know is this: when he is revealed, we will
be like him, for we will see him as he is.*
1 John 3:2, NRSV.

IRST John 3:1-3 quoted.] Here John has a view of the measureless love of an infinite God. John cannot find language to express it, and he calls upon the world to behold it. There were types and shadows that prefigured Christ in the Old Testament. Those who had been with Christ through His ministry recorded His works in the New Testament. For three and a half years the disciples were learning lessons from the lips of Christ, the greatest Teacher the world ever knew. . . . What brought Him here? Adam and Eve had transgressed the law of God in Eden. . . .

Christ looked upon our world before He came to it, and He saw that Satan's power was exercised upon the human family. And because of the transgression of Adam he claimed the whole human family. He pointed to their calamities and diseases and reflected them upon God. He said God would have no mercy upon them and they might as well be under his control. Jesus had enlisted to give His own life for the salvation of the human race. He laid aside His royal robe and royal crown that He might clothe humanity with divinity. . . .

Since the law of God was transgressed, the sentiment prevailed that it was impossible for human beings to keep the law of God. . . . The human and divine were combined in Jesus Christ. He came to our world to elevate humanity in the scale of moral value with God. He passed over the ground where Adam fell. He stood against the temptations of Satan and came off conqueror. He [Satan] approached the Son of God as an angel of light, just as he may tempt you.

Jesus Christ came off conqueror in the wilderness of temptation. When upon Jordan's banks, He offered such a prayer to heaven as heaven had never listened to before. His prayer penetrated through the darkness around Him and reached the highest heavens. The heavens were opened and the Holy Spirit, in appearance like a dove of burnished gold, descended upon Him, and from the lips of the Infinite One was heard these words, "This is my beloved Son, in whom I am well pleased." We have not understood how much this was saying to us. You are "accepted in the beloved.". . .

Christ came here to our atom of a world, and He honored it by taking human nature upon Himself. He honored humanity in the sight of all the created intelligences.—Manuscript 16, 1893.

July 22
OUR INFLUENCE IS A POWER FOR GOOD OR FOR EVIL

◆ *And they that be wise shall shine as the brightness of the firmament; and they that turn many to righteousness as the stars for ever and ever. Daniel 12:3.*

RUE Christians will have an experience like that of Christ in the wilderness of temptation, especially those who engage in rescuing souls from the snares of Satan. They will meet the assaults of the enemy of all righteousness; and as Christ overcame, so may they overcome through His grace. Christians should not feel that they are abandoned of God because they are subjected to sore temptations. If they remain unshaken by the temptations, Satan will leave them, and angels will minister to them as they did to Jesus. There is no comfort equal to that which Christians enjoy when the tempted soul has patiently suffered and Satan has been vanquished. They have borne witness for Jesus, relying wholly upon the Word of God, "It is written," and thus have resisted every advance of Satan, till they have beaten him back and gained the victory.

Let us in no case depreciate people because they are severely tempted and the billows seem to go over their head. We must remember that Jesus was sorely tempted in all points like as we are, so that He might succor all who should be tempted. . . .

We all have a personal influence. Our words and actions leave an indelible impress. It is our duty to live, not for self but for the good of others; to be controlled not by feelings, but by principle. We should consider that our influence is a power for good or for evil. We are either a light to cheer or a tempest to destroy. . . .

The law of God requires that we love one another as we love ourselves. Then every power and action of the mind must be put forth to that end—to do the greatest amount of good. . . . How pleasing to the Giver for us to hold the royal gifts of the soul so that they shall tell with power upon others! They are the connecting link between God and humans, and reveal the Spirit of Christ and the attributes of heaven. The power of holiness, seen but not boasted of, speaks more eloquently than the most able sermons. It speaks of God and opens to men and women their duty more powerfully than mere words can do.—Letter 39, 1887 (*Manuscript Releases,* vol. 20, pp. 137, 138).

July 23
**WE ARE TO
LIVE BY GOD'S
EVERY WORD**

◆ *This is my beloved Son, in whom I am
well pleased. Matthew 3:17.*

S Christ bowed upon Jordan's banks after His baptism, there was a bright light that descended like a dove of burnished gold and lighted upon Him, and from heaven was heard a voice saying, "This is my beloved Son, in whom I am well pleased." We read over these words, but do not take in their significance. We do not seem to understand their value to us. They are stating to you that you are accepted in the Beloved. Christ with His long human arm encircles the fallen race, while with His divine arm He grasps the throne of the Almighty, thus uniting earth with heaven, and fallen, finite human beings with the Infinite God. And this earth, which was divorced from heaven, is again united with heaven. A communication is opened with heaven through Jesus Christ [so] that the human race, which was fallen, is brought back again into favor with God. Here Jesus passed into the wilderness of temptation, and trial is brought to bear upon Him one hundred times more trying than that brought upon Adam and Eve in the Garden of Eden. . . .

If Adam and Eve had lived by every word that proceeded out of the mouth of God, they never would have fallen, never lost the right to the tree of life. All who will live by every word that proceedeth out of the mouth of God now will be brought back to the Eden home. . . .

There is happiness, hope, and peace for the desponding. We cannot afford to give our God-given ability and devote it to the commonplace things of this earth. We want a faith that will grasp the promise set before us in the gospel. . . .

I see matchless charms in Jesus. I never talk of any trials I cannot bear, or any self-sacrifice that I cannot make. I see One who died in my behalf, and He shall not die for me in vain. I will place myself in right relation to God, and I will have a right hold from above. I am not studying what the world will say of me, but my study is, Lord, how shall I please Thee? How shall I perform my mission in this world? . . .

If we are overcomers at last, there are battles for us to fight, and we will find that the flesh warreth against the Spirit and the Spirit against the flesh. It is for us to say which will triumph.—Manuscript 16, 1886 (*Sermons and Talks*, vol. 2, pp. 32-34).

July 24
JESUS OUR EXAMPLE ON HOW TO OVERCOME SATAN

◆ *All scripture is inspired by God and is useful for teaching, for reproof, for correction, and for training in righteousness, so that everyone who belongs to God may be proficient, equipped for every good work. 2 Timothy 3:16, 17, NRSV.*

HE great leading temptations wherewith we would be beset, Christ met and overcame in the wilderness. His coming off victor over appetite, presumption, and the world shows how we may overcome. Satan has overcome his millions in tempting the appetite and leading people to give up to presumptuous sins. There are many who profess to be followers of Christ, claiming by their faith to be enlisted in the warfare against all evil in their nature, yet who, with hardly a thought, plunge into scenes of temptation that would require a miracle to bring them forth unsullied. Meditation and prayer would have preserved them and led them to shun the dangerous positions in which they have placed themselves, and that give Satan the advantage over them.

The promises of God are not for us to claim rashly, to protect us while we rush on recklessly into danger, violating the laws of nature, or disregarding prudence and the judgment God has given us to use. This would not be genuine faith but presumption. The thrones and kingdoms of the world, and the glory of them, were presented to Christ. Never will we have temptations as strong as those that assailed Him.

But Satan comes to us with worldly honor, wealth, and the pleasures of life. These temptations are varied to meet people of every rank and degree, tempting them away from God to serve themselves more than their Creator. "All these things will I give thee," said Satan to Christ. "All these things will I give thee," says Satan to us. "All this money, this land, all this power, this honor, and these riches, will I give thee," and we are charmed, deceived, and treacherously allured on to our ruin. If we give ourselves up to worldliness of heart and of life, Satan is satisfied.

The Saviour overcame the wily foe, showing us how we may overcome. He has left us His example, to repel Satan with Scripture. He might have had recourse to His own divine power and used His own words, but His example would not then have been as useful to us. Christ used only Scripture. How important that the Word of God be thoroughly studied and followed, that in case of emergency we may be "throughly furnished unto all good works" and especially fortified to meet the wily foe.—*Letter 1a, 1872.*

July 25
OUR SAVIOUR
WAS TEMPTED
EXACTLY AS
WE ARE

◆ *Let him take hold of my strength, that he may make peace with me; and he shall make peace with me. Isaiah 27:5.*

*I*MAGINE, if you can, yourself in Christ's stead in the wilderness. There is no human voice you hear, but you are surrounded with demons under deceptive pretensions as angels from heaven, presenting in the most seducing attractions Satan's wily insinuations against God, as he did to our first parents. His sophistry is most deceiving and artful in undermining your confidence in God and destroying your faith and your trust. He keeps your mind on a constant strain so that he can get one clue that he can use to his own advantage to allure you into a controversy, as if reading your thoughts to which you will not give utterance, just as he did Eve.

He could not obtain from Christ one word to lead him on. The word, "It is written," was spoken from point to point as he tested Him. But only the quotation of His own words that He had inspired the holy men of old to write would come from Christ's lips. . . . In our Lord's great scene of conflict in the wilderness, apparently under the power of Satan and his angels, was He capable, in His human nature, of yielding to these temptations? . . .

As God He could not be tempted, but as a man He could be tempted, and that strongly, and could yield to the temptations. His human nature must pass through the same test and trial Adam and Eve passed through. His human nature was created; it did not even possess the angelic powers. It was human, identical with our own. He was passing over the ground where Adam fell. He was now where, if He endured the test and trial in behalf of the fallen race, He would redeem Adam's disgraceful failure and fall, in our own humanity.

A human body and a human mind were His. He was bone of our bone and flesh of our flesh. . . . He was subject to disappointment and trial in His own home, among His own brethren. He was not surrounded, as in the heavenly courts, with pure and lovely characters. He was compassed with difficulties. He came into our world to maintain a pure, sinless character, and to refute Satan's lie that it was not possible for human beings to keep the law of God. . . .

Through being partakers of the divine nature we may stand pure and holy and undefiled. The Godhead was not made human, and the human was not deified by the blending together of the two natures. Christ did not possess the same sinful, corrupt, fallen disloyalty we possess, for then He could not be a perfect offering.—Manuscript 94, 1893 (*Manuscript Releases*, vol. 6, pp. 110-112).

July 26
AT LAST WE SHALL SEE THE KING IN HIS BEAUTY

◆ *To everyone who conquers, I will give permission to eat from the tree of life that is in the paradise of God. Revelation 2:7, NRSV.*

IF you feel a spirit of controversy with anyone, just go out somewhere and speak of the love of Christ to souls who need a testimony in favor of the truth. Speak of the loveliness of Christ, and the wicked spirit that has been in your heart will depart. What we need is an experience in overcoming the enemy, and in clinging to the Mighty One. We cannot afford to lose everlasting life.

I must tell you that heaven is to be sought for, to be prayed for, to be worked for. We cannot, with our unconverted traits of character, drift into heaven. . . .

Do not spend time in controversy with those who bring up objections, for the enemy will suggest to other minds enough to occupy your time in combating them. Your strength is to keep to the affirmative. When the devil met Christ in the wilderness, Christ did not enter into controversy with him. Satan tempted Him to perform a miracle to create bread. Had Christ done this, He would have given the enemy a decided advantage, for Satan might have given a similar evidence of his own power. . . .

So today, if people bring to you objections to the truth, and try to stir you up, do not become excited. Keep on the track of the affirmative. Affirm the truth, "Thus saith the Lord," and let me tell you, the enemy will soon desire to get out of your presence. . . .

Let us lay aside the warfare the enemy would have us put on. Let us begin to work in earnest to overcome our hereditary and cultivated tendencies to evil. Let us plead with God to take away the wicked propensity to faultfinding, and in its place to give us life and the love of Christ. . . .

We have a heaven to win, and Christ wants us to have it. He died that we might have it. Every soul who is saved in the kingdom of God will give the glory to Him, not to any human being. Christ will open for us the golden gates; He will invite us to enter. . . .

And we must enter heaven here below or we shall never enter the heaven hereafter. Right here on this earth we must begin to live the life of Christ, and then it will be a heaven to you and it will be a heaven to those who associate with you. . . . And at last you will see the King in His beauty; you will behold His matchless charms and, touching the golden harp, fill heaven with rich music and songs to the Lamb.—Manuscript 97, 1906.

July 27
THROUGH DIVINE AID WE CAN BE VICTORS AGAINST SATAN

◆ *Thanks be to God, which giveth us the victory through our Lord Jesus Christ.*
1 Corinthians 15:57.

*I*T is at an immense cost that we have been placed on the high vantage ground where we can be liberated from the bondage of sin, which has been wrought by the fall of Adam. . . . Never can we understand the value of the human soul until we realize the great sacrifice made for the redemption of the soul upon Calvary. Adam's sin in Eden plunged the human race into hopeless misery. But in the scheme of salvation a way has been provided for all to escape if they comply with the requirements. A second probation has been granted by the sacrifice of the Son of God. We have a battle to fight, but we can come off victor through the merits of Christ's blood.

God saw that it was impossible for us to overcome and gain the victory in our own strength. The race has ever been growing weaker in every succeeding generation since the fall, and without the help of Christ we cannot resist the evil of intemperance. How thankful we should be that we have a Saviour and that He consented to lay off His royal robes and leave the royal throne, and to clothe His divinity with humanity and become a Man of sorrows and acquainted with grief. . . .

After His baptism, He was led by the Spirit into the wilderness and was tempted of the devil. Christ commenced the work of redemption just where the ruin began, and the future welfare of the world depended on that battle fought by the Prince of life in the wilderness. Thanks be to God that He came off victorious, passing over the same ground where Adam fell and redeeming Adam's disgraceful failure. Satan left the field of battle a conquered foe. This victory is an assurance to us that through divine help we may come off victorious in our behalf on our own account in the conflict with the enemy. . . .

Satan felt that all the power of this fallen planet was in his possession, but when Christ came to measure strength with the prince of darkness, Satan found One who was able to resist his temptations. The words of Christ are "The prince of this world cometh, and hath nothing in me.". . . All heaven was watching the result of the controversy between Christ and Satan. . . . Now the question is Will we take advantage of the situation and come off more than conqueror through Him who loved us?—Manuscript 26, 1887.

July 28
**ARE WE
PREPARED FOR
CHRIST'S RETURN?**

◆ *He was in the world, and the world was made by him, and the world knew him not. John 1:10.*

LL that the world could endure of their Redeemer was the few years He was with them upon the earth, and they wanted to get rid of Him almost as soon as His mission commenced. . . . The question that every one of us has to settle is: Am I prepared for the coming of the Son of man? If you have accepted your Saviour by living faith, if you have repented of your sins, then you are in a position of acceptance with God so that if Christ should come you would meet Him in peace. . . .

Let us notice the steps that the Son of man had to take in order to carry out the plan of salvation. He stepped down from the royal throne, laid aside His royal robes, clothed His divinity with humanity, and consented to come to this world. This world—right here—was to be the field of battle where Christ and Satan, the prince of this earth, should engage in conflict. And the question to be settled was How could God be just and true to His law and yet justify the sinner? This could be done only by the sacrifice of the Son of God. . . .

It was difficult to uproot Satan from the affection of the angels in heaven. He took the position that the law of God was against the heavenly intelligences, and the warfare and controversy between Christ and Satan was started in heaven and is going on in the earth to the present day. The controversy between Christ and Satan was witnessed not only by the heavenly intelligences but by all the worlds that God had created. Here the power arises that claims to have the right to change times and laws—it is the man of sin. But does he have power to change times and laws? No; because God's law is written in the tables of stone, engraven with His own finger, and placed in the temple of God in heaven. That great moral standard will be the criterion that will judge every being upon the face of the earth, both dead and living. . . .

Christ went into the wilderness of temptation to bear the severest temptations, He was tempted in all points as Adam was tempted, and He passed over the very ground where Adam stumbled and fell. . . . Christ was now to stand where Adam stood, bearing humanity and overcoming in behalf of the race where Adam fell. And Christ withstood the test on every point; He resisted on the point of appetite. . . . He was tempted upon the point of ambition, and presumption, and He overcame the enemy on these points. . . . The Saviour of the world overcame and obtained the victory on every point.—Manuscript 11, 1886.

216

July 29
**BETTER TO
SUFFER THAN
TO YIELD TO
TEMPTATION**

◆ *He humbled you . . . in order to make you
understand that one does not live by bread
alone, but by every word that comes from the
mouth of the Lord. Deuteronomy 8:3, NRSV.*

*T*HE duel between Christ and Satan was fought in the wilderness, Christ with apparently not a friend to aid Him. Satan was subtle; falsehood is his stock in trade. With all the power that he possessed he tried to overcome the humanity of Christ. . . .

Satan charmed the first Adam by his sophistry, just as he charms men and women today, leading them to believe a lie. Adam did not reach above his humanity for divine power; he believed the words of Satan. But the second Adam was not to become the enemy's bondslave.

Adam had the advantage over Christ in that, when he was assailed by the tempter, none of the effects of sin were upon him. He stood in the strength of perfect manhood, possessing the full vigor of mind and body. He was surrounded with the glories of Eden and was in daily communion with heavenly beings. It was not thus with Jesus when He entered the wilderness to cope with Satan. . . .

Every device that the enemy could suggest was brought against Him. It was when Christ was in a weakened condition, after His long fast of forty days, that the wisest of the fallen angels used the most enticing words at his command in an effort to compel the mind of Christ to yield to his mind. . . . "If thou be the Son of God," he said, "show thy power by relieving thyself of this pressing hunger." "Command that these stones be made bread.". . .

When Christ said to Satan, "Man shall not live by bread alone, but by every word that proceedeth out of the mouth of God," He repeated the words that, more than fourteen hundred years before, He had spoken to Israel. [Deuteronomy 8:3, quoted].

In the wilderness, when all means of sustenance failed, God sent His people manna from heaven; and a sufficient and constant supply was given. This provision was to teach them that while they trusted in God and walked in His ways, He would not forsake them. The Saviour now practiced the lesson He had taught to Israel. By the word of God succor had been given to the Hebrew host, and by the same word it would be given to Jesus. He awaited God's time to bring relief. He was in the wilderness in obedience to God, and He would not obtain food by following the suggestions of Satan. In the presence of the witnessing universe, He testified that it is a lesser calamity to suffer whatever may befall than to depart in any manner from the will of God.—Manuscript 113, 1902.

July 30
CHRIST KNOWS JUST HOW TO HELP US OVERCOME

◆ *Thou shalt fear the Lord thy God, and serve him. Deuteronomy 6:13.*

WE should not present our petitions to God to prove whether He will fulfill His word, but because He will fulfill it; not to prove that He loves us, but because He loves us.

"Again, the devil taketh him up into an exceeding high mountain . . . and saith unto him, All these things will I give thee, if thou wilt fall down and worship me."

This was Satan's crowning effort. Into this effort he threw all his beguiling power. It was the charm of the serpent. He exerted the power of his fascination upon Christ, striving to make Him yield His will to him. In His weakness Christ laid hold of God. Divinity flashed through humanity. Christ stood revealed as the Commander of heaven, and His words were the words of one who has all power. "Get thee behind me, Satan," He said, "for it is written, Thou shalt worship the Lord thy God, and him only shalt thou serve."

Satan had questioned whether Jesus was the Son of God. In his summary dismissal he had proof that he could not gainsay. He had no power to resist the command. Writhing with humiliation and rage, he was forced to withdraw from the presence of the world's Redeemer. Christ's victory was as complete as had been the failure of Adam.

Christ knew of the long years of conflict in the future between human beings and their subtle foe. He is the refuge of all who, beset by temptation, call upon Him. Temptation and trial will come to us all, but we need never be worsted by the enemy. Our Saviour has conquered in our behalf. Satan is not invincible. Day by day he meets those who are on trial, striving by his wiles to gain the mastery over them. His accusing power is great, and it is in this line that he wins more victories than in any other. Christ was tempted, that He might know how to help every soul that should afterward be tempted. Temptation is not sin; the sin lies in yielding. To the soul who trusts in Jesus, temptation means victory and greater strength.

Christ is ready to pardon all who come to Him confessing their sins. To the tried, struggling soul is spoken the word "Let him take hold of my strength, that he may make peace with me; and he shall make peace with me." Thank God, we have a high priest who is touched with the feelings of our infirmities, for He was in all points tempted as we are.—Manuscript 113, 1902.

July 31
JESUS GAINED THE VICTORY FOR US

◆ *The name of the Lord is a strong tower:*
the righteous runneth into it, and is safe.
Proverbs 18:10.

HERE was never a time when Christian men and women, in all walks of life, were in so great need of clear spiritual eyesight as now. It is not safe to lose sight of Christ for one moment. His followers must pray and believe and love Him fervently. . . .

Satan demanded of Christ a miracle as a sign of His divinity. But that which is greater than all miracles, a firm reliance upon a "Thus saith the Lord," was a sign that could not be controverted. So long as Christ held to this position, the tempter could gain no advantage.

It was in the time of greatest weakness that Christ was assailed by the fiercest temptations. Thus Satan thought to prevail. By this policy he had gained the victory over both men and women. When strength had failed and the willpower weakened, and faith ceased to repose in God, then those who had stood long and valiantly for the right were overcome. Moses was wearied with the forty years' wandering of Israel, when for the moment his faith let go its hold upon Infinite Power. He failed just upon the borders of the Promised Land. So with Elijah, who had stood undaunted before King Ahab; who had faced the whole nation of Israel with the four hundred fifty prophets of Baal at their head. After that terrible day upon Carmel when the false prophets had been slain and the people had declared their allegiance to God, Elijah fled for his life before the threats of idolatrous Jezebel. . . .

Whenever one is encompassed with clouds, perplexed by circumstances, or afflicted by poverty or distress, Satan is at hand to tempt and annoy. He attacks our weak points of character. He seeks to shake our confidence in God, who suffers such a condition of things to exist. We are tempted to distrust God, to question His love. . . .

Christ declared to the tempter, "Get thee behind me, Satan.". . . So we may resist temptation and force Satan to depart from us. Jesus gained the victory through submission and faith in God, and by the apostle He says to us, "Submit yourselves therefore to God. Resist the devil, and he will flee from you." We cannot save ourselves from the tempter's power; he has conquered humanity, and when we try to stand in our own strength, we shall become a prey to his devices; but "the name of the Lord is a strong tower: the righteous runneth into it, and is safe." Satan trembles and flees before the weakest soul who finds refuge in that mighty name.— Manuscript 15, 1908.

August 1
BELIEVE THAT CHRIST WILL GIVE US POWER TO OVERCOME

◆ *For we are his workmanship, created in Christ Jesus unto good works, which God hath before ordained that we should walk in them. Ephesians 2:10.*

*I*N your efforts to overcome, you will meet with many temptations; but if you continue to strive, Christ will give you great success. The more serious the trials, the more precious the victory you gain. If you will only flee to the Source of your strength, then you will receive a great blessing. But we must learn to cast all our cares upon Jesus Christ, who is our helper. All our sorrow and grief, take it to the Lord in prayer.

It is a great thing to believe in Jesus. We hear many say, "Believe, believe, all you have to do is to believe in Jesus." But it is our privilege to inquire, What does this belief take in, and what does it comprehend? There are many of us who have a nominal faith, but we do not bring that faith into our characters. The statement is made that the devil believed and trembled. While he was in heaven, he believed that Christ was the Son of God, and when upon this earth he was in conflict with Him here on the field of battle. He believed on Christ, but could this save him? No; because he did not weave Christ into his life and character. We must have that faith that works by love and purifies the soul, and this belief in Christ will lead us to put away everything that is offensive in His sight.

Unless we have this faith that works, it is of no advantage to us. You may admit that Christ is the Saviour of the world, but is He your Saviour? Do you believe today that He will give you strength and power to overcome every defect in your character? . . . We are to grow up to the full stature of men and women in Christ Jesus, and we are thus growing up a precious temple unto the Lord. He says, "I will dwell in them, and walk in them; and I will be their God, and they shall be my people.". . .

It makes every difference with us whether we are living righteously or in sin. To some of us Christ may say that He is ashamed to call us brothers and sisters; but to those who are loaded down with burdens, the pitying Saviour stands right by their side to help them. . . .

He took our nature upon Him, that He might come right down to us in the temptation wherewith we are beset. . . . Then shall we not accept Him as our Saviour? If you feel the wound and sting of sin, then it is for you to cry to the Saviour to help you.—Manuscript 5, 1886.

August 2
ALL MAY KNOW
GOD THE FATHER

◆ *For by grace are ye saved through faith; . . .*
it is the gift of God. Ephesians 2:8.

*J*ESUS Christ is our spiritual touchstone. He reveals the Father. . . . The mind must be prepared to appreciate the work and words of Christ, for He came from heaven to awaken a desire and to give the bread of life to all who hunger for spiritual knowledge. Inspiration declared that His mission was to preach the gospel to the poor, and to proclaim the acceptable year of the Lord. His Word declared that He should set judgment on the earth, and that the isles should wait for His law; that Gentiles should come to His light, and kings to the brightness of His rising. This was the Messenger of the Covenant yet to come, the Son of Righteousness yet to rise upon our world.

Adam and Eve were formed in the image of God. But Satan worked constantly to destroy the divine similitude. The holy pair yielded to temptation, and God's image was obliterated. Christ put His hand a second time to the work. He would re-create human beings. When the fullness of time came, God sent forth His Son. Hear, O heaven, and be astonished, O earth! The appointed Instructor appears, and He is no other than the Son of God; His divinity was clothed with humanity.

Christ came to reveal perfection amid the imperfection of a world corrupted by disobedience and sin. The eternal Word appeared in human form, bringing with Him all grace, all healing, all efficiency. He brought with Him the bread of life, which, if received, will be to us as the tree of life. The Inspired Word declares of this Teacher, "For Moses truly said unto the fathers, A prophet shall the Lord your God raise up unto you of your brethren, like unto me; him shall ye hear in all things whatsoever he shall say unto you. And it shall come to pass, that every soul, which will not hear that prophet, shall be destroyed from among the people."

The question of how to obtain a knowledge of God is to all a life-and-death question. Read Christ's prayer to His Father, intended not merely as an important lesson in education for the disciples, but to come down through all time for the benefit of those who would read the Inspired Writings. "Father," He prayed, "the hour is come; glorify thy Son, that thy Son also may glorify thee: as thou hast given him power over all flesh, that he should give eternal life to as many as thou hast given him. And this is life eternal, that they might know thee the only true God, and Jesus Christ, whom thou hast sent."—Manuscript 15, 1898.

August 3
HE WHO MADE THE WORLDS BECAME A HELPLESS BABE

◆ *And the child grew, and waxed strong in spirit, filled with wisdom: and the grace of God was upon him. Luke 2:40.*

E cannot understand how Christ became a little helpless babe. . . . His face could have been bright with light, and His form could have been tall and beautiful. He could have come in such a way as to charm those who looked upon Him; but this was not the way that God planned He should come among the human family. He was to be like those who belonged to the human family and to the Jewish race. His features were to be like those of other human beings, and He was not to have such beauty of person as to make people point Him out as different from others. He was to come as one of the human family, and to stand as a man before heaven and earth. He had come to take our place, to pledge Himself in our behalf, to pay the debt that sinners owed. He was to live a pure life on the earth, and show that Satan had told a falsehood when he claimed that the human family belonged to him forever, and that God could not take the race out of his hands.

People first beheld Christ as a babe, as a child. His parents were very poor, and He had nothing in this earth save that which the poor have. He passed through all the trials that the poor and lowly pass through from babyhood to childhood, from youth to manhood. . . .

The more we think about Christ's becoming a babe here on earth, the more wonderful it appears. How can it be that the helpless babe in Bethlehem's manger is still the divine Son of God? Though we cannot understand it, we can believe that He who made the worlds became, for our sakes, a helpless babe. Though higher than any of the angels, though as great as the Father on the throne of heaven, He became one with us. In Him God and humanity became one, and it is in this fact that we find the hope of our fallen race. . . .

From His earliest year, Christ lived a life of toil. In His youth He worked with His father at the carpenter's trade, and thus showed that there is nothing of which to be ashamed in work. . . . Those who are idle do not follow the example that Christ has given, for from His childhood He was a pattern of obedience and industry. He was as a pleasant sunbeam in the home circle. Faithfully and cheerfully He acted His part, doing the humble duties that He was called to do in His lowly life. Christ became one with us in order that He might do us good.—*Youth's Instructor, Nov. 21, 1895.*

August 4
CHRIST "GREW IN KNOWLEDGE" GOING ABOUT HIS FATHER'S BUSINESS

◆ *Wist ye not that I must be about my Father's business? Luke 2:49.*

VERY year His parents went to the city of Jerusalem to attend the feast of the Passover, and in His twelfth year Jesus went with them to the city. When the feast was over, the parents, forgetting all about Jesus, started on their road home with some of their relations, and did not know that Jesus was not with them. They supposed that He was in the company, and went a whole day's journey before they found out that He was not there. Frightened as to what had become of Him, they turned back to the city. . . .

Jesus knew that God had given Him this opportunity to give light to those who were in darkness, and He sought to do all in His power to open the truth to the rabbis and teachers. He led these men to speak about different verses in the Bible telling about the Messiah whom they expected to come. They thought that Christ was to come to the world in great glory at this time, and make the Jewish nation the greatest nation on the earth. But Jesus asked them what the Scriptures meant when they spoke of the humble life, the suffering and sorrow, the rejection and death, of the Son of God. Though Christ seemed like a child that was seeking help from those who knew a great deal more than He did, He was bringing light to their minds in every word He spoke. . . .

While Christ was teaching others, He Himself was receiving light and knowledge about His own work and mission in the world, for it is plainly stated that Christ "grew in knowledge." What a lesson there is in this for all the youth of our day! They may be like Christ, and by studying the Word of God, by receiving the light that the Holy Spirit can give them, they will be able to give light to others. . . .

The wise men were surprised at the questions that the child Jesus asked. . . . When there was a pause, Mary, the mother of Jesus, came up to her son and asked, "Son, why hast thou thus dealt with us? behold, thy father and I have sought thee sorrowing." Then a divine light shone from Jesus' face, as He lifted His hand and said, "How is it that ye sought me? wist ye not that I must be about my Father's business?". . . They did not know what He really meant by these words, but they knew He was a true son, who would be submissive to their commands. Though He was the Son of God, He went down to Nazareth and was subject to His parents.—*Youth's Instructor,* Nov. 28, 1895.

August 5
**JESUS AN
EXAMPLE
TO CHILDREN
AND YOUTH**

◆ *And Jesus increased in wisdom and
stature, and in favour with God and man.
Luke 2:52.*

*A*S Jesus looked upon the offerings that were brought
as a sacrifice to the temple, the Holy Spirit taught Him that His life was to
be sacrificed for the life of the world. . . . From His earliest years He was
guarded by heavenly angels; yet His life was one long struggle against the
powers of darkness. Satan sought in every way to tempt and try Him. He
caused people to misunderstand His words, so that they might not receive
the salvation He came to bring them. He was opposed both at home and
abroad, not because He was an evildoer, but because His life was free from
every taint of sin, and condemned all impurity. . . .

His stainless life was a rebuke, and many avoided His presence; but
there were some who sought to be with Him because they felt at peace where
He was. He was gentle, and never contended for His rights; but His own
brethren scorned and hated Him, showing that they did not believe in Him,
and casting contempt upon Him. . . . He lived above the difficulties of His
life, as if in the light of God's countenance. He bore insult patiently, and in
His human nature became an example for all children and youth. . . .

His life was as leaven, working amid the elements of society. Harmless
and undefiled He walked amid the careless, the thoughtless, the rude and
unholy. He mingled with the unjust publicans, the reckless prodigals, the
unrighteous Samaritans, the heathen soldiers, the rough peasants, and the
mixed multitudes. . . . He treated every human being as having great value.
He taught people to look upon themselves as persons to whom had been
given precious talents that, if rightly used, would elevate and ennoble
them, and secure for them eternal riches. By His example and character
He taught that every moment of life was precious, as a time in which to
sow seed for eternity.—*Youth's Instructor*, Dec. 12, 1895.

Jesus carried the burden of the salvation of the human family upon
His heart. He knew that unless people would receive Him, and become
changed in purpose and life, they would be eternally lost. This was the
burden of His soul, and He was alone in carrying this load. . . . From His
youth He was filled with a deep longing to be a lamp in the world, and He
purposed that His life should be "the light of the world." This He was, and
that light still shines to all who are in darkness. Let us walk in the light that
He has given.—*Ibid.*, Jan. 2, 1896.

August 6
JESUS PRESENTED TRUTH BY USING FAMILIAR OBJECTS

◆ *All these things spake Jesus unto the multitude in parables. Matthew 13:34.*

HE great Teacher proclaimed the truth to humanity, many of whom could not be educated in the schools of the rabbis, neither in Greek philosophy. Jesus uttered truth in a plain, direct manner, giving vital force and impressiveness to all His utterances. . . .

The rabbis and teachers had virtually shut up the kingdom of heaven from the poor and the afflicted, and left them to perish. In His discourses Christ did not bring many things before them at once, lest He might confuse their minds. He made every point clear and distinct. . . .

Christ was the originator of all the ancient gems of truth. Through the work of the enemy these truths had been displaced. They had been disconnected from their true position and placed in the framework of error. Christ's work was to readjust and establish the precious gems in the framework of truth. The principles of truth that had been given by Himself to bless the world had, through Satan's agency, been buried and had apparently become extinct. Christ rescued them from the rubbish of error, gave them a new, vital force, and commanded them to shine as precious jewels and stand fast forever. Christ Himself could use any of these old truths without borrowing the smallest particle, for He had originated them all. . . .

As Christ presented these truths to minds, He broke up their accustomed train of thought as little as possible. . . . He therefore aroused their minds by presenting truth through the agency of their most familiar associations. He used illustrations in His teaching that called into activity their most hallowed recollections and sympathies, that He might reach the inner temple of the soul. Identifying Himself with their interests, He drew His illustrations from the great book of nature, using objects with which they were familiar. The lily of the field, the seed sown by the sower, the springing up of the seed, and the harvesting of the grain, the birds of the air—all these figures He used to present divine truth, for these would remind them of His lessons whenever they should afterward look upon them. . . .

Although Satan has misrepresented God's purposes, falsified His character, and caused people to look upon God in a false light, yet through the ages God's love for His earthly children has never ceased. Christ's work was to reveal the Father as merciful, compassionate, full of goodness and truth. . . . The only begotten Son of God sweeps back the hellish shadow in which Satan has enveloped the Father, and declares, "I and My Father are one; look on Me and behold God."—Manuscript 25, 1890 (*Manuscript Releases*, vol. 13, pp. 240-243).

August 7
**PREFER TRADI-
TION RATHER
THAN OBEDIENCE
TO GOD'S LAW**

◆ *And he said unto them, Full well ye reject the commandment of God, that ye may keep your own tradition. Mark 7:9.*

*T*HE most learned men in the days of Christ—philosophers, legislators, priests, in all their pride and superiority—could not interpret God's character. . . . When, in the fullness of time, Christ came to our world, it was darkened and marred by the curse of apostasy and spiritual wickedness. The Jews had wrapped themselves about with the dark mantle of unbelief. They kept not the commandments of God. . . .

Those whom He addressed regarded themselves as exalted above all other peoples. To them, they proudly boasted, had been committed the oracles of God. The earth was languishing for a teacher sent from God, but when He came just as the living Oracles specified He would come, the priests and instructors of the people could not discern that He was their Saviour, nor could they understand the manner of His coming. Unaccustomed to accept God's Word exactly as it reads, or to allow it to be its own interpreter, they read it in the light of their maxims and traditions. So long had they neglected to study and contemplate the Bible that its pages were to them a mystery. They turned with aversion from the truth of God to the traditions of men.

The Jewish nation had reached a critical time in its history. Much was at stake. Would human ignorance give way? Would there be a thirsting for a deeper knowledge of God? Would this thirst develop into a longing for spiritual drink, as the thirst of David developed into a longing for water from the well of Bethlehem? Would the Jews turn from the influence of false teachers, which had perverted their senses, and call upon God for divine instruction? . . .

When Christ came as a human being, a flood of light was shed upon the world. Many would have received Him gladly, choosing to walk in the light, if the priests and the rulers had only been true to God and had guided the people aright by giving to them a true interpretation of the truths of the Word. But so long had the leaders misapplied the Scriptures that the people were misled by falsehoods. . . .

The Jews, as a nation, refused to accept Christ. They turned from the only One who could have saved them from eternal ruin. A similar condition of things exists in the so-called Christian world today. People who claim to understand the Scriptures are rejecting God's law and exerting a strong, determined influence against it. . . . What is the result? Look at the course of the youth growing up around us.—Manuscript 24, 1891 (*Manuscript Releases*, vol. 19, pp. 252-254).

August 8
MORTALS CAN OVERCOME ONLY THROUGH CHRIST

◆ *I will write upon him the name of my God, and the name of the city of my God, which is new Jerusalem, which cometh down out of heaven from my God: and I will write upon him my new name. Revelation 3:12.*

EVER will the human family—redeemed by the example of the Sent of God, the only begotten of the Father—understand and fully comprehend the terrible conflict waged with deceptive, alluring power and concealed, deadly hatred by Satan against our Lord when He lived upon earth. After the battle of the great day of God shall take place, when the power of rebellion is forever broken and Christ's mediatorial work in its magnitude is represented so plainly that all of the redeemed of God's family shall, with clear comprehension, understand the mission of His Son as the mediatorial remedy to make of the fallen race a repentant, humble, meek, reclaimed order of beings—then there will be seen developed the difference between the person that serveth God and the one that serveth Him not.

Rebellion will exist in our world until in heaven are spoken the words "It is done." Rebellion in the church is caused by its members feeling opposed to God and to His terms of salvation. Human beings want abundant room to express themselves and to attract attention. They do not know or understand that they are working out the plans of Satan. If they refuse to see and to become enlightened, if they refuse to be instructed, they reject the mediatorial remedy that has been given to save the sinner—not in sin but from sin. For the express purpose of saving sinners was the remedial work of Christ planned.

When Christ first announced to the heavenly host His mission and work in the world, He declared that He was to leave His position of dignity and disguise His holy mission by assuming the likeness of a man, when in reality He was the Son of the infinite God. And when the fullness of time was come, He stepped down from His throne of highest command, laid aside His royal robe and kingly crown, clothed His divinity with humanity, and came to this earth to exemplify what humanity must do and be in order to overcome the enemy and to sit with the Father upon His throne. . . . He made it possible for Himself to be buffeted by human agencies inspired by Satan, the rebel who had been expelled from heaven.

As the head of humanity, Christ lived on this earth a perfect, consistent life, in conformity with the will of His heavenly Father. . . . Always uppermost in His mind and heart was the thought "Not My human will, but Thy will, be done."—Letter 303, 1903.

August 9
JESUS TAUGHT BY
BOTH WORDS
AND EXAMPLE

◆ *For neither did his brethren believe in him. John 7:5.*

HE people saw that the Holy Spirit was resting upon Jesus at the age of twelve. He felt something of the burden of the mission for which He had come to our world. . . .

He understands the temptations of children, for He bore their sorrows and trials. Firm and steadfast was His purpose to do the right; though others tried to lead Him to do evil, yet He never did wrong, and would not turn away in the least from the path of truth and right. He always obeyed His parents, and did every duty that lay in His path.

But His childhood and youth were anything but smooth and joyous. His spotless life aroused the envy and jealousy of His brethren, for they did not believe on Him. They were annoyed because He did not act in all things as they did and would not become one with them in doing evil.—*Youth's Instructor,* Nov. 28, 1895.

Because He was so quick to see what was false and what was true, His brethren were greatly annoyed at Him, for they said that whatever the priest taught ought to be considered as sacred as a command of God. But Jesus taught both by His words and by His example that people ought to worship God just as He has directed them to worship Him, and not follow the ceremonies that religious leaders have said ought to be followed. . . .

The priests and the Pharisees also were annoyed because this Child would not accept their human inventions, maxims, and traditions. . . . Failing to convince Him that He ought to look upon human traditions as sacred, they came to Joseph and Mary and complained that Jesus was taking a wrong course in regard to their customs and traditions. Jesus knew what it was to have His family divided against Him on account of His religious faith. He loved peace; He craved the love and confidence of the members of His family; but He knew what it was to have them withdraw their affection from Him. He suffered rebuke and censure because He took a straightforward course and would not do evil because others did evil, but was true to the commandments of Jehovah. . . .

The scribes, rabbis, and Pharisees could not force Jesus to turn from the Word of God and follow human traditions, but they could influence His brethren in such a way that His life might become a very bitter one. His brethren threatened Him and sought to compel Him to take a wrong course, but He passed on, making the Scriptures His guide.—*Ibid.,* Dec. 5, 1895.

August 10
JESUS CARES ABOUT HUMAN PROBLEMS AND PERPLEXITIES

◆ *The steward called the bridegroom and said to him, "Everyone serves the good wine first, and then the inferior wine after the guests have become drunk. But you have kept the good wine until now." John 2:10, NRSV.*

*T*HE joyous festivities of a Jewish wedding were preceded by solemn religious ceremonies. In preparation for their new relationship, the parties performed certain rites of purification and confessed their sins.

A most interesting part of the ceremony took place in the evening when the bridegroom went to meet his bride and bring her to his home. At the house of the bride a company of invited guests awaited the appearance of the bridegroom. As he approached, the cry went forth, "Behold, the bridegroom cometh; go ye out to meet him." The bride, clothed in pure white, her head encircled with flowers, received the bridegroom, and, accompanied by the guests, they went from her father's house. By torchlight, with impressive display, with sounds of singing and instruments of music, the procession slowly proceeded to the house of the bridegroom, where a feast was provided for the guests.

For the feast the best food that could be secured was provided. Unfermented wine was used as a beverage. It was the custom of the time for marriage festivities to continue several days. On this occasion, before the feast ended it was found that the supply of wine had failed. When a call was made for more wine, Jesus' mother, thinking that He might suggest something to relieve the embarrassment, came to Him and said, "They have no wine.". . . The active part that Mary took in this feast indicates that she was not merely a guest, but a relative of one of the parties. As one having authority, she said to the servants, "Whatsoever he saith unto you, do it.". . .

Jesus said unto them, "Fill the waterpots with water. And they filled them up to the brim. And he saith unto them, Draw out now, and bear unto the governor of the feast.". . . The action of Christ at this time was left on record for all ages, that we might see that Christ did not fail even in such a perplexity as arose on this occasion. Yet He never worked a miracle to help Himself. A few days before this He had refused to satisfy His own hunger by changing a stone into bread at Satan's suggestion.—Manuscript 126, 1903.

August 11
WATER TO WINE

◆ *This beginning of miracles did Jesus in Cana of Galilee, and manifested forth his glory; and his disciples believed on him. John 2:11.*

*J*ESUS Christ is the originator of all missionary work done in our world. He worked miracles to heal the sick, but He never worked a miracle in His own behalf. His first noted miracle was performed at a marriage feast in Cana, when He turned water into wine. . . .

By this miracle Christ wished to teach that unfermented wine is far preferable to fermented wine. Christ never created fermented wine. The wine made on this occasion was exactly like the wine that comes fresh from the cluster. Christ knew the influence of fermented wine, and by giving them pure, unfermented wine, He showed them the only safe way in which to use grape juice.

Christ did not draw attention to this act to receive public notice. He wished to teach an important lesson. He did not make or use fermented wine. . . . Christ did turn water into wine, but He used wine fresh from the grapes, and never any other. He is our example in all things, and before His death He left as a last legacy to His church the bread, representing His body given for the sins of the world, and the wine, representing His spilt blood. But nothing but unleavened bread and unfermented wine could be used. Nothing of a fermented character is to be used in the Communion service, for fermented wine would destroy the figure representing the blood of Christ. We may all look upon this question as forever settled.

Christ wrought this miracle to teach still another lesson. He would not yield to the enemy when tempted to perform a miracle to supply His own necessities by converting a stone into bread. But on the occasion of the marriage feast He desired to express His sympathy with, and approval of, those at the wedding. Christ did not come to this world to forbid marriage or to break down or destroy the relationship and influence that exist in the domestic circle. He came to restore, elevate, purify, and ennoble every current of pure affection, that the family on earth might become a symbol of the family in heaven. In the Christian home the grace of God is to subdue and transform human character, and then the church will become an active, living, working church. In such families the song may well be sung, "There are angels hovering round; there are angels hovering round. Go, carry the tidings home."—Manuscript 22, 1898.

August 12
THE LIVING WATER COMES FROM JESUS

◆ *There cometh a woman of Samaria to draw water: Jesus saith unto her, Give me to drink. John 4:7.*

ONSIDER how circumstances that occur bring truth before the minds of others. Call to mind the woman of Samaria who came, as was her usual custom, to draw water. A stranger sitting on the well asks her for a drink. A conversation begins. Jesus says to her, "If thou knewest the gift of God, and who it is that saith to thee, Give me to drink; thou wouldst have asked of him, and he would have given thee living water." "Whosoever drinketh of this water shall thirst again: but whosoever drinketh of the water that I shall give him shall never thirst; but the water that I shall give him shall be in him a well of water springing up into everlasting life."

Remembering the weary work that she had to repeat day after day, and thinking what an advantage it would be if she could have water without all this trouble, the woman said, "Sir, give me this water, that I thirst not, neither come hither to draw." She did not realize that Jesus was presenting to her the soul's highest interest, the water of life.

The words spoken by Christ were the living water. But she soon became so interested that she left her water pot and, going into the city, bore the words to her countrymen, "Come, see a man, which told me all things that ever I did: is not this the Christ?"

The woman had come for water, and she heard of the water of life. She had been convinced of sin, and believed on Jesus Christ. Thus the holy oil is emptied, by the holy messengers represented by the two olive trees, into the golden tubes and from thence into the golden bowls. The emptying process goes on, from the receiving of the golden oil to the communicating of the same to others. Words are spoken; the unconscious influences that surround the soul are felt, although no words are designedly spoken. A word may be often spoken that will be as seed sown. . . .

The Lord has made ample provision that the heavenly graces shall be abundantly supplied to all, that the truth as it is in Jesus shall hold the first place in the heart and shall ever occupy the soul temple. Then there will be thorough devotion to God, and all true believers will become fishers of men. They will pray for wisdom, and will walk in accordance with the prayer: "Ye are the light of the world." "Let your light so shine before men, that they may see your good works, and glorify your Father which is in heaven."—Letter 48, 1897.

August 13
**NO POSITION
TOO LOWLY TO
BE HONORABLE
IN CHRIST**

◆ *Is not this the carpenter, the son of Mary,
the brother of James, and Joses, and of Juda,
and Simon? and are not his sisters here with
us? And they were offended at him. Mark 6:3.*

HRIST'S life of humiliation should be a lesson to all who desire to exalt themselves above others. Though He had no taint of sin upon His character, yet He condescended to connect our fallen human nature with His divinity. . . .

In humility Christ began His mighty work of lifting the fallen race from the degradation of sin, recovering them by His divine power, which He had linked with humanity. Passing by the grand cities and the renowned places of learning and supposed wisdom, He made His home in the humble and obscure village of Nazareth. The greater part of His life was passed in this place, from which it was commonly believed that no good could come. In the path that the poor, the neglected, the suffering, and the sorrowing must tread, He walked while on earth, taking upon Him all the woes that the afflicted must bear. . . . His family was not distinguished by learning, riches, or position. For many years He worked at His trade as a carpenter.

The Jews had proudly boasted that Christ was to come as a king, to conquer His enemies and tread down the heathen in His wrath. But the humble, submissive life our Saviour led, which should have enshrined Him in the hearts of the people and given them confidence in His mission, offended and disappointed the Jews, and we all know of the treatment He received from them. . . .

Christ did not exalt people by ministering to their pride. He humbled Himself, and became obedient to death, even the death of the cross. Unless human pride is humbled and subdued, unless the stubborn heart is made tender by the Spirit of Christ, it is not possible for Him to impress His divine similitude upon us. He, the humble Nazarene, might have poured contempt upon the world's pride, for He was commander in the heavenly courts. But He came to our world in humility, in order to show that it is not riches or position or authority or honorable titles that the universe of heaven respects and honors, but those who will follow Christ, making any position of duty honorable by the virtue of their character through the power of His grace.

No human being is warranted to uplift self in pride. "For thus saith the high and lofty One that inhabiteth eternity, whose name is Holy; I dwell in the high and holy place, with him also that is of a contrite and humble spirit, to revive the spirit of the humble, and to revive the heart of the contrite ones."—Letter 81, 1896.

August 14
CHRIST WILL CREATE A NEW HEART IN HIS FOLLOWERS

◆ *Jesus answered and said unto him, Verily, verily, I say unto thee, Except a man be born again, he cannot see the kingdom of God. John 3:3.*

*T*HE change that must come to the natural, inherited, and cultivated tendencies of the human heart is that change of which Jesus spoke when He said to Nicodemus, "Except a man be born again, he cannot see the kingdom of God.". . . He virtually said to Nicodemus, It is not controversy that will help your case. Arguments will not bring light to your soul. You must have a new heart, or you cannot discern the kingdom of heaven. It is not greater evidence that will bring you into a right position, but new purposes, new springs of action. You must be born again. Until this change takes place, until all things are made new, the strongest evidence that could be presented would be useless. . . .

To Nicodemus this was a very humiliating statement, and with a feeling of irritation he took up the words of Christ, saying, "How can a man be born when he is old?". . . But the Saviour did not meet argument with argument. Raising His hand in solemn, quiet dignity, He pressed home the truth with greater assurance, "Verily, verily, I say unto thee, Except a man be born of water and of the Spirit, he cannot enter into the kingdom of God.". . .

Christ's words conveyed the lesson that instead of feeling irritated over the plain words of truth and indulging in irony, Nicodemus should have a far more humble opinion of himself because of his spiritual ignorance. Yet the words of Christ were spoken with such solemn dignity, and both look and tone expressed such earnest love that Nicodemus was not offended as he realized his humiliating position. . . .

This lesson to Nicodemus I present as highly applicable to those who today are in responsible positions as rulers in Israel, and whose voices are often heard in council, giving evidence of the spirit that Nicodemus possessed. The words of Christ are spoken just as verily to presidents of conferences, elders of churches, and those occupying responsible positions in our churches. . . .

Nicodemus was converted as the result of this interview. In that night conference with Jesus, the convicted man stood before the Saviour under the softening, subduing influence of the truth that was shining into the chambers of his mind and impressing his heart. . . . Jesus told Nicodemus not only that he must have a new heart in order to see the kingdom of heaven, but how to obtain this new heart.—Letter 54, 1895.

August 15
**"NEVER MAN
SPAKE LIKE
THIS MAN"**

◆ *Then came the officers to the chief priests
and Pharisees; and they said unto them,
Why have ye not brought him? The officers
answered, Never man spake like this man.
John 7:45, 46.*

CHRIST came to this world just as the Old Testament
Scriptures foretold that He would come, but notwithstanding this, He was
misapprehended and misjudged. The Pharisees were filled with a frenzy of
hatred against Him, because they could see that His teaching had a power
and an attractiveness of which their words were utterly devoid. They decided that the only way to cut off His influence was to pass sentence of
death upon Him, and therefore they sent officers to take Him. But when
these officers came within hearing of His voice, and listened to His gracious words, they were charmed into forgetting their errand. . . .

"Are ye also deceived?" the elders asked. . . . Nicodemus saith unto
them, "Doth our law judge any man, before it hear him, and know what
he doeth?"

The lesson that Christ had given to Nicodemus had not been in vain.
Conviction had fastened upon his mind, and in his heart he had accepted
Jesus. Since his interview with the Saviour, he had earnestly searched the
Old Testament Scriptures, and he had seen truth placed in the setting of
the gospel.

The question asked by him was wise and would have commended itself to those presiding at the council had they not been deceived by the
enemy. But they were so filled with prejudice that no argument in favor of
Jesus of Nazareth, however convincing, had any weight with them. The
answer that Nicodemus received was "Art thou also of Galilee? Search, and
look; for out of Galilee ariseth no prophet."

The priests and rulers had been deceived, as Satan meant them to be,
into believing that Christ came out of Galilee. Some who knew that He
had been born in Bethlehem kept silent, that the falsehood might not be
robbed of its power.

The facts were plain. There was no dimness of the light. But the work
of Christ was interpreted by different ones in accordance with the state of
their minds. . . .

The Prince of Peace came to proclaim truth that was to bring harmony
out of confusion. But He who came to bring peace and goodwill started a
controversy that ended in His crucifixion.—Manuscript 31, 1889.

August 16
**WE ARE
SANCTIFIED
THROUGH THE
TRUTH IN JESUS**

◆ *Sanctify them through thy truth: thy word is truth. John 17:17.*

*E*VERY soldier engaged in the spiritual conflict must be brave in God. Those who are fighting the battles for the Prince of life must point their weapons of warfare outward, and not form a hollow square and aim their missiles of destruction at those who are serving under the banner of the Prince Emmanuel. We have no time for wounding and tearing down one another. How many there are who need to heed the words that Christ spoke to Nicodemus, . . . "Except a man be born of water and of the Spirit, he cannot enter into the kingdom of God.". . .

There are many who claim to be followers of Christ, whose names are enrolled on the church books, who have not been a strength to the church. They have not been sanctified through the truth. . . . It is not receiving the truth simply, but practicing the truth, that sanctifies the soul. Let those who would be sanctified through the truth search carefully and prayerfully both the Old and New Testaments that they may know what is truth. . . .

Those who are truly converted to Christ [must] keep on constant guard lest they shall accept error in place of truth. Those who think that it matters not what they believe in doctrine, so long as they believe in Jesus Christ, are on dangerous ground. There are some who think that they will be just as acceptable to God by obeying some other law than the law of God—by meeting some other conditions than those He has specified in the gospel—as if they obeyed His commandments and complied with His requirements. But they are under a fatal delusion, and unless they renounce this heresy and come into harmony with His requirements, they cannot become members of the royal family. . . .

Those who claim to be sanctified, and who give no heed to the words of divine authority spoken from Mount Sinai, make it manifest that they will not render to God the obedience that the Lawgiver requires. . . . "Without me," Christ says, "ye can do nothing." Provision for our perfection is found in union with Christ. "I in them, and thou in me, that they may be made perfect in one.". . .

What pleasure could [heaven] possibly be to souls who would not be drawn to Jesus in this life, to study His character and to be with Him in the life that is to come? They would prefer to be anywhere else than in the presence and companionship of Him in whom they have no delight. They did not know Him while in the world and could not learn to know Him in heaven.—Manuscript 40, 1894.

August 17
THE LORD TRUSTS US TO SOW GOOD SEED FOR A GOOD HARVEST

◆ *The kingdom of heaven may be compared to someone who sowed good seed in his field; but while everybody was asleep, an enemy came and sowed weeds among the wheat, and then went away. Matthew 13:24, 25, NRSV.*

*T*HE Lord has a work to do in our world, but He will not trust His work in the hands of people who know nothing of the Bible or of the mysteries of the kingdom of heaven. The Lord presents in parables the rise and progress of the work that results from the preaching of His Word, the present truth for this time. He brings before us the fashioning of a church that shall stand before the world as chosen and faithful. The parable of the sower shows the manner in which we should work. The work of the gospel ministry is the sowing of the seed. . . .

The parable of the wheat and the tares shows the mystery of the divine and the satanic agencies working in direct opposition, in vital conflict. The conflict continues till the close of this earth's history. The incorruptible seed is the living Word of God, which works in the personal sanctification of the receivers, elevating them by bringing them into the participation of the divine nature.

Many matters need to be considered. Those who have all their lifetime been the servants of sin, desiring to act in direct opposition to the divine will, need to be most thoroughly converted. Otherwise the leaven of evil will work under cover, as Satan appearing like an angel of light tempted Christ to oppose the divine will. God's great standard of righteousness is obnoxious to the tastes and appetites of sinful men and women. The active energy of the Saviour and that of the destroyer are in conflict.

The wheat is to be gathered for Christ's garner. The tares have the appearance of wheat, but when the harvest comes they must be rejected. Yet there is an imitation of the wheat through a long period of time. Satan puts forth a determined effort to deceive and lead into strange paths those who have any connection with the Word of God, and he will devise every possible scheme to lengthen the period of his control. The Lord God of heaven gives no sanction to mix and corrupt church associations. The Lord would have His work in the preaching of the gospel so done that there will be no encouragement to evil workers, no toleration of evil associations in Christian assemblies.—Manuscript 7, 1900.

August 18
CHRIST HEALED THE PALSIED MAN AND FORGAVE HIS SINS

◆ *And, behold, they brought to him a man sick of the palsy, lying on a bed: and Jesus seeing their faith said unto the sick of the palsy; Son, be of good cheer; thy sins be forgiven thee. Matthew 9:2.*

WHEN Jesus came as a man to our world, Satan had led the Jews into the practice of a religion that pleased the powers of darkness. The professed people of God had departed from God and were following another leader. Through their own perversity, they were going on to destruction, but Christ came to dispute the authority of Satan. . . .

The life of Christ was made one long scene of conflict. Satan stirred up the evil hearts of people, and set envy and prejudice at work against the Son of God, the Saviour of the world. He caused people to question and to doubt the word, works, and mission of Christ. . . . They [the Jews] followed Christ from place to place, in order that, if possible, they might catch some word from His lips to misstate, misconstrue, and publish abroad, giving it a meaning that had neither been expressed nor intended. Thus the way of Christ was hedged up by people who claimed to be just and holy. . . .

In this way Satan led people who might have been a power for Christ to work on the enemy's side in the controversy, and to become agents whereby he instilled into the hearts of the people questioning, suspicion, doubt, and hatred. . . .

The leaders of the people were ever watching for an excuse for their attitude of unbelief, and when He wrought His most convincing miracles, they were ready to catch up anything that would appear like an objection to His divine claims. When Jesus had healed the palsied man, He had said to him, "Son, thy sins be forgiven thee.". . .

In the miracle that Christ had wrought, He had changed the man's heart and had renewed him in mind and body, thus demonstrating to the Pharisees the fact that He had power to forgive sins, and to bring righteousness and peace to the sinner. Yet the Pharisees saw in His words of divine power a matter for unbelief and accusation. . . . Jesus saw that however deeply rooted were the principles that were set in opposition to the principles He proclaimed, yet they were delusion and falsehood, and had originated in the enemy of all righteousness. Jesus said to the people, "Every one that is of the truth heareth my voice."—Manuscript 65, 1895 (*Signs of the Times*, Apr. 25, 1895).

August 19
HEART MUST BE REFILLED WITH LOVE OF GOD

◆ *Then goeth he, and taketh with himself seven other spirits more wicked than himself, and they enter in and dwell there. Matthew 12:45.*

*T*HE man in the parable broke with Satan, refused to do his work, but the trouble with him was that after the heart was swept and garnished he failed to invite the heavenly Guest. It is not enough to make the heart empty; we must have the vacuum filled with the love of God. The soul must be furnished with the graces of the Spirit of God. People may leave off many bad habits and yet not be truly sanctified, because they do not have a connection with God; they do not unite with Christ. . . .

Satan, the great rebel, is ever seeking to entice us to sin against God. He will introduce false imaginings, arming the understanding against the revealed will of God, the lower passions against purity and self-denial, the will against God's will, setting up a wisdom from beneath to conflict with the wisdom from above. . . . Shall God's will be put in the background and our will be held as supreme? Can this be the controlling power in God's great contest for the recovery of His own? . . .

I have been warned that henceforth we shall have a constant contest. Science, so-called, and religion will be placed in opposition to each other, because finite beings do not comprehend the power and greatness of God. These words of Holy Writ were presented to me: "Of your own selves shall men arise, speaking perverse things, to draw away disciples after them." This will surely be seen among the people of God. There will be those who are unable to perceive the most wonderful and important truths for this time, truths that are essential for their own safety and salvation, while matters that are in comparison as the merest atoms, matters in which there is scarcely a grain of truth, are dwelt upon and magnified by the power of Satan so that they appear of the utmost importance. . . .

As the lovers of the world make religion subservient to the world, God requires His worshipers to subordinate the world to religion.—Manuscript 16, 1890.

August 20
**THE TOUCH OF
FAITH IS HEALING**

◆ *But Jesus turned him about, and when he saw her, he said, Daughter, be of good comfort; thy faith hath made thee whole. Matthew 9:22.*

*S*ATAN is the destroyer; the Lord is the Restorer. The Lord has not worked as a physician in the way that He desires to work, because, He says, Ye will not come to Me, that I may give you life. We look to every source for relief except to the One who proclaimed over the rent sepulcher of Joseph, "I am the resurrection, and the life." . . .

Christ met one poor soul who had spent all her living in order that she might be cured of a physical malady. The statement is that she had spent all that she had on many physicians, and was nothing better, but rather made worse. But one touch of Christ by faith took away the infirmity of long years. This suffering woman came behind Christ and touched His garment, [having] faith in the Person whom the garment covered, and instantly she was made whole. "Who touched me?" said Christ. Peter was astonished. He answered, "Thou seest the multitude thronging thee, and sayest thou, Who touched me?"

Christ desired to give a lesson that all present would never forget. He would show the difference between the touch of living faith and a casual touch. He said, "Somebody hath touched me: for I perceive that virtue is gone out of me." When the woman saw that she could not be hid, she came forward trembling, and throwing herself at His feet, told her pitiful story. Christ comforted her. "Daughter," He said, "thy faith hath made thee whole; go in peace, and be whole of thy plague."

Why do we not come to Jesus in faith? Many give Him a casual touch, coming in contact only with His person. The woman did more than this. She put forth her hand in faith and was healed instantly. . . . The friends of the truth will honor Him who is the Author and Finisher of their faith. Christ will prove Himself a physician in restoring the body as well as the soul. The workers together with God will yoke up with Christ and place themselves, soul, body, and spirit, in right relation to God. . . .

The will of men, women, and children must be trained by cooperation with God. . . . The melody of spiritual joy, and spiritual as well as physical health, will be revealed and will promote that blessedness that the Lord Jesus came to our world to impart to every individual who will believe.—Letter 106, 1898.

August 21
THE SERMON ON THE MOUNT

◆ *And seeing the multitudes, he went up into a mountain: and when he was set, his disciples came unto him. Matthew 5:1.*

HRIST'S sermon on the mount was designed to enter into our everyday life. The commandments are so broad that they take hold of even our thoughts. But how few take heed to the words of our Saviour! Consequently we shall have objections to meet. Some will claim that they are wholly led by the Spirit, and consequently they have not much use for the law of God or any portion of God's Word. Those who claim great light and are not sanctified through the truth are dangerous people, but they can be easily tested. "To the law and to the testimony: if they speak not according to this word, it is because there is no light in them." Isaiah 8:20. . . .

We must expect to be assailed by the powers of darkness, but if we successfully resist, then there will be rejoicing in heaven. The souls of human beings are valued by the heavenly host. . . . We must not be under anyone's banner but Christ's.—Manuscript 45, 1886.

Christ spake as never man spake. To the multitude that listened to His sermon on the mount—His lessons illustrated by things with which they were familiar—the law of God, with its living, matchless principles, was brought home to their minds and consciences. Among the thousands who were converted in a day, after Christ had risen from the tomb and ascended to the Father, were the very ones who had heard and believed the words spoken on that occasion.

As Jesus stood among the people, clothed with the garb of humanity, He longed to unfold to His disciples the deep mysteries of the plan of redemption; but with sadness He was forced to say, "I have yet many things to say unto you, but ye cannot bear them now." The temporal, the earthly, was so mingled in their minds with the spiritual and the eternal that the sacred and heavenly were eclipsed. . . .

The soul must be infused with the Spirit of the great Teacher if the mind would penetrate into the deep things of God. The truth will enlarge and enrich the mind. Its beauty, its purity, its holiness, [and] its invigorating power, will inspire the receivers, and they will not be content to be circumscribed in their work. The yearning soul will cry out after the living God, Show me Thy glory.—Manuscript 104, 1898.

August 22
PURE, UNSELFISH FAITH HONORED BY HEAVEN

◆ *There came unto him a centurion, beseeching him, and saying, Lord, my servant lieth at home sick of the palsy, grievously tormented. And Jesus saith unto him, I will come and heal him. Matthew 8:5-7.*

HE centurion felt his unworthiness. He was a man of contrite spirit although he was a man of authority. He felt unworthy to have Jesus Christ, with His miracle-working power, come under his roof, but His word spoken would be all that was essential, just as the centurion could say to his soldiers under him, "Go, and he goeth; and to another, Come, and he cometh; and to my servant, Do this, and he doeth it."

He had confidence in the merely spoken words of Christ to restore his servant. When Jesus heard it, He marveled. "Verily I say unto you, I have not found so great faith, no, not in Israel.". . .

The Jewish nation would not receive their promised Messiah when He came in just the manner prophecies declared He would come. Here was a man, not professedly of Israel, who had not had the opportunities that Israel had abundantly received, who in faith and appreciation of Christ was far in advance of the people of Israel, whom the Lord had made the repository of most sacred, precious truth.

Who were Israelites indeed—Jew or Gentile, barbarian, Scythian, bond or free? Jesus "was in the world, and the world was made by him, and the world knew him not. He came unto his own, and his own received him not." John 1:10, 11. But this Roman, a commander in authority, came to Jesus with a most earnest entreaty for one of his servants, sick of palsy, grievously tormented with pain. His faith in its simplicity was a pure, unselfish faith. He asks not of Jesus, "Show me a sign from heaven," but solicits Him to work a cure for his suffering servant. He tells Him he feels unworthy to have Him come under his roof. He who dwells in the high and lofty place, yet will He come and make His abode with the humble and contrite in heart. . . .

Let people receive the light as presented in the Word of God, in truth, and there will be a steadfastness of purpose that will enable them to stand erect in moral independence amid difficulties and danger. A character is formed, barricaded by truth—a character that will abide the day of trial and test before us, however dark may be the pressure, however severe the tribulation that the day of God's preparation may bring forth. The principle of righteousness works outward from within and makes itself felt.—Letter 114, 1895.

August 23
JESUS WALKS WITH US THROUGH ALL THE STORMS OF LIFE

◆ *But straightway Jesus spake unto them, saying, Be of good cheer; it is I; be not afraid. Matthew 14:27.*

I was today to write upon Christ walking on the sea and stilling the tempest. . . . How vividly before my mind was the boat, with the disciples, buffeted by the waves. The night was dark and tempestuous. Their Master was absent. The sea was strong, the winds contrary. Had Jesus, their Saviour, been with them, they would have felt safe. All through the long and tedious night they bend to their oars, forcing their way against wind and waves. They are beset with danger and horror. These were strong men, accustomed to hardships and perils, and not easily intimidated with danger.

They had expected to take their Saviour on board the ship at a certain designated point, but how could they even reach that spot without Him? All [seemed] in vain, [for] the wind was against them. The strength of the rowers was exhausted, and yet the merciless storm had not abated, but was lashing the waves into a fury as though to engulf the boat and themselves. Oh, how they longed for Jesus. In the hour of their greatest peril, when they had given up all for lost, amid the lightning flashes in the fourth watch of the night Jesus is revealed to them walking upon the water. Oh, then, Jesus had not forgotten them. His watchful eye of tender sympathy and pitying love had watched them all through that fearful storm. In their greatest need He was close by them. . . .

At the very point when despair was taking the place of hope, when they felt that they were utterly deserted, the eye of the world's Redeemer was watching them with a compassion that was as tender as a mother watching over a suffering child, and this love is infinite. The disciples were at first affrighted, but above the roaring of the angry tempest is heard the words the disciples longed most to hear, "Be of good cheer, it is I; be not afraid." Their confidence is restored. "Jesus; it is Jesus!" was spoken from one to the other. "Be not afraid; it is Jesus, the Master."

Jesus said to winds and waves, to the troubled waters, "Peace, be still." Oh, how many times have we in our experience been in a similar position as were these disciples. How many times has Christ revealed Himself to us and turned our sorrow into joy. Oh, powerful Redeemer, gracious and compassionate Saviour, able with Thine infinite power to calm all tempests, able to revive all hearts. He is our Redeemer. We may trust Him in the storm as well as the sunshine.—Letter 5, 1876.

August 24
THE MESSIAH OF PROPHECY REJECTED

◆ *And he said, Verily I say unto you, No prophet is accepted in his own country. Luke 4:24.*

ITH what intense interest was this controversy watched by the heavenly angels and the unfallen worlds as the honor of the law was being vindicated. Not merely for this world, but for the universe of heaven and the worlds that God had created, was the controversy to be forever settled. The confederacy of darkness was watching for the semblance of a chance to rise and triumph over the divine and human Substitute and Surety of the human race, that the apostate might shout, Victory, and the world and its inhabitants forever become his kingdom. But Satan reached only the heel; he could not touch the head. Now he sees that his true character is clearly revealed before all heaven, and that the heavenly beings and the worlds that God has created would be wholly on the side of God. He sees that his prospects of future influence with them will be entirely cut off. Christ's humanity will demonstrate for eternal ages the question that settled the controversy. . . .

What was it that moved His own nation to throw such scorn upon Jesus? The Jews were expecting an earthly prince who would deliver them from the power that God had declared would rule over them if they refused to keep the way of the Lord and obey His statutes, His commandments, and His laws. They had made their proud boast that Israel's king, the star arising from Judah, would break their thraldom, and make of them a kingdom of priests.

But it was not the absence of external honor and riches and glory that caused the Jews to reject Jesus. The Sun of Righteousness shining amid the moral darkness in such distinct rays revealed the contrast between sin and holiness, purity and defilement, and such light was not welcome to them. . . .

That which Christ had specified would be His work was fulfilled. The sick were healed, demoniacs were restored, lepers and paralytics were made whole. The dumb spake, the ears of the deaf were opened, the dead were brought to life, and the poor had the gospel preached to them. . . . Every miracle wrought by Christ convinced some of them of His true character, which answered to the specifications of the Messiah of prophecy, but those who did not receive the light of heaven set themselves more determinedly against this evidence. . . .

The teachings of Christ, in precept and example, were the sowing of the seed to be afterward cultivated by His disciples.—Manuscript 143, 1897.

August 25
SINGING DRIVES BACK THE POWER OF SATAN

◆ *The Lord is my strength and my shield; my heart trusted in him, and I am helped: therefore my heart greatly rejoiceth; and with my song will I praise him. Psalm 28:7.*

HE Lord Jesus came to the world to live the life that it will be for the interest of every being on earth to live—that of humble obedience. Those to whom Christ has given a probation in which to form characters for the mansions He has gone to prepare are to enter into His life example. If they are indeed learners in the school of Christ, they will not exalt themselves because they are possessors of houses and lands, because the Lord has in His providence lent them His goods to trade upon. . . .

Christ took upon Him human nature, that He might be able to sympathize with all hearts. . . . His spirit was never so full of worldly cares that He had no time or thought for the heavenly. He could give evidence of His cheerfulness by singing psalms and heavenly songs. The people of Nazareth often heard His voice raised in praise and thanksgiving to God. He often held communion with heaven in song, and all who were associated with Him, who often complained of their weariness of labor, were cheered by the sweet melody that fell from His lips. His praises seemed to drive away the evil angels and, as incense, filled the room with sweet fragrance.

This, too, had its lesson. It taught that people could commune with God in words of holy song. Christ carried the minds of His hearers away from their earthy exile to their future eternal home. . . . The house of God may be very humble in comparison with the temple of Solomon, but it is no less acknowledged by God. To those who worship there it is the gate of heaven, if they worship God in spirit and in truth, and in the beauty of holiness. As songs of praise are sung, as earnest fervent prayers arise to heaven, as lessons are repeated of the wondrous works of God, as the heart's gratitude is expressed in prayer and song, angels from heaven take up the strain and unite in praise and thanksgiving to God.

These exercises drive back the power of Satan. They expel murmuring and complaints, and Satan loses ground. God teaches us that we should assemble in His house to cultivate the attributes of perfect love. This will fit the dwellers of earth for the mansions Christ has gone to prepare for them that love Him. Then they will assemble in the sanctuary from Sabbath to Sabbath, from one new moon to another, to unite in loftier strains of song, in thanksgiving and praise to Him who sitteth upon the throne, and to the Lamb forever and ever.—Manuscript 24, 1898.

August 26
PHARISEES REFUSED TO ACKNOWLEDGE CHRIST'S POWER

◆ *But the Pharisees said, He casteth out devils through the prince of the devils. Matthew 9:34.*

*I*N Christ's mighty works there was sufficient evidence for faith. But these people did not want truth. They could not but acknowledge the reality of the works of Christ, but they cast condemnation upon them all. They must acknowledge that supernatural power attended His work, but this power, they declared, was derived from Satan. Did they really believe this? No; but they were so determined that the truth should not affect their hearts and they be converted that they charged the work of the Spirit of God to the devil. . . .

All-compassionate Redeemer! What love, what matchless love, was Thine! Charged by the great men of Israel with doing His works of mercy through the prince of devils, scorned and maligned, He was yet as one who saw and heard not. The work He came from heaven to do must not be left undone. He saw that truth must be unfolded to the people. The Light of the world must flash His beams into the darkness of sin and superstition and reveal error in contrast with truth. . . .

Christ does not use force or compulsion in drawing people to Him. But while truth was being proclaimed, the hearts of those who professed to be children of God were barricaded against it, and those who had not been so highly privileged, those who were not clothed with the garment of self-righteousness, were drawn to Christ. Their minds were convinced and quickened into activity, and light and truth vibrated through the universe. . . .

Satan endeavored to keep hidden from the world the great atoning sacrifice, which reveals the law in all its sacred dignity and impresses hearts with the force of its binding claims. He was warring against the work of Christ and united all his evil angels with human instrumentalities in opposition to that work. But while he was carrying on this work, heavenly intelligences were combining with human instrumentalities in the work of restoration. . . .

Here are the two great powers, the power of truth and righteousness and the working of Satan to make of none effect the law of God. The human agent, magnetized by the power of Satan, works in the lines of the enemy; the Saviour employs His human instrumentalities to be laborers together with God. . . . Those who expect to be children of God are not to expect an easy time in this life. . . . We are not left alone to engage in this conflict. Jesus Christ is the Captain of our salvation.—Manuscript 61, 1899.

August 27
ADAM'S DISGRACEFUL FALL REDEEMED BY CHRIST

◆ *For as in Adam all die, even so in Christ shall all be made alive. 1 Corinthians 15:22.*

CHRIST is called the second Adam. In purity and holiness, connected with God, and beloved by God, He began where the first Adam began. But the first Adam was in every way more favorably situated than was Christ. The wonderful provision made in Eden for the holy pair was made by a God who loved them. Everything in nature was pure and undefiled. Fruits, flowers, and beautiful, lofty trees flourished in the Garden of Eden. With everything that Adam and Eve required, they were abundantly supplied.

But Satan came, and insinuated doubts of God's wisdom. He accused Him, their heavenly Father and Sovereign, of selfishness, because to test their loyalty, He had prohibited them from eating the fruit of the tree of knowledge. Eve fell under the temptation, and Adam accepted the forbidden fruit from his wife's hand. He fell under the smallest test that the Lord could devise to prove his obedience, and the floodgates of woe were opened upon our world. He was furnished with a holy nature, sinless, pure, undefiled; but he fell because he listened to the suggestions of the enemy; and his posterity became depraved. . . .

When Christ came, He entered a world disloyal to God, a world all seared and marred by the curse of rebellion against the Creator. The archdeceiver had carried on his work with intense vigor, until the curse of transgression had fallen upon the earth. People were corrupted by Satan's inventions. . . . Claiming for himself the attributes of mercy, goodness, and truth, Satan attributed his own attributes to God. These misrepresentations must be met and demonstrated as false, by Christ in human nature.

Christ was tempted by Satan in a hundredfold more severe manner than was Adam, and under circumstances in every way more trying. . . . He redeemed Adam's disgraceful fall and saved the world. There is hope for all who will come to Christ and receive Him as their personal Saviour. . . .

By transgression the world had been divorced from heaven. Christ bridged the gulf and connected earth with heaven. In human nature He maintained the purity of His divine character. He lived the law of God, and honored it in a world of transgression, revealing to the worlds unfallen, to the heavenly universe, to Satan, and to all the fallen sons and daughters of Adam that through His grace humanity can keep the law of God! He came to impart His own divine nature, His own image, to the repentant, believing soul.—Manuscript 20, 1898 (*Manuscript Releases*, vol. 8, pp. 39-41).

August 28
BELIEVE THE TRUTH AND PRACTICE IT

◆ *For ye are all the children of God by faith in Christ Jesus. Galatians 3:26.*

*J*ESUS Christ is the Restorer. Satan, the apostate, is the destroyer. Here is the conflict between the Prince of life and the prince of this world, the power of darkness. . . . The world's Redeemer did not design that His purchased inheritance should live and die in their sins. What, then, is the matter? Why are so few reached and saved? It is because so many of those who profess to be Christians are working in the same lines as the great apostate. They let Satan devise and plan for them. He makes them apostates, disloyal to God, rebels against His precepts and laws. This brings severe, taxing labor upon the true Christian. He must convince the transgressor that he is a sinner, because "sin is the transgression of the law."

How much more might be done for Christ if all who have had the light and the truth set before them, and who profess to believe the Word, would practice the Word and adorn the doctrine of Christ our Saviour. . . . There are many earnest, prudent, warmhearted men and women who could do much for Christ if they would first give themselves to God and draw nigh to Him, seeking Him with their whole hearts. . . .

As a people we have to meet that which Christ met. The lukewarm, the covetous, the self-righteous, the impure, were the chief stumbling blocks He had to encounter, and those who work with Him will find the same discouraging hindrances in their experiences. . . . All who engage in this work as colaborers with Christ must be willing not only to preach the truth but to practice it. . . . There will be no change made in the divine economy in order to bring about marked changes in the religious world. Men and women must arise to the emergency; they must receive the golden oil, the divine communication, in rich blessings. This will enable them to arise and shine, because their light has come, and the glory of the Lord has risen upon them.

Those who claim to believe the Word of God, and yet cherish their own hereditary and cultivated traits of character, are the greatest stumbling blocks we shall meet as we present the grand, holy truths for this time. Those who believe present truth are to practice the truth, live the truth. They are to study the Word and eat the Word, which means eating the flesh and drinking the blood of the Son of God. They are to bring that Word, which is Spirit and life, into their daily, practical life. It is the bread from heaven, and it will give life to the world.—Letter 34, 1896.

August 29
**PERSECUTION
IN JESUS' DAY;
PERSECUTION NOW**

◆ *If they have persecuted me, they will also persecute you. John 15:20.*

*W*E read in Luke where Christ, in the synagogue of Nazareth, announced Himself as the Anointed One, as He read from the prophet Isaiah: "The Spirit of the Lord is upon me, because he hath anointed me to preach the gospel to the poor; he hath sent me to heal the brokenhearted, to preach deliverance to the captives, and recovering of sight to the blind, to set at liberty them that are bruised, to preach the acceptable year of the Lord.". . .

Then Satan whispered his unbelief, and [those in the synagogue] said, "Is not this Joseph's son?". . . How quickly the current changed, and they were filled with madness and rage because Jesus set before them their true spiritual apostasy. They "rose up, and thrust him out of the city, and led him unto the brow of the hill whereon their city was built, that they might cast him down headlong." But Jesus was protected in His mission by the heavenly angels. Passing through the midst of them unobserved, He went His way. . . .

Herod and the wicked authorities killed the Just One, but Christ never killed anyone, and we may attribute the spirit of persecution—because men and women want liberty of conscience—to its origin, Satan. He is a deceiver, a liar, a murderer, an accuser of the brethren. He loves to see human misery. He exults in distress, and as we view the cruel persecutions of those who would obey God according to the dictates of their own consciences, we may know that this is the mystery of iniquity. . . .

This conflict was opened upon the Son of God. He was afflicted, He was despised and rejected, a man of sorrows and acquainted with grief. The Majesty of heaven had to leave the scene of His labor again and again because of Satan's bruising His heel, and finally Satan's malignity reached its utmost power when Satan inspired and controlled the minds of wicked men to crucify Him. . . .

The enmity of Satan will continue, fierce and determined, against the followers of Jesus. Christ has said to His faithful ones, "They have persecuted Me; they will also persecute you." There can be no enmity between fallen angels and fallen human beings who have practiced the very works and sport of Satan. . . . Evil—wherever it exists, in rejecting light and truth and departing from the living God—will always league against the righteous and obedient.—Manuscript 62, 1886.

August 30
LEARN OF JESUS

◆ *Take my yoke upon you, and learn of me; for I am meek and lowly in heart: and ye shall find rest unto your souls. Matthew 11:29.*

HE great controversy between the Prince of light and the prince of darkness has not abated one jot or tittle of its fierceness as time has gone on. The stern conflict between light and darkness, between error and truth, is deepening in its intensity. The synagogue of Satan is intensely active, and in this age the deceiving power of the enemy is working in the most subtle way. Every human mind that is not surrendered to God, and is not under the control of the Spirit of God, will be perverted through satanic agencies.

The enemy is working continually to supplant Jesus Christ in the human heart, and to place his attributes in the human character in the place of the attributes of God. He brings his strong delusions to bear upon the human mind in order that he may have a controlling power. He seeks to obliterate the truth and abolish the true pattern of goodness and righteousness, in order that the professed Christian world shall be swept to perdition through separation from God. He is working in order that selfishness shall become worldwide, and thus make of no effect the mission and work of Christ.

Christ came to the world to bring back the character of God to humankind, and to retrace on the human soul the divine image. Through His entire life Christ sought by continuous, laborious efforts to call the world's attention to God and to His holy requirements in order that people might be imbued with the Spirit of God, might be actuated by love, and might reveal in life and character the divine attributes. . . .

In the character of Christ majesty and humility were blended. Temperance and self-denial were seen in every act of His life. But there was no taint of bigotry, no cold austerity manifested in His manner to lessen His influence over those with whom He came in contact. The world's Redeemer had a greater-than-angelic nature, yet united with His divine majesty were meekness and humility that attracted all to Himself. . . .

Christ, our Redeemer, comprehended all the necessities of humanity. He formulated the mighty plans by which the fallen race is to be uplifted from the degradation of sin. In every circumstance, however trivial, He represented the Father. Though upholding the world by the word of His power, yet He would stoop to relieve a wounded bird.—Manuscript 39, 1894.

August 31
JESUS WILL GIVE
US LIFE ETERNAL

◆ *And this is life eternal, that they might know thee the only true God, and Jesus Christ, whom thou hast sent. John 17:3.*

HE Lord Jesus said to His disciples when He was with them, "I have yet many things to say unto you, but ye cannot bear them now." He could have made disclosures which would have absorbed the attention of the disciples and caused them to lose sight of His former instruction that He wished to be the subject of their most earnest thought. But He withheld those things that they would have been amazed to hear, and that would have afforded them opportunity to cavil, to create misunderstanding and disaffection. He would give no occasion for persons of little faith and piety to mystify and misrepresent the truth, and thus create factions.

Jesus could have presented mysteries that would have given subject for thought and investigation for generations, even to the close of time. Himself the source of all true science, He could have led people to the investigation of mysteries, and age after age their minds would have been so thoroughly absorbed that they would have felt no desire to eat the flesh and drink the blood of the Son of God.

Jesus well knew that Satan is constantly working to excite curiosity, and to busy people with conjecture. Thus he seeks to eclipse the grand and momentous truth that Christ wished to be ever prominent before their minds. "For this is life eternal, that they might know thee the only true God, and Jesus Christ, whom thou hast sent."

There is a lesson for us in those words of Christ spoken after the feeding of the five thousand. He said, "Gather up the fragments that remain, that nothing be lost." These words meant more than that the disciples should gather the broken pieces of bread into baskets. Jesus meant that they should mark His words, should study the Scriptures, and treasure every ray of light. Instead of searching for a knowledge of something that God had not revealed, they were carefully to gather up what He had given them.

Satan had tried to eclipse from human minds the knowledge of God, and to eradicate from their hearts the attributes of God. . . . That which God had revealed was misconstrued, misapplied, and mingled with satanic delusions. Satan will quote Scripture in order to deceive. He tried to deceive Christ in this way. So he still tries to deceive. . . . Christ came to adjust truths that had been misplaced and made to serve the cause of error. He recalled them, repeated them, . . . and bade them stand fast forever.—Manuscript 32, 1896 (*Manuscript Releases,* vol. 17, pp. 20, 21).

September 1
**CHRIST
IDENTIFIES WITH
OUR SORROWS**

◆ *Jesus said, Take ye away the stone.*
Martha, the sister of him that was dead, saith
unto him, Lord . . . he hath been dead four
days. John 11:39.

CHRIST alone was able to bear the afflictions of the many. "In all their affliction he was afflicted." He never bore disease in His own flesh, but He carried the sickness of others. With tenderest sympathy He looked upon the suffering ones who pressed about Him. He groaned in spirit as He saw the work of Satan revealed in all their woe, and He made every case of need and of sorrow His own. . . . The power of love was in all His healing. He identified His interests with suffering humanity.

Christ was health and strength in Himself, and when sufferers were in His immediate presence, disease was always rebuked. It was for this that He did not go at once to Lazarus. He could not witness his suffering and not bring him relief. He could not witness disease or death without combating the power of Satan. The death of Lazarus was permitted that through his resurrection the last and crowning evidence might be given to the Jews that Jesus was the Son of God.

And in all this conflict with the power of evil, there was ever before Christ the darkened shadow into which He Himself must enter. Ever before Him was the means by which He must pay the ransom for these souls. As He witnessed the suffering of humanity, He knew that He must bear a greater pain, mingled with mockery, that He would suffer the greatest humiliation. When He raised Lazarus from the dead, He knew that for that life He must pay the ransom on the cross of Calvary. . . .

Christ was strong to save the whole world. He wept at the grave of Lazarus at the thought that He could not save everyone whom Satan's power had laid low in death. . . . From the light of His exalted purity, the world's Redeemer could see that the maladies from which the human family were suffering were brought upon them by transgression of the law of God. Every case of suffering He could trace back to its cause. . . . He knew that He alone could rescue them from the pit into which they had fallen. He alone could place their feet in the right path. His perfection alone could avail for their imperfection. He alone could cover their nakedness with His own spotless robe of righteousness. . . .

By actual experience He knew nothing of sin; He stood before the world the spotless Lamb of God. When suffering humanity pressed about Him, He who was in the health of perfect manhood was as one afflicted with them. This was essential, that He might express His perfect love in behalf of humanity.—Manuscript 18, 1898.

September 2
**JESUS VALUES
OUR GIFTS OF
LOVING SERVICE**

◆ *Now when Jesus was in Bethany, in the house of Simon the leper, there came unto him a woman having an alabaster box of very precious ointment, and poured it on his head, as he sat at meat. Matthew 26:6, 7.*

HIS incident is full of instruction. Jesus, the world's Redeemer, is drawing close to the time when He will give His life for a sinful world. Yet how little did even His disciples realize what they were about to lose. Mary could not reason upon this subject. Her heart was filled with pure, holy love. The sentiment of her heart was "What shall I render unto the Lord for all His benefits toward me?" This ointment, costly as it was estimated by the disciples, was but a poor expression of her love for her Master. But Christ could appreciate the gift as an expression of her love, and Mary's heart was filled with perfect peace and happiness.

Christ delights in the earnest desire of Mary to do the will of her Lord. He accepts the wealth of pure affection which His disciples did not, could not, understand. . . . Mary's ointment was the gift of love, and this gave it its value in the eyes of Christ. . . . Jesus saw Mary shrink away abashed, expecting to hear reproof from the One she loved and worshiped. But instead of this she hears words of commendation. "Why trouble ye the woman?" He said, "for she hath wrought a good work upon me. For ye have the poor always with you; but me ye have not always. For in that she hath poured this ointment on my body, she did it for my burial. Verily I say unto you, Wheresoever this gospel shall be preached in the whole world, there shall also this, that this woman hath done, be told for a memorial of her." No other anointing would Jesus receive, for the Sabbath was nigh at hand, and they kept the Sabbath according to the commandment. . . . The desire that Mary had to do this service for her Lord was of more value to Christ than all the spikenard and precious ointment in the world, because it expressed her appreciation of the world's Redeemer. It was the love of Christ that constrained her. . . .

Mary, by the Holy Spirit's power, saw in Jesus One who had come to seek and to save the souls that were ready to perish. Every one of the disciples should have been inspired with a similar devotion.—Manuscript 28, 1897.

September 3
JESUS'
TRIUMPHAL
ENTRY WIT-
NESSED BY MANY

◆ *Ye shall find an ass tied, and a colt with her: loose them, and bring them unto me. And if any man say aught unto you, ye shall say, The Lord hath need of them. Matthew 21:2, 3.*

HE time of Christ's triumphal entry into Jerusalem was the most beautiful season of the year. The Mount of Olives was carpeted with green, and the groves were beautiful with varied foliage. Very many had come to the feast from the regions round about Jerusalem with an earnest desire to see Jesus. The crowning miracle of the Saviour in raising Lazarus from the dead had a wonderful effect upon minds, and a large and enthusiastic multitude was drawn to the place where Jesus was tarrying.

The afternoon was half spent when Jesus sent His disciples to the village of Bethphage. . . . This was the first time during His life of ministry that Christ had consented to ride, and the disciples interpreted this move to be an indication that He was about to assert His kingly power and authority, and take His position on David's throne. Joyfully they executed the commission. They found the colt as Jesus had said. . . .

As Jesus takes His seat on the animal, the air becomes vocal with acclamations of praise and triumph. . . . He bears no outward sign of royalty. He wears no dress of state, nor is He followed by a train of men of arms. Instead He is surrounded by a company wrought up to the highest pitch of excitement. They cannot restrain the joyous feeling of expectancy that animate their hearts. . . .

The shout echoes from mountain and valley, "Hosanna to the son of David: . . . Hosanna in the highest." "Blessed is he that cometh in the name of the Lord.". . . Those who have once been blind . . . are the first to lead the way in that wonderful procession. . . . One whom He has raised from the dead leads the animal on which He is seated. The once deaf and dumb, with ears opened and tongues unloosed, help swell the glad hosannas. Cripples, with buoyant steps and grateful hearts, are now most active in breaking down the palm branches and strewing them in His path as their tribute of homage to the mighty Healer. The leper, who has listened to the dread words of the priest, "Unclean," . . . is there. The widow and the orphan are there to tell of His wonderful works. The restored dead are there. Their tongues, once palsied by the power of Satan, take up the song of rejoicing. . . . The demoniac is there, not now to have the words wrenched from his lips by Satan's power. . . . On the crest of Olivet the procession pauses.—Manuscript 128, 1899.

September 4
THE SAVIOUR HAS INTENSE SORROW WHEN WE REJECT HIS LOVE

◆ *He came unto his own, and his own received him not. John 1:11.*

EFORE them [the crowd with Jesus at His triumphal entry] lies the city of Jerusalem, with the temple of pure white marble, which is gilded with glory by the rays of the setting sun. It is a picture of unsurpassed loveliness, and well might the people apply to her the words of the prophet, "A crown of beauty in the hand of the Lord, and a royal diadem in the hand of thy God." At the entrancing sight, the throng joins with renewed fervor in their shouts of praise. . . . They suppose that Christ is now to take the throne of David and reign as a temporal prince. Their eyes turn to Him to see how He is impressed by the scene. But lo, the Son of man is in tears!

As Christ's eyes rest upon the temple, so soon to be desolated and its veil rent when the final act of the Jews would consummate His death, He wept over the disobedient city. . . . In a few short hours the world's Redeemer would be taken by wicked hands and crucified. Not the Roman nation, not the Gentiles, but the people for whom He had done so much, and from whom He had hoped for so much, were to be His murderers. . . .

The grace that bringeth salvation would no longer be heard in the city. This was the cause of the Saviour's intense sorrow. . . . The tender tears He shed over Jerusalem were the last tears of rejected love. . . . The glad throng could not understand the cause of the Saviour's sorrow. They did not know that the iniquities of Israel were bringing her final calamities upon her. But a mysterious awe falls upon the procession, and calms in a degree its enthusiasm. . . . A large number in that throng bear in their own bodies the evidence that divine power is among them, and each has a story to tell of the merciful works of Christ. The relation of those wonderful works increases the fervor of their feelings until it reaches an intensity that is indescribable. Disciples and people join in the songs of praise.

Then came the priests and rulers to Him, requesting Him to silence these acclamations of praise. "Master, rebuke thy disciples," they say. Christ answered them, "If these should hold their peace, the stones would immediately cry out."

Christ had come to earth to reveal the principles of the kingdom of heaven. His character as Saviour and Life-giver had been demonstrated only a short time before at the grave of Lazarus, but in their pride the Jews rejected the One who was mighty and having salvation. How different would have been Christ's attitude had the priests and rulers been true to the trust reposed in them. —Manuscript 128, 1899.

September 5
**"MY HOUSE
SHALL BE
CALLED A HOUSE
OF PRAYER"**

◆ *And Jesus went into the temple of God,
and cast out all them that sold and bought in
the temple, and overthrew the tables of the
moneychangers, and the seats of them that
sold doves. Matthew 21:12.*

*T*HE temple courts were filled with cattle, sheep, oxen, and doves. Above the noise of the lowing of cattle, the bleating of the sheep, and the cooing of the doves could be heard the voice of the traffickers as they offered for sale the animals and birds, at the highest rates, to those who had come to the Passover to offer sacrifice. Jesus said, "It is written, My house shall be called the house of prayer; but ye have made it a den of thieves."

This act on the part of Christ was deeply significant, more significant than any of the beholders realized. When the priests and Pharisees had recovered from the terror that had taken possession of their guilty souls at the words of Christ, they returned to the temple. They were not converted or even humbled. They determined to challenge Christ as to His authority for expelling them from the temple courts. When they reached the temple they found that a wonderful work had been done during their absence. The sick and dying had been restored to health. They were astonished, but they would not yield their stubborn unbelief. They had already determined to put Christ to death, and Lazarus also, who had been raised from the dead. They knew that the people would still believe in Christ as long as there lived among them one who had been raised from the dead by His power.

The evidence Christ had given was calculated to convince every sincere mind, but it was not evidence that these people wanted. It was the rejection and condemnation of Christ by the people for which they were seeking. Every additional evidence given only increased their aversion to Christ. To have Christ in the world performing His wonderful works, to have Him live before the people His life of goodness and self-denial and self-sacrifice, to have Him exercise for others the tender compassion that had long since departed from their lives, was the very thing they did not want.

Christ was fulfilling the commission given Him of His Father. "The Spirit of the Lord God is upon me; because the Lord hath anointed me to preach good tidings unto the meek; he hath sent me to bind up the brokenhearted, to proclaim liberty to the captives, and the opening of the prison for them that are bound; to proclaim the acceptable year of the Lord."—Manuscript 128, 1899.

September 6
GOD'S PEOPLE NOT TO MAKE A PRETENTIOUS SHOW

◆ *And when he saw a fig tree in the way, he came to it, and found nothing thereon, but leaves only, and said unto it, Let no fruit grow on thee henceforward for ever. And presently the fig tree withered away. Matthew 21:19.*

T was not a common thing for a fig tree to present full foliage at that early period of the season. The fruit of the fig tree makes its appearance before the leaves; therefore a fig tree in full leaf might be expected to have fruit upon it. Christ approached the tree, expecting to find fruit there, but searching from the lowest bough to the topmost branch, He found nothing but leaves, and His curse fell upon it.

This instance in the ministry of Christ is a singular one. It was unlike the ways and works of Christ. . . . Wherever He went He scattered mercy in words of counsel and deeds of goodness. He was the Restorer, the Healer. He came not to condemn the world but that the world through Him might be saved. The disciples could not understand the action of Christ in punishing a tree for its barrenness, and they said unto Him, "How soon is the fig tree withered away!"

Just before this Christ had made His triumphal entry into Jerusalem. For the second time He had cleansed the temple and had driven out from its courts the traffickers. . . . Dishonest dealing was practiced by the people who brought cattle to sell in the temple courts, but the word of command was given; divinity flashed through humanity, and no priest in his gorgeous dress, or trafficker looking on that countenance, dared to remain. . . .

This was a parable of the dispersion of the Jews. Now Christ, under the symbol of the blighted tree, presents before His disciples the righteous anger of God as He sees the temple courts desecrated to obtain unlawful gain, and the destruction of the Jewish nation. That tree, flaunting its pretentious foliage in the very face of Christ, was a symbol of the Jewish nation, which had been separating from God until, in their pride and apostasy, they had lost their power of discernment and knew not their Redeemer. . . .

This blighted fig tree with its pretentious branches is to repeat its lesson in every age to the close of this earth's history. . . . If the spirit of Satan entered unto unsanctified hearts in the days of Christ to counterwork the requirements of God in that generation, it will surely enter into the professed Christian churches in [our day]. History will repeat itself. . . . But the people who obey the commandments of God have no controversy. They take the Word of God for their guide.—Manuscript 32, 1898.

September 7
CHRIST WANTS US TO BEAR FRUIT BY WORKING FOR HIM

◆ *Every branch in me that beareth not fruit he taketh away: and every branch that beareth fruit, he purgeth it, that it may bring forth more fruit. John 15:2.*

I have been thinking about the lesson that Christ gave to His disciples just prior to His entering the Garden of Gethsemane, knowing it would be His last opportunity to instruct His disciples before His crucifixion. He says to them, as He points to a vine—and the vine is something that the Jews greatly prized and respected and considered very beautiful—"I am the true vine, and my Father is the husbandman. Every branch in me that beareth not fruit he taketh away."

Now, here is something for us to study. . . . We have our opportunities now to bear fruit; we can reveal that we are fruit-bearing branches of the vine. And if we go on now in a careless and indifferent manner, then what will be our position? He tells us He will take us away, for we cannot do anything without Christ, and if we are as a dead branch and do not draw sap and nourishment from the living Vine, we shall become withered branches. He says that every branch that beareth fruit, He purgeth it (pruneth it), that it may bring forth more fruit. . . .

We have the enemy in our world to contend with. We have the powers of darkness to meet. We have to be in this conflict as long as time shall last. Our Saviour was in the conflict with the powers of darkness, and the powers of darkness were in conflict with Him, even after He entered our world. Satan was in conflict with Him. And then just as soon as His reasoning powers were exercised, He was in conflict with the powers of darkness. His very coming—as a babe in Bethlehem—was to set up a standard against the enemy. . . .

And when He went away, what did He do? Who is to take up the controversy? Who are the visible ones who are to take up the controversy here in this world and carry it through to the very end? They are those who are Christ's followers, every soul of them. It is not merely the delegated ministers. There is where our people make a grand mistake. They seem to think that day by day, hour by hour, minute by minute in the conflict, the ministers must take care of them. It belongs to every soul of us.

We do not know what work God has for us to do. . . . If we have only the one talent and we begin to put that to the exchangers, and then we begin to work with that one talent, and God sees that we are faithful in that which is least, then He will give us another talent. . . . And thus the talent keeps increasing and growing; and the more we put it to the exchangers, the more talents we have to employ to the glory of God.—Manuscript 56, 1890.

September 8
**BELIEVERS SHOULD
HAVE PERSONAL
KNOWLEDGE
OF CHRIST**

◆ *Behold, what manner of love the Father
hath bestowed upon us, that we should be
called the sons of God: therefore the world
knoweth us not, because it knew him not.
1 John 3:1.*

*H*OW many today see Jesus Christ, the Saviour of the
world, as He is! How few know Him! How few know the Father! Everyone
that knows Christ has a knowledge of the Father. To see Christ as He is is
one of the greatest blessings that can ever come to fallen humanity; the
precious Saviour, to see Him as He is! How many have partial views of
Jesus Christ. How many acknowledge Him as the world's Redeemer, but
they know Him not as a personal Saviour; and this is essential—the
knowledge of God in Jesus Christ. . . .

"And every man that hath this hope in him purifieth himself." What
hope? Why, of seeing Jesus as He is, the living faith that lays hold of the arm
of the infinite God, the living faith that takes Christ as our personal
Saviour. Who knows Him as thus? All your casual views of Christ will not
save a single soul. Do you know Him by the living connection of faith? . . .

There was a wondrous work for Him to perform here when He came to
our earth. Satan was having things about as he pleased. He claimed this
earth's territory as his, the prince of the world. Christ came to dispute his
power and his claim. Christ came to rescue the human race from his oppressive power. . . . The battlefield was right here in this little world; the conflict went on between the Prince of life and the powers of darkness. Which
shall triumph? All the heavenly universe, the heavenly intelligences, were
looking upon Christ and taking cognizance of the battle. Here was Christ
disputing the authority of Satan, and Satan was following Him at every step,
determined to overthrow Him with his temptations, determined that he
would weary and exhaust the patience and forbearance of God for the
human family so that he should be able to ruin every one of them. . . .

Whatever may be your weakness, [however] compassed with infirmities, there is hope for you in God. Our precious Saviour came to save to
the utmost every soul that will come unto Him. . . . To those who have
their minds engrossed with earthly pleasures He comes and lifts the voice
of warning, and He presents eternity to your view; He there opens before
you heaven, the threshold lightened and brightened with His glory, and
the glory streams through the open door. The door is ajar, thank God.—
Manuscript 86, 1894.

September 9
BY HIS DEATH THE SAVIOUR ENDED SATAN'S POWER OVER US

◆ *Hereafter I will not talk much with you: for the prince of this world cometh, and hath nothing in me. John 14:30.*

$\mathcal{T}$HE Commander of heaven was assailed by the tempter. He had no clear, unobstructed passage through the world. He was not left free and without hindrance to win to His kingdom the souls of people by His gracious mercy and loving-kindness. . . . No human being had come into the world and escaped the power of the deceiver. The whole forces of the confederacy of evil were set upon His track to engage in warfare against Him, and, if possible, to prevail over Him. . . .

Satan saw the image of God in the character and person of Jesus Christ. He knew that if Christ carried out His plan, his satanic authority would be at an end. Therefore, the life of Christ was a perpetual warfare against satanic agencies. . . . The conflict increased in fierceness and malignity as again and again the prey was taken out of his hands. . . .

Just previous to His crucifixion the Saviour said, "The prince of this world cometh, and hath nothing in me." Though it was the hour of the power of darkness, yet in anticipation of His triumph Christ could say, "The prince of the world is judged." "Now is the judgment of this world: now shall the prince of this world be cast out." Viewing the work of redemption as completed, He could, even in death, speak of the great final deliverance and represent things that were future as if [they were] present. The only begotten Son of the infinite God could successfully carry through the great plan that made humanity's salvation sure. . . .

The condition of the world previous to the first appearing of Christ is a picture of the condition of the world just previous to His second advent. The same iniquity will exist; Satan manifests the same delusive power upon human minds. . . . He is securing his army of human agents to engage in the last conflict against the Prince of life, to overthrow the law of God, which is the foundation of His throne. Satan will work with miraculous presentations to confirm people in the belief that he is what he claims to be—the prince of this world—and that victory is his. He will turn his forces against those who are loyal to God; but though he may cause pain, distress, and human agony, he cannot defile the soul. . . . The people of God in these last days must expect to enter into the thick of the conflict, for the prophetic Word says, "The dragon was wroth with the woman, and went to make war with the remnant of her seed, which keep the commandments of God, and have the testimony of Jesus Christ."—Letter 43, 1895 (*Review and Herald,* Oct. 29, 1895).

September 10
CHRIST CAME TO IMPART PEACE TO HIS PEOPLE

◆ *Peace I leave with you, my peace I give unto you: not as the world giveth, give I unto you. Let not your heart be troubled, neither let it be afraid. John 14:27.*

N the East the customary greeting when visiting the house of a friend was "Peace be to this house," and in leaving it the same words were used. But Christ's farewell is of an altogether different character. [John 14:27 quoted.] Much is embodied in these words. They are of richest import, and will be reechoed to earth's remotest bounds. . . .

Christ brought that peace with Him to the world. He came to impart that peace, that all who will believe on Him might have a peace that passeth understanding. He, the world's Redeemer, had carried that peace with Him throughout His earthly life, and now He had come to the time when He must give His life so that the treasure of peace might ever abide in the heart by faith. He left that peace with His disciples, and He is implanting and maintaining it in the hearts of all who will welcome its presence. . . .

The time had come for Satan's last attempt to overcome Christ. But Christ declared, He hath nothing in Me, no sin that brings Me in his power. He can find nothing in Me that responds to his satanic suggestions. . . .

Why this severe conflict with the prince of the world when Jesus, through His childhood, youth, and manhood, had lived the law of God? . . . By a word Christ could have mastered the powers of Satan. But He came into the world that He might endure every test, every provocation, that it is possible for human beings to bear and yet not be provoked or impassioned, or retaliate in word, in spirit, or in action. For the honor and glory of God He was to offer Himself a living, spotless sacrifice to the Father. . . . The worlds unfallen, the heavenly angels, and the fallen race were watching every movement made by the Representative of the Father, and the Representative of perfect humanity. And His character was without a flaw. . . .

The last assault would soon come. The great victory to be achieved was union with His chosen people so that, although Christ was to be removed from earth to heaven, His church might have communion with Him. . . .

At times our trials do not come singly, followed by a period of peace and rest; temptations come in as an overwhelming wave to destroy all before it. The afflictions do not create Christians, but simply develop in them the mind and will of Christ, the living principles of virtue and holiness.—Manuscript 44, 1897.

September 11
JESUS, THE TRUE
PASSOVER LAMB,
WAS SLAIN FOR
OUR SINS

◆ *Then came the day of unleavened bread, when the passover must be killed. And he sent Peter and John, saying, Go and prepare us the passover, that we may eat. Luke 22:7, 8.*

CHRIST had chosen Peter and John, who were to be closely associated in labor, to prepare for the supper. . . . "And he said unto them, Behold, when ye are entered into the city, there shall a man meet you, bearing a pitcher of water; follow him into the house where he entereth in. And ye shall say unto the goodman of the house, The Master saith unto thee, Where is the guestchamber, where I shall eat the passover with my disciples?". . .

Christ desired to guard against any premature movements that might be made by traitors coming to the supper and reciprocating the action designed by Judas. It was customary for those living in the metropolis to accommodate strangers desirous of celebrating the Passover. The message took the form of a command. It might seem to us to be unbecoming for these two Galileans to speak thus to a stranger. But circumstances happened as Christ foretold. The disciples met a man carrying a pitcher. They followed him and entered the house that he entered and repeated their message, and it met a ready assent on the part of the master of the house. . . .

It was the last Passover that Jesus would keep with His disciples. He knew that His hour was come; He Himself was the true Paschal Lamb, and on the day the Passover was eaten He was to be sacrificed. He knew that the circumstances connected with this occasion would never be forgotten by His disciples.

Christ's first words after they had gathered about the table were "With desire I have desired to eat this passover with you before I suffer: for I say unto you, I will not any more eat thereof, until it be fulfilled in the kingdom of God.". . .

On this last evening with His disciples, Jesus had much to tell them. If they had been prepared to receive what He longed to impart, they would have been saved from heartbreaking anguish, from disappointment and unbelief. But Jesus saw that they could not bear what He had to say. As He looked into their faces, the words of warning and comfort were stayed upon His lips. Moments passed in silence. Jesus appeared to be waiting. The disciples were ill at ease. The glances they cast at each other told of jealousy and contention. . . . The disciples clung to their favorite idea that Christ would assert His power and take His position on the throne of David. And in heart each still longed for the highest place in the kingdom.—Manuscript 106, 1903.

September 12
IF WE WANT TO BE GREAT, WE MUST GIVE HUMBLE SERVICE

◆ *And there was also a strife among them, which of them should be accounted the greatest. Luke 22:24.*

*T*HE request of James and John to sit on the right and left of Christ's throne had excited the indignation of the others. That the two brothers should presume to ask for the highest position so stirred the ten that alienation threatened. They felt that they were misjudged, that their fidelity and talents were not appreciated. Judas was the most severe upon James and John.

When the disciples entered the upper room, their hearts were full of resentful feelings. Judas pressed next to Christ on the left side; John was on the right. If there was a highest place, Judas was determined to have it, and that place was thought to be next to Christ. And Judas was a traitor.

Another cause of dissension had arisen. At a feast it was customary for a servant to wash the feet of the guests, and on this occasion preparation had been made for the service. The pitcher, the basin, and the towel were there, but no servant was present, and it was the disciples' part to perform it. But each of the disciples, yielding to wounded pride, determined not to act the part of a servant. . . .

Looking at the disturbed countenances of His disciples, Christ rose from the table, and, laying aside His outer garment, which would have impeded His movements, He took a towel and girded Himself. . . .

Judas was the first whose feet Jesus washed. Judas had already closed the contract to deliver Jesus into the hands of the priests and scribes. Christ knew his secret. Yet He did not expose him. He hungered for his soul. His heart was crying, How can I give thee up? He hoped that His act in washing Judas' feet would touch the heart of the erring disciple and save him from completing his act of disloyalty. And for a moment the heart of Judas thrilled through and through with the impulse then and there to confess his sin. But he would not humble himself. He hardened his heart against repentance. He made no remonstrance, no protestation against the Saviour thus humiliating Himself. He was offended at Christ's act. If Jesus could so humble Himself, he thought, He could not be Israel's king. . . .

Even Judas, had he repented, would have been received and pardoned. The guilt of his soul would have been washed away by the atoning blood of Christ. But, self-confident and self-exalted, cherishing a high estimate of his own wisdom, he justified his course.—Manuscript 106, 1903.

September 13
WE ARE TO BE WASHED IN THE GREAT FOUNTAIN

◆ *Then cometh he to Simon Peter: and Peter saith unto him, Lord, dost thou wash my feet? John 13:6.*

HEN Peter's turn came, he was unable to restrain himself and exclaimed with astonishment, "Lord, dost thou wash my feet?". . .

Calmly Jesus replied, "What I do thou knowest not now; but thou shalt know hereafter." Feeling keenly the humiliation of his Lord, and filled with love and reverence for Him, Peter with great emphasis exclaimed, "Thou shalt never wash my feet."

Solemnly Jesus said to Peter, "If I wash thee not, thou hast no part with me."

A ray of light penetrated the mind of the disciple. He saw that the service that he refused was the type of a higher cleansing—the spiritual cleansing of mind and heart. He could not endure the thought of separation from Christ; that would have been death. "Not my feet only," he said, "but also my hands and my head."

"Jesus saith to him, He that is washed needeth not save to wash his feet, but is clean every whit.". . .

Every person who came from the bath was clean, but the sandaled feet soon became dusty and again needed to be washed. So Peter and his brethren had been washed in the great fountain opened for sin and uncleanness. Christ acknowledged them as His. But temptation had led them into evil, and they still needed His cleansing grace. When Jesus girded Himself with a towel to wash the dust from their feet, He desired by this very act to wash the alienation, jealousy, and pride from their hearts. This was of far more consequence than the washing of their dusty feet. With the spirit they had then, not one of them was prepared . . . to partake of the Paschal supper or to share in the memorial service that Christ was about to institute. Their hearts must be cleansed. Pride and self-seeking create dissension and hatred, but all this Jesus washed away in washing their feet.

A change of feeling was brought about. Looking upon them, Jesus could say, "Ye are clean." Now there was union of heart, love for one another. They had become humble and teachable. Except Judas, each one was ready to concede to another the highest place. . . .

Before the emblems of Christ's broken body and shed blood are partaken of, every difference existing between brother and brother is to be removed. . . . We are to seek for a preparation to sit with Christ in His kingdom.—Manuscript 106, 1903.

September 14
COVETOUSNESS AND GREED WILL LEAD TO RUIN IF INDULGED

◆ *Verily, verily, I say unto you, that one of you shall betray me. John 13:21.*

*T*HE disciples had searched one another's faces closely as they asked, "Lord, is it I?" Until now Judas had sat silent, as if unconcerned. Now his silence drew all eyes to him. To escape the scrutiny of the disciples, he nerved himself to ask, as they had done, "Master, is it I?" Jesus solemnly replied, "Thou hast said.". . .

Even now Judas could have acknowledged his guilt, even now broken the spell upon him. Christ was close beside him, ready to aid him. But his pride and the temptation of the enemy were so strong that he had no power to escape from the snare. Instead of casting himself upon the mercy of a compassionate Saviour, he braced himself in resistance. . . .

The history of Judas presents the sad ending of a life that might have been honored of God. . . . Judas had himself solicited a place in the inner circle of disciples. With great earnestness and apparent sincerity he declared, "Master, I will follow thee whithersoever thou goest.". . .

The disciples were anxious that Judas should become one of their number. He was a man of commanding appearance, a man of keen discernment and executive ability, and they commended him to Jesus as one who would greatly assist Him in His work.

The face of Judas was not repulsive. It was keen and intelligent, but it lacked the tenderness and compassion that is seen in a truly converted person. . . . In ministering to others, Judas might have developed an unselfish spirit. But though listening daily to the lessons of Christ, and witnessing His unselfish life, Judas indulged his covetous disposition. . . .

Christ read his heart, and in His teaching He dwelt upon the principles of benevolence that strike at the very root of covetousness. He presented before Judas the heinous character of greed, and many a time the disciple realized that his character had been portrayed and his sin pointed out. But he did not confess and forsake his unrighteousness. He was self-sufficient, and instead of resisting temptation he continued to follow his fraudulent practices. . . .

Though Jesus knew Judas from the beginning, He washed his feet. And the betrayer was privileged to unite with Christ in partaking of the sacrament. . . . To him had been offered the bread of life and the water of salvation. To him the Saviour's lesson had been given. But Judas refused to be benefited.—Manuscript 106, 1903.

September 15
WE DO THE WORK OF SATAN SOWING SEEDS OF DOUBT AND UNBELIEF

◆ *Have not I chosen you twelve, and one of you is a devil? He spake of Judas Iscariot the son of Simon: for he it was that should betray him. John 6:70, 71.*

*J*UDAS was one who exerted a large influence over the disciples. He was of commanding appearance and had excellent qualifications. But these endowments had not been sanctified to God. Judas had opened the chambers of his mind, the door of his heart, to the temptations of Satan. His energies were devoted to self-serving, self-exaltation, and the love of money. . . .

That poor, independent soul, separate from the spirit and life of Christ, had a hard time. He was ever under condemnation, because the lessons of Christ were always cutting him. Yet he did not become transformed and converted into a living branch through connection with the True Vine. Oh, if Judas had only humbled his heart before God under this divine instruction that pointed so plainly to himself in the principles set forth. Then he would no longer have remained a tempter to his brother disciples, sowing the seed of unbelief in their hearts.

Satan sowed in the heart and mind of Judas the seed that he communicated to his brethren. The questioning doubts that were passed from the devil into the mind of Judas, he passed on to the minds of his brethren. He presented so much accusation of his brethren that he was counterworking the lessons of Christ. This is why Jesus called Judas a devil. . . .

There is no such thing as occupying a neutral position. Each will have given to Him his or her work according to his or her ability. And all will, through faith in Christ, have a sense of their privilege in being connected with Him. . . . The disciple whose religion is a profession only is distinguished from the true. . . .

The hearing of the Word of God is not enough. Unless taught of God, the truth will not be accepted to the saving of the soul. It must be brought into the life practice. The human agent will reveal whether he or she is taught of God. And if not, it is not because God is not willing to teach, but because the person is not willing to receive His teaching and eat of the Bread of Life.

"Every one that doeth evil hateth the light [that God sends], neither cometh to the light, lest his deeds should be reproved." He or she hates reproof. . . . The self-righteous will not search for light. They love darkness rather than light, because they do not want to see themselves as God sees them. "But he that doeth truth cometh to the light that his deeds may be made manifest, that they are wrought in God."—Manuscript 67, 1897 (see also *Review and Herald,* Nov. 2, 1897).

September 16
IN GETHSEMANE OUR DESTINY HUNG IN THE BALANCE

◆ *And they came to a place which was named Gethsemane: and he saith to his disciples, Sit ye here, while I shall pray. Mark 14:32.*

S Christ left the disciples, bidding them pray for themselves and for Him, He selected three—Peter, James, and John—and went still farther into the seclusion of the garden. These three disciples had seen His transfiguration; they had seen the heavenly visitors, Moses and Elias, talking with Jesus, and Christ desired their presence with Him on this occasion also. . . .

Christ expressed His desire for human sympathy, and then withdrawing Himself from them about a stone's cast, He fell on His face and prayed, saying, "Father, if thou be willing, remove this cup from me; nevertheless not my will, but thine, be done.". . .

The superhuman agony with which He had been wrestling had brought Him to His disciples, longing for human companionship. But He was disappointed; they did not bring to Him the help He expected from them. . . .

Hear that agonizing prayer of Christ in the garden of Gethsemane! While the disciples were sleeping beneath the spreading branches of the olive trees, the Son of man—a man of sorrows and acquainted with grief—was prostrate upon the cold earth. As the agony of soul came upon Him, large blood drops of perspiration were forced from His pores, and with the falling dew moistened the sod of Gethsemane. . . .

Here the mysterious cup trembled in His hand. Here the destiny of a lost world was hanging in the balance. Should He wipe the blood drops from His brow and root from His soul the guilt of a perishing world, which was placing Him, all innocent, all undeserving, under the penalty of a just law? Should He refuse to become sinners' substitute and surety? Refuse to give them another trial, another probation?

Separation from His Father, the punishment for transgression and sin, was to fall upon Him in order to magnify God's law and testify to its immutability. And this was to settle forever the controversy between the Prince of God and Satan in regard to the changeless character of that law.

The Majesty of heaven was as one bewildered with agony. No human being could endure such suffering; but Christ had contemplated the struggle. He had said to His disciples, "I have a baptism to be baptized with; and how am I straitened till it be accomplished!" Now is the "hour, and the power of darkness."—Manuscript 42, 1897.

September 17
**CHRIST WAS
NOT FORCED TO
BEAR THE GUILT
OF THE WORLD**

◆ *And being in an agony he prayed more
earnestly: and his sweat was as it were great
drops of blood falling down to the ground.
Luke 22:44.*

CHRIST had not been forced to do this [bear the guilt of a perishing world]. He had volunteered to lay down His life to save the world. The claims of God's government had been misapprehended through the deceptive words and works of Satan, and the necessity of a mediator was seen and felt by the Father and the Son. . . .

The universe of heaven had watched with intense interest the entire life of Christ—every step from the manger to the present awful scene of momentous interest. The unfallen worlds were watching the result of this controversy. They beheld the Son of God, their loved Commander, in His superhuman agony, apparently dying on the field of battle to save a lost and perishing world. . . .

Satan was urging upon Him all the force of his temptations. He presented before Him that the sin of the world, so offensive to God, was chastisement too great. He would never again be looked upon as pure and holy and undefiled, as God's only begotten Son.

Christ was now standing in a different attitude than He had ever done before. Hitherto He had stood as an intercessor for others; now He longs for an intercessor for Himself. Could His human nature bear the strain? Shall the sins of an apostate world, since Adam's transgression to the close of time, be laid upon Him? . . .

In the supreme crisis, when heart and soul are breaking under the [world's] load of sin, Gabriel is sent to strengthen Him. And while the angel supports His fainting form, Christ takes the bitter cup and consents to drink its contents. Before the suffering One comes up the wail of a lost and perishing world, and the words come from the bloodstained lips, "Nevertheless, if the fallen race must perish unless I drink this cup, Thy will, not Mine, be done." . . .

There was silence in heaven; no harp was touched. They see their Lord enclosed by legions of satanic forces, His human nature weighed down with a shuddering, mysterious dread. . . . Strengthened by the angel sent from heaven, Jesus arises in sweat and blood and agony and for the third time returns to His disciples. . . . But He was disappointed. He found them sleeping in the hour of His bitterest agony. And the sight made angels grow sad. . . . Prophecy had declared that the "Mighty One". . . was to tread the winepress alone; "of the people there was none" with Him.—Manuscript 42, 1897.

September 18
WHEN HE WAS BETRAYED, CHRIST FELT WHAT WE WOULD FEEL

◆ *Rise up, let us go; lo, he that betrayeth me is at hand. Mark 14:42.*

*A*ND now they hear the heavy tramp of soldiers in the garden. . . . "And he that betrayed him had given them a token, saying, Whomsoever I shall kiss, that same is he; take him, and lead him away safely. And as soon as he was come, he goeth straightway to him, and saith, Master; master; and kissed him." "But Jesus said unto him, Judas, betrayest thou the Son of man with a kiss?". . .

To the multitude Jesus said, "Are ye come out, as against a thief, with swords and with staves to take me? I was daily with you in the temple teaching, and ye took me not: but the scriptures must be fulfilled."

John's record of this event is "Judas then, having received a band of men and officers from the chief priests and Pharisees, cometh thither with lanterns and torches and weapons. Jesus therefore, knowing all things that should come upon him, went forth, and said unto them, Whom seek ye? They answered him, Jesus of Nazareth. Jesus saith unto them, I am he. And Judas also, which betrayed him, stood with them. As soon then as he had said unto them, I am he, they went backward, and fell to the ground. . . . Then Simon Peter having a sword drew it, and smote the high priest's servant, and cut off his right ear. The servant's name was Malchus. Then said Jesus unto Peter, Put up thy sword into the sheath: the cup which my Father hath given me, shall I not drink it?"

At this saying terror seized upon the disciples. They were now all together again, surrounding their Lord; but at the proposition of Peter, they "all . . . forsook him, and fled."

The human nature of Christ was like unto ours. And suffering was really more keenly felt by Him, for His spiritual nature was free from every taint of sin. The aversion to suffering was in proportion to its severity. His desire for the removal of suffering was just as strong as human beings experience. . . .

How intense was the desire of the humanity of Christ to escape the displeasure of an offended God; how His soul longed for relief is shown in the words of the Sufferer, "Father, if it be possible, let this cup pass from me; nevertheless not as I will, but as thou wilt.". . . All the accumulated sin of the world was laid upon the Sinbearer, the One who was innocent of all sin, the One who alone could be the propitiation for sin, because He Himself was obedient. His life was one with God. Not a taint of corruption was upon Him.—Manuscript 42, 1897.

September 19
OUR PLACE IN HISTORY WILL BE DETERMINED BY OUR CHARACTERS

◆ *Consider that it is expedient for us, that one man should die for the people, and that the whole nation perish not. John 11:50.*

*W*ITH Caiaphas the Jewish high priesthood ended. This proud, overbearing, wicked man proved his unworthiness ever to have worn the garments of the high priest. He had neither capacity nor authority from heaven for doing the work. . . . Virtually, Caiaphas was no high priest. He wore the priestly robes, but he had no vital connection with God. . . .

The mock trial of Christ shows how base the priesthood had become. The priests hired people to testify under oath to falsehood, that Jesus might be condemned. But on this occasion, truth came to the help of Christ. . . . Thus it was shown that the testimonies borne against Him were false, that the witnesses had been hired by men who cherished in their hearts the basest elements of corruption. It was God's design that the men who delivered Jesus should hear the testimony of His innocence. "I find no fault in him," Pilate declared. And Judas, throwing at the feet of the priests the money he had received for betraying Christ, bore testimony, "I have sinned in that I have betrayed the innocent blood."

Previously, when the Sanhedrin had been called together to lay plans for waylaying Christ and putting Him to death, Caiaphas said, Cannot ye see that the world is gone after Him? The voices of some members of the council were heard, pleading with the others to check their passion and hatred against Christ. They wished to save Him from being put to death. In reply to them, Caiaphas said, "Ye know nothing at all, nor consider that it is expedient for us [he might have said "a corrupted priesthood"] that one man should die for the people, and that the whole nation perish not."

These words were uttered by one who knew not their significance. . . . He was condemning One whose death would end the need for types and shadows, whose death was prefigured in every sacrifice made. But the high priest's words meant more than he, or those who were combined with him, knew. By them he bore testimony that the time had come for the Aaronic priesthood to cease forever. . . .

Caiaphas was the one that was to be in office when types and shadow were to meet the reality, when the true High Priest was to come into office. . . . People of all characters, righteous and unrighteous, will stand in their positions. With the characters they have formed, they will act their part in the fulfillment of history.—Manuscript 101, 1897.

September 20

LIKE PILATE, WE CONDEMN CHRIST BY OUR SILENCE

◆ *Knowest thou not that I have power to crucify thee, and have power to release thee? Jesus answered, Thou couldest have no power at all against me, except it were given thee from above. John 19:10, 11.*

EFORE the judgment seat Christ stands bound as a prisoner. The judge looks upon Him with suspicion and severity. The people are fast gathering, and spectators are on every side as the charges against Him are read: "He says he is the king of the Jews." "He refuses to pay tribute to Caesar." "He makes himself equal with God.". . . .

Pilate was convinced that no evidence of the guilt of Christ could be substantiated, notwithstanding the priests and rulers had declared that He had spoken blasphemy. But the Jews were under the inspiration of Satan as was Cain and other murderers who have determined to destroy life rather than to save it. "And they were the more fierce, saying, He stirreth up the people, teaching throughout all Jewry, beginning from Galilee to this place."

Here Pilate thought he saw a chance how he might rid himself of the whole matter of the trial of Christ. He perceived clearly that the Jews had delivered Christ up from envy. . . . "As soon as he knew that he [Christ] belonged unto Herod's jurisdiction, he sent him to Herod, who himself also was at Jerusalem at that time."

This was the Herod whose hands were stained with the blood of John. "And when Herod saw Jesus, he was exceeding glad: for he was desirous to see him of a long season, because he had heard many things of him; and he hoped to have seen some miracle done by him. . . ."

The work and mission of Christ in this world was not to gratify the idle curiosity of princes, rulers, scribes, priests, or peasants. He came to heal the brokenhearted. . . . Could Christ have spoken any word to heal the bruises of sin-sick souls, He would not have kept silent. But the precious gems of truth, He had instructed His disciples, were not to be cast before swine. And Christ's deportment and silence before Herod made His silence eloquent.

The Jewish people had brought their long-looked-for Messiah for condemnation to the power to which they themselves were in bondage. They sought to obtain the condemnation of the Prince of life—the only One who could deliver them from their bondage.—Manuscript 112, 1897.

September 21
HISTORY IS REPEATED; CHRIST'S FOLLOWERS PERSECUTED

◆ *And Herod with his men of war set him at nought, and mocked him, and arrayed him in a gorgeous robe, and sent him again to Pilate. Luke 23:11.*

AST history will be repeated. A determined conflict is to be waged in the Christian world. People who are disloyal to the commandments of the living God will, in their supposed self-importance, be inspired by Satan to war against those who follow the Lamb of God which taketh away the sin of the world. . . . The result will be that people will become inhuman in their actions toward other people. . . .

If the professed Christian world would take a lesson from the Jews' treatment of Christ, and resolve in God never themselves to tread over the same ground, they would not make themselves responsible for the death of Christ in the person of His saints.

A large company of the priests and elders accompanied Christ to Herod. And when Christ was brought before Herod, these priests and rulers and scribes were all speaking excitedly, bringing in their accusations against Him. But the tetrarch paid little regard to the charges brought against Christ. He found Him to be innocent of all crime.

The Roman soldiers knew that they would please the low, coarse, hardened rabble and the priests and rulers if they should show Christ all the contempt that a wicked, corrupt soldiery could instigate. And they were helped on by the Jewish dignitaries themselves. . . . They set the Majesty of heaven, the King of glory, before them as a pretender, and treated Him as an object of derision.

They made the King of glory appear in as ridiculous a light as possible. They clothed Him with an old purple, kingly robe, which had done service to some king. They placed in His hands an old reed, and on His divine head a crown of cruel thorns, which pierced the holy temples and sent the blood trickling down His face and beard. The most contemptuous speeches were made before Him. But Christ did not cast upon them one reproachful look. They covered His face with an old garment and struck Him in the face, saying, "Prophesy, who is it that smote thee?" Then snatching the garment rudely away, they spat in His face, and smote Him with the reed with all the brutal force of a corrupt soldiery. The most grotesque attitude and the most vile language were used, while in mock humility they bowed before Him. . . .

The Jews had desired evidence of His divinity by working a miracle, but here they had far greater evidence than any miracle that could have been wrought.—Manuscript. 112, 1897.

September 22
AGAINST OVERWHELMING EVIDENCE PILATE STILL WAVERED

◆ *And from henceforth Pilate sought to release him: but the Jews cried out, saying, If thou let this man go, thou art not Caesar's friend: whosoever maketh himself a king speaketh against Caesar. John 19:12.*

FTER Herod had done his satanic work, he sent Christ, without having pronounced judgment upon Him, back to Pilate, a man convinced, a man convicted, of the truth but unwilling to yield. Pilate seemed wrought upon by unseen influences to acknowledge his convictions in regard to the Holy One of Israel. His wavering mind was compelled to acknowledge that Christ was no pretender, that not a single trace of deception could be found in His words or deportment. . . . Before that satanic, maddened throng, he pleaded for the scourge in the place of the cross.

The determined priests and rulers designed that the scourge should not be left out, but nothing short of the cross would they consent to be His punishment. This is human nature today when under the control of Satan. . . .

Pilate was unwilling to condemn Christ, and he thought he could, irrespective of the rulers, make an appeal to the sympathy of the human side of the character of the mob. He knew he had nothing to hope for in this line from the priests and rulers. He made a short speech declaring that he found no fault in Christ at all. He confirmed the testimony of Herod that the witnesses against Christ were worthless—they did not agree. . . .

Pilate was moving against light and overwhelming evidence and conviction. The priests and rulers saw that they could obtain all that they desired. Pilate had evidence and justice on his side, and if he had taken his stand firmly on the ground of Christ's innocence, he would have saved himself the afterremorse and despair of a man who had sacrificed innocence to the deadly enmity and hatred of an envious, professedly religious people. Jesus was scourged.

A message from God warned Pilate from the deed he was about to commit. . . . While Pilate was examining the prisoner, his wife was visited by an angel from heaven, and in a vision of the night she beheld Jesus and conversed with Him. . . . She heard the condemnation of Pilate and saw him give Christ up to His murderers. She awoke with a cry of horror. Calling for pen and paper, she wrote him words of warning. Now, in Pilate's dilemma, a messenger makes his way to him with the message from his wife, "Have thou nothing to do with that just man: for I have suffered many things this day in a dream because of him."—Manuscript 112, 1897.

September 23
THE WORLD'S REDEEMER REJECTED BY HIS OWN PEOPLE

◆ *Pilate said unto them, Whom will ye that I release unto you? Barabbas, or Jesus which is called Christ? Matthew 27:17.*

NE other course suggested itself to Pilate whereby he might save Him whom he dared not give up to that maddened power, knowing that for envy they had brought Jesus to the judgment hall. Pagan invention, without one particle of justice in it, had made a custom that at the great national festival there should be set at liberty one prisoner who had been condemned to death. Could the convicted Pilate make use of this subterfuge and bring about that which he desired—save an innocent man, whose power, even while bound and under accusation, he knew to be the power of no common man, but of God? His soul was in terrible conflict. He would present the true and innocent Christ side by side with the notable Barabbas, and he flattered himself that the contrast between innocence and guilt would be so convincing that Jesus of Nazareth would be their choice.

Barabbas had pretended to be Christ and had done great wickedness. Under satanic delusion he claimed that whatever he could obtain by theft and robbery and murder was his own. A most striking contrast was presented between the two. Barabbas was a notorious character who had done wonderful things through satanic agencies. He claimed to have religious power, a right to establish a different order of things. . . .

This false Christ was claiming what Satan claimed in heaven—a right to all things. Christ in His humiliation was possessor of all things. In Him was no darkness at all. . . .

Barabbas and Christ stood side by side, and the whole heavenly universe beheld them. The people looked upon the two. Where now were the voices that a few days before were loud in proclaiming the wonderful works that Christ had done? . . . Then the fickle multitude had been imbued with the enthusiasm of heavenly impulse to pour forth in sacred song their praise and hosannas as Christ rode into Jerusalem. Now the choice was given them. Pilate asks, "Whom will ye that I release unto you, Barabbas, or Jesus which is called Christ?". . .

There arose to heaven a cry of tremendous significance to all the world. All heaven heard that cry in which all seemed to join with a zeal and desperation born of their choice. "Not this man," they said, pointing to Jesus, "but Barabbas.". . . The world's Redeemer was rejected, the guilty murderer spared.—Manuscript 112, 1897.

273

September 24
WILL YOU CHOOSE JESUS?

◆ *But ye have a custom, that I should release unto you one at the passover: will ye therefore that I release unto you the King of the Jews? John 18:39.*

*T*HE great controversy between the Prince of light and the prince of darkness has not abated one jot or tittle of its influence as time has gone on. . . .

In our behalf Christ met the specious temptations of Satan and left to us an example as to how to overcome Satan in the conflict. He exhorts His followers, saying, "Be of good cheer; I have overcome the world." Satan has made masterly efforts to perpetuate sin. He arrayed all his evil agencies to war against Jesus Christ in an active, desperate conflict, in order that he might bruise the heart of infinite Love. He seduced the people to bow to idols, and thus gained supremacy over earthly kingdoms. He considered that to be the god of this world was the next best thing to gaining possession of the throne of God in heaven. In a large measure he has been successful in his plans. When Jesus was on earth Satan led the people to reject the Son of God and to choose Barabbas, who in character represented Satan, the god of this world.

The Lord Jesus Christ came to dispute the usurpation of Satan in the kingdoms of the world. The conflict is not yet ended, and as we draw near the close of time, the battle waxes more intense. As the second appearing of our Lord Jesus Christ draws near, satanic agencies are moved from beneath. Not only will Satan appear as a human being, but he will personate Jesus Christ, and the world who has rejected the truth will receive him as the Lord of lords and the King of kings. He will exercise his power and work upon human imagination. He will corrupt both the minds and the bodies of people, and will work through the children of disobedience, fascinating and charming, as does a serpent. What a spectacle will the world be for heavenly intelligences! What a spectacle for God, the Creator of the world, to behold!

The form Satan assumed in Eden when leading our first parents to transgress was of a character to bewilder and confuse the mind. He will work in [just] as subtle a manner as we near the end of earth's history. All his deceiving power will be brought to bear upon human subjects, to complete the work of deluding the human family. So deceptive will be his working that people will do as they did in the days of Christ, and when asked, "Whom shall I release unto you, Christ or Barabbas?" the almost universal cry will be "Barabbas, Barabbas!" And when the question is asked, "What will ye then that I shall do unto him whom ye call the King of the Jews?" the cry again will be "Crucify Him!"—Manuscript 39, 1894 (*Review and Herald,* Apr. 14, 1896).

September 25
EACH OF US NEEDS TO KNOW OUR OWN WEAKNESSES

◆ *And the Lord said, Simon, Simon, behold, Satan hath desired to have you, that he may sift you as wheat: but I have prayed for thee, that thy faith fail not: and when thou art con- verted, strengthen thy brethren. Luke 22:31, 32.*

ATAN is ever intruding himself between the human soul and God. He is ever seeking to make the human agent voice his sug- gestions rather than the words of God. . . .

How little did Peter understand his own weakness. He could not dis- cern but that his spirit was all right, even when he sought to make of none effect the solemn words of Christ that opened to them [the disciples] a fu- ture full of sorrow and of suffering, both to Him and to them. Christ saw that unless Peter was changed in spirit, he would not be able to endure the test and the trial of his Lord's rejection, humiliation, condemnation, and death. To his Master's warning words he responded, "Lord, I am ready to go with thee, both into prison, and to death. And he said, I tell thee, Peter, the cock shall not crow this day, before that thou shalt thrice deny that thou knowest me."

We see how human nature can be deceived, how human nature can be misled, because Satan is allowed to step in between the human soul and Jesus. The word of Christ needs to be spoken with authority, "Get thee be- hind me, Satan." Let Me come close to My servants, that they may not be overcome, that they may believe My words rather than the words of de- ceivers, for what I speak is truth and righteousness. . . .

God's people, rescued from the fire by Jesus Christ, have a sense of their sin, and feel humbled and ashamed. God sees and recognizes their repen- tance and notes their sorrow for sin, which they cannot remove or cancel themselves; but as they pray, their prayers are heard, and this is the reason that Satan stands by to resist Christ. . . . He steps in between the repenting, believing soul and Christ. He seeks to cast his hellish shadow before that soul, to dampen faith, and to make of none effect the words of God. . . .

If Satan stands between the soul and Jesus Christ, then the love and ac- ceptance and pardon of Christ is eclipsed. Men and women will be con- stantly striving to prepare a robe of righteousness to cover their deformity and sin, whereas Christ wants them to come to Him just as they are, and believe in Him as their personal Saviour. In His tender love a forgiving Father brings forth His best robe in which to array His returning child.— Letter 65, 1894 (*Manuscript Releases,* vol. 7, pp. 201-203).

September 26
WHILE WE LOOK TO GOD SATAN HAS NO POWER OVER US

◆ *Wherefore let him that thinketh he standeth take heed lest he fall. 1 Corinthians 10:12.*

*J*UST before Peter's fall, Christ said to him, "Simon, behold, Satan hath desired to have you, that he may sift you as wheat." How true was the Saviour's friendship for Peter! How compassionate His warning! But the warning was resented. In self-sufficiency Peter declared confidently that he would never do what Christ had warned him against. "Lord," he said, "I am ready to go with thee, both into prison, and to death." His self-confidence proved his ruin. He tempted Satan to tempt him, and he fell under the arts of the wily foe. When Christ needed him most, he stood on the side of the enemy and openly denied his Lord.

But even when Peter was denying Him, Christ showed that He still loved him. In the judgment hall, surrounded by those who were clamoring for His life, Jesus thought of His suffering, erring disciple, and turning, He looked at him. In that look Peter read the Saviour's love and compassion, and a tide of memories rushed over him. . . . He saw that he was doing the very thing that he had declared he would not do. . . . Once more he looked at his Master and saw a sacrilegious hand raised to smite Him in the face. Unable longer to endure the scene, he rushed heartbroken from the hall.

He pressed on in solitude and darkness, he knew not and cared not whither. At last he found himself in Gethsemane. The scene of a few hours before came vividly to his mind. He thought of how the Saviour, during His agony in the garden, had come for sympathy and comfort to those who had been so closely connected with Him in labor. . . .

On the very spot where Jesus poured out His soul in agony, Peter fell upon his face and wished that he might die. . . . Had Peter been left to himself, he would have been overcome. But One who could say, Father, I know "that thou hearest me always," One who is mighty to save interceded for him. Christ saves to the uttermost all who come to Him.

Many today stand where Peter stood when in self-confidence he declared that he would not deny his Lord. And because of their self-sufficiency they fall an easy prey to Satan's devices. Those who realize their weakness trust in a power higher than self. And while they look to God, Satan has no power against them. . . .

There are some lessons that will never be learned except through failure. Peter was a better man after his fall. . . . As fire purifies gold, so Christ purifies His people by temptation and trial.—Manuscript 115, 1902.

September 27
CHRIST
CRUCIFIED
FOR US

◆ *And when they were come to the place, which is called Calvary, there they crucified him, and the malefactors, one on the right hand, and the other on the left. Luke 23:33.*

OR transgression of the law of God, Adam and Eve were banished from Eden. Christ, our substitute, was to suffer without the boundaries of Jerusalem. He died outside the gate, where felons and murderers were executed. Full of significance are the words "Christ hath redeemed us from the curse of the law, being made a curse for us."—*The Desire of Ages*, p. 741.

Upon Christ as our substitute and surety was laid the iniquity of us all. He was counted a transgressor, that He might redeem us from the condemnation of the law. The guilt of every descendant of Adam was pressing upon His heart. The wrath of God against sin, the terrible manifestation of His displeasure because of iniquity, filled the soul of His Son with consternation. All His life Christ had been publishing to a fallen world the good news of the Father's mercy and pardoning love. Salvation for the chief of sinners was His theme. But now with the terrible weight of guilt He bears, He cannot see the Father's reconciling face. The withdrawal of the divine countenance from the Saviour in this hour of supreme anguish pierced His heart with a sorrow that can never be fully understood by us. So great was this agony that His physical pain was hardly felt.

Satan with his fierce temptations wrung the heart of Jesus. The Saviour could not see through the portals of the tomb. Hope did not present to Him His coming forth from the grave a conqueror, or tell Him of the Father's acceptance of the sacrifice. He feared that sin was so offensive to God that Their separation was to be eternal. Christ felt the anguish that the sinner will feel when mercy shall no longer plead for the guilty race. It was the sense of sin, bringing the Father's wrath upon Him as the sinner's substitute, that made the cup He drank so bitter, and broke the heart of the Son of God.—*Ibid.*, p. 753.

Amid the awful darkness, apparently forsaken of God, Christ had drained the last dregs in the cup of human woe. In those dreadful hours He had relied upon the evidence of His Father's acceptance heretofore given Him. He was acquainted with the character of His Father; He understood His justice, His mercy, and His great love. By faith He rested in Him whom it had ever been His joy to obey. And as in submission He committed Himself to God, the sense of the loss of His Father's favor was withdrawn. By faith, Christ was victor.—*Ibid.*, p. 756.

September 28
JESUS BECAME SIN FOR US AND SUFFERED ALONE

◆ *Reproach hath broken my heart; and I am full of heaviness: and I looked for some to take pity, but there was none; and for comforters, but I found none. Psalm 69:20.*

HE spotless Son of God hung upon the cross, His flesh lacerated with stripes; those hands so often reached out in blessing, nailed to the wooden bars; those feet so tireless on ministries of love, spiked to the tree; that royal head pierced by the crown of thorns; those quivering lips shaped to the cry of woe. And all that He endured—the blood drops that flowed from His head, His hands, His feet, the agony that racked His frame, and the unutterable anguish that filled His soul at the hiding of His Father's face—speaks to each child of humanity, declaring, It is for thee that the Son of God consents to bear this burden of guilt; for thee He spoils the domain of death, and opens the gates of Paradise.—*The Desire of Ages,* p. 755.

In the sufferings of Christ upon the cross prophecy was fulfilled. Centuries before the crucifixion, the Saviour had foretold the treatment He was to receive. He said, "Dogs have compassed me: the assembly of the wicked have inclosed me: they pierced my hands and my feet. I may tell all my bones: they look and stare upon me. They part my garments among them, and cast lots upon my vesture." The prophecy concerning His garments was carried out without counsel or interference from the friends or the enemies of the Crucified One. To the soldiers who had placed Him upon the cross, His clothing was given. Christ heard the men's contention as they parted the garments among them. His tunic was woven throughout without seam, and they said, "Let us not rend it, but cast lots for it, whose it shall be."

To those who suffered death by the cross, it was permitted to give a stupefying potion, to deaden the sense of pain. This was offered to Jesus; but when He had tasted it, He refused it. He would receive nothing that could becloud His mind. His faith must keep fast hold upon God. This was His only strength. To becloud His senses would give Satan an advantage.

The enemies of Jesus vented their rage upon Him as He hung upon the cross. Priests, rulers, and scribes joined with the mob in mocking the dying Saviour. At the baptism and at the transfiguration the voice of God had been heard proclaiming Christ as His Son. Again, just before Christ's betrayal, the Father had spoken, witnessing to His divinity. But now the voice from heaven was silent. No testimony in Christ's favor was heard. Alone He suffered abuse and mockery from wicked men.—*Ibid.,* p. 746.

September 29
"WOUNDED FOR OUR TRANSGRESSIONS"

◆ *But he was wounded for our transgressions, he was bruised for our iniquities: the chastisement of our peace was upon him; and with his stripes we are healed. Isaiah 53:5.*

*G*OD has a controversy with the inhabitants of this world. Satan has come to them disguised as an angel of light, and under his direction the majority of Christians bow at idolatrous shrines and worship an unknown god. . . .

The human family broke the law of God and defied His will. This law reveals to the world the attributes of God's character, and not a jot or tittle of it could be changed to meet humankind in its fallen condition. But God gave men and women unmistakable evidence that He loved them, and that justice is the foundation of His throne and the evidence of His love. He carried out the penalty of transgression, but let it fall upon a Substitute, even His only begotten Son.

God could not abolish His law to save the human race, for this would immortalize transgression and place the whole world under Satan's control. But He "so loved the world, that he gave his only begotten Son, that whosoever believeth in him should not perish, but have everlasting life." In this wonderful gift is shown the depth of God's goodness. He so loved sinful people that He gave Himself in His Son, that they might have another opportunity, another trial, another chance to show their obedience. He so loved men and women that in order to save them He gave His Son to the world, and in that gift He gave all heaven! This was the only provision God could make. By this gift a way was provided for sinners to return to their loyalty.

God is calling upon all to behold the Lamb of God, which taketh away the sin of the world. Christ lifts the guilt of sin from the sinner, standing Himself under the condemnation of the Lawgiver. He came to this world to live the law in humanity, that Satan's charge that human beings cannot keep the law of God might be demonstrated as false.

He kept the law in humanity, and when He was accused falsely by the Pharisees, He turned to them, asking with a voice of authority and power, "Which of you convinceth me of sin?" He came to reveal to the heavenly universe, to the worlds unfallen, and to sinful people, that every provision had been made by God in behalf of humanity, and that through the imputed righteousness of Christ all who receive Him by faith can show their loyalty by keeping the law. As repenting sinners lay hold of Christ as their personal Saviour, they are made partakers of the divine nature.— Manuscript 63, 1897.

September 30
CHRIST'S FOLLOWERS WILL BE HATED BY THE WORLD

◆ *If the world hate you, ye know that it hated me before it hated you. . . . because ye are not of the world, but I have chosen you out of the world, therefore the world hateth you.* John 15:18, 19.

HE followers of Christ should bear in mind that all the evil speeches made against Christ, all the abuse that He received, they must, as His followers, endure for His name's sake. The piety of the church may professedly be of a high order, but when the truth of the Word of God is brought to bear upon the heart, and when conviction of truth is rejected and despised so that they may keep in friendship with the majority, they place themselves . . . as rejecters of truth and light, on the side of the enemy. Satan stirs them up by a power from beneath, with an intensity that reveals his enmity to God and His laws. They enact human laws that are oppressive and galling. . . .

As Christ was hated without cause, so will His people be hated without cause, merely because they are obedient to the commandments of God and do His works in the place of working directly contrary to them. If He who was pure, holy, and undefiled, who did good and only good in our world, was treated as a base criminal and condemned to death without a vestige of evidence against Him, what can His disciples expect but similar treatment, however faultless may be their life and blameless their character? Human enactments, laws manufactured by satanic agencies under a plea of goodness and restriction of evil, will be exalted while God's holy enactments are despised and trampled underfoot. . . .

We see how professedly righteous people can act out the spirit of Satan to carry their wicked purposes through envy and jealousy and religious bigotry. . . . There is no warfare between Satan and the sinner, between fallen angels and fallen humans. Both possess the same attributes, both are evil through apostasy and sin. . . .

The prediction given in Eden refers in a special manner to Christ, and to all who accept and confess Him as the only begotten Son of God. Christ has pledged Himself to engage in the conflict with the prince and power of darkness and to bruise the serpent's head. All who are the sons and daughters of God are His chosen ones, His soldiers, to war against principalities and powers, against the rulers of the darkness of this world, against spiritual wickedness in high places. It is an unwearied conflict of which there is to be no end until Christ shall come the second time.—Manuscript 104, 1897.

October 1
**TEMPLE SERVICE
ENDED AT DEATH
OF CHRIST**

◆ *And, behold, the veil of the temple was rent in twain from the top to the bottom; and the earth did quake, and the rocks rent. Matthew 27:51.*

*T*HE next day the courts of the Temple were filled with worshipers. . . . But never had the service been performed with such conflicting feelings. The trumpets and musical instruments and the voices of the singers were as loud and clear as usual, but a sense of strangeness pervaded everything. One after another inquired about the strange event that had taken place. Hitherto the Most Holy Place had always been most sacredly guarded from intrusion. . . .

Only once a year was it entered, and then by the high priest. But now a curious horror was seen on many countenances, for this apartment was open to all eyes. At the very moment that Christ had expired, the heavy veil of tapestry, made of pure linen, and beautifully wrought with scarlet and purple, had been rent from top to bottom. The place where Jehovah had met with the priest, to communicate His glory, the place that had been God's sacred audience chamber, lay open to every eye—a place no longer recognized by the Lord.

Many who at that time united in the services of the Passover never again took part in them. Light was to shine into their hearts. The disciples were to communicate to them the knowledge that the great Teacher had come.

According to their practice, the people brought their sick and suffering to the Temple courts, inquiring, Who can tell us of Jesus of Nazareth, the Healer? Some had come from far to see and hear Him. . . . They would not be turned away. But they were driven from the Temple courts, and the people of Jerusalem could not fail to see the contrast between this scene and the scenes of Christ's life.

On every side was heard the cry "We want Christ, the Healer." A world without a Christ was blackness and darkness, not only to the disciples and to the sick and suffering, but to the priests and rulers. The Jewish leaders and even the Roman authorities found it harder to deal with a dead Christ than with a living Christ. The people learned that Jesus had been put to death by the priests. Inquiries were made regarding His death. The particulars of His trial were kept as private as possible, but during the time that He was in the grave, His name was on thousands of lips, and reports of His mock trial and of the inhumanity of the priests and rulers were circulated everywhere.—Manuscript 111, 1897 (*Manuscript Releases,* vol. 12, pp. 417-419).

October 2
**MEN AND
WOMEN TO
STAND BOLDLY
FOR CHRIST**

◆ *He went to Pilate, and begged the body of Jesus. . . . And when Joseph had taken the body, he wrapped it in a clean linen cloth, and laid it in his own new tomb, which he had hewn out in the rock. Matthew 27:58-60.*

Y those of intellect the priests were called upon to explain the prophecies of the Old Testament concerning the Messiah, and while trying to frame some falsehood in reply, the priests became like men insane. Upon many minds the conviction rested that the Scriptures had been fulfilled. . . .

Joseph was a disciple of Christ, but in the past he had not identified himself with Him for fear of the Jews. He now went boldly to Pilate and asked for the body of Christ. He was a rich man, and this gave him influence with the governor. Had he delayed, the body of the Saviour would have been placed with the bodies of the thieves in a dishonored grave.

Nicodemus, a chief ruler and a rabbi, was also a disciple of Christ. He had come to the Saviour by night, as if afraid to have it known that his heart was troubled. That night he listened to the most important discourse that ever fell from human lips. [See John 3.] The words he heard had penetrated his soul. He had been enlightened by them, but still he had not identified himself with Christ. He had been among the number spoken of by John. "Among the chief rulers also many believed on him; but because of the Pharisees they did not confess him, lest they should be put out of the synagogue." But Nicodemus had endeavored, as far as he could, to defend Christ. On one occasion he had asked the priests, "Doth our law judge any man, before it hear him, and know what he doeth?". . .

After the crucifixion Nicodemus came to the cross, bringing a mixture of myrrh and aloes to embalm Christ's body. He had witnessed the cruel treatment of the priests; he had marked Christ's patience and Godlike bearing, even in His humiliation. He now saw more clearly the real character of the high priest, and he came boldly to take the bruised body of his Saviour, looked upon as the body of a malefactor. Thus he identified himself with Christ in His shame and death.

With the death of Christ the hopes of the disciples had perished. Often they repeated the words "We trusted that it had been he which should have redeemed Israel.". . . They met together in the upper chamber, and closed and fastened the doors, knowing that the fate of their beloved Teacher might at any time be theirs.—Manuscript 111, 1897 (*Manuscript Releases,* vol. 12, pp. 419, 420).

October 3
**THERE IS
ALWAYS LIGHT
AMID DARKNESS**

◆ *And, behold, there was a great earthquake: for the angel of the Lord descended
from heaven, and came and rolled back the
stone from the door, and sat upon it.
Matthew 28:2.*

*I*F, after His crucifixion and burial, in the place of giving way to their sorrow the disciples had carefully reviewed what Christ had told them to prepare them for this time, they would have seen light amid the darkness. They need not have been in such apparently hopeless discouragement.

Before anyone had reached the sepulcher, there was a great earthquake. The mightiest angel from heaven, he who held the position from which Satan fell, received his commission from the Father, and, clothed with the panoply of heaven, he parted the darkness from his track. His face was like lightning, and his garments white as snow. As soon as his feet touched the ground it quaked beneath his tread. The Roman guards were keeping their weary watch when this wonderful scene took place, and they were enabled to endure the sight, for they had a message to bear as witnesses of the resurrection of Christ.

The angel approached the grave, rolled away the stone as though it had been a pebble, and sat upon it. The light of heaven encircled the tomb, and the whole heaven was lighted by the glory of the angels. Then his voice was heard, "Thy Father calls thee, come forth." And Jesus came forth from the grave with the step of a mighty Conqueror. There was a burst of triumph, for the heavenly family was waiting to receive Him, and the mighty angel, followed by the army of heaven, bowed in adoration before Him as He, the Monarch of heaven, proclaimed over the rent tomb of Joseph, "I am the resurrection and the life."

When Christ upon the cross cried out, "It is finished," there was a mighty earthquake that rent open the graves of many who had been faithful and loyal, bearing their testimony against every evil work, and magnifying the Lord God of hosts. Now as the Life-giver came forth from the sepulcher, proclaiming, "I am the resurrection and the life," He summoned these saints from the grave. When alive, they had, at the cost of their lives, borne their testimony unflinchingly for the truth. Now they were to be witnesses of Him who had raised them from the dead. These, said Christ, are no longer the captives of Satan. I have redeemed them; I have brought them from the grave as the firstfruits of My power, to be with me where I am, nevermore to see death or experience sorrow.—Manuscript 115, 1897.

October 4
"HE IS RISEN!"

◆ *He is not here, but is risen: remember how he spake unto you when he was yet in Galilee, saying, The Son of man must be delivered into the hands of sinful men, and be crucified, and the third day rise again. Luke 24:6, 7.*

*T*HE Sabbath was past, and Mary Magdalene came early in the morning, when it was yet dark, unto the sepulcher. Other women were to meet her there, but Mary was the first at the sepulcher. They had prepared the sweet spices to anoint the body of their Lord. The women were greatly terrified, and buried their faces in the earth, for the sight of the angels was more than they could endure. The angels were compelled to hide their glory yet more decidedly before they could converse with the women. The women trembled with awe. The angels said, "Fear not ye: for I know that ye seek Jesus, which was crucified. He is not here: for he is risen, as he said. Come, see the place where the Lord lay.". . .

There was no more weeping for Mary. Her heart was filled with joy and rejoicing. . . . While Mary was absent, He [Christ] appeared to the women who had come to the sepulcher from another direction. . . . "Go quickly, and tell his disciples that he is risen from the dead; and behold, he goeth before you into Galilee; there shall ye see him." As yet there had been no revelation of Christ to the eleven, and the women went to tell the disciples the wondrous news. . . . Thus Christ made an appointment for a public meeting with His followers in Galilee. Who was it that reminded the women who were seeking Christ in the tomb of what the Saviour had said to them previously? It was Christ who had risen, as He had told them He would.

In this connection Mark gives a most precious statement that must not be overlooked. The angel said to the women, "Go your way, tell his disciples and Peter that he goeth before you into Galilee." What a comforting message was thus given to the women to give to Peter. The last look Jesus had given Peter was after the disciple's thrice-repeated denial. Peter was not forgotten by Christ, and this mention of his name signified to him that he was forgiven. . . .

The wonderful instruction that Christ had given His disciples was never to lose its force, but they had to be reminded of the lessons that Christ had repeatedly given them while He was yet with them. "Remember," said the angel, "how he spake unto you when he was yet in Galilee, saying, The Son of man must be delivered into the hands of sinful men, and be crucified, and the third day rise again." The disciples were surprised that they had not thought of these things before.—Manuscript 115, 1897.

October 5
**WITNESS OF
THE GUARDS
AT THE TOMB**

◆ *And for fear of him the keepers did shake,
and became as dead men. Matthew 28:4.*

UT where were the Roman guards? They had been enabled to view the mighty angel who sang the song of triumph at the birth of Christ. The angels now sang the song of redeeming love. . . .

When the heavenly train was hidden from their sight, they arose to their feet and made their way as quickly as their tottering limbs would carry them to the gate of the garden. As they came up, staggering like blind or drunken men, their faces pale as the dead, they told those they met of the wonderful scenes they had witnessed. Messengers preceded them quickly to the chief priests and rulers, declaring as best they could, the incidents that had taken place. The guards were making their way first to Pilate, but the priests and rulers sent word for them to be brought into their presence. The hardened soldiers presented a strange appearance, as they bore testimony both to the resurrection of Christ and also of the multitude whom He brought forth with Him as the One who holds life-giving power. . . .

They had not time to think or speak anything but the truth. They thought their story would at once commend itself to the supposedly righteous men who had employed them. But the rulers were not pleased by the report. . . .

The soldiers were bribed to report a falsehood, and the priests guaranteed that if the matter came to Pilate's ears, as it most assuredly would, they would be responsible for the actions of the soldiers. They bribed Pilate to silence. They did more. By special messengers they sent the report that they had prepared to every part of the country. . . .

Many had believed on Jesus as they saw the terrible sights that took place. They remembered the voice that was heard at the foot of the cross amid the noise and confusion: "When the centurion, and they that were with him, watching Jesus, saw the earthquake, and those things that were done, they feared greatly, saying, Truly this was the Son of God.". . . All eyes were turned to the place from whence came the voice. Who had spoken? It was the centurion and the Roman soldiers, heathen and idolaters. . . .

What so enlightened and convinced these men that they could not refrain from confessing their faith in Jesus? It was the sermon that was given in every action of Christ and in His silence under cruel abuse. . . . In that lacerated, bruised, broken body hanging on the cross, the centurion recognized the form of the Son of God.—Manuscript 115, 1897.

October 6
FIRSTFRUITS
OF VICTORY
OVER DEATH

◆ *And the graves were opened; and many*
bodies of the saints which slept arose, and
came out of the graves after his resurrection,
and went into the holy city, and appeared
unto many. Matthew 27:52, 53.

*D*URING His ministry Jesus raised the dead to life. He raised the son of the widow of Nain and Jairus' daughter and Lazarus. But these were not clothed with immortality. After they were raised they continued to be subject to death and decay. But those who came forth from the grave at Christ's resurrection were raised to everlasting life. They were the multitude of captives who ascended with Him as trophies of His victory over death and the grave. . . .

These went into the city, and appeared unto many, declaring, "Christ has risen from the dead, and we be risen with him." Some were terrified at the sight. They bore the most undeniable evidence not only of their own resurrection, but of the resurrection of the crucified Redeemer. After His resurrection, Christ did not show Himself to any save His followers, but testimony in regard to His resurrection was not wanting. It came from various sources, [including] from the five hundred who assembled in Galilee to see their risen Lord. This testimony could not be quenched. The sacred facts of Christ's resurrection were immortalized.

Those who had been raised were presented as trophies to the heavenly universe—samples of the resurrection of all who receive and believe in Jesus Christ as their personal Saviour. They were a symbol of the final resurrection of the righteous. That same power that has raised Christ from the dead will raise His church—as His bride—and glorify it, with Christ, above all principalities, above all powers, above every name that is named, not only in this world, but in the heavenly courts, the world above. . . .

Christ was the firstfruits of them that slept. This very scene, the resurrection of Christ from the dead, was observed in type by the Jews at one of their sacred feasts, called the feast of the Jews. They came up to the temple when the firstfruits had been gathered in, and held a feast of thanksgiving. The firstfruits of the harvest crop was sacredly dedicated to the Lord. . . .

As Christ ascends while in the act of blessing His disciples, an army of angels encircles Him as a cloud. Christ takes with Him the multitude of captives as His trophy. He will Himself bring to the Father the firstfruits of them that slept, to present [them] to God as an assurance that He is conqueror over death and the grave.—Manuscript 115, 1897.

October 7
JESUS WILL GIVE US POWER TO OVERCOME

◆ *To him that overcometh will I grant to sit with me in my throne, even as I also overcame, and am set down with my Father in his throne. Revelation 3:21.*

*S*ATAN is wrestling and battling for our souls. He casts his hellish shadow right athwart our pathway. . . . Look away from his power to the One that is mighty to save to the utmost. Why doesn't your faith plow through the shadow to where Christ is? He has led captivity captive and given gifts unto His followers. He will teach you that Satan claims every soul that does not join with him as his property.

Satan is the author of death. What did Christ do after He brought Satan under the dominion of death? The very last words of Christ while expiring on the cross were "It is finished" (John 19:30). The devil saw that he had overdone himself. Christ by dying accomplished the death of Satan and brought immortality to light.

And after Christ came up from the resurrection, what did He do? He grasped His power and held His scepter. He opened the graves and brought up the multitude of captives, testifying to everyone in our world, and in creation, that He had the power over death and that He rescued the captives of death.

Not all who believed in Jesus were brought to life at that time. It was only a specimen of what would be, that we may know that death and the grave are not to hold the captives, because Christ took them to heaven. And when He comes again with power and great glory, He will open the graves. Again the prison house will be opened, and the dead will come forth to a glorious immortality.

Here are the trophies that Christ took up with Him and presented to the universe of heaven and the worlds that God had created. Any affection that they ever had for Lucifer, who was the covering cherub, is now destroyed. God gave him a chance to work out his character. If He had not done this, there might have been those who felt the accusation he [Lucifer] brought against God, that He didn't give him a fair chance, was justified.

The Prince of life and the prince of darkness were in conflict. The Prince of life prevailed, but at an infinite cost. His triumph is our salvation. . . . Did not our Saviour have something to overcome? Did He not keep up the battle with the prince of darkness until He was a victor on every point? Then He left the work right in the hands of His followers. We have something to do.—Manuscript 1, 1889.

October 8

THE QUESTION OF GOD'S SUPREMACY SETTLED

◆ *Lift up your heads, O ye gates; and be ye lift up, ye everlasting doors; and the King of glory shall come in. Psalm 24:7.*

LL heaven is watching the controversy.... Here upon the earth Satan stirs up the enmity that is in the human mind to resist the salvation that has been brought to them at such an infinite cost. He [Christ] was the light of the world, and yet the world knew Him not. He created the world, and yet the world would not acknowledge Him. But when His life was sought for, the Majesty of heaven had to go from place to place; heaven marked this. And He was despised and rejected; He was mocked at, reviled; but when He was reviled, He reviled not again. But Satan did not stop his persecutions until Christ hung upon the cross of Calvary. All heaven, and all the worlds God had created, were watching the controversy; would Christ carry out the plan He had undertaken to lift lost souls from the pit of sin? ...

The great rebel was uprooted from the thoughts of everyone as they saw Christ's resurrection; the question was settled that the law of God was immutable and covered all that were in heaven and in earth, and all the created intelligences. Christ was with His disciples forty days and forty nights and then ... He was taken up from them into heaven; and the multitude of captives were with Him; and a multitude of heavenly host was around Him; and as they approached the city of God, the angel that was accompanying Him said, "Lift up your heads, O ye gates; and be ye lifted up, ye everlasting doors; and the King of glory shall come in.". ...

Now this Saviour is our intercessor, making an atonement for us before the Father. ... And that precious Saviour is coming again. ... When He cometh the second time, it is not to wear the crown of thorns, it is not to have that old purple robe placed upon His divine form. The voices will not be raised, Crucify Him, Crucify Him, but there is a shout from the angelic host and from those who are waiting to receive Him, Worthy, Worthy is the Lamb that was slain. A divine Conqueror, in the place of the crown of thorns He will wear a crown of glory; in the place of that old kingly robe that they put upon Him in mockery, He will wear a robe whiter than the whitest white. And those hands that were bruised with the cruel nails will shine like gold. ...

The righteous dead come forth from their graves, and they that are alive and remain are caught up together with them to meet the Lord in the air, and so shall they ever be with the Lord. And they will listen to the voice of Jesus, sweeter than any music that ever fell on mortal ear, ... "Come, ye blessed of my Father, inherit the kingdom prepared for you from the foundation of the world."—Manuscript 11, 1886.

October 9
THE BOTTOM LINE: "SIN IS THE TRANSGRESSION OF THE LAW"

◆ *For God so loved the world, that he gave his only begotten Son, that whosoever believeth in him should not perish, but have everlasting life. John 3:16.*

HE rebellion against God's law was begun by Satan in heaven. By this rebellion sin was brought into existence. . . . Satan insisted that God had not dealt with him justly. He criticized God's plan of government. He declared the divine law to be arbitrary, detrimental to the interests of the heavenly universe, and in need of change.

Vital interests were at stake in the worlds that God had created. Would these supposed defects be made so apparent that the inhabitants of the heavenly universe would be justified in claiming that the law could be improved? Would Satan succeed in undermining their confidence in the law?

God in His wisdom did not use measures of force to suppress Satan's rebellion. Such measures would have aroused sympathy for Satan, strengthening his rebellion rather than changing his principles. If God had summarily punished him, many would have looked upon him as one who had been dealt with unjustly, and he would have carried a much larger number with him in his apostasy.

It was necessary to give Satan time to develop his principles. He has had every opportunity to present his side of the question. He has been artful. As often as his position has been seen in its true light, he has changed to some other position. By making false charges, and by misstating the purposes and declared will of God, he has secured sympathizers.

Adam and Eve were placed on trial and failed. . . . Satan deceived Eve, and she disobeyed God. The holy pair, not resisting temptation, were brought under Satan's jurisdiction. The enemy gained supremacy over the human race, bringing in death, the penalty of disobedience.

Jesus declared that He would bear the penalty for sin and that He would conquer Satan by coming to the world and meeting the foe on his own battlefield.

When Christ entered upon His campaign, Satan met Him and contested every inch of ground, exerting his utmost powers to conquer Him. Much was involved in this controversy. . . . The questions to be answered were: Is God's law imperfect, in need of being amended or abrogated? Or is it immutable? Is God's government stable? Or is it in need of changes? Not only before those living in the city of God, but before the inhabitants of all the heavenly universe, were these questions to be answered.— Manuscript 1, 1902.

October 10
ALL CREATION AFFECTED BY THE GREAT CONTROVERSY

◆ *It is finished. John 19:30.*

ROM the manger to the cross Satan followed the Son of God. Temptations beat upon Him like a tempest. But the more fierce the conflict, the more familiar He became with the temptations wherewith human beings are beset, and the better prepared He was to succor the tempted. The severity of the trial through which Christ passed was proportionate to the value of the object to be gained or lost by His success or failure. Not merely the interests of one world were involved. This world was the battlefield, but all the worlds that God had created were affected by the result of the conflict.

In order that he might reign as supreme ruler, Satan sought to overthrow Christ. And he planned and carried out the murder of Christ for no other reason than that to the last he entertained the hope that Christ would not endure a death made as horrible as infernal wisdom could make it. He endeavored to prove the correctness of his assertion that Christ was not self-sacrificing.

Actuated by satanic influences, the crowd clamored for the crucifixion of Christ. All heaven watched the successive steps of Christ's humiliation— His trial, rejection, and death. When on the cross He exclaimed, "It is finished," the warfare was ended. The blood of the Innocent was shed for the guilty. The life that He gave up ransomed the human race from eternal death and sealed the doom of him who had the power of death—the devil.

Satan sought to make it appear that he was working for the liberty of the universe. Even while Christ was on the cross, the enemy was determined to make his arguments so varied, so deceptive, so insidious, that all would be convinced that God's law was tyrannical. He himself laid every scheme, planned every evil, inflamed every mind to bring affliction on Christ. He himself instigated the false accusations against One who had done only good. He himself inspired the cruel deeds that added to the suffering of the Son of God—the pure, the holy, the innocent.

By this course of action Satan has forged a chain by which he himself will be bound. The heavenly universe will bear witness to the justice of God in punishing him. Heaven itself saw what heaven would be if he were in it. The hearts of all in the heavenly universe were united in regarding God's law as changeless. They supported the government of Him who, to redeem the transgressor, spared not His own Son from suffering the penalty of sin.

In His ministry, Christ by word and deed vindicated the honor of God's law. It was for this purpose that He came into the world.—Manuscript 1, 1902.

October 11
**GOD'S LAW
FINALLY
VINDICATED**

◆ *Give me understanding, and I shall keep
thy law; yea, I shall observe it with my whole
heart. Psalm 119:34.*

$\mathcal{W}$HEN Christ ascended and laid open before the heavenly intelligences the scene of the conflict and the fierce attacks that Lucifer made against Him to prevent Him from accomplishing His work on the earth, all the prevarications and accusations of him who had been an exalted angel were seen in their true light. It was seen that his professedly spotless character was deceptive. His deeply laid scheme to exalt himself to supremacy was now fully discerned. . . . When the issue was finally settled, every unfallen being expressed indignation at the rebellion. With one voice they extolled God as righteous, merciful, self-denying, just. His law had been vindicated.

In the beginning Satan's purpose was to separate the human family from God. And in every age he has carried out this same purpose. The same method of deception, the same logic that he used to deceive the holy pair in Eden, he has used in all succeeding ages. His plan of work has ever been one of deception. He claims to be religious. He has a synagogue in which there are worshipers. . . . He sways all classes.

Constantly Satan works among people of all ages. At times he assumes a cloak of piety, purity, and holiness. Often he transforms himself into an angel of light. He has blinded the eyes of men and women so that they cannot see beneath the surface and discern his real purposes.

God is omnipotent, omniscient, immutable. He always pursues a straightforward course. His law is truth—unchanging, eternal truth. His precepts are consistent with His attributes. But Satan makes them appear in a false light. By perverting them he seeks to give human beings an unfavorable impression of God. Throughout his rebellion he has sought to represent God as an unjust, tyrannical being.

But Satan's hypocrisy has been unmasked by Christ's life, trial, and death. Christ took upon Himself human nature, and by His perfect life demonstrated the falsity of the claims of him who constantly accuses those who are trying to obey God's law. And the blood of Christ shed on the cross is the everlasting, incontrovertible testimony that God's law is as immutable as is His own character. The crucifixion of Christ was a murder instigated by Satan and carried out by people who had separated themselves from God. In the day of judgment, when the death of Christ upon the cross is seen in all its reality, every voice will be hushed. Everyone will see that Satan is a rebel.—*Manuscript 1, 1902.*

October 12
THE SON OF GOD WAS BRUISED AND SCARRED IN OUR PLACE

◆ *Who his own self bear our sins in his own body on the tree, that we, being dead to sins, should live unto righteousness: by whose stripes ye were healed. 1 Peter 2:24.*

*W*ELL might all heaven be astonished at the reception their loved Commander received in the world! That a nation claiming to believe prophecy should deny Him, that they should go forward in face of warnings and predictions, close their eyes to light and fulfill the prophecies' every specification, and yet be so blind, so deluded by the enemy of souls that they claimed to be doing God service! And how amazing that a world should reject Him, as did one nation! . . .

His hands were pierced with nails, His holy temples were crowned with thorns. He was indeed bruised by Satan, who nerved his agents to do most cruel things. . . . Our salvation was wrought out by infinite suffering to the Son of God. . . . The heel of Christ was indeed bruised when His humanity suffered, and grief heavier than that which ever oppressed the [human] beings He had created weighed down His soul as He was engaged in paying the vast debt that sinners owed to God, which they could never pay to redeem themselves from bondage. On Him was laid the transgression and grief of us all. . . .

Can men and women for whom Christ died have any just sense of the sufferings of God's dear Son to bring salvation within their reach, that the sons and daughters of Adam might be brought back again to their Eden home? . . .

The conflict was so severe that He was fainting and apparently dying on the field of battle, when angels from the world of light came to the royal Sufferer and ministered unto Him and strengthened Him with food.

Jesus ascended on high from the field of conflict, bearing in His own person His bruises and scars as trophies of His victory, which was to result in annihilating the power of the first rebel, who [before he rebelled] was a chieftain in glory, an exalted angel in heaven. There was rejoicing in heaven, and the proclamation was carried to all worlds that the ruined race was redeemed. The gates of heaven were thrown open to the repentant race who would cease their rebellion and return to their allegiance to the law of God. . . .

The great Head of the church left His work with His delegated servants to carry forward in His name. . . . Christ's followers are not left to carry on this conflict against Satan in their own finite strength; the Captain of our salvation stands at the head, unseen by human vision. The eye of faith discerns their Captain and obeys His orders.—Manuscript 75, 1886.

October 13
**HEAVEN'S
TRIUMPHAL
RECEPTION
OF CHRIST**

◆ *Lift up your heads, O ye gates; even lift them up, ye everlasting doors; and the King of glory shall come in. Psalm 24:9.*

HRIST longed for careworn, oppressed, weary human beings to come to Him, that He might give them the light and life and joy and peace that is to be found nowhere else. The veriest sinners were the objects of His deep, earnest interest, pity, and love. But when in the greatest need of human sympathy, in the hour of His greatest trial and heaviest temptation, the most promising of His disciples left Him. He was indeed compelled to tread the winepress alone, and of the people there was none with Him. An atmosphere of apostasy surrounded Him. On every side could be heard sounds of mockery, taunting, and blasphemy. What then was the outlook for His disciples, left in a world that would not tolerate the Son of the living God? . . .

Christ's work was finished when He expired on the cross, crying with a loud voice, "It is finished." The way was laid open; the veil was rent in twain. Sinners could approach God without sacrificial offerings, without the service of a priest. Christ Himself was a priest forever after the order of Melchizedek. Heaven was His home. He came to this world to reveal the Father. His work on the field of His humiliation and conflict was now done. He ascended up into the heavens, and is forever set down on the right hand of God. . . .

In Joseph's tomb He wrapped Himself in the garment of immortality, and then waited in the world for a sufficient length of time to put beyond doubt the evidence that He was indeed risen from the dead. . . . He rose from the dead to become familiar with His disciples preparatory to His ascension, when He should be glorified before the heavenly universe. . . .

All heaven waited with eager earnestness for the end of the tarrying of the Son of God in a world all seared and marred with the curse of transgression. He ascended from the Mount of Olives in a cloud of angels, who triumphantly escorted Him to the City of God. . . . What a contrast was Christ's reception on His return to heaven to His reception on this earth. . . . There was no sorrow, no suffering, to meet Him at every turn. There were no scowling priests to exercise their ingenuity in finding some word of His that they could misinterpret and thus gain opportunity to harass, abuse, insult, and deride Him. . . .

In proportion to Christ's humiliation and suffering is His exaltation. He could have become the Saviour, the Redeemer, only by first being the Sacrifice.—Manuscript 128, 1897.

October 14
THE PROMISE OF DIVINE POWER

◆ *And, behold, I send the promise of my Father upon you: but tarry ye in the city of Jerusalem, until ye be endued with power from on high. Luke 24:49.*

*H*AVING magnified the law and made it honorable by accepting its conditions in saving a world from ruin, Christ hastened to heaven to perfect His work, and to accomplish His mission by sending the Holy Spirit to His disciples. Thus He would assure His believing ones that He had not forgotten them, though now in the presence of God where there is fullness of joy forevermore.

The Holy Spirit was to descend on those in this world who loved Christ. By this they would be qualified, in and through the glorification of their Head, to receive every endowment necessary for the fulfilling of their mission. The Life-giver held in His hands not only the keys of death but a whole heaven of rich blessings. All power in heaven and earth was given to Him, and having taken His place in the heavenly courts, He could dispense these blessings to all who receive Him. . . .

The Holy Spirit was sent as the most priceless treasure the world could receive. The church was baptized with the Spirit's power. The disciples were fitted to go forth and proclaim Christ, first in Jerusalem, where the shameful work of dishonoring the rightful King had been done, and then to the uttermost parts of the earth. The evidence of the enthronement of Christ in His mediatorial kingdom was given. . . .

The Father gave all honor to His Son, seating Him at His right hand, far above all principalities and powers. He expressed His great joy and delight in receiving the crucified One and crowning Him with glory and honor. And all the favors He has shown to His Son in His acceptance of the great atonement are shown to His people. Those who have united their interests in love with Christ are accepted in the Beloved. They suffered with Christ in His deepest humiliation, and His glorification is of great interest to them, because they are accepted in Him. God loves them as He loves His Son. Christ, Emmanuel, stands between God and the believer, revealing the glory of God to His chosen ones, and covering their defects and transgressions with the garments of His own spotless righteousness. . . .

If God's people will sanctify themselves by obedience to His precepts, the Lord will work in their midst. He will renew humble, contrite souls, making their characters pure and holy.—Manuscript 128, 1897.

October 15
TWO DISCIPLES WENT FROM DESPAIR TO HOPE

◆ *Two of them went that same day to a village called Emmaus, which was from Jerusalem about threescore furlongs. And they talked together of all these things which had happened. Luke 24:13, 14.*

N the first day of the week after Christ's crucifixion, the disciples had everything to fill their hearts with rejoicing. But this day was not a day of joy to all. To some it was a day of uncertainty, confusion, and perplexity. . . . The women brought tidings that . . . positively affirmed that Christ had risen from the dead, and that they themselves had seen Jesus alive in the garden.

But still the disciples seemed unbelieving. Their hopes had died with Christ. And when the news of His resurrection was brought to them, it was so different from what they had anticipated that they could not believe it. . . . From eyewitnesses some of the disciples had obtained quite a full account of the events of Friday. Others beheld the scenes of the crucifixion with their own eyes. In the afternoon of the first day of the week, two of the disciples, restless and unhappy, decided to return to their home in Emmaus, a village about eight miles from Jerusalem. . . .

They had not advanced far on their journey when they were joined by a stranger. But they were so absorbed in their gloom and disappointment that they did not observe Him closely. They continued their conversation, expressing the thoughts of their hearts. . . . Jesus knew that their hearts were bound up with Him in love, and He longed to take them in His arms and wipe away their tears, and put joy and gladness in their hearts. But He must first give them lessons that they would never forget. . . .

They told Him of their disappointment in regard to their Master, "how the chief priests and our rulers delivered him to be condemned to death, and have crucified him." With hearts sore with disappointment and with quivering lips they said, "We trusted that it had been he which should have redeemed Israel: and beside all this, today is the third day since these things were done."

Why did not the disciples remember Christ's words, and realize that events were to be as they had been? Why did not they realize that the last part of His disclosure would be just as verily fulfilled as the first part, that the third day He would rise again? This was the part they should have remembered. The priests and rulers did not forget this.—Manuscript 113, 1897.

October 16
THE DISCIPLES ENLIGHTENED ON CHRIST'S IDENTITY

◆ *And beginning at Moses and all the prophets, he expounded unto them in all the scriptures the things concerning himself.*
Luke 24:27.

HE disciples wondered what this stranger could know that He should penetrate to their very souls and speak with such earnestness, tenderness, sympathy, and with such hopefulness. For the first time since Christ's betrayal in the garden, they began to feel hopeful. Often they looked earnestly at their Companion, and thought that His words were just the words that Christ would have spoken. They were filled with amazement, and their hearts began to throb with expectation, hope, and joy. . . .

There are many who discount Old Testament history. They advocate the idea that the New Testament takes the place of the Old, and that therefore the Old Testament is no longer of any use. But Christ's first work with His disciples was to begin at the Alpha of the Old Testament to prove that He was to come to this world and pass through the experiences that had taken place in His incarnation. The rejection of the Son of God was plainly seen by the prophets. . . .

Christ would have the ideas of His disciples pure and true in every specification. They must understand, as far as possible, in regard to the cup of suffering that was apportioned to Him. He showed them that the awful conflict that they could not yet understand, but that they should understand, was the fulfillment of the covenant made before the foundation of the world was laid. Christ must die as all transgressors of the law will die if they continue in sin. All this should be, but it would not end in defeat but in glorious, eternal victory. . . .

As the disciples were about to enter their house, the Stranger appeared as though He would continue His journey. But the disciples felt drawn to Him. . . . "Abide with us," they said, "for it is toward evening, and the day is far spent." Christ responded to the invitation without making any excuses. "He went in to tarry with them."

Had the disciples failed on this occasion to press their invitation, they would not have known that their traveling Companion was no other than the risen Lord. Christ never forces His company upon anyone. He interests Himself in those who He knows need Him. But if they pass along, indifferent and careless, never thinking of the heavenly Guest, or asking Him to abide with them, He passes on. Thus many meet with great loss. They do not know Christ any more than did the disciples as He walked and talked with them by the way.—Manuscript 113, 1897.

October 17
JESUS REVEALS HIMSELF TO THE DISCIPLES

◆ *And it came to pass, as he sat at meat with them, he took bread, and blessed it, and brake, and gave to them. And their eyes were opened, and they knew him; and he vanished out of their sight. Luke 24:30, 31.*

HE simple evening meal of bread is prepared. It is placed before the Guest, and He puts forth His hands to bless the food. Why do the disciples start back in astonishment? Their companion spreads forth His hands in exactly the same way as their Master used to do. They look again, and lo, they see in His hands the print of nails. Both exclaim at once, It is the Lord Jesus. He has risen from the dead.

They rise to cast themselves at His feet and worship Him. But He has vanished out of their sight. They look at the space that had been occupied by One whose body had lately lain in the grave, and say to each other, "Did not our heart burn within us, while he talked with us by the way, and which he opened to us the scriptures?"

But with this great news to communicate, they cannot sit and talk. Their weariness and hunger have gone. Full of joy, they immediately set out again on the same path by which they came, hurrying to tell the tidings to His disciples in the city. The moon has set, but the Sun of Righteousness has shone upon them. Their hearts leap for joy. They seem to be in a new world. Christ is a living Saviour. They no longer mourn over Him as dead, but rejoice over a living Redeemer. . . .

In some parts the road was not safe or secure, but they climbed over the steep places, slipping on the smooth rocks. They did not know, they did not see, that they had the protection of Him who had just traveled the road with them. With their pilgrim's staff in hand, they press on, desiring to go faster than they dare. They lose their track, but find it again. Sometimes running, sometimes stumbling, they urge their way forward, their unseen Companion close beside them.

Entering Jerusalem, they go to the upper chamber where Christ spent the hours of the last evening before His death instructing His disciples. It is late, but they know that the disciples will not sleep till they know for a certainty what has become of the body of their Lord. They find the door of the chamber securely barred. They knock for admission, but no answer comes. All is still. Then they give their names. The door is carefully unbarred, but as soon as they have entered it is again fastened to keep out spies.—Manuscript 113, 1897.

October 18
"THE LORD IS RISEN INDEED!"

◆ *And they told what things were done in the way, and how he was known of them in breaking of bread. And as they thus spake, Jesus himself stood in the midst of them, and saith unto them, Peace be unto you. Luke 24:35, 36.*

*T*HE travelers find all in surprised excitement. The voices of those in the room break out into thanksgiving and praise, saying, "The Lord is risen indeed, and hath appeared unto Simon." Then the travelers, panting from the haste with which they have made their journey, tell the wondrous story of how, as they were journeying along full of discouragement and hopelessness, they were joined by a Stranger. With wonder and hope they relate how He opened the Scriptures to them, and how they invited Him to abide with them. They tell how they prepared the evening meal, and when, as their Guest had extended His hands to bless the food, they recognized Him. . . .

They have just finished their story, and some are saying they could not believe it, for it is too good to be true, when behold, another Person stands before them. Every eye is fastened upon the Stranger. No one has knocked for entrance. No footstep has been heard. The disciples are startled, and wonder what it means. Then they hear a voice that is no other than the familiar voice of their Master. Clear and distinct the words fall from His lips, "Peace be unto you."

"Then," John states, "were the disciples glad, when they saw the Lord. Then said Jesus to them again, Peace be unto you: as my Father hath sent me, even so send I you. And when he had said this, he breathed on them, and saith unto them, Receive ye the Holy Ghost.". . .

No one is to venture presumptuously into the work of God. Men and women are not to go unless the Holy Spirit is evidently upon them. Only under the supervision of the Holy Spirit can Christ's followers work as He worked.

That evening Christ showed His disciples His hands and His feet so that no doubt that He was the Christ might exist in their minds. "Behold my hands and my feet," He said, "that it is I myself: handle me, and see; for a spirit hath not flesh and bones, as ye see me have. . . . These are the words which I spake unto you, while I was yet with you, that all things must be fulfilled, which were written in the law of Moses, and in the prophets, and in the psalms, concerning me. Then opened he their understanding, that they might understand the scriptures, and said unto them, Thus it is written, and thus it behoved Christ to suffer, and to rise from the dead the third day."—Manuscript 113, 1897.

October 19
JESUS OPENED THE UNDER-STANDING OF HIS FOLLOWERS

◆ *Then opened he their understanding, that they might understand the scriptures. Luke 24:45.*

*T*HE sayings of Christ are to be valued, not merely in accordance with the measure of the understanding of those who hear; they are to be considered in the important bearing that Christ Himself attaches to them. He took the old truths, of which He Himself was the originator, and placed them before His hearers in heaven's own light. How different was their representation. What a flood of meaning and brightness and spirituality was brought in by their explanation.

After His resurrection Christ opened the understanding of His followers, that they might understand the Scriptures. Everything had been transformed by the working of the arts of Satan. Truth was covered up by the rubbish of error, and hidden from finite sight. When Christ referred to His humiliation, rejection, and crucifixion, the disciples could not take in His meaning. It had been a part of their education to expect Christ to set up a temporal kingdom, and when He spoke of His sufferings they could not understand His words. . . .

Christ had many truths to give to His disciples of which He could not speak, because they did not advance with the light that was flashed upon the Levitical laws and the sacrificial offerings. They did not embrace the light, advance with the light, and follow on to still greater brightness as Providence should lead the way.

And for the same reason Christ's disciples today do not comprehend important matters of truth. So dull has been the comprehension of even those who teach the truth to others that many things cannot be opened to them until they reach heaven. It ought not to be so. But as minds become narrow, they think they know it all, and set one stake after another in points of truths of which they have only a glimpse. People close their minds as though there were no more for them to learn, and should the Lord attempt to lead them on they would not take up with the increased light. They cling to the spot where they think they see a glimmer of light, when it is only a link in the living chain of truths and promises to be studied. . . .

The development of truth will be the reward to the humble-hearted seeker who will fear God and walk with Him. The truth that the mind grasps as truth is capable of constant expansion and new development. . . . As the mind grasps it in its preciousness, it becomes elevated, ennobled, and sanctified.—Manuscript 143, 1897 (*Manuscript Releases*, vol. 16, pp. 122, 123).

October 20
WHEN THE HOLY SPIRIT COMES AS THE COMFORTER

◆ *But when the Comforter is come, whom I will send unto you from the Father, even the Spirit of truth, which proceedeth from the Father, he shall testify of me. John 15:26.*

*I*T is not right for us to devote time, brain, bone, and muscle to gathering in the things of earth and drop eternity out of our reckoning, but we should gather sheaves for the Master's garner. . . . The Lord wants us to expand, to grow like the seed introduced into the soil—first the blade, then the ear, then the full corn in the ear. . . .

Some have asked, What shall I do to receive the Holy Ghost? Ask God to search your hearts as with a lighted candle. Do nothing for selfish gratification. Suppose that Christ's professed followers were representatives of Christ in our earth; would not worldlings see this and take knowledge of such that they had learned of Jesus? Will not such be a power? We want the religion of Christ. This will bring forth the fruits of love, joy, and peace. The desire of the Master is not for a scanty supply, but to bear it in abundance.

John 15:17-21 points to the opposition between Christ and the world, and to the persecution inflicted upon Christ and His followers. . . . We want to know Christ, whom to know aright is life eternal. In John 15 He points to trials, to conflicts. He asks if you can endure the conflict; then He points to eternal realities and shows you the thousands of angels sent to be ministers to those who are heirs of salvation. Though He shows the armies arrayed against you, yet He tells you that you need not be discouraged, for the Captain of the Lord's host is with you, as with the Lord's people in Joshua's time. . . . What we want is to know how to fight the battle. The victory is not in the minister or the layperson, but in the Captain of the Lord's host who fights the battle for us. . . .

We fight not against flesh and blood, but against principalities, and powers, and spiritual wickedness in high places, and God is with us.

We are not to consider that the smartness of men and women will bring success. People may have all the learning possible for a human being to comprehend, and yet they may be alone; without Christ they can do nothing. Do you walk humbly before Him? Have you a cherishing of inward sins, heartburnings against anyone? Are you seeking God with all your heart? We can bear to be separated from everything else but the Spirit of God. We want the inspiration of the cross, making us to fall helpless, and the Lord will lift us up.—Manuscript 27, 1891.

October 21
THE PROMISE OF THE HOLY SPIRIT: "YE SHALL RECEIVE POWER"

◆ *But ye shall receive power, after that the Holy Ghost is come upon you: and ye shall be witnesses unto me both in Jerusalem, and in all Judaea, and in Samaria, and unto the uttermost part of the earth. Acts 1:8.*

FTER His resurrection, Christ ascended to His appointed honor. Before the heavenly universe and the worlds unfallen He was to be enthroned. The Father would impress the minds of the believers with the glorious reception of His Son in the home He had left. For our sake He became poor, that we through His poverty might be made rich. . . .

As Christ ascended, His hands were outstretched in blessing upon His disciples. While they stood gazing upward to catch the last glimpse of their ascending Lord, He was received by the heavenly throng into the rejoicing ranks of cherubs and seraphs. And as they escorted Him to His heavenly home, they sang in triumph, "Sing unto God, ye kingdoms of the earth; O sing praises unto the Lord; . . . that rideth upon the heavens of heavens."

Christ determined to bestow a gift on those who had been with Him and on those who should believe on Him, because this was the occasion of His ascension and inauguration, a jubilee in heaven. What gift could Christ bestow rich enough to signalize and grace His ascension to the mediatorial throne? It must be worthy of His greatness and His royalty. Christ gave His representative, the third person of the Godhead, the Holy Spirit. This Gift could not be excelled. . . .

On the day of Pentecost Christ gave His disciples the Holy Spirit as their Comforter. It was ever to abide with His church. During the whole Jewish economy the influence of this Spirit has often been revealed in a marked manner, but not in full. The Spirit had been waiting for the crucifixion, resurrection, and ascension of Christ. For ages prayers had been offered for the fulfillment of the promise, for the impartation of the Spirit; and not one of these earnest supplications had been forgotten. Now for ten days the disciples sent up their petitions, and Christ in heaven added His intercession. He claimed the gift of the Spirit, that He might pour it out upon His people. . . . [Christ] having reached His throne, the Spirit was given as He had promised, and like a rushing, mighty wind, it fell upon those assembled, filling the whole house. It came with a fullness and power, as if for ages it had been restrained, but was now poured forth upon the church, to be communicated to the world. What followed this outpouring? Thousands were converted in a day.—Manuscript 44, 1898.

October 22
THE POWER THAT SHOOK THE WORLD

♦ *I will pour out of my Spirit upon all flesh: and your sons and your daughters shall prophesy, and your young men shall see visions, and your old men shall dream dreams. Acts 2:17.*

FTER the outpouring of the Holy Spirit, the disciples, clothed with the divine panoply, went forth as witnesses to tell the wonderful story of the manger and the cross. They were humble men, but they went forth with the truth. After the death of their Lord, they were a helpless, disappointed, discouraged company—as sheep without a shepherd; but now they go forth as witnesses for the truth, with no weapons but the Word and the Spirit of God, to triumph over all opposition. . . . They were transformed in character and united in the bonds of Christian love. . . . From their lips came words of divine eloquence and power that shook the world.

The third, fourth, and fifth chapters of Acts give an account of their witnessing. Those who had rejected and crucified the Saviour expected to find His disciples discouraged, crestfallen, and ready to disown their Lord. With amazement they heard the clear, bold testimony given under the power of the Holy Spirit. The words and works of the disciples represented the words and works of their Teacher, and all who heard them said, They have learned of Jesus; they talk as He talked. "And with great power gave the apostles witness of the resurrection of the Lord Jesus: and great grace was upon them all."

The chief priests and rulers thought themselves competent to decide what the apostles should do and teach. As they went forth preaching Jesus everywhere, the men who were worked by the Holy Spirit did many things that the Jews did not approve. There was danger that the ideas and doctrines of the rabbis would be brought into disrepute.

The apostles were creating a wonderful excitement. The people were bringing their sick folk . . . and those that had been healed were shouting the praises of God and glorifying the name of Jesus, the very One whom the Jews had condemned, scorned, spit upon, crowned with thorns, and caused to be scourged and crucified. This Jesus was extolled above the priests and rulers. The apostles were even declaring that He had risen from the dead. The Jewish rulers decided that this work must be stopped, for it was proving them guilty of the blood of Jesus.—Letter 38, 1896.

October 23
OPPOSED BY RELIGIOUS LEADERS

◆ *The Sadducees, came upon them, being grieved that they taught the people, and preached through Jesus the resurrection from the dead. And they laid hands on them, and put them in hold unto the next day. Acts 4:1-3.*

HE assertions made by the apostles that they had seen Jesus after His resurrection, and that He had ascended to heaven, were overthrowing the fundamental principles of the Saducean doctrine. This was not to be allowed. The priests and rulers were filled with indignation, and laid their hands on the apostles and put them in the common prison. The disciples were not intimidated or cast down. . . .

"The angel of the Lord by night opened the prison doors, and brought them forth, and said, Go, stand and speak in the temple to the people all the words of this life." We see here that persons in authority are not always to be obeyed, even though they may profess to be teachers of Bible doctrines. There are many today who feel indignant and aggrieved that any voice should be raised presenting ideas that differ from their own in regard to points of religious belief. Have they not long advocated their ideas as truth? So the priests and rabbis reasoned in apostolic days. What mean these men who are unlearned, some of them mere fishermen, who are presenting ideas contrary to the doctrines that the learned priests and rulers are teaching the people? They have no right to meddle with the fundamental principles of our faith.

But we see that the God of heaven sometimes commissions people to teach that which is regarded as contrary to the established doctrines. Because those who were once the depositories of truth became unfaithful to their sacred trust, the Lord chose others who would receive the bright beams of the Sun of Righteousness, and would advocate truths that were not in accordance with the ideas of the religious leaders. And then these leaders, in the blindness of their minds, give full sway to what is supposed to be righteous indignation against the ones who have set aside cherished fables. . . .

But the Holy Spirit will from time to time reveal the truth through its own chosen agencies; and no one, not even a priest or ruler, has a right to say, You shall not give publicity to your opinions, because I do not believe them. That wonderful "I" may attempt to put down the Holy Spirit's teaching.—Letter 38, 1896.

October 24
**"WE MUST
OBEY GOD"**

◆ *But Peter and the apostles answered, "We must obey God rather than any human authority." Acts 5:29, NRSV.*

*I*N most of the religious controversies, the foundation of the trouble is that self is striving for the supremacy. About what? About matters that are not vital points at all, and that are regarded as such only because people have given importance to them. See Matthew 12:31-37; Mark 14:56; Luke 5:21; Matthew 9:3.

But let us follow the history of the men whom the Jewish priests and rulers thought so dangerous because they were bringing in new and strange teaching on almost every theological subject. The command given by the Holy Spirit, "Go, stand and speak in the temple to the people all the words of life," was obeyed by the apostles. . . .

If the priests and rulers had dared act out their own feelings toward the apostles, there would have been a different record, for the angel of God was a watcher on that occasion, to magnify His name if any violence had been offered to His servants.

"And when they had brought them, they set them before the council: and the high priest asked them, saying, Did not we straitly command you that ye should not teach in this name? . . . Then Peter and the other apostles answered and said, We ought to obey God rather than men. . . . And we are his witnesses of these things; and so is also the Holy Ghost, whom God hath given to them that obey him. When they heard that, they were cut to the heart, and took counsel to slay them."

Then the Holy Spirit moved upon Gamaliel, a Pharisee, a doctor of the law, who had a reputation among all the people. His advice was "Refrain from these men, and let them alone: for if this counsel or this work be of men, it will come to nought. But if it be of God, ye cannot overthrow it; lest haply ye be found even to fight against God. And to him they agreed."

Yet the attributes of Satan so controlled their minds that notwithstanding the wonderful miracles that had been wrought in healing the sick and in releasing God's servants from prison, the priests and rulers were so filled with prejudice and hatred they could hardly be restrained. "When they had called the apostles, and beaten them, they commanded that they should not speak in the name of Jesus, and let them go. And they departed from the presence of the council, rejoicing that they were counted worthy to suffer shame for his name. And daily in the temple, and in every house, they ceased not to teach and preach Jesus Christ."—Letter 38, 1896.

October 25
**THERE IS
DANGER IN
REFUSING
TO REPENT**

◆ *But if it be of God, ye cannot overthrow it; lest haply ye be found even to fight against God. Acts 5:39.*

E can see what evidence was given the priests and rulers and how firmly they resisted the Spirit of God. Those who claim superior wisdom and piety may make most terrible and (to themselves) fatal mistakes if they allow their minds to be molded by another power, and pursue a course in resistance to the Holy Spirit. The Lord Jesus, represented by the Holy Spirit, was in the presence of that assembly [of priests trying the apostles], but they did not discern Him. For a moment they had felt the conviction of the Spirit, that Jesus was the Son of God, but they stifled conscience and became blinder and more hardened than before. Even after they had crucified the Saviour, God in His mercy had sent them . . . another call to repentance, even in the terrible charge brought against them by the apostles, that they had killed the Prince of life.

It was not alone the sin of putting to death the Son of God that cut them off from salvation, but their persistence in rejecting light and the conviction of the Holy Spirit. The spirit that works in the children of disobedience worked in them, leading them to abuse the men through whom God was giving a testimony to them. The malignity of rebellion reappeared and was intensified in every successive act of resistance against God's servants and the message He had given them to declare.

Every act of resistance makes it harder to yield. Being the leaders of the people, the priests and rulers felt it incumbent on them to defend the course they had taken. They must prove that they had been in the right. Having committed themselves in opposition to Christ, every act of resistance became an additional incentive to persist in the same path. The events of their past career of opposition were as precious treasures to be jealously guarded. And the hatred and malignity that inspired those acts was concentrated against the apostles.

The Spirit of God revealed its presence unto those who, irrespective of the fear or favor of the public, declared the truth that had been committed to them. Under the demonstration of the Holy Spirit's power, the Jews saw their guilt in refusing the evidence that God had sent; but they would not yield their wicked resistance. Their obstinacy became more and more determined, and worked the ruin of their souls. It was not that they could not yield, but that they could and would not.—Letter 38, 1896.

October 26
IN OUR TIME THE HOLY SPIRIT WILL COME AGAIN

◆ *Be patient therefore, brethren, unto the coming of the Lord. Behold, the husbandman waiteth for the precious fruit of the earth, and hath long patience for it, until he receive the early and latter rain. James 5:7.*

$\mathcal{W}$E have taught, we have expected, that an angel is to come down from heaven, that the earth will be lightened with his glory. Then we shall behold an ingathering of souls similar to that witnessed on the day of Pentecost. This mighty angel comes bearing no soft, smooth message, but words that are calculated to stir the hearts of men and women to their very depths. . . . Are we, indeed, as human agencies to co-operate with the divine instrumentalities in sounding the message of this mighty angel who is to lighten the earth with His glory?

How great and widespread must be the power of the prince of evil, which can be subdued only by the mighty power of the Spirit. Disloyalty to God, transgression in every form, has spread over our world. Those who would preserve their allegiance to God, who are active in His service, become the mark of every shaft and weapon of hell. If those who have had great light have not corresponding faith and obedience, they soon become leavened with the prevailing apostasy; another spirit controls them. While they have been exalted to heaven in point of opportunities and privileges, they are in a worse condition than the most zealous advocates of error. . . .

Others who have not had so great light, who have never identified themselves with the truth, will, under the influence of the Spirit, respond to the light when it shines upon them. Truth that has lost its power upon those who have long slighted its precious teaching appears beautiful and attractive to those who are ready to walk in the light. . . .

Amid the confusion of delusive doctrines, the Spirit of God will be a guide and a shield to those who have not resisted the evidences of truth. . . . We have no time to confer with flesh and blood. The power of Satan is apparently in the supremacy; he is seeking to convert all things in the world to his own purpose, to imbue human beings with his own spirit and nature. The conflict will be terrible. . . . The confederacy of satanic agencies, united with evil persons, are as instruments of unrighteousness, throwing their whole force into the battlefield, evil against good. . . .

When the Spirit was poured out from on high, the church was flooded with light, but Christ was the Source of that light. His name was on every tongue; His love filled every heart. So it will be when the angel that comes down from heaven having great power shall lighten the whole earth with His glory.—Letter 25b, 1892.

October 27
**STEPHEN, THE
FIRST CHRISTIAN
MARTYR**

◆ *Then they cried out with a loud voice, and
stopped their ears, and ran upon him with one
accord, and cast him out of the city, and stoned
him. Acts 7:57, 58.*

TEPHEN was the first Christian martyr. . . . The enemies of God and the truth felt stirred with hatred and opposition. Satan impelled them to resist the truth. Stephen had to meet in argument the most artful, deceptive disputants, hoping to confuse and put down his arguments. If Stephen had not searched the Scriptures and himself become fortified with the evidence of God's Word, he could not have borne the test; but he knew the foundation of his faith and was firm, and he was ready to answer his opponents.

Stephen came off victorious. He spoke with assurance and wisdom and power that astonished and confounded the enemies of truth. When they found themselves baffled and defeated at every attempt, then they were bent on his destruction. Had these professedly honest and wise men been really seeking for the truth, they would have admitted evidence that they could not controvert. . . . But such was not their purpose or character. They hated Christ, they hated all His followers, and they put Stephen to death.—Manuscript 17, 1885.

Stephen, a man loved by God, and one who was laboring to win souls to Christ, lost his life because he bore a triumphant testimony of the crucified and risen Saviour. The record states that he was full of faith and power, and that he did great wonders and miracles among the people. . . . But the spirit that had manifested itself in bitter opposition to the world's Redeemer was still working in the children of disobedience. The hatred that the enemies of truth had shown for the Son of God, they revealed in their hatred for His followers. . . .

In the light that they saw in the face of Stephen, the men of authority had evidence from God. But they despised the evidence. Oh, that they would heed! Oh, that they would repent! But they would not; and the rebuke of God came from the lips of the faithful witness: "Ye stiffnecked and uncircumcised in heart and ears, ye do always resist the Holy Ghost: as your fathers did, so do ye.". . .

Here two armies were in conflict, the army of heaven and the army of false religious zealots. On which side would this company forever after stand? It was still possible for them to repent and be forgiven even after having done this terrible evil against Christ in the person of His saint.—Manuscript 11, 1900.

October 28
PHILIP THE EVANGELIST

◆ *A man of Ethiopia, an eunuch of great authority, . . . was returning, and sitting in his chariot read Esaias the prophet. Then the Spirit said unto Philip, Go near, and join thyself to this chariot. Acts 8:27-29.*

heavenly messenger was sent to Philip [one of the chosen deacons] to show him his work for the Ethiopian. The evangelist was directed: "Arise, and go toward the south unto the way that goeth down from Jerusalem unto Gaza, which is desert.". . .

Today, just as much as then, the angels are leading and guiding those who will be guided and led. This angel could have done the work himself, but this is not God's way of working. Believers must connect with other believers, and as God's instrumentalities work in behalf of the lost.

Philip understood his work. This man of high authority was being drawn to the Saviour, and he did not resist the drawing. He did not make his high position an excuse why he could not accept the crucified One. The evangelist asked him, "Understandest thou what thou readest? And he said, How can I, except some man should guide me? And he desired Philip that he would come up and sit with him" and explain to him the Word of God. . . .

"Then Philip opened his mouth, and began at the same scripture, and preached unto him Jesus. And as they went on their way, they came unto a certain water: and the eunuch said, See, here is water; what doth hinder me to be baptized? And Philip said, If thou believest with all thine heart, thou mayest. . . . And they went down both into the water, both Philip and the eunuch; and he baptized him.". . .

While angels from heaven are doing their work, evil agencies are working to draw the mind to something else. Satan is interposing obstacles, so that the inquiring mind that would understand the Word of God shall become confused. Thus he worked with Christ in the wilderness of temptation. The experience of Christ is placed on record that we may understand the methods and plans of Satan. Had Philip left the eunuch with his case hanging in the balance, he might never have accepted the Saviour. Evil angels were waiting for their opportunity when they could press in their falsehoods and divert the newly awakened mind from seeking after truth. The Lord's agencies must be wholly consecrated to His service, that they may be quick to understand their work. As wise stewards they must take advantage of every circumstance to teach the grace of God and draw people to Christ.—Manuscript 11, 1900.

October 29
SAUL BECOMES PAUL, APOSTLE TO THE GENTILES

◆ *And he fell to the earth, and heard a voice saying unto him, Saul, Saul, why persecutest thou me? And he said, Who art thou, Lord? And the Lord said, I am Jesus whom thou persecutest. Acts 9:4, 5.*

AUL had been educated by the most learned teachers of the age. He had been taught by Gamaliel. Saul was a rabbi and a statesman. He was a member of the Sanhedrin and was very zealous for the suppression of Christianity. He acted a part in the stoning of Stephen, and we read further of him, "As for Saul, he made havock of the church, entering into every house, and haling men and women committed them to prison." But he was stopped in his career of persecution.

As he was on his way to Damascus to arrest any Christians he could find, "suddenly there shined round about him a light from heaven: and he fell to the earth, and heard a voice saying unto him, Saul, Saul, why persecutest thou me?". . .

Saul converted was called Paul. He united with the disciples and was among the chief of the apostles.—Manuscript 95, 1899.

Although the apostles were often cast down in the conflict with evil people and the powers of darkness, yet they were enabled to press again to the conflict, having before them triumph or death in the effort. In their bodies, in bruises and wounds and stripes received for the sake of Jesus, they carried the evidence of the crucifixion of Christ, that they were partakers with Him of His sufferings.

Their very deliverance and preservation under manifold difficulties and trials testified that Jesus lived, and because of His power they lived also.—Manuscript 58, 1900.

A true and faithful Stephen was stoned to death by the enemies of Christ. Surely it did not appear that God was strengthening His cause in the earth by thus permitting wicked men to triumph. But from this very circumstance, Paul was converted to the faith, and through his words thousands were brought to the light of the gospel.—Letter 10, 1879.

Those selected for the work of God should be men and women who are faithful and true, workers whom God can instruct, who will impart what they receive, proclaiming without reserve the will of God, pointing out the better way to all with whom they come in contact. New men and women in Christ are born to conflict, toil, and labor, born to engage in the good fight of faith. There is ever within their reach a power by which they may obtain the victory at every onset, power that will enable them to be more than conquerors over the difficulties they meet.—Letter 150, 1900.

October 30
TIMOTHY, AN EXEMPLARY YOUTH

◆ *Let no man despise thy youth; but be thou an example of the believers, in word, in conversation, in charity, in spirit, in faith, in purity. 1 Timothy 4:12.*

IMOTHY'S] principles had been so established by a correct education that he was fitted to be placed as a religious teacher in connection with Paul, the great apostle to the Gentiles. He was a mere youth, yet he bore his great responsibilities with Christian meekness. He was faithful, steadfast, and true; and Paul made him his companion in labor and travel, that he might have the benefit of his experience in preaching the gospel and establishing churches. . . .

Paul loved Timothy because Timothy loved God. His intelligent knowledge of experimental piety and of the truth gave him distinction and influence. . . . The moral influence of his home was substantial, not fitful, not impulsive, not changeable. The Word of God was the rule that guided Timothy. . . .

There are many who move from first impulse rather than from experience and judgment. But Timothy exercised consideration and calm thought, inquiring at every step, "Is this the way of the Lord?". . . He had no specially wonderful talents; but his work was valuable because he used his God-given abilities as consecrated gifts in the service of God. The Holy Spirit found in Timothy a mind that could be molded and fashioned to become a temple for the indwelling of the Holy Spirit, because he submitted to be molded.

The highest aim of our youth should not be to strain after something novel, but to place themselves under the teaching of the Holy Scriptures. Then they may possess the attributes classed as highest in the heavenly courts. They will hide themselves in God, and in all their teaching will simplify the original truth so that it will not appear strange but familiar to other minds. They will weave it into their daily thoughts and practical life.

We see the advantage that Timothy had in a correct example of piety and true godliness. . . . The manifest spiritual power of the piety in the home kept him pure in speech and free from all corrupting sentiments. From a child Timothy had known the Holy Scriptures. He had the benefit of the Old Testament Scripture, and the manuscript of part of the New, the teachings and lessons of Christ. . . .

A noble, all-round character does not come by chance. It is the result of the molding process of character-building in the early years of youth, and a practice of the law of God in the home.—Letter 33, 1897.

October 31
JOHN THE BELOVED BECOMES JOHN THE REVELATOR

♦ *The Revelation of Jesus Christ, which God gave unto him, to shew unto his servants things which must shortly come to pass; and he sent and signified it by his angel unto his servant John. Revelation 1:1.*

*A*FTER Christ had ascended, John's testimony concerning Christ disturbed those in authority. With power he bore witness that Christ was a risen Saviour. To please the Jews, the Romans had crucified Christ, and now they sought still further to please them by placing John where his voice would not be heard by Jew or Gentile. He was banished to the Isle of Patmos.

Apparently the Lord permitted His enemies to triumph, as far as outward appearance was concerned. But God's hand was moving unseen in the darkness. God permitted His faithful servant to be placed where Christ could give him a more wonderful revelation of Himself to give to the world. . . . He was hidden as it were on a desert island, and here Christ visited him, giving him a most wonderful view of His glory, and making known to him what was to come upon the earth. . . .

John was deprived of the society of his brethren and of the pleasure of association. But no one could deprive him of the light and revelation of Christ. A great light was to shine from Christ to His servant. Richly favored was this beloved disciple. With the other disciples he had traveled with Jesus, learning of Him and feasting on His words. . . . On the holy Sabbath day the risen Saviour made His presence known to John; and the testimony then given him is given also to us. God would have us search the Scriptures, that we may know what will be in the last days of this earth's history. . . .

[Portions of Revelation 1 are quoted.] This is a most powerful testimony, but its true significance is but dimly discerned. Let every student of Scripture carefully ponder every word in the first chapter of Revelation, for every sentence and every word is of weight and consequence.

The appearance of Christ to John should be to all, believers and unbelievers, an evidence that we have a risen Christ. It should give living power to the church. At times dark clouds surround God's people. It seems as though oppression and persecution would extinguish them. But at such times the most instructive lessons are given. As in the darkest night the stars shine the brightest, so the most brilliant beams of God's glory are revealed in the deepest gloom. The darker the sky, the more clear and impressive are the beams of the Sun of Righteousness, the risen Saviour.—Manuscript 106, 1897.

311

November 1
GOD'S MESSAGE FOR HIS PEOPLE

◆ *The devil shall cast some of you into prison, that ye may be tried; and ye shall have tribulation ten days: be thou faithful unto death, and I will give thee a crown of life. Revelation 2:10.*

*J*OHN had been closely associated with the Saviour during His life of ministry. He had heard His wonderful words and had seen His wonderful deeds, and his testimony was given in clear lines. Out of the abundance of a heart overflowing with love for Christ he spoke, and no power could stay his words. . . .

Like his Master, John patiently submitted to every attempt to put him to death. When his enemies cast him into the cauldron of boiling oil, they thought to hear no more from him. But as the words of satanic origin were spoken, "Thus perish all who believe in that deceiver, Jesus Christ of Nazareth," John declared, "My Master patiently submitted to all that Satan and his angels could devise to humiliate and torture Him. He gave His life to save the world. He died that we might live. I am honored in being permitted to suffer for His sake. I am only a weak, sinful man, but Christ was holy, harmless, undefiled, separate from sinners. He did no sin, neither was guile found in His mouth." John's words, while suffering at the hands of his enemies, had an influence, and he was removed from the cauldron by the very ones who had cast him in.

It was after this that John was sent to the Isle of Patmos, where, separated from his companions in the faith, his enemies supposed that he would die from hardship and neglect. But John made friends and converts even there. They thought that they had at last placed the faithful witness where he could no longer trouble Israel or the wicked rulers of the world. . . .

God and Christ and the heavenly host were John's companions on the Isle of Patmos. From them he received instruction that he imparted to those separated with him from the world. There he wrote out the visions and revelations he received from God, telling of the things that would take place in the closing period of this earth's history. When his voice would no longer witness for the truth, when he could no longer testify of the One he loved and served, the messages given to him on that rocky, barren coast were to go forth as a lamp that burneth. Every nation, kindred, tongue, and people would learn the sure purpose of the Lord, not concerning the Jewish nation merely, but every nation upon the earth.—Manuscript 150, 1899.

November 2
REVELATION AN OPEN BOOK FOR OUR STUDY

◆ *Blessed is he that readeth, and they that hear the words of this prophecy, and keep those things which are written therein: for the time is at hand. Revelation 1:3.*

ANY have entertained the idea that the book of Revelation is a sealed book, and they will not devote time and study to its mysteries. They say that they are to keep looking to the glories of salvation, and that the mysteries revealed to John on the Isle of Patmos are worthy of less consideration than these.

But God does not so regard this book. He declares: "I testify unto every man that heareth the words of the prophecy of this book, If any man shall add unto these things, God shall add unto him the plagues that are written in this book: and if any man shall take away from the words of the book of this prophecy, God shall take away his part out of the book of life, and out of the holy city, and from the things which are written in this book.". . .

The Lord revealed to His servant John the mysteries of the book of Revelation, and He designs that they shall be open to the study of all. In this book are depicted scenes that are now in the past and some of eternal interest that are taking place around us; other of its prophecies will not receive their complete fulfillment until the close of time, when the last great conflict between the powers of darkness and the Prince of heaven will take place. . . .

Many of the prophecies are about to be fulfilled in quick succession. Every element of power is about to be set to work. Past history will be repeated, old controversies will arouse to new life, and peril will beset God's people on every side. Intensity is taking possession of the human family. It is permeating everything upon the earth. And for what? Games, plays, amusements; people are rushing and crowding and contending for the mastery. That which is common and perishable is absorbing their attention, so that things of eternal interest are scarcely thought of.

Human beings, possessed with energy, zeal, and perseverance, will place all their God-given powers in cooperation with Satan's despotism to make void the law of God. Impostors of every caste and grade will claim to be worthy and true, and there will be a magnifying of the common and impure against the true and the holy. Thus the spurious is accepted, and the true standard of holiness is discarded, as the word of God was discarded by Adam and Eve for the lie of Satan.—Manuscript 143, 1901.

November 3
TESTIMONY OF JESUS REVEALS GOD'S ETERNAL LOVE

◆ *I John, who also am your brother, and companion in tribulation, and in the kingdom and patience of Jesus Christ, was in the isle that is called Patmos, for the word of God, and for the testimony of Jesus Christ. Revelation 1:9.*

IT is through one who is "a brother, and companion in tribulation" that Christ reveals to His people the fearful conflict that they must meet before His second coming. Before the scenes of their bitter struggle are opened to them, they are reminded that other believers also have drunk of the cup and been baptized with the baptism. He who sustained these early witnesses to the truth will not forsake His people in the final conflict.

It was in a time of fierce persecution and great darkness, when Satan seemed to triumph over the faithful witnesses for God, that John in his old age was sentenced to banishment. He was separated from his companions in the faith, and cut off from his labors in the gospel; but he was not separated from the presence of God. The desolate place of his exile proved to him to be the gate of heaven. He says, "I was in the Spirit on the Lord's day"—the holy day that God had blessed and set apart as His own—"and heard behind me a great voice, as of a trumpet, saying, I am Alpha and Omega, the first and the last: and, What thou seest, write in a book. . . . And I turned to see the voice that spake with me. And being turned, I saw seven golden candlesticks; and in the midst of the seven candlesticks one like unto the Son of man.". . .

Christ walks in the midst of the golden candlesticks. Thus is symbolized His relation to the churches. He is in communion with His people. . . . Although He is High Priest and Mediator in the sanctuary above, yet He walks up and down in the midst of the churches on earth. . . .

Again, as the Holy Spirit rested upon the prophet, he sees a door opened in heaven, and hears a voice calling him to look upon the things which shall be hereafter. And he says, "Behold, a throne was set in heaven, and one sat on the throne. And he that sat was to look upon like a jasper and a sardine stone." Ministering angels were around about Him, waiting and eager to do His will, while the rainbow of God's promise, which was a token of His covenant with Noah, was seen by John encircling the throne on high—a pledge of God's mercy to every repentant, believing soul. It is an everlasting testimony that "God so loved the world, that he gave his only begotten Son, that whosoever believeth in him should not perish, but have everlasting life." It declares to the whole world that God will never forget His people in their struggle with evil.—Manuscript 100, 1893.

314

November 4
CHRIST'S WORK FOR OUR REDEMPTION IS DESCRIBED

◆ *Behold, the Lion of the tribe of Juda. . . . And in the midst of the elders stood a Lamb as it had been slain. Revelation 5:5, 6.*

*T*HE Saviour was presented to John under the symbols of the "Lion of the tribe of Juda," and "a Lamb as it had been slain." Here the whole work of redemption was expressed. These symbols represent the union of omnipotent power and self-sacrificing love. As the Lion of Judah, Christ will defend His chosen ones and bring them off victorious, because they accepted Him as "the Lamb of God, which taketh away the sin of the world." Christ the slain Lamb—who was despised, rejected, the victim of Satan's wrath, of human abuse and cruelty—how tender was His sympathy with His people who were in the world! And according to the infinite depths of His humiliation and sacrifice as the Lamb of God will be His power in glory as the Lion of Judah, for the deliverance of His people.

To John were opened the great events of the future that were to shake the thrones of kings and cause all earthly powers to tremble. He beheld the close of all earthly scenes, the ushering in of His reign who is to be King of kings, and whose kingdom shall endure forever. . . . He saw Christ receiving the adoration of all the hosts of heaven and heard the promise that whatever tribulation might come upon God's people, if they would but patiently endure they should be more than conquerors through Him that loved them. . . .

John was now prepared to witness the thrilling scenes in the great conflict between those who keep the commandments of God and those who make void His law. He saw the wonder-working power arise that was to deceive all who should dwell upon the earth who were not connected with God, "saying to them that dwell on the earth, that they should make an image to the beast, which had the wound by a sword, and did live.". . .

Of the loyal and true who do not bow to the decrees of earthly rulers against the authority of the King of heaven the revelator says, "Here is the patience of the saints: here are they that keep the commandments of God, and the faith of Jesus."

These lessons are for our benefit. We need to stay our faith upon God, for there is just before us a time that will try every soul. Christ upon the Mount of Olives rehearsed the fearful judgments that were to precede His second coming. . . . While these prophecies received a partial fulfillment at the destruction of Jerusalem, they have a more direct application in the last days.—Manuscript 100, 1893.

November 5
LOOKING INTO THE FUTURE

◆ *There will be signs. . . . People will faint from fear and foreboding of what is coming upon the world. Luke 21:25, 26, NRSV.*

*J*OHN also was a witness of the terrible scenes that will take place as signs of Christ's coming. He saw armies mustering for battle, and people's hearts failing them for fear. He saw the earth moved out of its place, the mountains carried into the midst of the sea, the waves thereof roaring and troubled. He saw the vials of wrath opened, and pestilence, famine, and death come upon the inhabitants of the earth.

Already the restraining Spirit of God is being withdrawn from the world. Hurricanes, storms, tempests, fire and flood, disasters by sea and land, follow each other in quick succession. Science seeks to explain all these. The signs thickening around us, telling of the near approach of the Son of God, are attributed to any other than the true cause. People cannot discern the sentinel angels restraining the four winds, that they shall not blow until the servants of God are sealed. But when God shall bid His angels loose the winds, there will be such a scene of strife as no pen can picture.

We are standing on the threshold of great and solemn events. Prophecy is fast fulfilling. The Lord is at the door. There is soon to open before us a period of overwhelming interest to all who are living. The controversies of the past are to be revived. New controversies will arise. The scenes to be enacted in our world are not even dreamed of. Satan is at work through human agencies.

But God's servants are not to trust to themselves in this great emergency. The program of coming events is in the hands of the Lord. The world is not without a ruler; the Majesty of heaven has the destiny of nations, as well as the concerns of His church, in His own hands. . . .

The important future is before us. To meet its trials and temptations, and to perform its duties, will require great faith and perseverance. But we may triumph gloriously, for not one watching, praying, believing soul will be ensnared by the devices of the enemy. All heaven is interested in our welfare and waits our demand upon its wisdom and strength. In the time of trial just before us, God's pledge of security will be placed upon those who have kept the word of His patience.—Manuscript 100, 1893.

November 6
WE ARE ACCOUNTABLE FOR THE LIGHT WE HAVE BEEN GIVEN

◆ *Strait is the gate, and narrow is the way, which leadeth unto life, and few there be that find it. Matthew 7:14.*

HE mild, beloved disciple [John] has said, "He that saith, I know him, and keepeth not his commandments, is a liar, and the truth is not in him" (1 John 2:4). The Word of God is very plain and pointed. It is dangerous business to profess to be a follower of Jesus and in works deny Him by indifference to even one of His requirements.

The history of the Reformation teaches us that the church of Christ is never to come to a standstill and cease reforming. God stands at the head, saying to them as He did to Moses, "Go forward." "Speak unto the children of Israel, that they go forward." God's work is onward; step by step His people advance onward through conflict and trial to final victory. The history of the church teaches us that God's people are not to be stereotyped in their theories of faith, but to be prepared for new light, for opening truth revealed in His Word.

The past history of the advancement of truth amid error and darkness shows us that sacred truth is not cherished and sought after by the majority. Those who have advanced in reform, obeying the voice of God—"Go forward"—have been subject to opposition, torture, and death; and in the face of gaping prisons and threatened torture and death, they deemed the truth for their time of sufficient importance to hold tenaciously, yielding their life rather than to sacrifice their faith. They counted not their life dear unto them if sacrificed for the truth of God. The truth in our day is as important as it was in the days of the martyrs. . . .

What if in Luther's day people had taken a position to cover their disobedience to God's requirement with: "God is too merciful to condemn me for not taking unpopular truth. Our intellectuals and our religious leaders do not accept it. I will run the risk of transgressing God's law because the world rejects it. . . . I am satisfied with my religion; . . . I will risk going with the crowd."

If I go with the crowd, the Bible tells me I am in the broad road to death. Said the Majesty of heaven, "Strait is the gate, and narrow is the way, which leadeth unto life, and few there be that find it." We are accountable for the light that shines in our day. Christ wept in agony over Jerusalem because they knew not the time of their visitation. It was their day of trust, their day of opportunity and privilege. . . . The foul ingratitude, the hollow formalism, and the hypocritical insincerity of hundreds of years called these tears of irrepressible anguish from His eyes.—Letter 35a, 1877.

November 7
**DANGER OF
INDIFFERENCE
TO LIGHT**

◆ *And this is the judgment, that the light
has come into the world, and people loved
darkness rather than light. John 3:19, NRSV.*

HE loss of one soul is represented as a catastrophe in comparison with which the gain of a world sinks into insignificance. . . . In Jerusalem is represented every soul who neglects present privileges and refuses the light that God sends them. Have the counsels of God been cherished? Have the entreaties and warnings of His servants been accepted? Has remonstrance been heeded? Oh, that we may individually improve the golden moments of this "thy day" lest the word shall come, "but now they are hid from thine eyes." If light shines in our day we are to receive the light, appreciate it, and walk in the light without waiting to see whether prominent people or scholars accept it. . . .

The words of Christ [are]: "Think not that I am come to destroy the law, or the prophets: I am not come to destroy, but to fulfil.". . . Jesus looked down through the centuries and saw that the Christian world would think and teach that the death of Christ abrogated the Father's law. He therefore makes a plain statement to undeceive all minds that want to be undeceived upon this point. . . .

Men and women have died without keeping the seventh-day Sabbath. They were good people and lived up to all the light they had. They could not be responsible for the light that they never had. We are accountable for the light that shines in our day. To excuse our transgression of God's law because good people in generations past did not keep it would be folly. . . .

It is never safe to be indifferent to light. If professedly great and good people do not obey the law of God, is it any reason we should transgress? . . . It was the scribes, the rulers, the priests, men in holy office, men who believed their righteousness was above the whole world, who persecuted Christ. These pious pretenders were the fiercest persecutors Jesus had. . . . It was the teachers of the people that mocked Him while He hung upon the cross.

Professed Christians of today who reject light will be no more favorable to those who receive and rejoice in the light of truth than were the Jews in the days of Christ. If they had known that He was the Prince of life, they would not have crucified Him. Why did they not know? Because they refused every evidence given them that Christ was the Messiah. . . . They will look upon the believers as a little, weak people, a few fanatics, and will speak derisively of them.—Letter 35a, 1877.

November 8
**PERSECUTION IN
EARLY CENTURIES**

◆ *And others had trial of cruel mockings
and scourgings, yea, moreover of bonds and
imprisonment. Hebrews 11:36.*

*W*HEN Jesus revealed to His disciples the fate of Jerusalem and the scenes of the Second Advent, He foretold also the experience of His people from the time when He should be taken from them to His return in power and glory for their deliverance. From Olivet the Saviour beheld the storms about to fall upon the apostolic church, and, penetrating deeper into the future, His eye discerned the fierce, wasting tempests that were to beat upon His followers in the coming ages of darkness and persecution. . . .

The history of the early church testified to the fulfillment of the Saviour's words. The powers of earth and hell arrayed themselves against Christ in the person of His followers. . . . Christians were stripped of their possessions and driven from their homes. . . . Great numbers sealed their testimony with their blood. . . .

Under the fiercest persecution these witnesses for Jesus kept their faith unsullied. . . . With words of faith, patience, and hope they encouraged one another to endure privation and distress. The loss of every earthly blessing could not force them to renounce their belief in Christ. Trials and persecutions were but steps bringing them nearer their rest and their reward. . . .

In vain were Satan's efforts to destroy the church of Christ by violence. The great controversy in which the disciples of Jesus yielded up their lives did not cease when these faithful standard-bearers fell at their post. By defeat they conquered. God's workmen were slain, but His work went steadily forward. The gospel continued to spread, and the number of its adherents to increase. . . . Said a Christian, expostulating with the heathen rulers who were urging forward the persecution: "You may torment, afflict, and vex us. Your wickedness puts our weakness to the test, but your cruelty is of no avail. It is but a stronger invitation to bring others to our persuasion. The more we are mowed down, the more we spring up again. The blood of the Christians is seed."

Thousands were imprisoned and slain; but others sprang up to fill their places. And those who were martyred for their faith were secured to Christ, and accounted of Him as conquerors. They had fought the good fight, and they were to receive the crown of glory when Christ should come. The sufferings that they endured brought Christians nearer to one another and to their Redeemer.—*The Spirit of Prophecy,* vol. 4, pp. 39-42.

November 9

EARLY CHURCH CORRUPTED BY SATAN'S FOLLOWERS

◆ *I have a few things against thee, because thou sufferest that woman Jezebel, which calleth herself a prophetess, to teach and to seduce my servants to commit fornication, and to eat things sacrificed unto idols. Revelation 2:20.*

HEIR [the martyrs'] living example and dying testimony were a constant witness for the truth; and, where least expected, the subjects of Satan were leaving his service and enlisting under the banner of Christ. . . .

The great adversary now endeavored to gain by artifice what he had failed to secure by force. Persecution ceased, and in its stead were substituted the dangerous allurements of temporal prosperity and worldly honor. Idolaters were led to receive a part of the Christian faith, while they rejected other essential truths. They professed to accept Jesus as the Son of God, and to believe in His death and resurrection; but they had no conviction of sin, and felt no need of repentance or of a change of heart. With some concessions on their part, they proposed that Christians should make concessions, that all might unite on the platform of belief in Christ.

Now was the church in fearful peril. Prison, torture, fire, and sword were blessings in comparison with this. Some of the Christians stood firm, declaring that they could make no compromise. Others reasoned that if they should yield or modify some features of their faith, and unite with those who had accepted a part of Christianity it might be the means of their full conversion. . . . Under a cloak of pretended Christianity Satan was insinuating himself into the church, to corrupt their faith and turn their minds from the word of truth.

At last the larger portion of the Christian company lowered their standard, and a union was formed between Christianity and paganism. Although the worshipers of idols professed to be converted, and united with the church, they still clung to their idolatry, only changing the objects of their worship to images of Jesus, and even of Mary and the saints. The foul leaven of idolatry, thus introduced into the church, continued its baleful work. Unsound doctrines, superstitious rites, and idolatrous ceremonies were incorporated into her faith and worship. As the followers of Christ united with idolaters, the Christian religion became corrupted, and the church lost her purity and power. There were some, however, who were not misled by these delusions.—*The Spirit of Prophecy*, vol. 4, pp. 42, 43.

November 10

THERE ARE TWO CLASSES AMONG CHRIST'S FOLLOWERS

◆ *Then shall the kingdom of heaven be likened unto ten virgins, which took their lamps, and went forth to meet the bridegroom. And five of them were wise, and five were foolish. Matthew 25:1, 2.*

*T*HERE have ever been two classes among those who profess to be followers of Christ. While one class study the Saviour's life and earnestly seek to correct their defects and conform to the Pattern, the other class shun the plain, practical truths that expose their errors. Even in her best estate the church was not composed wholly of the true, pure, and sincere. Our Saviour taught that those who willfully indulge in sin are not to be received into the church; yet He connected with Himself men who were faulty in character, and granted them the benefits of His teachings and example, that they might have an opportunity to see and correct their errors.

Among the twelve apostles was a traitor. Judas was accepted, not because of his defects of character, but notwithstanding them. He was connected with the disciples that through the instruction and example of Christ he might learn what constitutes Christian character, and thus be led to see his errors, to repent, and, by the aid of divine grace, to purify his soul "in obeying the truth."

But Judas did not walk in the light so graciously permitted to shine upon him. By indulgence in sin he invited the temptations of Satan. His evil traits of character became predominant. He yielded his mind to the control of the powers of darkness, he became angry when his faults were reproved, and thus he was led to commit the fearful crime of betraying his Master. In like manner do all who cherish evil under a profession of godliness hate those who disturb their peace by condemning their course of sin. When a favorable opportunity is presented, they will, like Judas, betray those who for their good have sought to reprove them.

The apostles encountered those in the church who professed godliness while they were secretly cherishing iniquity. Ananias and Sapphira acted the part of deceivers, pretending to make an entire sacrifice for God, when they were covetously withholding a portion for themselves. . . . As trials and persecution came upon His [Christ's] followers, those only who were willing to forsake all for the truth's sake desired to become His disciples. Thus, as long as persecution continued, the church remained comparatively pure. But as it ceased, converts were added who were less sincere and devoted, and the way was opened for Satan to obtain a foothold.—*The Spirit of Prophecy*, vol. 4, pp. 44, 45.

November 11
THEY ALSO WILL PERSECUTE YOU

◆ *Yea, and all that will live godly in Christ Jesus shall suffer persecution. 2 Timothy 3:12.*

*H*EROD and the wicked authorities killed the Just One, but Christ never killed anyone, and we may attribute the spirit of persecution—because people want liberty of conscience—to its origin, Satan. He is a deceiver, a liar, a murderer, and accuser of the brethren and sisters. He loves to see human misery. He exults in distress, and as we view the cruel persecutions of those who would obey God according to the dictates of their own consciences, we may know that this is the mystery of iniquity. The Lord said to Satan, that old serpent, "It [the Seed of the woman] shall bruise thy head, and thou shalt bruise his heel" (Gen. 3:15). Christ in a special manner bruised the head of the serpent, but the prophecy is far-reaching. It is a declaration of an unwearied conflict between Christ and His followers, and Satan and his angels and human agencies on this earth, to the close of time.

This conflict was opened upon the Son of God. He was afflicted; He was despised and rejected of men, a man of sorrows and acquainted with grief. The Majesty of heaven had to leave the scene of His labor again and again because of Satan's bruising His heel, and finally Satan's malignity reached its utmost power when Satan inspired and controlled the minds of wicked men to crucify Him. He has followed the children of God, causing them disaster and death. . . . Isaiah, Daniel, and John have in prophecy announced these very struggles and conquests that God's people would pass through, and the triumph of Satan in his supposed victories.

The enmity of Satan will continue fierce and determined against the followers of Jesus. . . . Evil, wherever it exists, in rejecting light and truth and departing from the living God, will always league against the righteous and obedient. Fallen angels and fallen human beings join in a desperate companionship. This is the very union that the persecutors of the faithful entered into.

Satan made his calculations that if he could induce men and women, as he deceived and induced the angels in his warfare, he should have them as his allies in every enterprise against heaven. . . .

The truth does not present ideas mingled with traditions and fables. The religion of Jesus Christ presents the truth, pure and undefiled. It will bear investigation, and honest seekers after the truth will have it. True religion does not excite the mind and feelings, but appeals to the intellect and to the heart. It is constantly developing and rising higher and higher heavenward.—Manuscript 62, 1886.

November 12
REFORMATION PRINCIPLES ARE TO BE UPHELD TODAY

◆ *Write the things which thou hast seen, and the things which are, and the things which shall be hereafter. Revelation 1:19.*

*T*HE principle that we are called to uphold at this time is the same that was maintained by the adherents of the gospel in the days of the great Reformation. When the princes assembled at the Diet of Spires in 1529, it seemed that the hope of the world was about to be crushed out. To this assembly was presented the emperor's decree restricting religious liberty, and prohibiting all further dissemination of the reform doctrines. . . .

Mighty issues for the world depended upon the action of a few heroes of faith. Those who had accepted the truths of the Reformation met together, and their unanimous decision was "Let us object to the decree. In matters of conscience the majority has no power." They drew up their protest and submitted it to the assembled states. . . .

In this last conflict God has committed to our hands the banner of truth and religious liberty that these reformers held aloft. Those whom He has blessed with the knowledge of His Word are held responsible for this great gift. We are to receive God's Word as supreme authority. We must accept its truths for ourselves, as our own individual act. And we shall be able to appreciate these truths only as we shall search them out for ourselves, by personal study of the Word of God. . . .

The Protestant churches, having received doctrines that the Word of God condemns, will bring these to the front and force them upon the consciences of the people, just as the papal authorities urged their dogmas upon the advocates of truth in Luther's time. The same battle is again to be fought, and every soul will be called upon to decide upon which side of the controversy he or she will be found.

When people are not willing to see the truth and receive it because it involves a cross, they are opening the door to Satan's temptations. He will lead them, as he led Eve in Eden, to believe a lie. The truth through which they might have been sanctified is set aside for some pleasing delusion presented by the destroyer of souls.

It is often the case that the most precious truth appears to lie close by the side of fatal errors. The rest that Christ promised to all who should learn of Him lies close beside indifference and carnal quietude, and multitudes overlook the fact that this rest is found only in wearing Christ's yoke and bearing His burden, in possessing His meekness and lowliness.—Manuscript 100, 1893.

November 13
**UNDERSTAND
THE DIFFERENCE
IN FAITH AND
PRESUMPTION**

◆ *Keep back thy servant also from presumptuous sins; let them not have dominion over me: then shall I be upright, and I shall be innocent from the great transgression. Psalm 19:13.*

*T*HE great truth of our entire dependence upon Christ for salvation lies close to the error of presumption. Freedom in Christ is by thousands mistaken for lawlessness; and because Christ came to release us from the condemnation of the law, many declare that the law itself is done away, and that those who keep it are fallen from grace. And thus, as truth and error appear so near akin, minds that are not guided by the Holy Spirit will be led to accept the error and, in so doing, place themselves under the power of Satan's deceptions. In thus leading people to receive error for truth, Satan is working to secure the homage of the Protestant world.

Every soul needs to be on guard against his devices. We must be Bible readers, and obedient to the Scriptures. . . . The inquiry should rise from every heart, What is truth? If we would stand against the deceptive teaching that now meets us on every side, that is turning the truth of God into a lie, we must have the heavenly anointing. . . .

Those early reformers, whose protests have given us the name of Protestant, felt that God had called them to give the light of the gospel to the world, and in doing this they were ready to sacrifice their possessions, their liberty, and their own lives. Are we, in this, the last conflict of the great controversy, as faithful to our trust? . . .

Luther's pen was a power, and his writing, scattered broadcast, stirred the world. The same agencies are at our command, with facilities multiplied a hundredfold. Bibles and publications in many languages setting forth the truth for this time are at our hand and can be swiftly carried to every part of the world. . . .

The truth must be proclaimed in the dark places of the earth. Obstacles must be met and surmounted. A great work is to be done, and those who know the truth should make mighty intercession for help now. . . . The Spirit of Christ must be poured out upon them, and they must be making ready to stand in the judgment. While they are consecrating themselves to God, a convincing power will attend their efforts to present the truth to others. We must sleep no longer on Satan's enchanted ground, but call into requisition all our resources, and avail ourselves of every facility with which Providence has furnished us. . . . And the promise is given, "Lo, I am with you alway, even unto the end of the world."—Manuscript 100, 1893.

November 14
BE FAITHFUL
UNTO DEATH

◆ *He shall cover thee with his feathers, and under his wings shalt thou trust: his truth shall be thy shield and buckler. Psalm 91:4.*

HE body of [John] Huss was consumed. The council had done all that they could do with the man whose only crime was that he could not accept as infallible the Council of Constance, and he could not let their voice stand above the voice of God in His Word. But God seeks again "that which is past," recalling all the proceedings whether of judgment or of mercy. . . . The biography of the righteous is among the best treasures that the church can possess. We have the benefit of the accounts of the workings of the power of evil in contrast to the deeds of those who through many centuries were living by every word that proceedeth out of the mouth of God.

This rich experience is bequeathed to us as a legacy of great value. When history shall be repeated, when the great men and women of earth will not come to the Bible for light and evidence and truth, when human commandments shall be exalted above the commandments of God, and when it shall be regarded a crime to obey God rather than civil laws, then we shall not have to tread a path in which we have had but few examples of others who have gone before us.

The Lord supported His faithful ones to the end. This should be an encouragement. It should give confidence to the righteous in all ages that the Lord is unchangeable. He will manifest for His people in this age His grace and His power as He has done in past ages. The declarations of God's Word and the accuracy with which He has made them good in history combine to give us assurance and instruction of greatest value. . . .

In the experience of Huss was a witness, a monument erected, calling the attention of the world to the promise: "Be thou faithful unto death, and I will give thee a crown of life" (Rev. 2:10). Registered in the history of nations, John Huss lives. His godly works and steadfast faith, his pure life and conscientious following of the truth that was unfolded to him, these he would not yield even to be saved a cruel death. That triumphant death was witnessed by all heaven, by the whole universe. Satan bruised the heel of the seed of the woman, but in the act of Huss his head was bruised. . . .

The battlements of heaven are thronged with a great crowd of angels watching the conflict of human beings with the prince of darkness. . . . With intense interest they watch to see if the child of God, harassed, perplexed, persecuted, denounced, defamed, and condemned as was the Master, will look to heaven for strength. Heaven waits our demand upon its resources.—Manuscript 38, 1887.

325

November 15

FOLLOWERS OF JESUS FACE A LIFE-AND-DEATH STRUGGLE

◆ *I will lift up mine eyes unto the hills, from whence cometh my help. My help cometh from the Lord, which made heaven and earth. Psalm 121:1, 2.*

S the cars [of the train] glided slowly along we had a fine opportunity of seeing the country [Switzerland] through which we passed. . . .

Here among the rocks and caverns of the earth the Lord has provided a hiding place for His people. These chapels, built so high upon the precipitous rocks that seem inaccessible to humans, were thus arranged for safety and protection. They testify to us that there was a time when the people of God were suffering because they, like Daniel of old, purposed in their hearts that they would worship God according to the dictates of their own consciences. They could not consent that any person should be conscience for them, and they felt more secure in the wildness of rocks and mountains, where the wild beasts make their home from the snare of the fowler, than to trust themselves to the mercy of human beings who were infected with an erroneous religion and satanic zeal to maintain human customs and traditions that were in direct opposition to the religion of the Bible. These were cruel as bloodthirsty wolves to extirpate all who should dare to differ with the doctrines of papists—men and women who would take the Bible and the Bible alone as their foundation, until its glorious beams scattered human tradition from their path, making clear the way of the Lord. . . .

The man of sin is Satan's agent. He sets his inventive powers to work, and Satan plans; then the followers of Jesus must prepare for a life-and-death struggle. The authority of the church, combined with the authorities of the nation, set themselves to work to cripple the conscience—to be themselves conscience for everybody. For anyone to differ, and stand in opposition to these great men of the world in their religious faith and worship, would raise endless questions, and they could not keep this light to themselves. The more they pondered the question, the more they saw was involved in turning from old traditions to the Word of God. But they must face the conflict, harness for battle, rise above human littleness, and not have thoughts of self-preservation detain them in the prospect of unmeasurable danger and peril. The world's Redeemer had given them in His life an example of what they must do and what they must be in order to win eternal life.—Manuscript 52, 1886.

November 16
**GOD REVEALS
HIS SECRETS
IN EVERY AGE**

◆ *But there is a God in heaven that revealeth secrets, and maketh known to the
king Nebuchadnezzar what shall be in the
latter days. Daniel 2:28.*

*I*N past ages the Lord God of heaven revealed His se-
crets to His prophets, and this He does still. The present and the future are
equally clear to Him, and He shows to His servants the future history of
what shall be. The Omniscient looked down the ages and predicted
through His prophets the rise and fall of kingdoms hundreds of years before the events foretold took place. The voice of God echoes down the
ages, telling earth's inhabitants what is to take place. Kings and princes
take their places at their appointed time. They think they are carrying out
their own purposes, but in reality they are fulfilling the word God has
given through His prophets. . . .

The unbelieving and godless do not discern the signs of the times. In
ignorance they may refuse to accept the inspired record. But when professed Christians speak sneeringly of the ways and means employed by the
great I AM to make His ways and purposes known, they show themselves
to be both ignorant of the Scriptures and of the power of God. . . . The
Christian who accepts the truth, the whole truth, and nothing but the
truth will look at Bible history in its true bearing. The past, the history of
the Jewish economy from the beginning to the end, instead of being spoken of contemptuously and sneered at as "the dark ages," will reveal light,
and still more light, as it is studied.

The word of men and women fails, and those who take their assertions
as their dependence may well tremble, for they will one day be as ship-
wrecked vessels. But God's Word is infallible and endures forever. . . .

God lives and reigns. His glory is not confined to the temple made
with hands. He has not closed heaven against His people. As in the Jewish
age, so in this age God reveals His secrets to His servants the prophets.

The image shown to Nebuchadnezzar [Daniel 2] in the visions of the
night represents the kingdoms of the world. The metals in the image, sym-
bolizing the different kingdoms, became less and less pure and valuable.
The head of the image was of gold, the breast and arms of silver, the sides
of brass, [the legs of iron], and the feet and toes of iron mingled with clay.
So the kingdoms represented by them deteriorated in value. . . . If they had
kept the fear of the Lord ever before them, they would have been given wisdom and power which would have bound them together and kept them
strong.—Manuscript 39, 1899 (see also *Review and Herald,* Feb. 6, 1900).

November 17
GOD CALLS US TO BE CHILDREN OF THE LIGHT

◆ *Ye are all the children of light, and the children of the day: we are not of the night, nor of darkness. 1 Thessalonians 5:5.*

HE Bible is God's great director. It is a lamp to our feet, a light to our path. It flashes its light ahead, that we may see the path by which we are traveling; and its rays are thrown back on past history, showing the most perfect harmony in that which to the mind in darkness appears like error and discord. In that which seems to the worldling an inexplicable mystery, God's children see light and beauty. . . .

The Israelites placed over their doors a signature of blood, to show that they were God's property. So every child of God in this age will bear the signature God has appointed. . . . God declares, "I gave them my sabbaths, to be a sign between me and them, that they might know that I am the Lord that doth sanctify them." When people say that the law of God is abrogated by the testimonies of "the fathers," they are teaching for doctrine the commandments of men. . . .

We are living in a momentous period in this earth's history. The great conflict is just before us. . . . The man of sin has worked with a marvelous perseverance to exalt a spurious sabbath, and the disloyal Protestant world has wondered after the beast and has called obedience to the Sabbath instituted by Jehovah disloyalty to the laws of the nations. Kingdoms have confederated to sustain a false sabbath institution, which has not a word of authority in the oracles of God. . . .

The great conflict now being waged is not merely a strife of humans against humans. On the one side stands the Prince of Life, acting as our substitute and surety; on the other [stands] the prince of darkness, with the fallen angels under his command. . . . "Put on the whole armour of God, that ye may be able to stand against the wiles of the devil."

There will be a sharp conflict between those who are loyal to God and those who cast scorn upon His law. The church has joined hands with the world. Reverence to God's law has been subverted. The religious leaders have taught for doctrine the commandments of men. As it was in the days of Noah, so it is in this age of the world. . . . The truly loyal will not be carried away by the current of evil. They will not throw scorn and contempt on that which God has set apart as holy. The test comes to everyone. There are only two sides. Which are you on?—Manuscript 39, 1899 (see also *Review and Herald*, Feb. 6, 1900).

November 18
**MAKE NO HASTY,
RASH MOVES**

◆ *Ye ought to be quiet, and to do nothing
rashly. Acts 19:36.*

*L*ET Christ be seen in all that you do. Let all see that
you are living epistles of Jesus Christ. . . . Let your life win the hearts of all
who are brought in contact with you. There is too little done at the present time to render the truth attractive to others. There have been some
who have, in speaking to the people, felt like making a raid on the
churches. They sour minds by their censoriousness. We want our hearts
mellowed by the love of Jesus. That is in God's order. If not presented in
the most pleasant, acceptable form, truth will be unpalatable to many.
While we must present the truth in contrast with error, let it be presented
in a manner that shall create as little prejudice as possible. . . .

While we will not violate the Sabbath, which a despotic power will seek to
compel us to do, we will be wise in Christ—Christ's wisdom—and not in our
own spirit. A consistent, substantial, lovable Christian is a powerful argument
for the truth. We must say no words that will do ourselves harm, for this would
be bad enough, but when we speak words, and when we do presumptuous
things that imperil the cause of God, we are doing a cruel work, for we give
Satan advantage. We are not to be rash and impetuous, but always learning
of Jesus and how to act in His Spirit, presenting the truth as it is in Jesus. . . .

Let everyone be careful and not step off the ground where God is, onto
Satan's ground. Many did this in the ranks of the Reformers of past ages.
Luther had great trouble because of these elements. Rash persons stepped
out of their place, when God did not send them, and rushed heedlessly
forward to do a very objectionable, impulsive work. They ran ahead of
Christ and provoked the devil's wrath. In their untimely, misguided zeal,
they closed the door to great usefulness of many souls who might have
done great good for the Master. . . .

There are those who will, through hasty, unadvised moves, betray the
cause of God into the enemy's power. There will be people who will seek
to be revenged, who will become apostates and betray Christ in the person
of His saints. All need to learn discretion; then there is danger on the other
hand of being conservative, of giving away to the enemy in concession.
Our brethren and sisters should be very cautious in this matter for the
honor of God. . . . The two armies will stand distinct and separate, and this
distinction will be so marked that many who shall be convinced of truth
will come on the side of God's commandment-keeping people.—
Manuscript 6, 1889.

November 19
**AVOID CONTEN-
TION; PROMOTE
HARMONY**

◆ *Only by pride cometh contention: but with the well advised is wisdom. Proverbs 13:10.*

HE Reformation was greatly retarded by making prominent differences on some points of faith and each party holding tenaciously to those things where they differed. We shall see eye-to-eye erelong, but to become firm and consider it your duty to present your views in decided opposition to the faith or truth, as it has been taught by us as a people is a mistake and will result in harm, and only harm, as in the days of Martin Luther. Begin to draw apart and feel at liberty to express your ideas without reference to the views of your associates, and a state of things will be introduced that you do not dream of.

My husband had some ideas on some points differing from the views taken by his brethren. I was shown that however true his views were, God did not call for him to put them in front before his brethren and create differences of ideas. . . .

Speculative ideas should not be agitated, for there are peculiar minds that love to get some point that others do not accept, and argue and attract everything to that one point, urging that point, magnifying that point, when it is really a matter that is not of vital importance and will be understood differently. Twice I have been shown that everything of a character to cause our ministers to be diverted from the very points now essential for this time should be kept in the background.

Christ did not reveal many things that were truth, because it would create a difference of opinion and get up disputations. But young men who have not passed through the experience we have had would as soon have a brush as not. Nothing would suit them better than [to] have a sharp discussion. . . .

We are in the great day of atonement, a time when we must be afflicting our souls, confessing our sins, humbling our hearts before God, and getting ready for the great conflict. When these contentions come in before the people, they will think one has the argument, and then that another directly opposed has the argument. The poor people become confused, and the conference will be a dead loss, worse than if they had had no conference.

Now when everything is dissension and strife, there must be decided efforts to handle, to publish with pen and voice, these things that will reveal only harmony.—Letter 37, 1887 (*Manuscript Releases,* vol. 15, pp. 20-22).

November 20
WE ARE TO KNOW THE TRUTH AND PRACTICE IT

◆ *Anyone who resolves to do the will of God will know whether the teaching is from God or whether I am speaking on my own. John 7:17, NRSV.*

E are not to set our stakes and then interpret everything to reach this set point. Here is where some of our great Reformers have failed, and this is the reason that many who today might be mighty champions for God and the truth are warring against the truth. . . . God designs we should be learners, first from the living oracles, and second from our associates. This is God's order.

The Word of God is the great detector of error; to it we believe everything must be brought. The Bible must be our standard for every doctrine. We must study it reverentially. We are to receive no one's opinion without comparing it with the Scriptures. Here is divine authority, which is supreme in matters of faith.

It is the Word of the living God that is to decide all controversies. It is when people mingle their own human smartness with God's words of truth, in giving sharp thrusts to those who are in controversy with them, that they show that they have not a sacred reverence for God's Inspired Word. They mix the human with the divine, the common with the sacred, and they belittle God's Word. . . .

The correct interpretation of the Scriptures is not all that God requires. He enjoins upon us that we should not only know the truth, but that we should practice the truth as it is in Jesus. We are to bring into our practice, in our association with others, the spirit of Him who gave us the truth. We must not only search for the truth as for hidden treasures, but it is a positive necessity, if we are laborers together with God, that we comply with the conditions laid down in His Word, and bring the spirit of Christ into our hearts, that our understanding may be strengthened and we become apt teachers to make known to others the truth revealed to us in His Word. . . .

There is no assurance that our doctrine is right and free from all chaff and error unless we are daily doing the will of God. If we do His will, we shall know of the doctrine. We shall see the truth in its sacred beauty. We shall accept it with reverence and godly fear, and then we can present to others that which we know is truth. . . .

The soul that is in love with God and His work will be as candid as the day. There will be no quibbling, no evading the true bearing of Scripture. God's Word is our foundation of all doctrine.—Letter 20, 1888 (*The Ellen G. White 1888 Materials*, vol. 1, pp. 42-44).

November 21
**PEOPLE TO BE
EDUCATED TO
SEARCH THE
SCRIPTURES**

◆ *Search the scriptures; for in them ye think
ye have eternal life: and they are they which
testify of me. John 5:39.*

*T*HE present is a time of great peril to the people of
God. God is leading out a people, not an individual here and there. . . .
"Take heed, therefore, how ye hear" is an admonition of Christ. We are to
hear for the sake of learning the truth, that we may walk in it. And again:
"Take heed what ye hear." Examine closely, "prove all things," "believe not
every spirit.". . . This is the counsel of God; shall we heed it?

A person may hear and acknowledge the whole truth, and yet know
nothing of personal piety and true experimental religion. He or she may
explain the way of salvation to others, and yet be a castaway. . . . "Why,"
asked a man who had been and still was practicing wickedness, "are souls
converted to the truth through my influence?" I answered, "Christ is constantly drawing souls to Himself, and flashing His own light in their path.
The seeker after salvation is not permitted to read the character of him
who teaches him. If he himself is sincere, if he draws nigh to God, believing in Him, confessing his sins, he will be accepted.". . .

In the time of the Reformers, some were afraid of the influence on the
church of those in error, and hence special pain was taken to make iron rules
that the common people should not read and interpret the Scriptures for
themselves. Thus the church came to exercise tyranny over dissenters. . . .

We should never let the impression prevail that only a privileged few
have a knowledge of the Scriptures and that others must refer to these—
one or another of their favorite ministers—as authority for their doctrines.
People should be educated to search the Scriptures for themselves, to dare
to think for themselves, taking the Bible as their guidebook, their standard
of faith. Although heresy may lift its head boldly, and insult the truth by
perverted ideas and false interpretations and misapplication of Scripture,
there should be no suppression of religious freedom by reformers.

The church should ever bear in mind that they are never to ascribe to
fallible mortals the unerring wisdom of the one living God. . . . We want
all souls to have a pure gospel and to feel the necessity of searching the
Scriptures for themselves, to know what saith the voice of the Eternal, and
bind themselves to the great heart of Infinite Love.—Letter 12, 1890.

November 22
**GOOD AND
EVIL ANGELS
ALWAYS PRESENT**

◆ *For we wrestle not against flesh and blood, but against principalities, against powers, against the rulers of the darkness of this world. Ephesians 6:12.*

NGELS from heaven communicate with the human family, and not one of us by anything we can do may uphold or keep ourselves. We are where we are, kept every moment by the power of God. I have thought that we do not make the ministration of heavenly angels as important as we should. . . . What would we do without them? I want you to consider what kind of position we should be left in if we had not the ministry of holy angels. . . .

We meet the opposition of men and women, but there is someone behind that opposition. It is the prince of the powers of darkness, with his evil angels, who is constantly at work. . . . Who is it that is ruling the world today? And who is it that has chosen to stand under the banner of the prince of darkness? Why, it is nearly the whole world at large. All the world that has not accepted Jesus Christ has chosen for their leader the prince of darkness, and just as soon as they stand under his banner, they have connection with evil angels.

Either the evil angels or the angels of God are controlling all human minds. . . . Every provision has been made; everything in God's plan has been arranged so that we should not be left to our own impulses, to our own finite powers, to carry on the warfare against the powers of darkness in our own finite strength, because we would certainly fail if we were thus left to ourselves. . . .

In the Psalms David speaks of God's being a refuge and a strong tower, a refuge and a fortress; unto Him we can run and we can be saved. How precious is the thought that God is our refuge and that He will be our helper in all times and in all places, and that in every emergency we have God with us. He says that He will give His angels charge over us to keep us in all our ways. . . . In our God we have a helper, and we will trust in Him. We must constantly look in that direction, believing that the angels of God are round about us, and that heaven is in communication with us, because these heavenly messengers are ascending and descending upon the ladder of shining brightness. . . .

How is it with us? Are we standing with the whole armor on, so that we can work in harmony with the angels of God who are working for us? If we separate ourselves from these angels by taking our own course of action, then we place ourselves where the wicked one can tempt us.— Manuscript 1, 1890 (*Sermons and Talks*, vol. 2, pp. 57-59).

November 23
STUDY DANIEL AND REVELATION TOGETHER

◆ *Now I am come to make thee understand what shall befall thy people in the latter days: for yet the vision is for many days. Daniel 10:14.*

*D*ANIEL identified himself with Israel's sins, and confessed their sins as his own. He prayed, "O Lord, hear; O Lord, forgive; O Lord, hearken and do; defer not, for thine own sake, O my God: for thy city and thy people are called by thy name." Yet Gabriel, the heavenly messenger, thrice called him a man greatly beloved. . . .

How can we but see how closely the universe of heaven is connected with this fallen world! These communications given to Daniel should fill our souls with awe, with humility, with meekness, and lay our pride low in the dust. . . .

A wonderful connection is here seen between the universe of heaven and this world. The things revealed to Daniel were afterward complemented by the revelation made to John on the isle of Patmos. These two books should be carefully perused. Twice Daniel inquired, How long shall it be to the end of time? "And I heard, but I understood not: then said I, O my Lord, what shall be the end of these things? And he said, Go thy way, Daniel: for the words are closed up and sealed till the time of the end. Many shall be purified, and made white, and tried; but the wicked shall do wickedly: and none of the wicked shall understand; but the wise shall understand. . . . But go thou thy way till the end be: for thou shalt rest, and stand in thy lot at the end of the days."

It was the Lion of the tribe of Judah who unsealed the book and gave to John the revelation of what should be in these last days. Daniel stood in his lot to bear his testimony, which was sealed until the time of the end, when the first angel's message should be proclaimed to our world. These matters are of infinite importance in these last days. . . . The book of Daniel is unsealed in the revelation to John, and it carries us forward to the last scenes of this earth's history.

The case of Daniel reveals to us the fact that the Lord is always ready to hear the prayers of the contrite soul, and when we seek the Lord with all our hearts, He will answer our petitions. Here is revealed where Daniel obtained his skill and understanding; and if we will only ask of God wisdom, we may be blessed with increased ability, and with power from heaven. If we will come to God just as we are, and pray to Him in faith as did Daniel, we shall see of the salvation of God. We need to pray as we never prayed before.—Letter 59, 1896 (*Manuscript Releases*, vol. 18, pp. 14-16).

November 24
**BOOK OF DANIEL
NOW UNSEALED
FOR STUDY**

◆ *But thou, O Daniel, shut up the words, and seal the book, even to the time of the end: many shall run to and fro, and knowledge shall be increased. Daniel 12:4.*

HERE is need of a much closer study of the Word of God; especially should Daniel and the Revelation have attention as never before in the history of our work. We may have less to say in some lines, in regard to the Roman power and the papacy, but we should call attention to what the prophets and apostles have written under the inspiration of the Spirit of God. . . .

Read the book of Daniel. Call up, point by point, the history of the kingdoms there represented. Behold statesmen, councils, powerful armies, and see how God wrought to abase pride and lay human glory in the dust. God alone is represented as great. In the vision of the prophet He is seen casting down one mighty ruler and setting up another. He is revealed as the monarch of the universe, about to set up His everlasting kingdom—the Ancient of days, the living God, the Source of all wisdom, the Ruler of the present, the Revealer of the future. Read and understand how poor, how frail, how short-lived, how erring, how guilty, are mortals. . . .

The light that Daniel received direct from God was given especially for these last days. The visions he saw by the banks of the Ulai and the Hiddekel, the great rivers of Shinar, are now in process of fulfillment, and all the events foretold will soon have come to pass.

Consider the circumstances of the Jewish nation when the prophecies of Daniel were given. The Israelites were in captivity, their temple had been destroyed, their temple services suspended. Their religion had centered in the ceremonies of the sacrificial system. They had made the outward forms all-important, while they had lost the spirit of true worship. . . . The Lord wrought to bring the people into captivity, and to suspend the services of the temple, in order that the outward ceremonies might not become the sum total of their religion. . . . The outward glory was removed, that the spiritual might be revealed. . . .

In giving the light to His people, God did not work exclusively through any one class of persons. Daniel was a prince of Judah. Isaiah also was of the royal tribe. David was a shepherd boy, Amos a herdsman, Zechariah a captive from Babylon, Elisha a tiller of the soil. The Lord raised up as representative leaders the prophets and princes, the noble and the lowly, and by inspiration taught them truths to be given to His people.—Letter 57, 1896 *(Manuscript Releases, vol. 16, pp. 333-335).*

November 25
EARLY OPPONENTS RIDICULED ADVENTISTS

◆ *Who shall separate us from the love of Christ? shall tribulation, or distress, or persecution, or famine, or nakedness, or peril, or sword? Romans 8:35.*

*I*NSTEAD of arguments from the Scriptures, the opponents of the Advent faith chose to employ ridicule and scoffing. The careless and ungodly, emboldened by the position of religious teachers, resorted to opprobrious epithets, to base and blasphemous witticisms, in their efforts to heap contumely upon William Miller and his work. The gray-headed man who had left a comfortable home to travel at his own expense from city to city, from town to village, toiling unceasingly to bear to the world the solemn warning of the judgment near, was sneeringly denounced as a fanatic, a liar, a speculating knave.

Time, means, and talents were employed in misrepresenting and maligning Adventists, in exciting prejudice against them, and holding them up to public contempt. Ministers occupied themselves in gathering up damaging reports, absurd and malicious fabrications, and dealing them out from the pulpit. Earnest were the efforts put forth to draw away the minds of the people from the subject of the Second Advent. But in seeking to crush out Adventism, the popular ministry undermined faith in the Word of God. It was made to appear a sin, something of which people should be ashamed, to study the prophecies that relate to the coming of Christ and the end of the world. This teaching made some infidels, and many took license to walk after their own ungodly lusts. Then the authors of the evil charged it all upon Adventists.

The Wesleys encountered similar accusations from the ease-loving, godless ministers who were constantly intercepting their labors and seeking to destroy their influence. They were pronounced uncharitable, and accused of pride and vanity, because they did not pay homage to the popular teachers of their time. They were accused of skepticism, of disorderly practices, and of contempt of authority. John Wesley fearlessly threw back these charges upon those who framed them, showing that they themselves were responsible for the very evils of which they accused the Methodists. . . . The great controversy between truth and error has been carried forward from century to century since the fall of man. God and angels, and those united with them, have been inviting, urging people to repentance and holiness and heaven; while Satan and his angels, and human agents inspired by them, have been opposing every effort to benefit and save the fallen race.—*The Spirit of Prophecy,* vol. 4, pp. 218-220.

November 26
THE WITNESS OF WILLIAM MILLER

◆ *We are troubled on every side, yet not distressed; we are perplexed, but not in despair; persecuted, but not forsaken; cast down, but not destroyed. 2 Corinthians 4:8, 9.*

*W*ILLIAM Miller was disturbing Satan's kingdom, and the archenemy sought not only to counteract the effect of the message, but to destroy the messenger himself. As Father Miller made a practical application of Scripture truth to the hearts of his hearers, the rage of professed Christians was kindled against him, even as the anger of the Jews was excited against Christ and His apostles. Church members stirred up the baser classes, and upon several occasions enemies plotted to take his life as he should leave the place of meeting. But holy angels were in the throng, and one of these, in the form of a man, took the arm of this servant of the Lord and led him to safety from the angry mob. His work was not yet done, and Satan and his emissaries were disappointed in their purpose.

Comparing his own expectations as to the effect of his preaching with the manner in which it had been received by the religious world, William Miller said: "It is true, but not wonderful, when we become acquainted with the state and corruption of the present age, . . . that I have met with great opposition from the pulpit and professed religious press; and I have been instrumental, through the preaching of the Advent doctrine, of making it quite manifest that not a few of our theological teachers are infidels in disguise. . . .

"Surely, we have fallen on strange times. I expected, of course, that the doctrine of Christ's speedy coming would be opposed by infidels, blasphemers, drunkards, gamblers, and the like; but I did not expect that ministers of the gospel and professors of religion would unite with characters of the above description, at stores and public places, in ridiculing the solemn doctrine of the Second Advent." . . .

Now, as in the time of our Saviour, people build the sepulchers and sound the praises of the dead prophets, while they persecute the living messengers of the Most High. William Miller was despised and hated by the ungodly and unbelieving; but his influence and his labors were a blessing to the world. Under his preaching, thousands of sinners were converted, backsliders were reclaimed, and multitudes were led to study the Scriptures and to find in them a beauty and glory before unknown.—*The Spirit of Prophecy*, vol. 4, pp. 220, 221.

November 27
THREE ANGELS' MESSAGES—A CALL TO THE WORD OF GOD

◆ *And I saw another angel fly in the midst of heaven, . . . saying with a loud voice, Fear God, and give glory to him; for the hour of his judgment is come. Revelation 14:6, 7.*

HE proclamation of the first, second, and third angels' messages has been located by the Word of Inspiration. Not a peg or pin is to be removed. No human authority has any more right to change the location of these messages than to substitute the New Testament for the Old. The Old Testament is the gospel in figures and symbols. The New Testament is the substance. One is as essential as the other. The Old Testament presents lessons from the lips of Christ, and these lessons have not lost their force in any particular.

The first and second messages [Revelation 14:6-8] were given in 1843 and 1844, and we are now under the proclamation of the third; but all three of the messages are still to be proclaimed. It is just as essential now as ever before that they shall be repeated to those who are seeking for the truth. By pen and voice we are to sound the proclamation, showing their order and the application of the prophecies that bring us to the third angel's message. There cannot be a third without the first and second. . . .

The book that was sealed was not the book of Revelation, but that portion of the prophecy of Daniel that related to the last days. . . . When the book was opened, the proclamation was made, "Time shall be no longer." The book of Daniel is now unsealed, and the revelation made by Christ to John is to come to all the inhabitants of the earth. By the increase of knowledge a people is to be prepared to stand in the latter days.

[Revelation 14:6, 7 quoted.] This message, if heeded, will call the attention of every nation and kindred and tongue and people to a close examination of the Word, and to the true light in regard to the power that has changed the seventh-day Sabbath to a spurious sabbath. . . . The Sabbath memorial, declaring who the living God is, the Creator of the heavens and the earth, has been torn down, and a spurious sabbath has been given to the world in its place. Thus a breach has been made in the law of God. . . .

In the first angel's message people are called upon to worship God, our Creator, who made the world and all things that are therein. . . . The message proclaimed by the angel flying in the midst of heaven is the everlasting gospel, the same gospel that was declared in Eden when God said to the serpent, "I will put enmity between thee and the woman, and between thy seed and her seed."—Manuscript 32, 1896 (*Manuscript Releases*, vol. 17, pp. 6, 7).

November 28
THE LAW OF
GOD NEEDS
NO REVISION

◆ *And they that shall be of thee shall build the old waste places: thou shalt raise up the foundations of many generations; and thou shalt be called, The repairer of the breach, The restorer of paths to dwell in. Isaiah 58:12.*

HRIST came to our world to represent the character of God as it is represented in His holy law, for His law is a transcript of His character. Christ was both the law and the gospel. . . .

In the fifty-eighth chapter of Isaiah the work of those who worship God, the Maker of the heavens and the earth, is specified: "They that shall be of thee shall build the old waste places: thou shalt raise up the foundations of many generations." God's memorial, His seventh-day Sabbath, will be uplifted. . . .

The history of the church and the world, the loyal and the disloyal, is here plainly revealed. The loyal, under the proclamation of the third angel's message, have turned their feet into the way of God's commandments, to respect, to honor and glorify Him who created the heavens and the earth. The opposing forces have dishonored God by making a breach in His law, and when light from His Word has called attention to His holy commandments, revealing the breach made in the law by the papal authority, then, to get rid of conviction, many have tried to destroy the whole law. But could they destroy it? No; for all who will search the Scriptures for themselves will see that the law of God stands immutable, eternal, and His memorial, the Sabbath, will endure through eternal ages, pointing to the only true God in distinction from all false gods.

Satan has been persevering and untiring in his efforts to prosecute the work he began in heaven, to change the law of God. He has succeeded in making the world believe the theory he presented in heaven before his fall, that the law of God was faulty and needed revising. A large part of the professed Christian church, by their attitude, if not by their words, show that they have accepted the same error. But if in one jot or tittle the law of God has been changed, Satan has gained on earth that which he could not gain in heaven. He has prepared his delusive snare, hoping to take captive the church and the world. But not all will be taken in the snare. A line of distinction is being drawn between the children of obedience and the children of disobedience, the loyal and true and the disloyal and untrue. Two great parties are developed, the worshipers of the beast and his image, and the worshipers of the true and living God.—Manuscript 32, 1896 (*Manuscript Releases*, vol. 17, pp. 8, 9).

November 29
THE ANGEL OF REVELATION 10 PROCLAIMS GOD'S LAST MESSAGE

◆ *And he set his right foot upon the sea, and his left foot on the earth. Revelation 10:2.*

*T*HE message of Revelation 14, proclaiming that the hour of God's judgment is come, is given in the time of the end. The angel of Revelation 10 is represented as having one foot on the sea and one foot on the land, showing that the message will be carried to distant lands, the ocean will be crossed, and the islands of the sea will hear the proclamation of the last message of warning to our world. . . .

"That there should be time no longer." This message announces the end of the prophetic periods. The disappointment of those who expected to see our Lord in 1844 was indeed bitter to those who had so ardently looked for His appearing. It was in the Lord's order that this disappointment should come, and that hearts should be revealed.

Not one cloud has fallen upon the church that God has not prepared for; not one opposing force has risen to counterwork the work of God that He has not foreseen. All has taken place as He has predicted through His prophets. He has not left His church forsaken in darkness, but has traced in prophetic declarations what would occur, and through His providence, acting in its appointed place in the world's history, He has brought about that which His Holy Spirit inspired the prophets to foretell. All His purposes will be fulfilled and established. His law is linked with His throne, and satanic agencies combined with human agencies cannot destroy it.

Truth is inspired and guarded by God; it will live, and will succeed, although it may appear at times to be overshadowed. The gospel of Christ is the law exemplified in character. The deceptions practiced against it, every device for vindicating falsehood, every error forged by satanic agencies, will eventually be eternally broken, and the triumph of truth will be like the appearing of the sun at noonday. The Sun of Righteousness shall shine forth with healing in His wings, and the whole earth shall be filled with His glory.

All that God has in prophetic history specified to be fulfilled in the past has been, and all that is yet to come in its order will be. Daniel, God's prophet, stands in his place. John stands in his place. In the Revelation the Lion of the tribe of Judah has opened to the students of prophecy the book of Daniel, and thus is Daniel standing in his place. He bears his testimony, that which the Lord revealed to him in vision, of the great and solemn events that we must know as we stand on the very threshold of their fulfillment.—Manuscript 32, 1896 (*Manuscript Releases*, vol. 17, pp. 9-11).

November 30
HOLD FAST TO THE TRUTH AS IT IS IN JESUS

◆ *And I took the little book out of the angel's hand, and ate it up; and it was in my mouth sweet as honey: and as soon as I had eaten it, my belly was bitter. And he said unto me, Thou must prophesy again. Revelation 10:10, 11.*

*I*N history and prophecy the Word of God portrays the long, continued conflict between truth and error. That conflict is yet in progress. Those things that have been will be repeated. Old controversies will be revived, and new theories will be continually arising. But God's people, who in their belief in fulfillment of prophecy have acted a part in the proclamation of the first, second, and third angels' messages, know where they stand. . . . They are to stand firm as a rock, holding the beginning of their confidence steadfast unto the end.

A transforming power attended the proclamation of the first and second angels' messages, as it attends the message of the third angel. . . . There was diligent study of the Scriptures, point by point. Almost entire nights were devoted to earnest searching of the Word. We searched for the truth as for hidden treasures. The Lord revealed Himself to us. Light was shed on the prophecies, and we knew that we received divine instruction. . . .

After the Great Disappointment there were few who set themselves to seek the Word with all their heart. But some souls would not settle down in discouragement and deny that the Lord had led them. To these the truth was opened point by point, and entwined with their most hallowed recollections and sympathies. . . . Truth was made to shine forth, beautiful in its simplicity, dignified with a power and invested with an assurance unknown before the Disappointment. We could then proclaim the message in unity. But among those who had not held fast their faith and experience there was great confusion. Every conceivable opinion was presented as the message of truth, but the Lord's voice was "Believe them not; for I have not sent them."

We walked carefully with God. The message was to be given to the world, and we knew that this present light was the special gift of God. . . . His disappointed ones, who were still seeking after truth, were led step by step to communicate to the world that which had been communicated to them. . . . The work moved hard at first. Often the hearers rejected the message as unintelligible, and the conflict began in decided earnest, especially upon the Sabbath question. But the Lord manifested His presence. At times the veil that concealed His glory from our eyes was drawn aside. We beheld Him in the high and holy place.—Manuscript 32, 1896 (*Manuscript Releases*, vol. 17, pp. 11, 12).

December 1
SEARCH THE SCRIPTURES TO CONFIRM TRUTH

◆ *Study to shew thyself approved unto God, a workman that needeth not to be ashamed, rightly dividing the word of truth.*
2 Timothy 2:15.

HE Lord will not lead minds now to set aside the truth that the Holy Spirit has moved upon His servants in the past to proclaim. Many will honestly search the Word for light as those in the past have searched it; and they see light in the Word. But they did not pass over the ground, in their experience, when these messages of warning were first proclaimed. Not having had this experience, some do not appreciate the value of the truths that have been to us as waymarks, and that have made us as a peculiar people what we are. They do not make a right application of the Scriptures, and thus they frame theories that are not correct. It is true that they quote an abundance of Scripture, and teach much that is true; but truth is so mixed with error as to lead to wrong conclusions. . . .

Satan is working [so] that the history of the Jewish nation may be repeated in the experience of those who claim to believe present truth. The Jews had the Old Testament Scriptures and supposed themselves conversant with them. But they made a woeful mistake. The prophecies that refer to the glorious second appearing of Christ in the clouds of heaven they regarded as referring to His first coming. Because He did not come according to their expectations, they turned away from Him. . . .

The very same Satan is at work to undermine the faith of the people of God at this time. There are persons ready to catch up every new idea. The prophecies of Daniel and the Revelation are misinterpreted. . . . These messages, received and acted upon, are doing their work to prepare a people to stand in the great day of God. If we search the Scriptures to confirm the truth God has given His servants for the world, we shall be found proclaiming the first, second, and third angels' messages.

It is true that there are prophecies yet to be fulfilled. But very erroneous work has been done again and again, and will continue to be done by those who seek to find new light in the prophecies, and who begin by turning away from the light that God has already given. The messages of Revelation 14 are those by which the world is to be tested; they are the everlasting gospel and are to be sounded everywhere.—Manuscript 32, 1896 (*Manuscript Releases*, vol. 17, pp. 12-15).

December 2
**GOD GIVES NO
AUTHORITY TO
SET A TIME FOR
CHRIST'S RETURN**

◆ *But about that day and hour no one knows,
neither the angels of heaven, nor the Son, but
only the Father. Matthew 24:36, NRSV.*

OUR views have found favor with some, but it is because these persons have not discernment to see the true bearing of the arguments you present. They have had but a limited experience in the work of God for this time, and they do not see where your views would lead them. They are ready to assent to your statements; they see nothing in them but that which is correct. But they are misled because you have woven together much Scripture in constructing your theory; your arguments appear conclusive to them.

Not so, however, with those who have an experimental knowledge of the truth that applies in the last period of this earth's history. While they see that you hold some precious truth, they see also that you have misapplied Scripture, placing it in a framework of error, where it does not belong, and making it give force to that which is not present truth. . . . The light God has given me is that the Scriptures you have woven together you yourself do not fully understand. . . .

I have had to speak plainly in regard to those who were then leading away from right paths. With pen and voice I have borne the message, "Go not ye after them." The hardest task I ever had to do in this line was in dealing with one who, I knew, wanted to follow the Lord. For some time he had thought he was obtaining new light. He was very ill, and must soon die. . . . Those to whom he presented his views listened to him eagerly, and some thought him inspired. He had a chart made and reasoned from the Scriptures to show that the Lord would come at a certain date, in 1894 I think. To many his reasoning seemed to be without a flaw. They told of his powerful exhortations in his sickroom. Most wonderful views passed before him. But what was the source of his inspiration? It was the morphine given him to relieve his pain. . . .

No one has a true message fixing the time when Christ is to come or not to come. Be assured that God gives no one authority to say that Christ delays His coming five years, ten years, or twenty years. "Be ye therefore ready also: for the Son of man cometh at an hour when ye think not.". . .

All who are laborers together with God will contend most earnestly for the faith once delivered to the saints. They will not be turned from the present message, which is already lightening the earth with its glory. Nothing is worth contending for but the glory of God. The only rock that will stand is the Rock of Ages. The truth as it is in Jesus is the refuge in these days of error.—Letter 32, 1896.

December 3
"TIME NO
LONGER"

◆ *And the angel which I saw stand upon the sea and upon the earth lifted up his hand to heaven, and sware by him that liveth for ever and ever, . . . that there should be time no longer. Revelation 10:5, 6.*

𝒯HE mighty Angel who instructed John was no less a personage than Jesus Christ. Setting His right foot on the sea, and His left upon the dry land, shows the part that He is acting in the closing scenes of the great controversy with Satan. This position denotes His supreme power and authority over the whole earth. The controversy has waxed stronger and more determined from age to age, and will continue to do so to the concluding scenes when the masterly working of the powers of darkness shall reach their height. . . .

After these seven thunders uttered their voices, the instruction comes to John, as to Daniel, in regard to the little book: "Seal up those things which the seven thunders uttered.". . . John sees the little book unsealed. . . . Then Daniel's prophecies have their proper place in the first, second, and third angels' messages to be given to the world. The unsealing of the little book was the message in relation to time.

The books of Daniel and the Revelation are one. One is a prophecy, the other a revelation; one a book sealed, the other a book opened. . . . The special light given to John, which was expressed in the seven thunders, was a delineation of events that would transpire under the first and second angels' messages. . . . The first and second angels' messages were to be proclaimed, but no further light was to be revealed before these messages had done their specific work. . . .

This time, which the Angel declares with a solemn oath, is not the end of this world's history, neither of probationary time, but of prophetic time, which would precede the advent of our Lord. That is, the people will not have another message upon definite time. After this period of time, reaching from 1842 to 1844, there can be no definite tracing of the prophetic time. The longest reckoning reaches to the autumn of 1844.

The Angel's position, with one foot on the sea, the other on the land, signifies the wide extent of the proclamation of the message. It will cross the broad waters and be proclaimed in other countries, even to all the world. The comprehension of truth, the glad reception of the message, is represented in the eating of the little book. The truth in regard to the time of the advent of our Lord was a precious message to our souls.—Manuscript 59, 1900 (*Manuscript Releases*, vol. 19, pp. 319-321).

December 4
WE ARE CALLED TO BE SEPARATE FROM THE WORLD

◆ *Who gave himself for us, that he might redeem us from all iniquity, and purify unto himself a peculiar people, . . . These things speak, and exhort, and rebuke with all authority. Let no man despise thee. Titus 2:14, 15.*

WHEN the truth we now cherish was first seen to be Bible truth, how strange it appeared, and how strong was the opposition we had to meet in presenting it to the people for the first time. But how earnest and sincere were the truth-loving, truth-obeying ones. We were indeed a peculiar people. We were few in numbers, without wealth, without worldly wisdom or worldly honors, and yet we believed God, and were strong and successful, a terror to evildoers. Our love for one another was firm; it was not easily shaken. The power of God was manifested in our midst, the sick were healed, and there was much calm, sweet, holy joy.

But while the light has continued to increase, the advancement of the church has not been proportionate to the light. The fine gold has gradually become dim, and deadness and formality have come in to cripple the energies of the church. Their abundant privileges and opportunities have not led His people onward and upward to purity and holiness. A faithful improvement of the talents entrusted to them by God would have increased those talents greatly. Where much is given, much will be required. Those only who faithfully accept and appreciate the light God has given us, and who will take a high, noble stand in self-denial and self-sacrifice, will be channels of light to the world. . . .

No one has a right to start out on his or her own responsibility and advance ideas in our papers on Bible doctrines and place them in the foreground when it is known that there are various opinions on the same subject and that it will create a controversy. The first-day Adventists have done this. Each one has followed his or her own independent judgment and sought to present original ideas, until there is no concentrated action among them except perhaps that of opposing Seventh-day Adventists. We should not follow their example. . . .

We cannot, my brethren and sisters, float along with the current of the world. The work for us to do is to come out and be separate. This is the only way we can walk with God as did Enoch. . . . Like Enoch we are called upon to have a strong, living, working faith; it is the only way we can be laborers together with God. We must meet the conditions laid down in the Word of God or die in our sins. We must know what moral changes are essential to be made in our characters through the grace of Christ in order to be fitted for the mansions above.—Letter 53, 1887.

December 5
LIVE EVERY DAY AS THOUGH IT MIGHT BE THE LAST

◆ *Watch therefore: for ye know not what hour your Lord doth come. . . . Therefore be ye also ready: for in such an hour as ye think not the Son of man cometh. Matthew 24:42-44.*

*G*OD gives no one a message that it will be ten or twenty years before this earth's history shall close. If it were forty or one hundred years, the Lord would not authorize anyone to proclaim it. He would not give any living being an excuse for delaying the preparation for His appearing. He would have no one say, as did the unfaithful servant, "My Lord delayeth his coming," for this leads to reckless neglect of opportunities and privileges to prepare for that great day. Every soul who claims to be a servant of God is called to do His service as if every day might be the last. . . .

Let everyone to whom the Lord has given light from His Word be sure to make a right use of that light. Let all be guarded that they do not presume to feed the flock of God with food that is not appropriate for the time.

Talk of the speedy appearing of the Son of man in the clouds of heaven with power and great glory. Put not off that day. God has given no one light to say, "My Lord delayeth his coming." Let the inquiry be made, Shall I stand at the right hand or at the left hand of the Judge at that day? . . .

It is essential that all shall know what atmosphere surrounds their own souls, whether they are in copartnership with the enemy of righteousness and unconsciously doing his work, or whether they are linked up with Christ, doing His work, and seeking to establish souls more firmly in the truth.

Satan would be pleased to have anyone and everyone become his allies to weaken the confidence believers have in one another, and to sow discord among those who profess to believe the truth. Satan can accomplish his purposes most successfully through professed friends of Christ who are not walking and working in Christ's lines. Those who in mind and heart are turning away from the Lord's special work for this time, those who do not cooperate with Him in establishing souls in the faith by leading them to heed His words of warning, are doing the work of the enemy of Christ. . . .

This is the day of the Lord's preparation. We have no time now to talk unbelief and to gossip, no time now to do the devil's work. . . . So long as the people of God are in this world they will have to meet conflict and trouble and deception, because many choose the attributes of Satan instead of the attributes of God.—Manuscript 32a, 1896 (*Manuscript Releases,* vol. 18, pp. 58-62).

December 6
NOW IS NOT A TIME TO COMPROMISE

◆ *The watchman said, The morning cometh, and also the night: if ye will inquire, inquire ye: return, come. Isaiah 21:12.*

E are pressing on to the final conflict, and this is no time to compromise; it is no time to hide your colors. When the battle rages sore, let no one turn traitor. It is no time to lay down or conceal our weapons and give Satan the advantage in the warfare, but unless you watch and keep your garments unspotted from the world, you will not stand true to your Captain. . . . Call to your fellow watchmen, crying, "The morning cometh, and also the night."

It is no time now to relax our efforts, to become dull and spiritless, no time to hide our light under a bushel, to speak smooth things, to prophesy deceit. Every power is to be employed for God. You are to maintain your allegiance, bearing testimony for God and for truth. Do not be turned aside by any suggestion the world may make. We cannot afford to compromise; there is a living issue before us, of vital importance to the remnant people of God to the very close of this earth's history, for eternal interests are involved. On the very eve of the crisis, it is no time to be found with an evil heart of unbelief, departing from the living God.

The original apostasy began in disbelief and denial of the truth; but if we would triumph, we must fix the eye of faith steadfastly upon Jesus, the Captain of our salvation. We are to follow the example of Christ. In all that Jesus did on earth, He had an eye single to the glory of God. . . . Divinity and humanity were united in Christ, that He might reveal to us God's purpose, and bring us into close union with Himself. This union will enable us to overcome the enemy, for through faith in Christ, we shall have divine power.

Our numbers are increasing; our facilities are enlarging, and all this calls for union among the workers, and for entire consecration and real devotion to the cause of God. There is no place in the work of God for halfhearted workers, for those who are neither hot nor cold.

Watchmen on the walls of Zion are to be vigilant, and sleep not day or night. But if they have not received the message from the lips of Christ, their trumpets will give an uncertain sound. Brethren and sisters, God calls upon you, both ministers and laypersons, listen to His voice, as speaking to you through His Word. Let His truth be received into your heart, that you may be spiritualized by His living, sanctifying power. Then let the distinct message for this time be sent from watchman to watchman on the walls of Zion.—Manuscript 152, 1897.

December 7
SOME WILL CHOOSE REBELLION RATHER THAN OBEDIENCE

◆ *And before him shall be gathered all nations: and he shall separate them one from another, as a shepherd divideth his sheep from the goats: and he shall set the sheep on his right hand, but the goats on the left. Matthew 25:32, 33.*

*T*HE world, under Satan's training, has become qualified to do the work that he has purposed—place rebellion on the judgment seat, and summon the Creator of the heavens and the earth to be judged according to human judgment. Satanic agencies confront God with the will of humankind. In the last great conflict, people will attempt to array God before their judgment seat and pronounce sentence against Him, judging His law by the standard of the world. But the supreme Ruler will judge every person according to his or her works. All heaven has been watching for this movement. Then everyone will have an opportunity to choose on whose side they will stand.

All are working out their own destiny at the present time. God brings the light of His Word before the world, but there are those who will choose rebellion rather than obedience, and this decision will be for all time. The sinner voluntarily turns from a "Thus saith the Lord" to the deceiving representations of Satan. Has not God spoken? Has He not presented before human minds the motives that are to bear upon human hearts? In their resistance, they are rebelling against the word and power and authority of God, saying, "We will not have this man to reign over us."

And you are taking sides. A reward is offered you if you are obedient—connected with God as His sons and daughters. On the other hand is presented the judgment scene. When the Son of man shall come in His glory and all the holy angels with Him, the judgment will sit, and the books will be opened, and everyone will be judged out of those things that are written in the books. . . .

The world is to be again destroyed as by the Flood, not by water, but by fire. . . . Fathers and mothers must awake to their responsibilities, lest by their own course of action they encourage rebellion in their children. We feel to the depths of our being the peril that meets us in these last days. But the Lord sees, He understands all our necessities. . . .

Left to yourselves, you will never exercise your reason correctly. But the Lord will not leave you to yourselves. He follows you by His Holy Spirit. He thrusts the subject upon you.—Manuscript 10a, 1898.

December 8
THOSE WHO KEEP GOD'S COMMANDMENTS ARE HIS JEWELS

◆ *And they shall be mine, saith the Lord of hosts, in that day when I make up my jewels; and I will spare them, as a man spareth his own son that serveth him. Malachi 3:17.*

*T*HERE are only two places in the universe in which we can place our treasures—in God's storehouse or in Satan's. God's work is moving slowly for want of means. Workers are not able to enter new fields. Yet there are millions under the undisturbed domination of Satan.

Satan is busily laying his plans for the last mighty conflict, when all will take sides. After the gospel has been traveling over the world for nearly two thousand years, Satan will present to men and women the same scene that he presented to Christ. In a wonderful panorama, he will cause the kingdoms of the world in their glory to pass before them. . . . He will present before them entrancing views of the kingdom of God, and he claims that these are views of His kingdom. But are they? No; no.

Look, oh, look. Listen to the voices and powers that prevail in the world. The heavenly Watcher sees the earth filled with violence and crime. Is there any voice of prayer? Do you see any sign that God is recognized? . . . Look, you who are hesitating between obedience and disobedience. Look in imagination at the vast multitudes worshiping at Satan's altar. Listen to the music, to the language—called higher education. But what has God written upon it? Mystery of iniquity.

The working of the power of iniquity seems to have taken the whole world captive. . . . Enumerate the vices of men and women, if you can. But it is of no use to try to number them. Wealth is obtained by every species of robbery—not robbery of people alone but of God. People are using His means to gratify their selfishness. Everything that they can grasp is made to minister to their greed. Avarice and sensuality prevail. . . .

But they do not see all things. . . . John saw this multitude. This demon worship was revealed to him, and it seemed as though the whole world was standing on the brink of perdition. But as he looked with intense interest, he beheld a company of God's commandment-keeping people. They had the sign of the living God upon their foreheads, and he exclaimed, "Here is the patience of the saints: here are they that keep the commandments of God, and the faith of Jesus."—Manuscript 122, 1898.

December 9
OUR WORK IS TO PROCLAIM THE THREE ANGELS' MESSAGES

◆ *Cry aloud, spare not, lift up thy voice like a trumpet, and shew my people their transgression, and the house of Jacob their sins. Isaiah 58:1.*

HE last great conflict will be short but terrible. Old controversies will be revived. New controversies will arise. The last warnings must be given to the world. There is a special power in the presentation of the truth at the present time, but how long will it continue? Only a little while. If ever there was a crisis, it is now.

Decided efforts should be made to bring the message for this time prominently before the people. The third angel is to go forth with great power. Let none ignore this work or treat it as of little importance. The truth is to be proclaimed to the world, that they may see the light.

This is our work. The light that we have upon the third angel's message is the true light. The mark of the beast is exactly what it has been proclaimed to be. All in regard to this matter is not yet understood, and will not be understood until the unrolling of the scroll, but a most solemn work is to be accomplished in our world. The Lord's command to His servants is "Cry aloud, spare not, lift up thy voice like a trumpet, and shew my people their transgression, and the house of Jacob their sins."

There is to be no change in the features of our work. It is to stand as clear and distinct as prophecy has made it. We are to enter into no confederacy with the world, supposing that by so doing we could accomplish more. If any stand in the way, to hinder the advancement of the work in the lines that God has appointed, they will displease God. No line of our faith that has made us what we are is to be weakened. We have the old landmarks of truth, experience, and duty; we are to stand firmly in defense of our principles, in full view of the world.

It is essential that workers be raised up to open the living oracles of God to all nations, tongues, and peoples. People of all ranks and capacities, with various gifts, are to stand in their God-given armor, to cooperate harmoniously for a common result. They are to unite in the work of bringing the truth to all nations and peoples, each worker fulfilling his or her own special appointment.

There is a wide field of action, and in their plans and devising, all need to consider the result. Everything is to move according to the divine plan. The whole body must be fitly joined together, that each member may promote the designs of Him who gave His life for the life of the world.—Manuscript 3, 1899.

December 10
"A NEW HEART ALSO WILL I GIVE YOU"

◆ *A new heart also will I give you, and a new spirit will I put within you: and I will take away the stony heart out of your flesh, and I will give you an heart of flesh. Ezekiel 36:26.*

*T*HE truths of the Word of God are not mere sentiments, but the utterances of the Most High. Anyone who makes these truths a part of the life becomes in every sense a new creature. The person is not given new mental powers, but the darkness, that through ignorance and sin has clouded the understanding, is removed.

The words "A new heart will I give you" mean "A new mind will I give you." This change of heart is always attended by a clear conception of Christian duty, an understanding of truth. The clearness of our view of truth will be proportionate to our understanding of the Word of God. A person who gives the Scriptures close, prayerful attention will gain clear comprehension and sound judgment, as if in turning to God he or she had reached a higher grade of intelligence. . . .

We are dependent on the Bible for a knowledge of the early history of our world, of the creation of Adam and Eve, and of their fall. Remove the Word of God, and what can we expect other than to be left to fables and conjectures, and to that enfeebling of the intellect which is the sure result of entertaining error? We need the authentic history of the origin of the earth, of the fall of the covering cherub, and of the introduction of sin into our world. Without the Bible we should be bewildered by false theories. . . .

Wherever Christians are they may hold communion with God. And they may enjoy the intelligence of sanctified science. Their minds may be strengthened even as Daniel's was. . . .

The mind in which error has once taken possession can never expand freely to truth, even after investigation. The old theories will claim recognition. The understanding of things that are true and elevated and sanctifying will be confused. Superstitious ideas will enter the mind to mingle with the true, and these ideas are always debasing in their influence. Christian knowledge bears its own stamp of unmeasured superiority in all that concerns the preparation for the future, immortal life. It distinguishes the Bible reader and believer, who has been receiving the precious treasures of truth, from the skeptic and the believer in pagan philosophy. . . .

In the cities and nations of our world, there will be found among unbelievers a remnant who will appreciate the blessed Word and who will receive the Saviour. Christ will give men and women power to become the sons and daughters of God.—Manuscript 42, 1904.

December 11
**GOD'S PEOPLE
NOT TO BE
HIDDEN AWAY**

◆ *Ye are the light of the world. A city that is
set on an hill cannot be hid. Matthew 5:14.*

*D*ANIEL was a statesman in Babylon. . . . By his faithful service he taught those in Babylon that his God was a living God, not an image such as they worshiped. It was God's design to show the Babylonians that there was a King above the king of Babylon—the God whom the Hebrew youth worshiped. These youth exalted God. They knew that they were to carry out the principles of truth, and therefore they refused the meat from the royal table and the wine from the royal cellar. Their abstinence from the prescribed bill of fare made a distinction in every way between their appearance and the appearance of those youth who indulged their appetite.

There were plenty to make remarks, but these youth were faithful even in little things. And in physical appearance they were far ahead of the youth who sat at the king's table. Their simple diet kept their minds clear. They were better prepared for their studies, for they never knew the oppression caused by eating luxurious food. They were better prepared physically for taxing labor, for they were never sick. With clear minds they could think and work vigorously. By obeying God, they were doing the very things that will give strength of thought and memory. God ordained Daniel and his fellows to be connected with the great men of Babylon, that these men might become acquainted with the religion of the Hebrews, and know that God reigns over all kingdoms. . . .

In like manner the Lord means that Seventh-day Adventists shall witness for Him. They are not to be hidden away from the world. They are to be in the world, but not of the world. They are to stand distinct from the world in their manner of dealing. They are to show that they have purity of character, that the world may see that the truth, which they conscientiously believe, makes them honest in their dealings; that those with whom they are connected may see that believers of truth are sanctified through the truth, and that the truth received and obeyed makes the receivers as sons and daughters of God, children of the heavenly King, members of the royal family, faithful, true, honest, and upright, in the small as well as the great acts of life. . . .

Whatever is worth doing is worth doing well. Let us be faithful in the smallest duties, as well as the work requiring the largest sacrifice. To all who follow Daniel's example, not only professing the truth but living the truth, acting in accordance with the principles of temperance, the Lord will give encouragement similar to the encouragement He gave Daniel.— Manuscript 47, 1898.

December 12
"WHEN SHALL THESE THINGS BE?"

◆ *The disciples came unto him privately, saying, Tell us, when shall these things be? And what shall be the sign of thy coming, and of the end of the world? Matthew 24:3.*

CHRIST warned His disciples of the destruction of Jerusalem as well as of the temple. This event was foretold by Daniel. The oblations and sacrifices were no more of value, for type had reached antitype in the one great oblation. . . .

When Christ referred to the destruction of Jerusalem, His prophetic words reached beyond that event to the final conflagration that will take place in that day when the Lord rises out of His place to punish the world for their iniquity, when the earth shall disclose her blood and shall no more cover her slain. This entire chapter is a warning to those who shall live in the last scenes of this earth's history.

Turning to His disciples, Christ said, "Take heed that no man deceive you. For many shall come in my name, saying, I am Christ; and shall deceive many." Many false messiahs will appear, claiming to work miracles, and declaring that the time of the deliverance of the Jewish nation has come. These will mislead many. These words were fulfilled. Between the death of Christ and the siege of Jerusalem, many false messiahs appeared. But this warning is given also to those who live in this age of the world. The same deceptions practiced prior to the destruction of Jerusalem will be practiced again. The same events that took place at the overthrow of Jerusalem will take place again. . . .

Prior to the destruction of Jerusalem human beings wrestled for the supremacy. Emperors were murdered. Those supposed to be standing next to the throne were slain. . . .

Through the apostles God gave the Jewish people a last opportunity to repent. He manifested Himself through His witnesses, in their arrest, in their trial, and in their imprisonment. Yet their judges pronounced on them the death sentence. . . .

So it will be again. Seventh-day Adventists will fight the battle over the seventh-day Sabbath. . . . Christ told His disciples that they would be delivered up to councils, but He told them also that they were not to be anxious as to how they might vindicate the truth, for He would give them a mouth and wisdom that all their adversaries could not gainsay nor resist. . . .

Magicians and sorcerers, claiming miraculous power, drew the people after them into the mountain solitudes. But this prophecy was spoken also for the last days. This sign is given as a sign of the Second Advent. Companies inspired by Satan will be formed to deceive and to delude.—Manuscript 78, 1897.

December 13
WE ARE SOLDIERS
OF THE LORD

♦ *For I reckon that the sufferings of this present time are not worthy to be compared with the glory which shall be revealed in us. Romans 8:18.*

𝒩O one would think of entering an army in time of war, hoping to have ease and self-indulgence and a real pleasant and profitable time. They know that hardships and privations are the liabilities; and as long as the war lasts, they will have coarse food and often short rations, long weary marches by day, enduring the heat of the burning sun, camping out at night in the open air, exposed to drenching rains and chilling frosts, venturing health and life itself as they stand as targets for the enemy.

The Christian life is compared to the life of a soldier, and there can be no bribes presented of ease and self-indulgence. The idea that Christian soldiers are to be excused from the conflicts, experiencing no trials, having all temporal comforts to enjoy, and even the luxuries of life, is a farce. The Christian conflict is a battle and a march, calling for endurance. Difficult work has to be done. It often proves fatal to the Christianity of those who, with false ideas of pleasantness and ease, enlist as soldiers in Christ's army and then experience trials. God does not present the reward to those whose whole life in this world has been one of self-indulgence and pleasure. . . .

Those who serve under the bloodstained banner of Prince Emmanuel are expected to do difficult work that will tax every power God has given them. They will have painful trials to endure for Christ's sake. They will have conflicts that rend the soul, but if they are faithful soldiers they will say with Paul, "For our light affliction, which is but for a moment, worketh for us a far more exceeding and eternal weight of glory.". . .

An army would be demoralized if it did not learn to obey the orders of the captain. Each soldier must act in concert. Union is strength; without union, efforts are meaningless. Whatever excellent qualities soldiers may possess, they cannot be safe, trustworthy soldiers if they claim a right to act independently of their comrades. This independent action cannot be maintained in the service of Christ. . . .

Those who prefer to act alone are not good soldiers; they have some crookedness in their character that needs to be straightened. They may think themselves conscientious, but they do not the works of Christ. They cannot render efficient service. Their work will be of a character to draw apart when Christ's prayer was that His disciples might be one as He was one with the Father.—Letter 62, 1886.

December 14
THE SEAL OF GOD IS THE SABBATH

◆ *I am the Lord your God; walk in my statutes, and keep my judgments, and do them; and hallow my sabbaths; and they shall be a sign between me and you, that ye may know that I am the Lord your God. Ezekiel 20:19, 20.*

HE Sabbath was given to all humankind to commemorate the work of creation. The great Jehovah, when He had laid the foundations of the earth, when He had dressed the whole world in its garb of beauty, and created all the wonders of the land and the sea, instituted the Sabbath day and made it holy. . . . God sanctified and blessed the day in which He had rested from all His wondrous work. And this Sabbath, sanctified of God, was to be kept for a perpetual covenant. It was a memorial that was to stand from age to age, till the close of earth's history. . . .

During their stay in Egypt, Israel had so long heard and seen idolatry practiced that to a large degree they had lost their knowledge of God and of His law, and their sense of the importance and sacredness of the Sabbath. The law was given a second time to call these things to their remembrance. In God's statutes was defined practical religion for all humankind. . . .

There are those who hold that the Sabbath was given only for the Jews; but God has never said this. He committed the Sabbath to His people Israel as a sacred trust, but the very fact that the desert of Sinai, and not Palestine, was the place selected by Him in which to proclaim His law reveals that He intended it for all humankind. The law of Ten Commandments is as old as creation. Therefore the Sabbath institution has no special relation to the Jews, any more than to all other created beings. God has made the observance of the Sabbath obligatory upon all people. "The Sabbath," it is plainly stated, "was made for man." Let everyone, therefore, who is in danger of being deceived on this point give heed to the Word of God rather than the assertions of humans. . . .

Every person has been placed on trial, as were Adam and Eve in Eden. As the tree of knowledge was placed in the midst of the Garden of Eden, so the Sabbath command is placed in the midst of the Decalogue. In regard to the fruit of the tree of knowledge, the restriction was made, Ye shall not eat of it . . . lest ye die. Of the Sabbath, God said, Ye shall not defile it, but keep it holy. . . . As the tree of knowledge was the test of Adam's obedience, so the fourth command is the test that God has given to prove the loyalty of all His people. The experience of Adam is to be a warning to us so long as time shall last. It warns us not to receive any assurance from the mouths of mortals or of angels that will detract one jot or tittle from the sacred law of Jehovah.—*Review and Herald,* Aug. 30, 1898.

December 15
BELIEVER OF PRESENT TRUTH MUST BE STRONG IN THE LORD

◆ *Finally, my brethren, be strong in the Lord, and in the power of his might.*
Ephesians 6:10.

RUE Christianity will always be aggressive, and wherever it exists it will arouse enmity. All who live a conscientious life, who bear testimony of the claims of God, of the evil of sin, of the judgment to come, will be called the disturbers of Israel. Those whose testimony awakens apprehension of the soul offend pride and arouse opposition. The hatred of evil against good exists as surely now as in the days of Christ when the multitudes cried, "Away with this man!" "Release unto us Barabbas." There is no kind of evil in our world but that some have an interest in maintaining it. Evil is ever warring against good. And since we know that the conflict with the prince of darkness is constant and must be severe, let us be united in the warfare. Cease to war against those of your own faith. Let no one help Satan in his work. We have all that we can do in another direction. . . .

The first thing recorded in Scripture history after the fall was the persecution of Abel. And the last thing in Scripture prophecy is the persecution against those who refuse to receive the mark of the beast. We should be the last people on the earth to indulge in the slightest degree the spirit of persecution against those who are bearing the message of God to the world. . . .

A passive piety will not answer for this time; let the passiveness be manifested where it is needed, in patience, kindness, and forbearance. But we must bear a decided message of warning to the world. The Prince of Peace thus proclaimed His work, "I came not to send peace [on earth], but a sword." Evil must be assailed; falsehood and error must be made to appear in their true character; sin must be denounced; and the testimony of every believer in the truth must be as one. All your little differences, which arouse the combative spirit among brethren and sisters, are devices of Satan to divert minds from the great and fearful issue before us. . . .

Those who profess to believe the special truths for this time need to be converted and sanctified by the truth. As Christians we are made depositories of sacred truth, and we are not to keep the truth in the outer court, but bring it into the sanctuary of the soul. Then the church will possess divine vitality throughout. . . . One question will be all absorbing—Who shall approach nearest the likeness of Christ? Who shall do most to win souls to righteousness? When this is the ambition of believers, contention is at an end; the prayer of Christ is answered.—Letter 25b, 1892.

December 16
**THE PAST
RECORDED IN
THE BIBLE IS ALSO
FOR OUR TIME**

◆ *Not unto themselves, but unto us they did
minister the things, which are now reported
unto you by them that have preached the
gospel unto you with the Holy Ghost sent
down from heaven. 1 Peter 1:12.*

EVER are we absent from the mind of God. God is
our joy and our salvation. Each of the ancient prophets spoke less for their
own time than for ours, so that their prophesying is in force for us. [First
Corinthians 10:11 and above text quoted.] The Bible has been your study
book. It is well thus, for it is the true counsel of God, and it is the con-
ductor of all the holy influences that the world has contained since its creation. We have the encouraging record that Enoch walked with God. If
Enoch walked with God in that degenerate age just prior to the destruction of the world by a flood, we are to receive courage and be stimulated
with his example that we need not be contaminated with the world, but
amid all its corrupting influences and tendencies we may walk with God.
We may have the mind of Christ.

Enoch, the seventh from Adam, was ever prophesying the coming of
the Lord. This great event had been revealed to him in vision. Abel, though
dead, is ever speaking of the blood of Christ, which alone can make our offerings and gifts perfect. The Bible has accumulated and bound up together its treasures for this last generation. All the great events and solemn
transactions of Old Testament history have been, and are, repeating themselves in the church in these last days. There is Moses still speaking, teaching self-renunciation by wishing himself blotted from the book of life for
his people so that they might be saved. David is leading the intercession of
the church for the salvation of souls to the ends of the earth. The prophets
are still testifying of the sufferings of Christ and the glory that should follow. There the whole accumulated truths are presented in force to us, that
we may profit by their teachings. We are under the influence of the whole.

What manner of persons ought we to be to whom all this rich light of
inheritance has been given? Concentrating all the influence of the past with
new and increased light of the present, accrued power is given to all who
will follow the light. Their faith will increase and be brought into exercise
at the present time, awakening an energy and an intensely increased
earnestness, and thorough dependence upon God for His power to replenish the world and send the light of the Sun of Righteousness to the ends of
the earth. God has enriched the world in these last days proportionately
with the increase of ungodliness if His people will only lay hold of His
priceless gift and bind up their every interest with Him.—Letter 74a, 1897.

December 17
**GIVE THE LAST
MESSAGE OF
WARNING TO
THE WORLD**

◆ *He that shall endure unto the end, the same shall be saved. And this gospel of the kingdom shall be preached in all the world . . . and then shall the end come. Matthew 24:13, 14.*

*I*T is not enough in this time of test and trial to have merely an intellectual knowledge of the truth. Heart work must be done. . . . The Lord cannot use the worker into whose experience true conversion has not entered. . . . The agencies of God and satanic agencies cannot combine. While so many are saying, Who is the Lord, that I should serve Him? While there prevails a lack of faith in God, let those who represent the work of the third angel's message act like converted people. . . . I am hoping that we may have the satisfaction of seeing a work done that is free from selfishness and that will rapidly advance work in missionary lines. . . .

If ever there was a time in the history of Seventh-day Adventists when they should arise and shine, it is now. No voice should be restrained from proclaiming the third angel's message. Let none, for fear of losing prestige with the world, obscure one ray of light coming from the Source of all light. It requires moral courage to do the work of God for these last days, but let us not be led by the spirit of human wisdom. The truth should be everything to us. Let those who want to make a name with the world go with the world.

The great conflict is right at hand in which all will take sides; in it the whole Christian world will be involved. Daily, hourly, we must be actuated by the principles of the Word of God. Self must be sanctified by the principles of the righteousness, the mercy, and the love of God. At every point of uncertainty, pray and earnestly inquire: Is this the way of the Lord? With your Bibles before you, consult with God as to what He would have you do. Holy principles are revealed in the Word of God. The source of all true wisdom is found in the cross of Calvary.

Everywhere we see increasing evidence that the message we have from God is to be the last message of warning to the churches of the world. Yet year after year is passing into eternity, and the churches are unwarned. I am instructed to speak to my brethren and sisters and to ask, Are we conscious of the neglect? I have been given message after message for our leaders, encouraging them to begin work in every place where the way shall open. If laborers would go forth to the work, the Lord would bless their own souls and would make their efforts fruitful. As the people hear the reasons of our faith, they will become interested and will be converted. There are many important places open to those who will work for souls.—Letter 94a, 1909.

December 18
THE PATH OF OBEDIENCE IS THE WAY TO HOLINESS

◆ *Many shall be purified, and made white, and tried; but the wicked shall do wickedly: and none of the wicked shall understand; but the wise shall understand. Daniel 12:10.*

HE world is a theater. The actors, the inhabitants of the world, are preparing to act their part in the last great drama. God is lost sight of. There is no unity of purpose, except as parties of people confederate to gain their ends. God is looking on. His purposes in regard to His rebellious subjects will be fulfilled. The world has not been given into human hands, though God is permitting the elements of confusion and disorder to bear sway for a season. A power from beneath is . . . working with all deceivableness of unrighteousness in those who are binding themselves together in secret societies. Those who are yielding to the passion for confederation are working out the plans of the enemy. The cause will be followed by the effect.

Transgression has almost reached its limit. Confusion fills the world, and a great terror is soon to come upon human beings. The end is very near. We who know the truth should be preparing for what is soon to break upon the world as an overwhelming surprise. . . .

The wicked have chosen Satan as their leader. Under his control, the wonderful faculties of the mind are used to construct agencies of destruction. God has given the human mind great power, power to show that the Creator has endowed human beings with ability to do a great work against the enemy of all righteousness, power to show what victories may be gained in the conflict against evil. . . .

But when those to whom God has entrusted capabilities give themselves into the hands of the enemy, they become a power to destroy. When people do not make God first and last and best in everything, when they do not give themselves to Him for the carrying out of His purposes, Satan comes in and uses in his service the minds that, given to God, could achieve great good. Under his direction they do an evil work with great and masterly power. God designed them to work on a high plane of action, to enter into His mind, and thus acquire an education that would enable them to work the works of righteousness. But they know nothing of this education. They are helpless. Their powers do not guide them aright, for they are under the enemy's control.

The way to holiness and heaven is found in the path of obedience. "God so loved the world, that he gave his only begotten Son, that whosoever believeth in him should not perish, but have everlasting life."—Letter 141, 1902.

359

December 19
**LET US STAND ON
THE SIDE OF
CHRIST**

◆ *Come unto me, all ye that labour and are
heavy laden, and I will give you rest. Take
my yoke upon you, and learn of me; for I am
meek and lowly in heart: and ye shall find
rest unto your souls. Matthew 11:28, 29.*

*A*LL who would work for the Master must submit to
the yoke of Christ. This submission involves self-sacrifice and entire consecration of body, soul, and spirit. As they learn of Christ, His meekness
and lowliness, they will find that His yoke is easy and His burden is light.
They will not become weary in His service. . . . Let all ask of God, and they
will receive wisdom to carry on His work under the ministration of the
Holy Spirit. . . .

Time is precious. The destiny of souls is in the balance. At infinite cost
a way of salvation has been provided. Shall Christ's great sacrifice be in
vain? Shall the earth be entirely controlled by satanic agencies? The salvation of souls is dependent upon the consecration and activity of God's
church. The Lord calls all who believe in Him to be workers together with
Him. While their life shall last, they are not to feel that their work is done.
Until the time comes when Christ shall say, "It is finished," His work for
the saving of souls will not decrease, but will grow in importance.

The mercy of God is shown by His long forbearance. He is holding
back His judgments, waiting for the message of warning to be sounded to
all. There are many who have not yet heard the testing truths for this time.
The last call of mercy is to be given more fully to our world. . . .

The terrible condition of the world today would indicate that apparently the death of Christ has been almost in vain, that Satan has triumphed. The great majority of the earth's inhabitants belong to Satan's
kingdom. . . . Christ has not yet set up His kingdom. "We see not yet all
things put under him."

But we have not been deceived. Notwithstanding the apparent triumph of Satan on the earth, Christ is carrying forward His mediatorial
work in the heavenly sanctuary. . . . As we see the fulfillment of prophecy,
our faith in the final triumph of Christ's kingdom should be increased. We
should go forth with courage to do our appointed work.

By the fragrance of our speech and the nobility of our characters, let
us make it clear that in the great conflict between good and evil we are on
the side of Christ. Let us express our faith in the triumph of the cross of
Calvary. Let all our people decide that in their life truth and righteousness
shall be magnified.—Manuscript 57, 1903.

December 20
WE ARE LABORERS TOGETHER WITH GOD

◆ *For we are labourers together with God: ye are God's husbandry, ye are God's building. 1 Corinthians 3:9.*

*T*HERE never will be a time in the history of the church when God's workers can fold their hands and be at ease, saying, "All is peace and safety." Then it is that sudden destruction cometh. Everything may move forward amid apparent prosperity; but Satan is wide awake and is studying and counseling with his evil angels another mode of attack where he can be successful. The contest will wax more and more fierce on the part of Satan, for he is moved by a power from beneath.

As the work of God's people moves forward with sanctified, resistless energy, planting the standard of Christ's righteousness in the church, moved by a power from the throne of God, the great controversy will wax stronger and stronger, and will become more and more determined. Mind will be arrayed against mind, plans against plans, principles of heavenly origin against principles of Satan. Truth in its varied phases will be in conflict with error in its ever-varying, increasing forms, and which, if possible, will deceive the very elect. . . .

There is danger now of our losing sight of the important truths applicable for this period of time, and seeking for those things that are new and strange and entrancing. Many, if reproved by the Spirit of God through His appointed agencies, refuse to receive correction, and a root of bitterness is planted in their hearts against the Lord's servants who carry heavy, disagreeable burdens. . . . They have not the moral courage to do the things that it is for their special benefit to do. They see no necessity for reform, and so they reject the words of the Lord and hate Him who reproveth at the gate. This very refusal to heed the admonitions that the Lord sends gives Satan every advantage to make them the bitterest enemies of those who have told them the truth.—Manuscript 92, 1897 (*Testimonies to Ministers,* pp. 406-408).

Our work must be an earnest one. We are not to fight as those who beat the air. The ministry, the pulpit, and the press demand people like Caleb, who will do and dare, people whose eyes are single to detect the truth from error, whose ears are consecrated to catch the words from the faithful Watcher. And the Spirit from the throne of God will make itself felt upon a degenerate Christianity, a corrupt world, ready to be consumed by the long-deferred judgments of an offended God.—Manuscript 92, 1897 (*Testimonies to Ministers,* p. 407).

December 21
**THERE WILL
NEVER BE A
TIME TO CHANGE
OUR MESSAGE**

◆ *In vain do they worship me,
teaching human precepts as doctrines.
Matthew 15:9, NRSV.*

*M*Y soul is much burdened, for I know what is before us. Every conceivable deception will be brought to bear upon those who have not a daily, living connection with God. Satan's angels are wise to do evil, and they will create that which some will claim to be advanced light and will proclaim it as new and wonderful; yet while in some respects the message may be truth, it will be mingled with human inventions and will teach for doctrine the commandments of men. . . . Many apparently good things will need to be carefully considered with much prayer, for they are specious devices of the enemy to lead souls in a path that lies so close to the path of truth that it will be scarcely distinguishable from it. . . .

A new order of things has come into the ministry. There is a desire to pattern after other churches, and simplicity and humility are almost unknown. The young ministers seek to be original, and to introduce new ideas and new plans for labor. Some open revival meetings, and by this means call large numbers into the church. But when the excitement is over, where are the converted ones? Repentance and confession of sin are not seen. The sinner is entreated to believe in Christ and accept Him, without regard to one's past life of sin and rebellion. The heart is not broken. There is no contrition of soul. The supposed converted ones have not fallen upon the Rock, Christ Jesus. . . .

The Lord desires His servants today to preach the old gospel doctrine, sorrow for sin, repentance, and confession. . . . Sinners must be labored for, perseveringly, earnestly, wisely, until they shall see that they are transgressors of God's law, and shall exercise repentance toward God and faith toward the Lord Jesus Christ. . . .

Workers should not feel that it is a virtue to stand apart because they do not see all minor points in exactly the same light. If they agree on fundamental truths, they should not differ and dispute about matters of little real importance. To dwell on perplexing questions, that after all are of no vital consequence, tends to call the mind away from truths vital to the saving of the soul. . . .

Unbelievers are critical, and they seek to frame some excuse for not receiving the truth as it is in Jesus. Where these differences exist among us, those who stand outside will say, "It will be time enough for us to believe as you do when you can agree among yourselves as to what constitutes truth." Thus the ungodly take advantage of the divisions and controversies among Christians.—Manuscript 82, 1894 (*Review and Herald,* Nov. 4, 1965).

December 22
**TAKE CARE
IN RECEIVING
"NEW LIGHT"**

♦ *We have not followed cunningly devised
fables, when we made known unto you the
power and coming of our Lord Jesus Christ.
2 Peter 1:16.*

E are to pray for divine enlightenment, and at the same time we should be careful about receiving everything termed new light. . . . I have been shown that it is the device of the enemy to divert minds to some obscure or unimportant point, something that is not fully revealed or is not essential to salvation. . . .

We must let the principles of the third angel's message stand out clear and distinct. The great pillars of our faith will hold all the weight that can be placed upon them.—Manuscript 82, 1894 (*Review and Herald,* Nov. 4, 1965).

Our ministers must cease to dwell upon their peculiar ideas, with the feeling, "You must see the point as I do, or you cannot be saved." Away with this egotism! The great work to be done in every case is to win souls to Christ. . . .

There is a time of trouble coming to the people of God, but we are not to keep that constantly before the people, and rein them up to have a time of trouble beforehand. There is to be a shaking among God's people; but this is not the present truth to carry to the churches; it will be the result of refusing the truth presented.

The ministers should not feel that they have some wonderful advanced ideas, and unless all receive these, they will be shaken out, and a people will arise to go forward and upward to the victory. Satan's object is accomplished just as surely when people run ahead of Christ and do the work He has never entrusted to their hands, as when they remain in the Laodicean state, lukewarm, feeling rich and increased with goods, and in need of nothing. The two classes are equally stumbling blocks.

Some zealous ones who are aiming and straining every energy for originality have made a grave mistake in trying to get something startling, wonderful, entrancing, before the people, something that they think others do not comprehend. But often they do not themselves know what they are talking about. . . .

Some are naturally combative. . . . They would like to enter into controversy, would like to fight for their particular ideas; but they should lay this aside, for it is not developing the Christian graces. Work with all your power to answer the prayer of Christ, that His disciples may be one as He is one with the Father.—*Ibid.* (*Review and Herald,* Nov. 11, 1965).

December 23
NOT ONLY BELIEVE, BUT DO THE WILL OF THE FATHER

◆ *Not everyone who says to me, "Lord, Lord," will enter the kingdom of heaven, but only the one who does the will of my Father in heaven. Matthew 7:21, NRSV.*

*H*OLINESS means perfect obedience to God's law— "Thou shalt" and "Thou shalt not." Those who pay no heed to this law, except to tear it down by their unsanctified actions, are in rebellion against God and cannot possibly be holy. . . .

Are those who so boldly claim to be sanctified doing the works of Christ? Are they holding up before the people the law of God given on Mount Sinai? They declare that they have with them the power of God, but the Scriptures declare: "To the law and to the testimony: if they speak not according to this word, it is because there is no light in them" (Isa. 8:20). . . .

Another doctrine that will be presented is that all we have to do is to believe in Christ—to believe that He has forgiven our sins, and that after we are forgiven, it is impossible for us to sin. This is a snare of Satan. It is true that we must believe in Christ. He is our only hope of salvation. But it also is true that we must work out our individual salvation daily in faith, not boastingly, but with fear and trembling. We are to use every power of our being in His service, and after we have done our utmost, we are still to regard ourselves as unprofitable servants. Divine power will unite with our efforts, and as we cling to God with the hand of faith, Christ will impart to us His wisdom and His righteousness. Thus, by His grace we shall be enabled to build upon the sure foundation.

It is not the purpose of God that we should be dwarfs in the religious life. He desires us to be constantly growing in grace and the knowledge of the truth. He wants us to be able to do better work for Him today than we did yesterday. He has for us a heaven full of blessings, and He wants us to claim these blessings, and . . . glorify God as His obedient disciples.

As we follow on step by step to know the Lord, we need not expect that the way will be free from hindrances. Just as surely as we strive to serve the Lord, so surely will Satan put forth every effort in his power to accomplish our ruin. But help has been laid upon One that is mighty, and to every struggling child of His who asks Him for grace, believing, He comes with the needed aid. We have an all-powerful Saviour who was victorious in His assumed humanity, and we are to press forward in the work of overcoming in the name of Jesus Christ of Nazareth. In His strength, which we claim by faith, we are gaining the victory over sin.—Manuscript 27, 1886.

December 24
**THE HOLY SPIRIT
HELPS DISCERN
TRUTH FROM
ERROR**

◆ *For our gospel came not unto you in word only, but also in power, and in the Holy Ghost, and in much assurance.*
1 Thessalonians 1:5.

T is the truth as it is in Jesus that quickens the conscience and transforms the mind, for it is accompanied to the heart by the Holy Spirit. Without the enlightenment of the Spirit of God, we shall not be able to discern truth from error, and shall fall under the masterful temptations and deceptions that Satan will bring upon the world. We are near the close of the controversy between the Prince of light and the prince of darkness, and soon the delusions of the enemy will try our faith, of what sort it is. . . .

But though the prince of darkness will work to cover the earth with darkness, and with gross darkness the people, the Lord will manifest His converting power. A work is to be accomplished in the earth similar to that which took place at the outpouring of the Holy Spirit in the days of the early disciples, when they preached Jesus and Him crucified. Many will be converted in a day, for the message will go with power. It can then be said: "Our gospel came not unto you in word only, but also in power, and in the Holy Ghost.". . .

The work of the Holy Spirit is immeasurably great. It is from this source that power and efficiency come to the worker for God; and the Holy Spirit is the Comforter, as the personal presence of Christ to the soul. Any person who looks to Christ in simple, childlike faith is made a partaker of the divine nature through the agency of the Holy Spirit. When led by the Spirit of God, Christians may know that they are made complete in Him who is the head of all things. As Christ was glorified on the day of Pentecost, so will He again be glorified in the closing work of the gospel, when He shall prepare a people to stand the final test in the closing conflict of the great controversy. . . .

The people of God are to be called out from their association with worldlings and evildoers to stand in the battle for the Lord against the powers of darkness. When the earth is lightened with the glory of God, we shall see a work similar to that which was wrought when the disciples, filled with the Holy Spirit, proclaimed the power of a risen Saviour. [After] the light of heaven penetrated the darkened minds of those who had been deceived by the enemies of Christ, the false representation of Him was rejected, for through the efficiency of the Holy Spirit they now saw Him exalted to be a Prince and Saviour, to give repentance unto Israel, and remission of sins.—Manuscript 143, 1901.

December 25
THE DEATH DECREE AGAINST GOD'S PEOPLE

◆ *And the letters were sent by posts into all the king's provinces, to destroy, to kill, and to cause to perish, all Jews, both young and old, little children and women, in one day. Esther 3:13.*

*S*ATAN will excite the indignation of apostate Christendom against the humble remnant who conscientiously refuse to accept false customs and traditions. . . . The church and the world will unite, and the world will lend to the church power to crush out the right of the people to worship according to His Word.

The decree that is to go forth against the people of God in the near future is in some respects similar to that issued by Ahasuerus against the Jews in the time of Esther. The Persian edict sprang from the malice of Haman toward Mordecai. . . . The king's decision against the Jews was secured under false pretenses, through a misrepresentation of that peculiar people. Satan instigated this scheme in order to rid the earth of those who preserved the knowledge of the true God. . . .

History repeats itself. The same masterful mind that plotted against the faithful in ages past is now at work to gain control of the fallen churches, that through them he may condemn and put to death all who will not worship the idol sabbath. We have not to battle with mortals, as it may appear. We war not against flesh and blood, but against principalities, against powers, against the rulers of the darkness of this world, against wicked spirits in high places. But if the people of God will put their trust in Him and by faith rely upon His power, the devices of Satan will be defeated in our time as signally as in the days of Mordecai.

The decree is to go forth that all who will not receive the mark of the beast shall neither buy nor sell and, finally, that they shall be put to death. But the saints of God do not receive this mark. The prophet of Patmos beheld those who had gotten the victory over the beast and over his image and over his mark and over the number of his name, standing on the sea of glass, having the harps of God and singing the song of Moses and the Lamb. . . .

Paul writes to the Romans, "If it be possible, as much as lieth in you, live peaceably with all men." But there is a point beyond which it is impossible to maintain union and harmony without the sacrifice of principle. Separation then becomes an absolute duty. The laws of nations should be respected when they do not conflict with the laws of God. But when there is collision between them, every true disciple of Christ will say, as did the apostle Peter when commanded to speak no more in the name of Jesus, "We ought to obey God rather than men."—Manuscript 51, 1899 (see also *Signs of the Times,* Nov. 8, 1899).

December 26
ALL REVELATION IN SCRIPTURE COMES FROM JESUS CHRIST

◆ *No prophecy of scripture is a matter of one's own interpretation, because no prophecy ever came by human will, but men and women moved by the Holy Spirit spoke from God. 2 Peter 1:20, 21, NRSV.*

HE whole Bible is a revelation, for all revelation to human beings comes through Christ and all centers in Him. God has spoken unto us by His Son, whose we are by creation and by redemption. Christ came to John, exiled on the isle of Patmos, to give him the truth for these last days, to show him that which must shortly come to pass. Jesus Christ is the great trustee of divine revelation. It is through Him that we have a knowledge of what we are to look for in the closing scenes of this earth's history. . . .

John, the beloved disciple, was the one chosen to receive this revelation. He was the last survivor of the first chosen disciples. Under the New Testament dispensation he was honored as the prophet Daniel was honored under the Old Testament dispensation.

The instruction to be communicated to John was so important that Christ came from heaven to give it to His servant, telling him to send it to the churches. This instruction is to be the object of our careful and prayerful study, for we are living in a time when persons who are not under the teaching of the Holy Spirit will bring in false theories. . . .

After the passing of the time [1844], God entrusted to His faithful followers the precious principles of present truth. . . . Those who passed through these experiences are to be as firm as a rock to the principles that have made us Seventh-day Adventists. . . . Those who took part in the establishment of our work upon a foundation of Bible truth, those who know the waymarks that have pointed out the right path, are to be regarded as workers of the highest value. They can speak from personal experience regarding the truths entrusted to them. These workers are not to permit their faith to be changed to infidelity; they are not to permit the banner of the third angel to be taken from their hands. They are to hold the beginning of their confidence firm unto the end.

The Lord has declared that the history of the past shall be rehearsed as we enter upon the closing work. Every truth that He has given for these last days is to be proclaimed to the world. Every pillar that He has established is to be strengthened. We cannot now step off the foundation that God has established. We cannot now enter into any new organization, for this would mean apostasy from the truth.—Manuscript 129, 1905.

December 27
ANGELS TO
ANSWER PRAYERS
OF UNSELFISH
WORKERS

◆ *The way of the just is uprightness: thou, most upright, dost weigh the path of the just. Isaiah 26:7.*

WE have before us in the Word of God instances of heavenly agencies working on the minds of kings and rulers, while at the same time satanic agencies were also at work on their minds. No human eloquence, in strongly set forth human opinions, can change the working of satanic agencies. Satan seeks continually to block the way, so that the truth shall be bound about by human devising, and those who have light and knowledge are in the greatest danger unless they constantly consecrate themselves to God, humiliating self, and realizing the peril of the times.

Heavenly beings are appointed to answer the prayers of those who are working unselfishly for the interests of the cause of God. The very highest angels in the heavenly courts are appointed to work out the prayers that ascend to God for the advancement of the cause of God. Each angel has a particular post of duty, and is not permitted to leave for any other place. If an angel should leave, the powers of darkness would gain an advantage. . . .

Day by day the conflict between good and evil is going on. . . . As a people we do not understand as we should the great conflict going on between invisible agencies, the controversy between loyal and disloyal angels. Evil angels are constantly at work, planning their line of attack, controlling as commanders, kings, and rulers, the disloyal human forces.

I call upon you who are not ready for the last great controversy to wake up. You are not watching for that which is soon coming upon the earth. Human instrumentalities under the control of fallen angels are seeking to gather in their harvest. Those who would find themselves under the protection of the angels of God must live wholly for God's glory, prepared to stand in their lot and in their place. . . .

Over every person good and evil angels strive. It is the person himself who determines which shall win. I call upon the ministers of Christ to press home upon the understanding of all who come within the reach of their voice the truth of the ministration of angels. Do not indulge in fanciful speculations. The written Word is our only safety. We must pray as did Daniel, that we may be guarded by heavenly intelligences. As ministering spirits, angels are sent forth to minister to those who shall be heirs of salvation. Pray . . . pray as you have never prayed before. We are not prepared for the Lord's coming. We need to make thorough work for eternity.—Letter 201, 1899.

December 28
CHRIST IS KNOCK-ING AT YOUR HEART'S DOOR; LET HIM IN

◆ *For it became him, for whom are all things, and by whom are all things, . . . to make the captain of their salvation perfect through sufferings. Hebrews 2:10.*

MONG the people of God there is to be no dissension, no controversy, no warfare against one another. The forces of righteousness are to be a unit in their conflict with evil. All the strength of God's people is to be directed against the forces of the enemy. The will of every child of God is to be placed on the side of God's will. Satan's strong efforts against good, and the terrible hatred of his agencies against God's agencies, show the need of union and harmony among the forces of righteousness.

A terrible contest is before us. We are nearing the battle of the great day of God Almighty. That which has been held in control is to be let loose. The angel of mercy is folding its wings, preparing to step down from the golden throne and leave the world to the control of Satan, the king they have chosen, a murderer and a destroyer from the beginning.

The principalities and powers of earth are in bitter revolt against the God of heaven. They are filled with hatred against all who serve Him, and soon, very soon, is to be fought the last great battle between good and evil. The earth is to be the battlefield—the scene of the final contest and the final victory. Here, where for so long Satan has led people against God, rebellion is to be forever suppressed.

Christ came to this earth in human form that He might stand as the Captain of our salvation, so that we should not be overcome by Satan's power. And when the enemy has seemed to be gaining a signal victory over righteousness, God has been working in mercy and power to counteract his designs. . . .

God's people are to bear a bold, decided testimony for the truth, unfolding the purposes of God by the witness of pen and voice. . . . When we consecrate ourselves to Christ, He speaks to the heart, filling it with His Spirit. We have no time to wrestle and contend among ourselves, no time to work on suppositions or cherish prejudices. It is too late for this . . . for Christ is at the door.

There is a reality in sound doctrine. It is not a vapor that passes away. Light is to shine forth from the Word of God. God calls upon His people to draw near to Him. Let no one interpose between Him and His people. Christ is knocking at the door of the heart, seeking for entrance. Will you let Him in?—Letter 153, 1901.

December 29
WE ARE ON THE BORDERS OF THE PROMISED LAND

♦ *And they brought up an evil report of the land which they had searched unto the children of Israel, saying, The land, through which we have gone to search it, is a land that eateth up the inhabitants thereof. Numbers 13:32.*

HE time when the work goes hardest is the very time to test the spiritual strength and the wisdom of every worker. . . . When difficulties arise in any branch of the cause—as they surely will, for the church militant is not the church triumphant—all heaven is watching to see what will be the course of those who are entrusted with sacred responsibilities. Some will stumble, some will give heed to seducing spirits; some will choose darkness rather than light because they are not true to God. Like their Master, those who are abiding in Christ will not fall nor be discouraged. . . .

Now when we are just on the borders of the Promised Land, let none repeat the sin of the unfaithful spies. They acknowledged that the land they went up to see was a good land, but they declared that the inhabitants were strong, the giants were there, and that they themselves were in comparison as grasshoppers in the sight of the people and in their own sight. All the difficulties were magnified into insurmountable obstacles. They made it appear as folly and presumption to think of going up to possess the land. . . . But Caleb stilled them before Moses, and said, "Let us go up at once, and possess it; for we are well able to overcome it."

This was the language of faith; but the spies who had spoken discouragingly were not to be baffled in their attempts to prevent the people from going forward in doing the word of the Lord. . . . They exaggerated the difficulties until all the congregation was crazed with discouragement and fear. . . .

Amid all the lamentations and bitterness of feeling, Caleb and Joshua spoke to the congregation, "The land, which we passed through to search it, is an exceeding good land." But the people wished to believe the worst, and while the ringing voice of Caleb was heard above the tumult, they stood with stones in their hands to batter down the men who bore the right testimony. . . .

While the people were cherishing doubts, and believing the unfaithful spies, the golden opportunity for Israel passed by. . . . Shall it be, in these last days just before we enter into the heavenly Canaan, that God's people shall indulge the spirit that was revealed by ancient Israel? People full of doubts and criticisms and complaints can sow seeds of unbelief and distrust that will yield an abundant harvest. The history of Israel was written for our admonition upon whom the ends of the world are come.— Manuscript 6, 1892.

December 30
**BAPTISM OF
THE HOLY GHOST
LEADS TO
TRUE RELIGION**

◆ *But the Comforter, which is the Holy
Ghost, whom the Father will send in my
name, he shall teach you all things, and bring
all things to your remembrance, whatsoever I
have said unto you. John 14:26.*

WHAT promise did our Lord Jesus Christ make to His disciples to furnish them with consolation in view of His departure from them? It was the promise of the Holy Spirit of God. The divine influence of the Holy Spirit was to cooperate with the human mind and bring to their remembrance whatsoever Christ had spoken unto them. The great need of this time of peril is the Holy Spirit, for it will bring to the receiver all other blessings in its train. The truth believed will transform the character.

In the light of the truth that is shining in our day, we are reproved for the dearth of the Holy Spirit. . . . As long as individuals are content with a mere theory of truth, and are yet lacking in the daily operation of the Spirit of God upon the heart, which is manifested in outward transformation of character, they are cutting themselves off from the qualification that would fit them for greater efficiency in the Master's work. . . .

The baptism of the Holy Ghost as on the day of Pentecost will lead to a revival of true religion, and to the performance of many wonderful works. Heavenly intelligences will come among us, and men and women will speak as they are moved upon by the Holy Spirit of God. But should the Lord work upon people as He did on and after the day of Pentecost, many who now claim to believe the truth would know so very little of the operation of the Holy Spirit that they would cry, "Beware of fanaticism." They would say of those who were filled with the Spirit, "They are filled with new wine" [Acts 2:13, NRSV]. . . .

When souls long after Christ, and seek to become one with Him, then those who are content with the form of godliness exclaim, "Be careful; do not go to extremes."

When angels of heaven come among us and work through human agents, there will be solid, substantial conversions, after the order of the conversions of the day of Pentecost. Now . . . be careful and do not go into human excitement. But while we should be careful not to go into human excitement, we should not be among those who will raise inquiries and cherish doubts in reference to the work of the Spirit of God, for there will be those who will question and criticize when the Spirit of God takes possession of men and women, because their own hearts are not moved, but are cold and unimpressible.—Letter 27, 1894.

December 31
THE CONTRO-VERSY BETWEEN CHRIST AND SATAN IS ENDED

◆ *And God shall wipe away all tears from their eyes; and there shall be no more death, neither sorrow, nor crying, neither shall there be any more pain: for the former things are passed away. Revelation 21:4.*

HE wicked receive their recompense in the earth. They "shall be stubble: and the day that cometh shall burn them up, saith the Lord of hosts." . . . The sins of the righteous having been transferred to Satan, he is made to suffer not only for his own rebellion, but for all the sins that he has caused God's people to commit. . . .

Satan's work of ruin is forever ended. . . . While God is to the wicked a consuming fire, He is to His people both a sun and a shield. . . . The fire that consumes the wicked purifies the earth. Every trace of the curse is swept away. No eternally burning hell will keep before the ransomed the fearful consequences of sin.

One reminder alone remains: Our Redeemer will ever bear the marks of His crucifixion. Upon His wounded head, upon His side, His hands and feet, are the only traces of the cruel work that sin has wrought. . . .

In the Bible the inheritance of the saved is called "a country.". . . The tree of life yields its fruit every month, and the leaves of the tree are for the service of the nations. There are ever-flowing streams, clear as crystal, and beside them waving trees cast their shadows upon the paths prepared for the ransomed of the Lord. . . .

In the City of God "there shall be no night." None will need or desire repose. There will be no weariness in doing the will of God and offering praise to His name. We shall ever feel the freshness of the morning and shall ever be far from its close. . . . All the treasures of the universe will be open to the study of God's redeemed. Unfettered by mortality, they wing their tireless flight to worlds afar—worlds that thrilled with sorrow at the spectacle of human woe and rang with songs of gladness at the tidings of a ransomed soul. . . .

The great controversy is ended. Sin and sinners are no more. The entire universe is clean. One pulse of harmony and gladness beats through the vast creation. From Him who created all flow life and light and gladness throughout the realms of illimitable space. From the minutest atom to the greatest world, all things, animate and inanimate, in their unshadowed beauty and perfect joy, declare that God is love.—*The Great Controversy,* pp. 673-678.

My Prayer List

My Prayer List

My Prayer List

My Prayer List

My Prayer List

My Prayer List

My Prayer List

My Prayer List

My Prayer List

My Prayer List

My Prayer List

My Prayer List